How Does It Feel?

**Elvis Presley, The Beatles, Bob Dylan,
and the Philosophy of Rock and Roll**

Grant Maxwell

ISBN 978-0692486269 (paperback)

TO GINNY

*Grant Maxwell examines the recorded music of popular culture
with the same subtlety and care as he brings to the literary and
philosophical texts of high culture. He seeks not just breadth of
knowledge but coherence of insight; not just accumulation of
knowledge but depth of understanding.*

Richard Tarnas, author of *The Passion of the Western Mind*

TABLE OF CONTENTS

PROLOGUE: "WHAT'S THAT SUPPOSED TO MEAN?"   1

I. "STANDING IN THE GATEWAY"
    CHAPTER 1: "LET'S GET REAL, REAL GONE   9
        FOR A CHANGE"
    CHAPTER 2: "A CREATIVE TENSION"   45
    CHAPTER 3: "LOOKING FOR THE INNER HEAT"   116

II. "YOU REALLY DON'T KNOW UNTIL YOU STEP INSIDE"
    CHAPTER 4: "A REVELATION TO BEHOLD"   176
    CHAPTER 5: "AN EXTREME SENSE OF DESTINY"   197

EPILOGUE: "THROUGH THE MIRROR"   220

NOTES   236

BIBLIOGRAPHY   275

ACKNOWLEDGEMENTS   281

INDEX   282

PROLOGUE
"WHAT'S THAT SUPPOSED TO MEAN?"

And this secret life itself spoke to me: "Behold," it said, "I am that which must always overcome itself."

Friedrich Nietzsche, *Thus Spoke Zarathustra*[1]

Only someone who has overcome himself is truly able to overcome.

Jean Gebser, *The Ever-Present Origin*[2]

Watching footage of Bob Dylan's performance at the Newport Folk Festival in 1965 when he "went electric," the viewer is immediately struck, as Dylan and his band begin their set with "Maggie's Farm," by the insistence, intensity, and sheer volume of the repetitive three-note bass line. This pounding heartbeat, conspiring with the primal, cutting snarl of Mike Bloomfield's lead guitar, must have been jolting for an audience expecting an acoustic folksinger. The sound is piercing and anxiety producing, urgent and fierce. Although Peter Yarrow of Peter, Paul, and Mary claims that "the volume of the blues band was kind of wild, you couldn't get the words too clearly,"[3] judging from the recording, while "wild" is an accurate description of the volume, the words were perfectly audible, an observation reinforced by the fact that Paul Rothchild, who would go on to produce the Doors, was engineering the sound.

However, although the folk audience might have been startled by the sheer magnitude of the noise coming from their beloved troubadour, it could not have been mere loudness that produced such a negative reaction from the crowd, as both the Paul Butterfield Blues Band and the Chambers Brothers had played loud electric sets earlier in the day, which had both been well-received.[4] While many in the audience were probably surprised by Dylan's thwarting of their expectations (despite the fact that Dylan had released *Bringing It All Back Home* about four months previously and "Like a Rolling Stone" a week before), contrary to popular belief, it does not seem to be the bare fact of Dylan playing loud rock and roll that caused the audience to start booing.[5]

Paying careful attention to the performance, as the band begins playing "Maggie's Farm," there is excited talking in the crowd, neither ecstatic nor critical, a clamor of expectant voices attempting to determine

1

the value of this new music, shouting to be heard over the strident rhythm section and guitar. Dylan is visibly a bit nervous, but the first verse sounds fine, if slightly uncertain, his powerful voice cutting through the rhythmic potency of the band.[6] This initial success appears to give Dylan courage, and he starts to smile as the song goes to the five at the end of the first verse on the word "bored," the dominant chord that universally releases tension in the blues, allowing the song to resolve back to the one, the tonic or root chord. But the bass, which has been thunderously dominating the feel of the band, and rather effectively up to this point, does not go to the five, and thus the tension is not released.[7]

This deviation from the recorded version of the song on *Bringing It All Back Home* does not seem premeditated as the musicians appear confused for a brief moment, Dylan deliberately finishing the phrase, and then looking uncomfortably over at Bloomfield as two unseen men in the audience start to boo about a second after the singer steps back from the microphone. Another second later, Dylan looks down, apparently toward the booing men, with a half-wounded, half-disdainful expression as others join in the booing, the singer seeming to realize that he has lost his audience for this first live performance with a band (at least since high school).[8] Although Dylan's guitar is barely audible, and his left hand is not visible during this critical moment of the first verse, the bass refuses to move to the five again at the end of the second verse, while Dylan's hand moves to what appears to be the A chord, the five for the key of D in which the song is played, which indicates that Dylan was performing the song as it was originally conceived, but that the sheer volume of the bass overruled his guitar.

While most commentators have implicitly assumed that Dylan meant the band to stay on the root chord as a planned assault on the audience, it seems far more likely, based on the subtle fluctuations in the band's playing, as well as on the gestural and facial cues from Dylan and Bloomfield, that the bass player simply did not know the changes of the song very well, which merely demonstrates how little rehearsal had gone into the performance. As organ player Al Kooper charitably, though somewhat inaccurately, expressed it: "We didn't especially play that good; the beat got turned around."[9] Similarly, musician Geoff Muldaur has said that "I don't believe people were booing because the music was revolutionary. . . . It was just that Dylan wasn't very good at it. He had no idea how to play the electric guitar, and he had very second-rate musicians with him, and they hadn't rehearsed enough. It just didn't work. The musicians didn't play good. There's no doubt in my mind, people were booing because it stank."[10] While many interpreters have differed from this assessment, based on the footage, it seems undeniable, though it also seems odd that, to my knowledge, it has never been mentioned in print that the specific musical problem was neither primarily the beat getting turned around nor Dylan's electric guitar-playing, but the bass player missing a change.

One suspects that the fact that the bass player, Jerome Arnold, was one of two African Americans performing with Dylan may have had something to do with this collective amnesia, the product of a condescending proto-political correctness that may have been justified at the time, but that is perhaps unnecessary in the post-Obama era, especially when so many of our greatest musicians are black. However, the fact remains that, although the booing seems to have begun as a reaction to the music's execution, it soon took on an entirely different significance, perhaps even by the end of that first song, but certainly by the time other audiences followed suit, culminating in the Manchester Free Trade Hall concert in 1966 when an audience member yelled "Judas!" before Dylan and the Hawks (later the Band) erupted into a volcanic performance of "Like a Rolling Stone." In both concerts, bookending what is probably the most inspired and volatile ten months of Dylan's performing career, high drama was played out on the stage of popular culture, requiring nearly as much conceit and suspension of disbelief as the theater for its effectiveness.[11]

The unvarnished truth about Dylan's performance at Newport in 1965 is that the young singer was accustomed to versatile session players and the ability to do multiple takes of songs in the studio, while this rhythm section, borrowed along with Bloomfield from the Butterfield Blues Band, was only prepared to play straight blues. But this was the leader of the band's fault, not the rhythm section's. Having worked with very few groups at that point, Dylan chose his musicians naively, thinking that they would be able to do his songs justice with very little rehearsal when this was just not the case. Playing alone, Dylan's confidence in his performance was unshakable because he had the exceptional capacity to rise to any occasion. But playing with a band suddenly made it necessary for him to consider the other musicians, even just enough to elicit a good performance from them. Thus, it seems that the simple fact, generally overlooked, is that members of the audience started booing not primarily because they felt betrayed by Dylan's embrace of rock and roll, but because Dylan was not yet a proficient band leader, so the bass player missed a change, which broke the momentum and made the performance feel wrong in a way that would have been difficult to define in the moment.

The myth that has grown up around this concert is that it was the symbolic enactment of an ideological schism between the folk purists and those favorably inclined toward rock and roll,[12] and it ultimately did come to symbolize this very thing for, according to folksinger Oscar Brand: "To the old left, Dylan was the second coming. . . . He was a kind of link to their own lost youth that validated them and gave them hope for their own resurgence." However, if Dylan's betrayal of this hopeful expectation was the source of the old guard's disapproval, it does not seem to have been the primary concern for the larger audience. As singer, novelist, and close Dylan friend Richard Farina insisted:

> We all grew up with . . . radio music—it was not traditional music. . . . Only when popular music was in its very worst period, when nothing was happening there, did we turn to folk music. [Rock and roll] was part of everybody's music when they were growing up in America. It was part of high school in America. The first person that Dylan and I ever talked about when we hung out together was Buddy Holly.[13]

Given their generation's deep affection for rock and roll, with the benefit of recording technology and a careful ear, one gets the distinct impression that the myth might have been rather different had Dylan and his band sounded as tight as they did on his latest record.

However, as was almost always the case, Dylan managed to transform this near disaster into a triumph, snatching victory from the jaws of defeat when he was called back out to perform two acoustic songs. After singing "Mr. Tambourine Man," he performed a weary, frustrated "It's All Over Now, Baby Blue" that perfectly encapsulated the transitional quality of that moment, the performance of the death and rebirth of American popular music from one genre into another, from one way of being into another. Having already recorded the song that *Rolling Stone* magazine would appropriately nominate the "greatest song of all time,"[14] "Like a Rolling Stone," Dylan had not quite mastered live rock and roll. However, this was the moment when the reigning "King of Folk Music"[15] declared unequivocally that he was no longer exclusively, or even primarily, a folk musician.

Speaking in Martin Scorsese's *No Direction Home* about that first electric performance at Newport, Dylan recalls:

> I was thinkin' that someone was shouting, 'Are you with us? Are you with us?' And, uh, you know, I don't know, what's that supposed to mean? I had no idea why they were booing. I don't think anybody was there having a

negative response to those songs, though. Whatever it
was about wasn't about anything that they were hearing.[16]

However, knowing Dylan's propensity for misdirection, and seeing the
subtle signs in the performance footage, it seems likely that Dylan
convinced himself in retrospect that the booing "wasn't about anything
that they were hearing," perhaps choosing to believe, or even just
claiming to believe the myth that his milieu had spontaneously created to
cover up the fact that the man they had elected their prophet was all too
human. Whatever Dylan's intention, though, his audience and his
generation apparently needed him to succeed, so rather than believe that
Dylan could make a mistake as basic as not having sufficiently
rehearsed, most of those involved seem to concur that Dylan made
intentionally alienating music to declare his independence from the folk
movement. While this supposition appears true to a limited extent, Dylan
almost certainly did not intend for the bass player to miss the chord
change, which sparked the booing and stalled the momentum of the
performance.[17]

Nevertheless, as Dylan's friend Paul Nelson observed a decade later:
"In the mid-Sixties Dylan's talent evoked such an intense degree of
personal participation from both his admirers and detractors that he could
not be permitted so much as a random action. Hungry for a sign, the
world used to follow him around, just waiting for him to drop a cigarette
butt. When he did they'd sift through the remains, looking for
significance. The scary part is they'd find it." Although one might
interpret this "hunger for a sign" in a less sinister light than Nelson does,
it seems clear that the audience so intensely wanted Dylan to succeed
that, by collectively creating a narrative near the factual truth, but not
quite identical with it, they allowed Dylan to carry on with his trajectory
toward greatness.

And this disjunction between the way the situation actually transpired
and the belief of the collective could conceivably be taken as proof that
everyone was participating in a mass delusion, as from a reductionist
perspective, the concert was just a lot of people making a lot of noise and
getting worked up about it. However, from a mythically and
narratologically informed perspective, the very fact that the audience
collectively and unconsciously saved Dylan from embarrassment,
transmuting what was simply a bad performance into an epochal rupture,
can be taken as evidence that Dylan really was, in some sense, destined
for great things. The myth of this moment is far more significant than the
way the music actually sounded whereas, by contrast, both the music and
the event were equally significant at the "Judas" concert the following

year, Dylan by then having drastically improved his approach to live rock and roll, not least by hiring one of his generation's greatest bands, but also by forging a performative mode markedly different than his acoustic folk persona.[18]

Legend has it that Pete Seeger, the embodiment of the old guard of folk music at that moment, was threatening to cut the cables with an axe while Dylan was playing with the band at Newport. Seeger and the rest of the folk community ultimately acquiesced to Dylan's revolution, though not without a great deal of resistance, a great deal of wailing and gnashing of teeth. However, if Seeger initially played the role of disapproving father, singer Maria Muldaur played the role of supportive sister. At a party later that night, Muldaur recalls seeing Dylan sitting by himself "looking really weird," so encouraged by Richard Farina, as she recalls: "I go over by myself, and I say, 'Hey, Bob, how you doing?' His legs were wiggling like they always did, and he was just brooding in the corner with his legs wiggling. I put my hand on his shoulder and said, 'Would you like to dance?' And he looked up at me, and he said, 'I would dance with you, Maria, but my hands are on fire.' . . . Bob was looking like he was really down after his whole experience with that band. He didn't look like a guy who thought he had very much to celebrate."[19] As Muldaur told Scorsese, Dylan's utterance may have been "cryptic," but she "kinda knew exactly what he meant." Muldaur apparently understood that Dylan's hands were burning with an archetypal, promethean flame, blazing with the magnitude of what he had just done, performing the necessary murder of the old order in an ugly, flawed, but ultimately effective—and era-defining—fifteen minutes of visceral intensity and sheer volume.

As Al Kooper, in his drolly humorous way, describes Dylan's next show a month after the Newport performance:

> When we played Forest Hills, "Like a Rolling Stone" was number one. And so when we played "Like a Rolling Stone," they stopped booing and sang along. And then when we finished they started booing again. I thought that was great. I enjoyed that. But at the party after the show, Bob came runnin' up to us and gave us big hugs. He said, "That was fabulous! It was great, it was like a carnival, it was fantastic." He really enjoyed the show.

Based on Kooper's observations, it seems clear that Dylan understood on a profound level that the booing was not really about him, that he was a catalyst for something profound occurring in his culture. In fact, Dylan seems at least temporarily to have attained a state approaching egoless consciousness such that he enjoyed the crowd booing him, at least for a time, not because he had a pathological need to be hated, but because he knew that he was playing a central role in the cultural drama. As Dylan recalls: "I had a perspective on the booing because you gotta realize you can kill somebody with kindness, too," which seems to indicate that Dylan did perhaps, on some level, see himself as something like a messianic figure despite his frequent protestations to the contrary, not primarily for the glory, but because he knew that he could fulfill that vital cultural function.[20]

In fact, this kind of deep humility and sense of service to the greater good is precisely how one might expect a messiah to conceive his role. Dylan, in his "perspective" on the resistance leveled against him, was putting into action the French proverb, "to understand all is to forgive all," for seemingly more than anyone else, he understood that the audiences were not booing because of who he was as a private individual, but because he was playing a necessary transformative role in the development of historical process.[21] And having rejected folk music, he was not about to settle into his role as "Rock and Roll King"[22] any more than he would accept the mantle of "Messiah."[23] Dylan, always refusing to be pinned down, rejected the labels "folk rock" and "rock and roll" for his new style, preferring to call it "vision music,"[24] which seems as accurate a description as any. As ever, Dylan's impulse was to transcend genre, identity, and even temporality to perform the "unceasing creation"[25] characteristic of humanity's greatest achievements, including the best of rock and roll.

I. "STANDING IN THE GATEWAY"

CHAPTER 1
"LET'S GET REAL, REAL GONE FOR A CHANGE"

In principle new points of view are not as a rule discovered in territory that is already known, but in out-of-the-way places that may even be avoided because of their bad name.

C.G. Jung, *Synchronicity*[26]

The story I will tell about Elvis Presley is not a story he would have told about himself, at least not in these words. However, I suspect that he would have been sympathetic to the general trajectory of my interpretation of him, though he may not have known much of the vocabulary used to contextualize the narrative arc of his life. Indeed, as the hermeneutic mode I am employing here suggests, the methods characteristic of literary interpretation can be applied just as fruitfully to biography, to the narrative construction of "real life." Presley and those who knew him felt that he was the catalyst for a profound transformation, not only in music, but in the American culture that the music both reflected and impelled. As Sam Phillips, Presley's first producer and mentor, articulated it, the singer "may not have been able to verbalize all that—but he damn sure wasn't dumb, and he damn sure was intuitive, and he damn sure had an appreciation for the total spirituality of the human existence, even if he would never have thought of the term."[27] Aside from situating this exposition within the proper scope of Presley's vital significance for understanding the last half-century of American culture, this observation by Phillips also serves to rectify a common misconception, namely, the stereotype of Presley as a dumb country boy.[28]

This clarification is particularly necessary because this book is written in a style, and for an audience, that often privileges the mode of intellectual analysis even while tracing a movement that implicitly pushes against the privileging of that mode, a precarious operation at best. As RCA promotion manager Chick Crumpacker noted: "He was so unassuming . . . but he had this quality—he was very, very smart behind it all." Similarly, according to one acquaintance, Presley knew "what he was doing at all times. I really believe he was like a novelist—he studied and watched what was going on, it was really just second nature with him."[29] Presley may have cultivated a "country dumb" persona, as the Ray Charles character describes it in the movie *Ray*, but, in fact, he appears to have been something of a genius in understanding how to

9

present himself physically and vocally in order to elicit a desired reaction from others.

Although Presley clearly stated "I don't dig the intellectual bit,"[30] he also explained:

> I've made a study of Marlon Brando. . . . I've made a study of poor Jimmy Dean. I've made a study of myself, and I know why girls, at least the young 'uns, go for us. We're sullen, we're broodin', we're something of a menace. I don't understand it exactly, but that's what the girls like in men. I don't know anything about Hollywood, but I know that you can't be sexy if you smile. You can't be a rebel if you grin.[31]

In a practical way rather than an intellectual way, Presley obsessively observed and emulated the physicality of his performative influences as much as he studied the vocal phrasing of his musical influences, which was a large contributing factor to the radically novel style that he did so much to create.[32] As has often been suggested, sexuality was one important component of the bodily epistemologies repressed in modernity, which Presley embodied in a qualitatively more concentrated way than his precursors.

However, Presley's appeal exceeded mere sexuality, for according to biographer Peter Guralnick, Presley's early manager, Bob Neal, saw the first few years of Presley's career as "an almost exponential progression . . . not just in his stage manner . . . but in an appetite for change and self-improvement that seemed to know no experiential bounds." In Neal's opinion, Presley would never "be mistaken for an intellectual—and he was far too jittery to be called introspective. But he soaked up influences like litmus paper; he was open to new people and new ideas and new experiences in a way that defied social stereotypes. He was *serious* about his work."[33] Similarly, Walter Matthau, who worked with Presley in his fourth film, *King Creole*, told an interviewer:

> I almost hesitate, I creep up to the sentence . . . he was an instinctive actor. Because that almost is a derogation of his talents. That's saying, 'Well, you know, he's just a dumb animal who does it well by instinct.' No, he was quite bright, too. He was very intelligent. Also, he was intelligent enough to understand what a character was and how to play the character simply by being himself *through* the means of the story.[34]

For those who were close to Presley, particularly in his early days, he was evidently a brilliant, intuitive, self-aware, hard-working, well-mannered, generous artist, "a beautiful human being"[35] who, in music and daily life as much as in his acting, intentionally projected a persona that was far less serious and complex than the young man underneath.

Presley once described a kind of meditative technique to early girlfriend June Juanico that he had developed as a child in which he would "look up at the moon" and feel himself to be floating "in the space between the moon and the stars." As he told her: "I learned a long time ago not to talk about it. People think you're crazy when you talk about things they don't understand,"[36] a scenario that suggests Presley was far more conscious than he is often given credit for because he learned to hide this serious, contemplative side of himself behind the persona that most people saw, and which ultimately resulted in the caricature of the "fat Elvis" in rhinestone jumpsuit and shades, dying on the toilet while eating a peanut-butter and banana sandwich.

"A Protean Hero"

Although there were many significant historical factors that contributed to the production of the material, political, and economic conditions under which rock and roll could emerge, the primary focus of this study is on the direct experience of Presley, his contemporaries, and their successors, attempting to think its way into the world view that these musicians inhabited in order to understand how they did what they did. Thus, this chapter's project is to draw out the philosophical subtleties implicit in Presley's radically novel mode of relating to experience, evident both in his life and in his music.[37]

Presley certainly inherited the crown of "American cool" after the death of James Dean left a void in that most intangible of kingdoms, but this succession was far more than merely a vapid fad or a trivial pop culture phenomenon as it was often portrayed, particularly in the first few decades of rock and roll.[38] Rather, I would contend, somewhat contrary to Simon Frith's argument in *Performing Rites*, that the apparent whims of the marketplace can fruitfully be seen as a metric of the deepest desires and needs of the individuals who make up that economy at any given historical moment.[39] Although this correlation between the profound yearnings of individuals and the commodities on which people spend their money is complicated by the often cynical realities of advertising, in some cases, as with the rise of Elvis Presley, the phenomenon defies the capability of corporate interests to create or control and, instead, reveals something authentic about the cultural psyche at that moment.[40]

I tend to agree with Anthony DeCurtis when he writes that, "as someone at play in the fields of popular culture, I care about everything that interests people. In a way that is antithetical to most rock criticism, I grow more curious about something the more popular it gets."[41] I generally relate to this sentiment and would go further in saying that, while there is certainly value in unearthing what Robert Palmer calls the "more rarefied epiphanies"[42] that have been marginalized or ignored (a tendency exemplified by the series of *Nuggets* compilations and the rock criticism of Lester Bangs), perhaps the best way to understand what the collective culture was going through at any particular moment is to look at the movements to which the most people were giving their attention.

Of course, the dichotomy that Frith, and to a lesser extent DeCurtis, sets up between "popular" and "avant garde" becomes largely moot in the case of Presley, the Beatles, and Dylan, as these three artists seem to epitomize both descriptors in a way that very few artists in the history of popular music have been able to achieve, though Presley was only able to maintain this quality for the first few years of his career. Thus, while there have been many periods when the avant garde was generally marginalized in American culture (the early fifties for instance), when Guralnick writes that Presley emerged in an era "that required a protean hero,"[43] he does not seem to be exaggerating or being facetious. Rather, Presley's primary biographer seems to be recognizing that mid-twentieth century America, like almost all cultures in all times, needed such a transformative figure to enact, perform, and catalyze the deepest impulses of that cultural moment.[44]

Indeed, the word "culture," related (via the Latin "cultura") to the "cults" of ancient Greece, is generally defined by the relation of a collective to a charismatic figure or set of figures. Although it could be argued that a number of other early rock and rollers, including Chuck Berry, Little Richard, Buddy Holly, and others surpassed Presley in a variety of ways, the fact remains that Presley's first single, "That's All Right," was released in July of 1954, a full year before Berry's first single, "Maybelline," a year and four months before Richard's first hit, "Tutti Frutti," and three years before Holly's "That'll Be the Day." Put simply, among those men generally considered the "founding fathers" of the genre, Elvis Presley has by far the strongest claim to having invented rock and roll in its fully realized form (as distinct from rhythm and blues) because he got there first by a long shot.[45] As Chuck Berry reportedly summed it up: "Describe Elvis Presley? He was the greatest who ever was, is or ever will be."[46]

"A Somewhat Different Musical Proposition"

To be fair, Bill Haley & His Comets recorded "Rock Around the Clock" three months before Presley recorded "That's All Right," though the song did not attain widespread success until the following year, after Presley's record had exploded into popular consciousness, at least in southeastern regional markets. Haley certainly did a great deal to popularize the genre, though to my ears, as well as to those of many critics, Haley's music is not truly rock and roll, but a sort of bridge or compromise formation between jazzy, rhythm & blues-inflected country music and the rock and roll that would find its first complete expression in "That's All Right."[47] As Haley himself put it: "We take a lot of care with lyrics because we don't want to offend anybody. The music is the main thing, and it's just as easy to write acceptable words."[48] Haley was clearly not a proponent of the rebellious quality that has characterized rock and roll since its inception.

In contrast, aside from the transgressive suggestiveness of the songs Presley would sing, Presley's first record possesses a manic energy and a dangerous intensity that Haley's music lacks, qualities that ultimately defined the emerging genre. All of the structural elements were present to render Haley's music technically identifiable as rock and roll—the more pronounced backbeat, the instrumental and vocal inflections derived simultaneously from country, blues, jazz, and gospel, and the inclusion of the verb "rock" in the lyrics—but the spark that would set the fire blazing was struck by Presley.

This is an exemplary instance of the radically different conclusions that can result from the modes of interpretation associated with rationality (which sociologist Max Weber defines as a "conceptual simplification and ordering" in service to "systematic regimentation") and with affectivity (which can be defined as "visceral forces beneath, alongside or generally *other than* conscious knowing, vital forces insisting beyond emotion"[49]). Although Haley's song might be considered the first rock and roll record by a rational accounting, it is Presley's song that remains the epochal initiatory act as it expresses not only the confluence of genres that Haley's song synthesizes, but also the affective tone and attitude of the new genre that Haley did not possess, but which Presley epitomized.[50]

Bluntly stated, Bill Haley was not very cool, a quality which forms the heart of the genre, for American cool is definable as affective authenticity in contradistinction to the more affected performativity exhibited by Haley, which was characteristic of the pre-rock and roll era's late orthodoxy in which he had one foot firmly planted. Indeed, the juxtaposition of "affectivity" and "affectedness" is striking, for while "affect" implies the authentic bodily feelings that produce one's activity, the quality of being "affected" indicates a more passive and inauthentic submission to culturally preconditioned roles and modes of engagement. Thus, the transition marked by the subtle difference between Haley's and Presley's performativities can be seen as an emblematic enactment of the profound shift from the mandates of rationalized culture determining one's identity, to allowing one's persona to result from one's intrinsic felt experience. This difference is primarily constituted in attention to the abstract conceptual mores of society being the predominant motivating factor for the rational mode, as opposed to attention focused on the nuances of one's bodily economy being the primary motive force in the affective mode. If Haley was hesitating in the doorway to the reemerging embodied mode, Presley leapt through with abandon into the new realm that he did so much to liberate. This subtle but crucial difference delineated the liminal cusp between "real" and "fake," between authenticity and its lack.

Similarly, the Moondog Coronation Ball in Cleveland in 1952, produced by disc jockey Alan Freed who popularized the term "rock and roll,"[51] was claimed by him to have been the "first rock and roll concert." Although the term "rock and roll" had been in use since the forties, and Freed had been using it on his radio show since 1951,[52] the performers who actually played at the Moondog event, like Paul "Huckleback" Williams and Tiny Grimes, were jazzy rhythm and blues musicians, both men having previous connections with Charlie Parker, for instance. Listening to their music, it sounds close to the rock and roll that would emerge a few years later, but not quite, an occasion of what philosopher Alfred North Whitehead describes as "that slightest change of tone which yet makes all the difference."[53] As Robert Palmer expresses it, by the mid-fifties, "Rock and roll had become, *in practice*, a somewhat different musical proposition from rhythm and blues. The beat tended to become heavier and more emphatic; blues- and gospel-derived melodic usages expanded to embrace more elements of pop songcraft; jazz content was minimized."[54] As with Haley, though to a lesser extent, many of the elements were present at the Moondog Coronation Ball that would define the emergent form.

However, also as with Haley's music, the musical enaction of Williams and Grimes presents as relatively affected, perhaps due in part to the structural elements delineated by Palmer, but also perhaps due to a relative lack of the willfully concentrated authenticity that Presley reintroduced into mainstream popular music, appropriating this essential element for the creation of the new genre from James Dean and Marlon

Brando as much as from musicians like Arthur "Big Boy" Crudup and Big Mama Thornton by whom he was influenced. Listening to their music and witnessing their visual performativity, it is clear that Williams and Grimes were still essentially in the jazz age, while Presley, a few years later, emerged fully formed as the prime exemplar of what would become the rock era. Although Presley's contribution is often summarized as having synthesized black and white musical modes, it seems that Presley's synthesis of the performativity characteristic of his musical precursors with that of the two actors mentioned above is nearly as significant a factor in Presley's production of rock and roll. Thus, rather than claiming the Moondog Coronation Ball as the "first rock and roll concert," it might be more accurate to say that the collective desire for the phenomenon of rock and roll was evinced in the Moondog Coronation Ball, but that it was a container waiting for something to fill it, as the new music did not truly emerge until Presley's moment of inspiration more than two years later in 1954.

"That Don't Move Me"

Presley's era-defining first recordings, collected in *Elvis at Sun*, can be grouped into two distinct categories. The first category is slow, sentimental ballads crooned largely in a saccharine imitation of the vocal jazz tradition exemplified by Frank Sinatra, Dean Martin, Bing Crosby, and Perry Como, though with a pronounced blues inflection.[55] However, the second kind of song was sung in the qualitatively new style created by Presley and his compatriots: not quite country, blues, jazz, or gospel, but a synthesis of all these styles, transubstantiated into something new by their rarefaction in the alembic of the new approach. Indeed, as Palmer observes, this new kind of song was fundamentally different from the more traditional fare, for "in a culture whose idea of musical entertainment was Perry Como, Doris Day, and 'Your Hit Parade,' the appearance of an Elvis Presley . . . was radical, unprecedented."[56] Although "That's All Right," discussed below, is considered by many to be the first true rock and roll record, correctly to my mind, "Milkcow Blues Boogie," recorded a few months later, is the record on which Presley explicitly enacts the leap from one genre into another.[57]

On this record, he starts out in the jazz age, which by now has settled into a safe orthodoxy, crooning in his quavering ballad-voice. Then, in what is clearly a staged, dramatic move, Presley "stops" the band (we know it is staged because the band quits playing before he tells them to) and, in a slightly harder, more commanding voice intones: "Hold it, fellas. That don't move me. Let's get real, real gone for a change,"[58] an invocation which calls into being a new approach to making music, and perhaps a novel way of relating to experience that shifts the focus of attention from rational thought to visceral motivity, to that which "moves" one. With this statement, Presley seems to be inciting his band, and himself, to make the potentially terrifying transrational leap, identifying for the length of the song with their bodies rather than their mental or critical faculties, which, for many in modernity exemplify the mode of consciousness that differentiates us from animals and justifies our very existence.

While the phrase "for a change" seems explicitly to suggest trying something new, there also appears to be an implication of consciously moving their centers of attention from egoic consciousness to a more embodied form of consciousness for the purpose of producing collective transformation ("for a change"). And when Presley tells his musicians to "hold it," it may not be too much to suggest that Presley is half-consciously admonishing his band to hold themselves back from being drawn into the gravity of the old way of being. Thus, this break in the song seems to be an intentional enactment of the moment when rock and roll is born by performing a rupture with the previous mode. Though all of the individual musical elements of rock and roll already existed in jazz, blues, country, and gospel, and those genres had cross-pollinated to a limited degree, it was not until Elvis Presley sang on these records, these Sun sessions, that an archetypal sun rose on a new day for American popular music.[59]

Presley was enacting a mode that he knew to be transgressive within his cultural milieu, one that reversed the privileging opposition characteristic of modernity, focusing on affect and intuition over rational and intellectual concerns, though, as seen below with the Beatles and Dylan, intellect would be reengaged by rock and roll in profound ways in the sixties. However, the very fact that Presley was consciously entering into the modes largely repressed and rendered unconscious in modernity through pervasive cultural rationalization suggests that his initiatory reversal was always already gesturing toward an integration of these modes.

In these early recordings, we hear Presley developing a persona, creating a semi-fictional character paradoxically more true to his affective authenticity, by means of which he enacts the emerging genre in songs such as "Milkcow Blues Boogie," "That's All Right," "Blue Moon of Kentucky," "Good Rockin' Tonight," and "Mystery Train" through the suggestive inflections and distinctive phrasing that he employs in his singing, as well as in the manic intensity of his guitar strumming. Indeed, in the two different versions of "I'm Left, You're

Right, She's Gone," one slow and one fast, Presley enacts this same transition between two stylistic eras, though "Milkcow Blues Boogie" remains the paradigmatic enactment aside from "That's All Right" as, in this case, he dramatically dismisses the old style in favor of the new within the space of a single recorded track.[60]

"The Sheer Enjoyment of the Moment"

In November 1954, Presley summed up his reason for making music and performing in a succinct and direct way: "I like to do these things because they make me feel good," which is a statement that comes as no surprise to anyone familiar with Presley's music. However, while one might be inclined to interpret this statement as a trivial insight, it is, in fact, a precise evocation of the repressed affective orientation that was then reemerging into mass consciousness largely through the catalyst of rock and roll in a further iteration of the more constrained emergences that had occurred in the popular music of earlier decades.[61] Similarly, as Guralnick describes a television appearance by Presley on the Dorsey brothers' *Stage Show*, the most striking element of the performance is "the sheer enjoyment of the moment."[62] Although the ultimate trajectory of Presley's life certainly was hedonistic, there is something more profound than mere hedonism gestured toward here.

Watched by an entire generation, Presley made the epochal discovery that one's activities should be affectively enjoyable, not just rationally intelligible, and that perhaps the best pragmatic metric for the value and efficacy of an activity is the question asked by Bob Dylan a decade later: "How does it feel?"[63] Or, to put it in Presley's terms from the spoken interregnum of "Milkcow Blues Boogie": Does it move you? In fact, this question appears to have been the guiding principle by which Presley pursued his musical vision. According to producer Bones Howe, in the recording studio:

> It was always about the music. He would keep working on a song, and he would listen to it played back, and his criterion was always: did it make him feel good? He didn't care if there were little mistakes, he was interested in anything that would make magic out of the record. The sessions were always fun, there was great energy, he was always doing something that was innovative. It was always about whether you had a feeling for music or not, whether you felt what he felt.[64]

Presley understood that precision and theoretical mastery are of secondary importance to the purpose of popular music, which can be expressed accurately as to "make magic," a phrase that might sound naïve to our ears, but which nevertheless articulates the irreducibly numinous quality of a truly great song. It has often been suggested that music is the purest of the arts because it has the ability to produce nearly unmediated feeling in the listener, to open up vast imaginal vistas, and to evoke ecstatic states of consciousness. At its best, rock and roll has epitomized this capacity, not only invoking depths of feeling, but inciting the listener out of stasis, the literal meaning of "ecstasy," and into motion.

Not only did Presley's instinct for the pursuit of such ecstatic enjoyment impel him to become a wildly successful performer, it also placed him directly at the center of what might be described as the deepest project of modernity, expressed by E.M. Forster in *Howard's End* as "only connect," to find meaningful relationality in a world that had seemingly been voided of intrinsic meaning by cultural rationalization, constituted largely in the repression of attention to bodily feeling. This impulse toward felt connection enacted by Presley is also evident in the initiatory declarations of the beats, particularly Allen Ginsberg's "Howl," in which the figure of Moloch exemplifies the extreme patriarchal, mechanistic, materialistic, rationalistic, and alienated state of affairs that Presley, Ginsberg, and many in their generation sought to overcome in different ways, through the pushing of language to transcend its inherently rational limitations in poetic and philosophical illumination as much as through the more purely visceral focus on modes other than intellect performed by early rock and roll.[65] Whereas Ginsberg articulated the reemergence of bodily knowledge in the more intellectual medium of poetry, Presley's rock and roll was an almost completely intuitive expression of the return of modes repressed in modernity.

Ultimately, it seems that in order to produce genuine novelty, whether in music or in thought, one must focus one's attention on one end of the dialectical polarity formed by affect and rationality, so that musicians must generally privilege intuition over intellect, while philosophers (even musically oriented ones) must privilege rational thought in their daily work. However, it seems that the most profound novelty in either domain results from the engagement of this kind of extremity with its polar opposite, in Presley's ongoing conversation with his critics and his push against the rationalized expectations of his culture's predominant sectors as much as in the project of the present study, which is to explicate the fundamental philosophical premises of rock and roll by means of intellectual analysis without vitiating the visceral intensity and irreducible spirit of the genre.

For Presley, the transgressive focus on pure affect, and the concomitant awareness of temporality as qualitative duration, of the lived experience of time rather than the quantitative measurability privileged by science, seems to have formed the crux of the method by which he made music. Guralnick explains: "Time meant nothing to him in the studio. If he felt like singing spirituals, he would sing spirituals to his heart's content. It was his way of finding his place." However, he continues, "if the feeling wasn't there, you waited until it *got* there, you didn't try to define it too precisely before it showed up—and if something else happened to show up while you were waiting, well, then, you took advantage of that."[66] Presley seems to have understood that, where musical inspiration is concerned, one cannot force the constantly shifting quality of temporal experience to do one's bidding as one can to a limited extent in the relatively narrow domain accessible to science.

Presley apparently found that he could induce in himself a state of meditative readiness so that, when inspiration struck, he would be prepared to perform the surge of novelty that he experienced as endemic to that moment. What a profoundly different approach this is from a science that generally constructs time as a quantitative, static medium for empirical testing and repeatability, often seeking to bring the world into compliance via technological instruments and mathematical models. Science is certainly a valid and noble enterprise, but apparently not the only valid way to approach understanding the world. Presley, only partially conscious of his role's significance, was one of the primary figures who seems to have initiated the emergence of a novel approach to experience that integrates the individuated, modern, rational mind with the more intuitive mode of consciousness, which had been the predominant mode of cognizance prior to the seventeenth century, and which is the appropriate approach for perceiving the qualitative nature of time. No wonder Presley and his group experienced apprehension as they created this audaciously new musical genre.

"You Didn't Have To Go Inside To Get the Feeling"

It seems to be the case that, in genuine cultural revolutions, a certain amount of uncertainty, even fear, is usually experienced by the would-be revolutionaries before the new mode finds footing in popular consciousness. The purpose of such revolutions appears to be to mediate the emergence of something that has never existed before in a sustained way, though all of the component parts are extant. Thus, there are often no institutions set up for the new mode's implementation, no ready-made audience or market, which is why it is so unusual for all of the necessary elements to come together to create a genuinely novel phenomenon like the one Presley and his compatriots enacted. As Sam Phillips expressed it: "what I was thinking was, where you going to go with this, it's not black, it's not white, it's not pop, it's not country."[67] The new music that Presley and his band created in the Sun sessions, despite the fact that they had planned and labored to bring it into being, did not fit into an easily accessible category precisely because it embodied the integration of the categories that Phillips mentions. There were no radio stations for music that sounded like the progeny of blues and country, though, as discussed above, there was a relatively recently invented name for the genre.[68]

Listening to the studio banter after an early take of "Blue Moon of Kentucky," Phillips can be heard saying "Hell, that's different. . . . That's a pop song now, nearly about,"[69] Presley, bassist Bill Black, and guitarist Scotty Moore laughing uneasily. They were not sure exactly what it was they had created, though they knew that they had never heard anything quite like it before. Indeed, it is easy to forget more than a half-century later in the culture that these men did so much to create the profoundly novel quality of this music, with all the difficulties and resistances that inevitably accompany novelty's ingression into historical process. Rock and roll was not just a revolution in musical style; it was a primary embodiment of a transformation in the way many people, in America and elsewhere, lived, felt about, and thought about their lives and their relation to immediate experience. At its deepest octave, rock and roll appears to have been the symbolic, narrative act of the paradigmatic European white man breaking out of exclusive identification with his rational intellect and the generally quantitative domains of experience to which this mode allows access, and into a centauric, dual identification of consciousness with an emergent self that encompasses both affectivity and mentality, both quality and quantity, a rupture whose shock waves are still rippling through our culture more than half a century later.

A central aspect of this integration effected by Presley and the other early rock and rollers was the synthesis of black and white music to create a genre, which, though it was not raceless, constituted a profound complication of the cultures of these two groups. By now, it is cliché to note that the original rock and roll, exemplified by Presley, was produced by the synthesis of music made by both black people and white people: blues and country, vocal jazz and gospel. It appears, though, that this synthesis implicitly gestured toward the integration of a profound bifurcation in American culture between intellect and intuition. However, it is important to be absolutely clear that the pernicious supposition that African Americans are biologically more intuitive or somatically gifted and that Americans of European descent are biologically more intellectual is an unsupportable assertion. Nevertheless, as theorists like Frantz Fanon and Amiri Baraka have articulated, there do seem to have been genuine cultural differences in these areas, though always already deconstructed by the many visible exceptions to this general cultural tendency, and largely integrated in the subsequent half century.[70]

Presley's constantly amused smirk seems to attest, in part, to the fact that he knew that emulating the mannerisms and stylistic tropes of African American rhythm and blues, as a white man, would be perceived as dangerous and subversive to the postwar order in which he lived. Of course, the emulation of black culture was already a widespread phenomenon, from the white jazz musicians who followed the lead of their African American counterparts, to Jackie Robinson who initiated a revolution in the way baseball was played by white athletes during the same period. However, Presley's emulation of black culture seems to have differed qualitatively from these instances in that he not only emulated the way African Americans played, as did Benny Goodman or numerous white baseball players; he actually *acted* black to some extent, not in the condescending mode of minstrelsy, but in genuine homage. That is, rather than limiting his emulation to a specific area of endeavor, Presley partially modeled his persona on the subtle gestural and vocal inflections characteristic of postwar African American culture. Although Presley was certainly not the only white person to carry the cultural emulation to this extent, he was perhaps the most visible, coming to symbolize this act of racial integration within himself for many observers, both sympathetic and otherwise.[71]

The Presleys, who lived in a primarily black area of Memphis, were as immersed in African American culture as it was possible for white people to be in the mid-twentieth century South. The preachers and the congregations who worshiped in the churches in Presley's neighborhood expressed their religious devotion in an decidedly physical way, singing, dancing, shouting, and testifying in cathartic, rhythmic rejoicing. Although Presley was a liminal figure between the black and white worlds, living in the neighborhood where this ecstatic embodiment predominated, but not actually venturing into these African American churches, "you didn't have to go inside to get the feeling." Living in the midst of this cultural milieu, Guralnick explains, "you breathed it in, as natural as air—after a while you got used to it, it became yours, too, *it was almost like being in church.*"[72] This was the culture in which Elvis Presley spent a significant portion of his formative years. A white boy in a primarily black community with all of the complex social dynamics that this immersion in otherness entailed, Presley was consistently embedded in the somatic modes that were generally more privileged in the black community than in its white counterpart.

By all accounts, Presley seems to have internalized those modes, integrating them to a high degree with the rationalized, post-Enlightenment mentality that had been inculcated into him as a nearly inescapable part of being white in postwar American culture, in his white schools and churches as much as through the increasingly pervasive media of radio and television. In a way that very few people were able to do at that time, Presley, partially by dint of his developmental environment, exemplified the integration of the opposed modes at the heart of a schizophrenic modernity. He may not have been particularly interested in verbally articulating this integration, but he enacted it in his singing, his physical movements when performing, and in his general mode of relating to his embodied experience. Although ultimately, as Palmer suggests, "white musicians have long since made the rock and roll idiom their own," to a great extent because of Presley's appropriation and synthesis of the genre's tropes from proto-rock and roll musicians, "the fact remains that the music's wellsprings, its governing aesthetic precepts, its 'deep structures,' are fundamentally African and African-American."[73]

Although Presley's white social circles in Memphis were, in fact, largely oriented toward music, particularly gospel, Presley necessarily participated to some degree in the mentality of the predominant streams of primarily white, national culture, which generally privileged logocentric rationality, first in school, but particularly once he expanded beyond his immediate milieu to become a perpetual presence in the press. Ultimately, this privileging of intellect produced a situation of profound unintelligibility. In articulating the cognitive dissonance produced by the epistemological bifurcation between affect and rationality, philosopher Richard Tarnas recognizes "the striking resemblance between this state of affairs and the condition that Gregory Bateson famously described as the 'double bind': the impossibly problematic situation in which mutually contradictory demands eventually lead a person to become schizophrenic." Although Presley does not seem to have been particularly troubled by this "impossibly problematic" situation, this incoherence permeated his culture for, as Tarnas continues: "The differences between Bateson's psychiatric double bind and the modern existential condition are more in degree than in kind: the modern condition is an extraordinarily encompassing and fundamental double bind, made less immediately conspicuous simply because it is so universal."[74] Indeed, the juxtaposition of the rationalized alienation that permeated much of mid-twentieth century American culture with the rhythmic, somatic, spiritual embodiment apparently enacted by African Americans in Presley's neighborhood is strikingly discordant.

Having emphasized the radical bifurcation between racially aligned cultures at this historical moment in the mid-fifties, it should also be mentioned that radio was at the forefront of enacting a reintegration of these artificially conditioned cultural modes in the United States. As a salesman for the station that would first play Presley's songs, WDIA, quipped, the letters stood for "We Done Integrated Already,"[75] and Presley was deeply immersed in this musical, cultural, and epistemological integration. In an interview in 1956, Presley explained:

> The colored folks been singing it and playing it just like I'm doin' now, man, for more years than I know. They played it like that in the shanties and in their juke joints, and nobody paid it no mind 'til I goosed it up. I got it from them. Down in Tupelo, Mississippi, I used to hear old Arthur Crudup bang his box the way I do now, and I said if I ever got to the place where I could feel all old Arthur felt, I'd be a music man like nobody ever saw.[76]

With characteristic modesty, Presley was aware that he was the propagator of a musical mode that had existed before him and that this mode had come to prominence through him, to some degree, because of his race.

However, the reality is somewhat more complex than Presley constructs it in the interest of self-effacement, as the very act of being a white man singing something that resembled what had previously been considered black music was profoundly courageous in the cultural climate of the mid-fifties. Although others were performing a similar act of racial integration, very few people carried this project to the level of overwhelming cultural visibility that Presley did, making him a lightning rod for this deeply divisive issue at the heart of American culture. And Presley certainly added a great deal to the primarily African American musical modes by synthesizing them with other, predominantly white genres, particularly country music, and adding his own distinctive inflections. Nevertheless, it is clear that the core of Presley's music was derived in large part from African American music, and specifically from the focus on "feel" that Presley emphasizes in relation to Crudup, which is the essence of the blues genre. As John Lennon would later recall:

"Somebody said that blacks gave the middle-class whites back their bodies," and Presley was one of the primary mediators of this profound gift.[77]

In a similar way to Presley, though in an opposite trajectory, black rock and rollers like Chuck Berry and Little Richard did a great deal to move African American music toward the embrace of previously white musical and cultural tropes. Indeed, Chuck Berry's first hit, "Maybellene," was a rewrite of Roy Acuff's "Ida Red." Whereas Presley was a white man playing largely rhythm and blues with a country inflection, Chuck Berry was an African American playing something close to country music, though inflected by the blues. Strategically orchestrated by Leonard Chess of Chess Records to appeal to a white audience, Berry's song was a huge hit among millions of mostly white teenagers, which "proved that they were ready to idolize an African American."[78] Although white jazz fans had long revered black musicians like Louis Armstrong, Duke Ellington, Billie Holiday, and Nat King Cole, Berry carried this reverence to a new level of intensity partially by appropriating the most distinctively "white" musical form, country music.

Thus, it would be misleading to suggest that Presley produced the integration of black and white musical modes single-handedly. For another instance, Sam Phillips was a curator of novelty who understood that African American music represented a profound mode of engagement largely unencumbered by the limiting assumptions produced by the exclusive privileging of intellect in the predominant, Eurocentric cultures of modernity. As Phillips articulated it with characteristically poetic bluntness, he was drawn to "genuine, untutored negro" music, to "negroes with field mud on their boots and patches in their overalls . . . battered instruments and unfettered techniques"[79] for, according to Phillips, he "was shooting for that damn row that hadn't been plowed."

Leaving aside the vestiges of the "noble savage" mythos in which Phillips seems to be engaging, the integration of epistemologies, associated in this particular context with the integration of racially overdetermined cultural tropes embodied in music, was the "middle way" toward the novelty for which Presley and Phillips were explicitly searching, following what amounts to an "almost subversive attraction not just to black music but to black culture, to an inchoate striving, a belief in the equality of man."[80] In the American culture of the mid-fifties, this fascination with African American culture was indeed subversive as, to many whites, black cultural modes seemed to possess an intrinsically deeper understanding of, and a more profound relationship with the body than did white culture, a difference that could be both frightening and enthralling for a cultural mode that had systematically repressed and othered bodily knowledge for centuries.

The courage required for Presley and his compatriots to delve into the modes that were primarily associated at that time with African American culture is evident in the great resistance, ridicule, and anger that were directed toward Presley, explicated more fully below, though of course this resistance pales in comparison to that experienced by many African Americans enacting a similar project of integration. Nevertheless, Presley apparently underwent what might be described as an echo of the black experience in the fifties, for, as Phillips explains, when the young singer first entered Sun Studio in 1953, "he tried not to show it . . . but he felt *inferior*. He reminded me of a black man in a way; his insecurity was so *markedly* like that of a black person."[81] Thus, it seems that it was not only the profound gifts of the African American experience, but also the deep burden of that experience that Presley carried more than most white men. However, despite the fact that he lived in an African American neighborhood, emulated black cultural and musical tropes, and even felt something like an echo of the African American experience, Presley enjoyed a largely unconscious cultural privilege shared by those with lighter skin tones and European features in American culture, a privilege that has still not been erased. Although Presley's racial identity was genuinely ambiguous, he lived in a culture that reified radical difference based almost exclusively on physical appearance.

Ultimately, one of Presley's primary contributions was carrying the rhythmic sophistication and intensity of black music into predominantly white musical domains, thereby complicating the overly simplistic distinctions between these musical forms and, ultimately, between these two American cultures. Indeed, this musical integration seems habitually to have entrained a visceral empathy between the two groups, comprising a necessary precondition for the socio-political integration of desegregation and Civil Rights that would culminate in the sixties.[82] As Ray Charles put it, the new style of music "meant that White America was getting hipper."[83]

"The Change That Was Coming To America"

Aside from the reactionary voices that condemned Presley based on racism, classism, conservatism, or simple misunderstanding, the most common descriptions of Presley were primarily focused on his intuitive brilliance and on the profoundly novel quality of his music. As Phillips expresses it, Presley had the most intuitive ability to hear songs without ever having to classify them, or *himself*, of anyone I've ever known outside of Jerry Lee Lewis and myself. It seemed like he had a photographic memory for every damn song he ever heard—and he was one of the most introspective human beings that I've ever met. You see, Elvis Presley knew what it was like to be poor, but that damn sure didn't make him prejudiced. *He didn't draw any lines.*[84]

Presley appears to have acted as something like an agent of boundary dissolution between the opposed modes of thought that had been artificially associated with black and white for centuries in American culture. Partially because he grew up, for a significant portion of his youth, in a primarily African American neighborhood, and partially because he had a profound sense of the radical equality of all humanity, derived largely from his devotion to the "do unto others" ethos of Christianity, Presley genuinely did not seem interested in racial distinctions, a fairly radical position at that moment in history. At the time when Presley emerged, racial integration was already beginning, particularly in music, and Presley himself became a prime focus and catalyst for this multi-leveled integration of races and of the epistemological modes that these racial identities had temporarily embodied.

However, Presley's novelty was not confined to the integration of this pervasive dichotomy in American culture. When speaking of Presley, observers consistently remark upon the quality of radical difference that he seemed to possess intrinsically.[85] Commentators have said that he "opened up new territory" and that "he was the change that was coming to America,"[86] that he was not only the agent of transformation, but that he actually embodied that transformation. Watch the full episodes of *The Ed Sullivan Show* in which Presley appears and one will comprehend, in a visceral way, what the beats and hippies meant when they called the main streams of mid-twentieth century American culture "straight" and "square." In fact, these spatial tropes seem to be precise descriptions of both the mental and physical qualities of most of the other performers besides Presley.

Physically, almost all of the various singers, in particular, seem stiff, constrained, and uncomfortable in their own skin, as if literally boxed in by their cultural assumptions, a situation alluded to above in relation to Bill Haley. Similarly, on a psychological level, these performers present as willfully naïve, trapped within elaborate constructions of race, gender, class, and sexuality. It is abundantly clear from watching this footage that Presley broke out of many of those rational bonds, smashing through restrictive barriers with a pelvic thrust of erotic force and an amused smirk. Where most of the other performers appear inauthentic to an early twenty-first century sensibility, playing culturally prescribed roles in which they do not seem to believe just below the surface, Presley comes off as authentic: conscious that he is playing a role and attempting to make that role coincide with how he feels in each moment.

It is a pleasure to watch Presley wrestle, or perhaps dance, with his fear and insecurity, striving to lose himself in the music and dialogically feeding off of the audience's reactions. He is such a magnetic performer, in part, because he periodically lets the audience know, through small physical gestures and facial expressions, shrugs and eye blinks, that he knows that they know down deep that they are all participating in a kind of play, a slightly ridiculous make-believe, but that this is precisely what makes it enjoyable. This telegraphing of self-awareness is something that few of the other performers do in these broadcasts, but which has become a standard mode of performance in the irony-drenched postmodern culture of the last few decades.

The other performers play their roles like actors in a classic Broadway musical, melodramatically projecting caricatures of emotion, while Presley has thrown aside the mask or, in the words of Bob Dylan, is beckoning his audience "through the mirror."[87] It is clear from watching Presley in this footage that a qualitatively new kind of person had been born and that Presley was one of the first people to bring this new style of being to primetime television.[88] It might even be said that Presley was the paradigmatic postmodern man in that he was constantly aware of the constructed quality of culture as well as the performative nature of physicality, the presentation of body.[89]

"Trying to Make It Live"

At the moment when Presley recorded his first songs at the Sun Studio in 1954-55, the world was apparently ripe for change. As Presley recognized: "I happened to come along at a time in the music business when there was no trend. The people were looking for something different, and I was lucky. I came along just in time."[90] Presley is here articulating the proverbial night that is darkest just before the dawn when the old order no longer contains the charged affect of profound, revolutionary significance that it once carried. Popular music at that moment in the mid-fifties was experienced by many of those in the cultural vanguard as a stale orthodoxy providing increasingly diminishing returns. However, as Presley's statement suggests, the absence of a vital "trend" provided the space within which the new genre could emerge.

Although rhythm and blues and country music were being played in clubs in Memphis, and around the nation, Presley had performed very little at the time of his early Sun sessions, so his musical style was created first in the recording studio, and only then was it brought onto the stage. In the studio, Presley was attempting to break through into a new affective realm, to birth a novel mode, though these attempts were met with what seemed like resistance from reality itself. Presley was persistently following his felt sense to overcome the current performative modes, though the "numbing familiarity" of the music he was singing made it difficult to find the novelty for which he and Phillips were explicitly searching, Guralnick's phrase "trying to make it live" evocative of birth, or perhaps of creation itself.

Presley was endeavoring to generate something new and vital, but the inertia of habit kept pulling his efforts into a mechanical, entropic monotony.[91] Indeed, Presley seems to have been enacting the vital impulse that Alfred North Whitehead describes as "an offensive, directed against the repetitious mechanism of the Universe,"[92] for as numerous theorists have suggested, the emergence of novelty does not happen gradually, though the preparation for revolution is gradual. Rather, as Whitehead observes: "new epochs emerge with comparative suddenness."[93] Thus, the creation of rock and roll by Presley and his friends was not a process of slow, steady development, but a sudden, revelatory moment of rupture and discontinuity with the past.

As Presley articulates his creation of "That's All Right," "this song popped into my mind that I had heard years ago, and I started kidding around with [it]." Presley had been almost physically hurling himself at a seemingly insurmountable internal obstacle until suddenly, for no discernible material reason, but bound up with "kidding around," there was a lightning strike of felicitous inspiration that catalyzed the transformation of what had seemed a fixed and immovable system. As Scotty Moore narrates the momentous discovery:

> All of a sudden . . . Elvis just started singing this song, jumping around and acting the fool, and then Bill picked up his bass, and he started acting the fool, too, and I started playing with them. Sam, I think, had the door to the control booth open—I don't know, he was either editing some tapes or doing something—and he stuck his head out and said, "What are you doing?" And we said,

"We don't know." "Well, back up," he said, "try to find a place to start, and do it again."

Moore is describing a process of intuitive creation that has more to do with playful experimentation than it does with theorizing. Although these four men knew intellectually that they wanted to create something new by fusing what had been considered black and white musical tropes, they did not know precisely how this integration would take place.

In fact, the integration seems to have required years of conscious, theoretical preparation, and then putting critical thought aside and simply being in the moment without observing that moment, allowing something to emerge that they did not consciously create, though they consciously laid the groundwork for its emergence. Sam Phillips' great genius was not in producing the new genre; it was in granting Presley, Moore, and Black the space to create novelty through "acting the fool," momentarily putting aside their rational considerations in favor of the abandon of absurdist physical humor, allowing something to spring forth that seemed to them to exceed their conscious volition. However, perhaps as significant as this moment of creation is that Phillips immediately saw the value of the novelty when it emerged.

All of the parties involved in this creative process agreed that there was something profoundly new about the music they had just produced through an unintentional moment of imaginative play, Phillips describing the new sound as "different" and as "itself," a collision of terms that suggests authentic novelty. The sound that Presley and his band discovered seems always to have existed *in potentia*, implicit in all of the elements that they had brought to the process of creation: their deep knowledge of different kinds of music, their theoretical preparation for the integration of these various musical modes and, perhaps most importantly, their inchoate desire for, or vision of, something as yet unrealized. They were able to create this music because they could feel the form of it pulling them magnetically into its event horizon, and Presley's ability to lose himself in ecstatic affect, to impel himself out of stasis, moved his band to a similar state of pure enjoyment, a process through which the vital creative impulse could locate a form for its expression. Whether one conceives this inspiration as coming from the unconscious or from something transcending individuality, as Presley saw it, this creative impulse does not appear to have been primarily the product of rational, egoic consciousness.

"A Certain . . . Feel"

Of course, it is imperative that those who receive such apparently transpersonal inspiration put in the work necessary not only to enact the moment of revelation, but to see it through to fruition, to uncover that which seems obvious in retrospect, but which is obscure until its annunciatory achievement. Thus, after Presley and the others received their initial epiphany, they played the song repeatedly, "refining" the strikingly new sound that had spontaneously emerged, though the central component of the music was always Presley's energetic strumming on his acoustic guitar, "up till this moment almost a handicap to be gotten over."[94] In fact, it is often the case that working within constraints, "tarrying with the negative" [95] as Hegel expresses it, is the very thing that impels the emergence of novelty.

Similarly to Presley's rather rudimentary guitar playing, all of the voices of the primary artists who are the subjects of this study—Presley, Lennon, McCartney, and Dylan—were not initially considered great instruments by the conventional standards of their day. Their voices were all constrained in ways that forced their owners to create exceptionally distinctive singing styles in order to make their vocal cords convey the affect that they felt impelled to express. As Presley put it: "I never sang like [that] in my whole life until I made that record."[96] Because, in his younger days, Presley's voice was somewhat limited in timbre and accuracy of pitch, he was instinctively driven to invent inflections and phrasings, his singular low swoops and high hiccups, that transmuted his liabilities into strengths.

In turn, the thrilling novelty of Presley's singing impelled Moore and Black to play in a new way, producing a "swinging gait that was the very epitome of what Sam had dreamt of but never fully imagined." When Phillips first played the take for the band, Bill Black asserts, "we couldn't believe it was us,"[97] Moore adding, "it just sounded sort of raw and ragged. . . . We thought it was exciting, but what was it? It was just so completely different. But it just really flipped Sam—he felt it really had something"[98] This collective narrative is a portrait of the process of transformation into novelty at its purest. Presley mediated this transformation, and he was a "different singer" because of what ultimately amounts to a moment of transduction between musical eras.

As in all such cases of rupture, "all the rules were out the window," for such moments of "phase transition" seem generally to be constituted in the supersession of the axioms of a system, the fundamental premises on which the system is based. Although "everything had changed,"[99] it was not necessary for the change to be articulated because it was a transformation that surpassed the scope of rational, analytic discourse. Indeed, this novelty *can* be articulated, which is the project of retroactive analysis like that found in the present work—a mode that exhibits its own kind of novelty—though the purest novelty is often prior to verbal formulation. As Palmer observes: "Plato warned in his *Republic* that changes in the modes and rhythms of popular music inevitably lead to changes in society at large,"[100] and this originary moment of rock and roll seems to be one of the clearest cases in musical history of a fundamentally new rhythmic, and thus affective, mode catalyzing an equally fundamental cultural transformation.

Referring to "That's All Right" and its flipside, "Blue Moon of Kentucky," Moore noted that "it's funny how they both come about by accident. There was nothing like a direction, there was just a certain . . . feel." Although Moore and Phillips had talked many times in the coffee shop next to the studio about creating something new that somehow combined black and white musical tropes, this ambition does not seem to have been at the front of their minds during the session. Certainly, there was a sense that they were trying to create a novel style out of known elements, but these men did not seem to know precisely what form that synthesis would take; they simply knew that they must keep experimenting, following the lure of intuition until it "felt" right. This process of creation was prepared intellectually by analyzing the various elements that they suspected would combine to create a new style, but the new style itself could only be discovered by leaving aside analysis and entering into a largely nonverbal engagement with experience.

Presley and the others carried the vision of what they intended to create—they could somatically sense its contours somewhere just over the temporal horizon—but the only way to bring their vision to fruition was to act in a primarily intuitive mode. Indeed, as Phillips' assistant Marion Keisker describes the creative process in the studio: "Sam would say, 'Well, let's go back, and you hold on to what you did there. I want that.' And Elvis would say, 'What did I do? What did I do?' Because it was all so instinctive that he simply didn't know." The primary criterion for judging their work was that it had to feel right, not knowing why it felt right, or even being conscious of what they had just done a moment before. All of the material components of composition, arrangement, and performance had to be organized spontaneously in such a way that these elements produced a bodily recognition in the participants of the achievement of the musical mode that they sensed clearly, but, until now, had not possessed the specific structural components to bring into concrete manifestation.

Positive affect constituted an indication that they were heading in the right direction, moving toward the new entity that they were attempting to body forth, for as Phillips puts it: "Every time we did a number I wanted to make sure to the best of my ability that everybody *enjoyed* it." As discussed above, to an intellectually privileging mode, this "organizing principle," as Guralnick puts it, may sound rather trivial, even hedonistic, but, in fact, it is coextensive with the recognition that attention to felt experience is indispensable for the production of the most profound kinds of novelty. Indeed, acting on this principle, according to Marion Keisker, "everyone was trying very hard to hang very loose through the whole thing,"[101] which suggests the participants' implicit knowledge that, in order to make good music, they had to abide in a kind of meditative state similar to Zen Buddhist *mushin* ("no mind") so that, in each moment, they would adjust not only their playing, but their posture, breathing, facial expression, and conscious attention in a continuous dance incorporating their different modes of engagement to follow what Whitehead calls the "lure of feeling"[102] leading them inexorably toward the production of novel musical forms.

Although the state of confluent creativity that Presley and his band enacted is usually accompanied by a feeling of autonomous intentionality and self-determination, it appears that one must paradoxically relinquish egoic control enough to allow something usually described as excessive of conscious volition to manifest through one's individuality in order for this kind of state to occur. This process seems temporarily to bring the affective modes of participants in the sort of phenomenon enacted by Presley and his compatriots into a kind of energetic resonance.[103]

In "Good Rockin' Tonight," for instance, analysis and doubt, indeed, conscious thought, appear consciously to have been put aside, allowing something to emerge from the band that resembles nothing so much as group awareness so that all three of the musicians seem willingly to have temporarily released their egoic minds to give themselves to the new form they are creating. The recognition that this intuitive enjoyment and fusion is "almost in defiance of societal norms" illustrates the transgressive quality of ecstatic, boundary-dissolving collective experience at that moment in American culture. By definition, only that which is taboo or repressed by a society can be transgressive and, in this moment of musical creation, American history witnessed a primary moment of ecstatic affect's reemergence. As with "That's All Right" and "Milkcow Blues Boogie," though in this case in the lyrics as well as the musical aspects of the song, Presley announces that "good rockin'," a term associated with physicality, and particularly sexuality, is the "news" that the culture had been waiting for.

However, it was not just in those initial sessions that these men effected a transformation in the music. It was over the sustained period of all the Sun sessions that Presley, Moore, Black, and Phillips worked out the form of the new genre they had initially stumbled upon the day they recorded "That's All Right." For instance, they produced a radical reimagining of "I Don't Care If the Sun Don't Shine," which had been an outtake from Disney's *Cinderella*, and was later popularized by Patti Page and Dean Martin. As Phillips describes Presley's reason for choosing to record the song: "That's what he heard in Dean . . . that little bit of mischievousness that he had in his soul when he cut up a little bit—[that's why] he loved Dean Martin's singing."[104] Presley took his admiration for Martin, certainly a prime exemplar of the musical orthodoxy at that moment, and recontextualized his vocal inflections, which carried the "mischievousness" that Phillips describes, within the rhythmic realm of what amounts to a close cousin of the "jump blues" exemplified by Louis Jordan to generate an emergent mode.[105]

Presley and his band were not creating this new style out of thin air. Rather, they were intuitively synthesizing disparate genres in novel ways to create, in Moore's words, "almost a total rhythm thing."[106] They appropriated the tropes of the country and vocal jazz styles that were popular in their predominantly white social milieu and placed these tropes in the context of predominantly African American rhythmic modes, particularly in Presley's vocalization, even *Time* magazine grudgingly admitting: "There is no denying that rock and roll evokes a physical response from even its most reluctant listeners, for that giant pulse matches the rhythmical operations of the human body."[107]

"They'll Run Us Out of Town!"

After the new music had been created in the studio, there was still the essential task of propagating this music to the public. As in almost all such revolutionary instances, one can see in this case the necessity of transmitting the revolution through established channels of communication. Indeed, another factor that made Sam Phillips the perfect mentor for Presley was that he was close friends with disc jockey Dewey Phillips (no relation), who had a popular radio show in Memphis. Once Sam persuaded Dewey to play "That's All Right" and "Blue Moon of Kentucky" on his show on July 7, 1954, dozens of calls and telegrams came pouring in, prompting Dewey to play the songs over and over again throughout the evening's program. Here we see the mythologizing already beginning with Dewey Phillips as champion and myth-purveyor, which illustrates that not only is it necessary for the new style to be created and concretized on tape, but in order for a new form of music to take root in collective awareness, there usually must be someone with influence promoting the new genre through existing avenues of transmission with the authority that this position implies.

It just so happens that this is one of those felicitous cases in which the distance between the artist and the people who could help present his art as a viable cultural commodity was very slight. It took Presley about a year to convince Sam Phillips to let him record at Sun Studio. But when he did, achieving the initial realization of his felt potential after some hard work and frustration, it seemed to be only a matter of time before the world recognized this music for the dramatic transformation that it represented, not only because the music is intrinsically great, but because Sam Phillips and Dewey Phillips were buddies. Once Dewey played the songs on his show, "the news traveled like wildfire,"[108] a strikingly appropriate image for the propagation of a promethean discovery through culture.

That Presley and his band, during the Sun sessions, recorded multiple versions of songs in the two different styles—jazzy blues balladry and the new, more upbeat rock and roll style—illustrates the tentativeness with which they approached this new genre. Although it is clear to most people listening more than a half century later that the rock and roll numbers are the truly exciting, ground-breaking performances from these sessions, while the slower songs are largely mediocre retreads of an existing genre, in 1954, the new style that these musicians had just created seemed frantic, even dangerous. According to Moore, after they played back a take of "That's All Right," they declared: "Well, that's fine, but good God, they'll run us out of town!"[109] It may seem ridiculous to us now, in an era when gangsta rap and death metal are the conventional orthodoxy, that this largely acoustic music derived primarily from country and blues should be so controversial. However, as anyone knows who studies the way revolutions in music occur, it is nearly impossible to overestimate the inertia of culture, but it is similarly impossible to halt the revolution once it is underway.

In retrospect, although rock and roll's success seems to have been inevitable, Presley and the genre that he largely initiated and represented in popular consciousness received a great deal of resistance from the existing powers in the press, the government, and even from musicians of a previous generation.[110] Once the new style had been created in the studio, Presley, Black, and Moore quickly began playing live shows, with Presley's effusive physicality an apparently natural outgrowth of his singing. Nevertheless, a review in the *New York Times* judged Presley as having "no discernible singing ability."[111] Similarly, another review in the *New York Journal-American* asserted that "the sight of young (21) Mr. Presley caterwauling his unintelligible lyrics in an inadequate voice, during a display of primitive physical movement difficult to describe in terms suitable to a family newspaper, has caused the most heated reaction."[112] And the *Daily News* declared that popular music "has reached its lowest depths in the 'grunt and groin' antics of one Elvis Presley," asserting that "Elvis, who rotates his pelvis, was appalling musically. Also, he gave an exhibition that was suggestive and vulgar, tinged with a kind of animalism that should be confined to dives and bordellos."[113]

Yet another critic wrote that Presley's music was "a terrible popular twist on darkest Africa's fertility tom-tom displays,"[114] and another that "if any further proof were needed that what Elvis offers is not basically music but a sex show, it was proved last night," claiming that his show recalled "one of those screeching, uninhibited party rallies which the Nazis used to hold for Hitler."[115] The press, in a panicked frenzy of incomprehension, many seeming personally threatened by Presley, could not decide if he was a "primitive" African, a Nazi, or a stripper, all similarly odious to the predominant cultural milieu of little more than half a century ago.[116] As New York Congressman Emanuel Celler stated, Presley's "animal gyrations . . . are violative of all that I know to be in good taste."[117]

Even, or perhaps especially Frank Sinatra, who was the primary precursor to the role that Presley now inhabited, declared ("in a ghost-written magazine article"[118]):

> Rock 'n' roll smells phony and false. . . . It is sung, played, and written for the most part by cretinous goons and by means of its almost imbecilic reiteration, and sly, lewd, in plain fact, dirty lyrics . . . it manages to be the martial music of every sideburned delinquent on the face of the earth. . . . [It] is the most brutal, ugly, desperate, vicious form of expression it has been my misfortune to hear.[119]

Reading this bile-filled utterance, one suspects that there is an element of jealousy involved in Sinatra's condemnation of the new musical genre, particularly since he later dedicated an entire season finale of his television show to welcoming Presley back from the army in 1960, implicitly acknowledging the younger singer as his legitimate successor.[120] Nevertheless, in the passage above, Sinatra articulates a sentiment about rock and roll that was ironically prevalent among the generation which had previously rebelled in a similar, though more constrained way through the catalyst of Sinatra's music.

Rock and roll was in fact partially responsible for "race mixing,"[121] as one critic opined, though the guardians of that moment's normative discourse generally interpreted this as a negative development, whereas most of us now see this integration as entirely positive. However, even such African American luminaries as Martin Luther King, Jr. and Langston Hughes decried rock and roll, apparently worried that the unsophisticated physicality of the genre would undermine their efforts toward racial equality, King going so far as to say that rock and roll "often plunges men's minds into degrading and immoral depths."[122] Clearly, Presley and rock and roll had become symbolic foci for the major issues that divided the younger generation from the older, generally constellated around attitudes toward race, sexuality, and affect.[123]

The vituperative litany from the old guard against the young upstarts proves that even such august cultural authorities as the *New York Times* and the United States Congress are not infallible. Although it may seem obvious to us now that these institutions have often served as platforms for reactionary oppression, corruption, and cynical self-interest, this view does not seem to have been the predominant one in the nineteen-fifties, though certain sectors of society, particularly the beats, expressed these kinds of sentiments openly. Thus, it is only right to condemn what can accurately be described as warfare by the reactionary right against emancipatory ideals. However, once one has acknowledged the moral turpitude of some within the prevailing institutions, it becomes apparent that these conservative agents were enacting an entrenched resistance and oppression that ultimately served the function of the Hegelian negative mentioned above, the obstacle that *Geist* or "Spirit," the vital impulse toward self-overcoming apparently intrinsic to temporality, must confront to be transformed.

According to Hegel: "Spirit . . . wins its truth only when, in utter dismemberment, it finds itself. . . . Spirit is this power only by looking the negative in the face, and tarrying with it. This tarrying with the negative is the magical power that converts it into being."[124] From a Hegelian perspective, Presley's critics were not merely short-sighted and mean-spirited, though they were certainly these things. Although the condemnation of such repressive attitudes is certainly justified, it must also be recognized that these conservative voices were performing a necessary function in what appears to be an essentially dialectical process of transformation. Understood in this way, the old order's repressive behavior becomes intelligible, not only because this *ancien regime* characteristically sought to conserve and protect its mode of thought embodied in established power structures, but because novel modes often seem a bit ridiculous, half-formed, overly idealistic, and naïve to the conservative mode of consciousness.

As Whitehead writes: "If you have had your attention directed to the novelties in thought in your own lifetime, you will have observed that almost all really new ideas have a certain aspect of foolishness when they are first produced."[125] Indeed, the moment of confluent inspiration when Presley "acted the fool" to create the new genre seems to confirm Whitehead's dictum beyond all reasonable expectation, proving foolishness and novelty to be intimately imbricated.[126] Ultimately, Sam Phillips' expression of the meaning of rock and roll's initial incarnation remains fairly definitive:

> We were all beginners, just beginners, and we were *making history*. Oh, there was all sorts of resentment. First it was 'sinful,' and second it was affecting our children. *Yes, it was*. But it was giving them some individuality, giving them some say-so about their emotions and not having them just be a product of their parents right up until they were twenty-five years old. All this had an awful lot to do with the total psychological change that took place in this country because of rock and roll and r&b—which was for the better, I don't give a damn what anybody says.[127]

It is to be expected that a fundamental transformation in world view, a "total psychological change," would be met with a great deal of fear and resistance. Thus, that the rock and roll revolution was ultimately successful, as Phillips insists, in mediating the affective liberation of American culture is a testament not only to the originality and brilliance of Presley and his cohort, but to the courage and persistence of these world-transforming outsiders.

"Like They Were Transformed"

However, it is also clear that Presley was the recipient of a gift that very few individuals are given, for according to Presley's early girlfriend Dixie Locke: "Right from the start it was as if he had a power over people, it was like they were transformed."[128] Indeed, Paul McCartney would declare that, after hearing Presley's "Hound Dog" for the first time: "We were like new people."[129] By many accounts, Presley seems to have possessed the ability to mediate what was experienced as a radical transformation in others, a potency that appears directly related to Presley's ability to put aside rational thought to become like an animal on stage, acting almost purely by instinct. As discussed above, Presley appears to have made a conscious decision to enact this role, which is how philosopher Henri Bergson describes intuition: the conscious, temporary relinquishment of intellect to engage with other domains of process, as opposed to prerational, unconscious instinct. It is Presley's undeniable animality relative to the culture in which he was embedded that elicited both erotic desire from his fans and accusations of bestial primitivity from his detractors.

However, as also mentioned above, I do not mean to suggest that Presley's primary effect on his audience was merely to serve as a catalyst for the release of repressed sexuality, though he certainly did this.[130] In fact, the mass erotic release that he produced in his admirers was but one manifestation of the affective force that many of his associates recognized in him. For instance, Marion Keisker describes Presley as having "an almost magical quality that both protected him and in turn brought out the best in others." Similarly, according to Jimmie Rodgers Snow: "I'd never seen anyone quite like him—even as a kid he had that something about him, he just *had* it." Presley possessed talent and drive, certainly, but he also possessed the courage necessary to transgress social mores intentionally to think like an animal. By consciously enacting certain aspects of instinctual animality, Presley seems to have been able to tap into an intuitive mode through his music that allowed him to see and express the "higher kind of—mystery, for want of a better word," as Guralnick puts it, that others could not, often constrained as they were in rationalized cultural assumptions by which Presley was relatively unencumbered.

As June Juanico recalls Presley's description of his performative experience: "I don't know, it's hard to explain. It's like your whole body gets goose bumps, but it's not goose bumps. It's not a chill either. It's like a surge of electricity going through you. It's almost like making love, but it's even stronger than that." Juanico asked him if this was a common feeling among performers: "I don't know," he replied "The few I've talked to experience excitement and nerves, but they must not feel the way I do. If they did, they would say more about it, don't you think? They say they get nervous, but after they sing a few lines, they calm down. Hell, I don't calm down till two or three hours after I leave the stage. Sometimes I think my heart is going to explode." Presley possessed an exceptional ability to mediate this "surge of electricity," and to communicate this energetic quality to his audience. He is only able to describe this experience through analogy to having "goose bumps" or a "chill" or "making love," though the phenomenon seems to elude the reach of Presley's vocabulary.[131]

However, it is not merely because Presley was not an intellectual that he lacked the words to describe his experience; it is also because his culture did not possess the language of this experience ready at hand outside of a few theorists like those referred to in the present work. Perhaps the closest analogy in his contemporary milieu for what Presley experienced was the feeling that can come over one in church, though he was at great pains to assert that his music was not religious, probably because he knew that such a claim would produce an immediate backlash. As he asserted in a 1956 interview: "There was some article came out where I got the jumping around from my religion. Well, my religion has nothing to do with what I do now. Because the type of stuff I do now is not religious music, and my religious background has nothing to do with the way I sing."[132] However, one suspects that this is a case of Presley protesting too much, for he would also claim that his music was a gift from God, and he would go on to record numerous gospel songs over the course of his career.

Nevertheless, though Presley may not have fully understood what it was that he was doing, he got better and better at doing it, at least until his induction into the army. In an interview in early 1956, Presley was asked: "Have you any idea just what it was that started the girls going crazy over you?" to which he replies: "No, I don't. I guess it's just something God gave me. I believe that, you know."[133] Similarly, in a 1957 interview, Presley states that "I lose myself in my singing," indicating an overcoming of egoic consciousness, which seems to be a precondition for the ingression of musical inspiration.[134] Contrary to the stereotype of Presley as an uncouth animal, to which many people still uncritically subscribe, Presley appears to have been a profoundly moral and empathetic young man who consciously enacted a transgressive role in his performance. According to Jimmie Rogers Snow: "This nice, polite, well-mannered boy became transformed onstage in a manner that seemed to contradict everything that you might discern about his private personality."[135] Essentially, Presley was, in most respects, a conscientious person who developed the ability to render himself a catalyst for the deepest yearnings of his cultural moment by consciously regressing to a prerational state, thereby embodying the expression of modes that had been repressed and systematically denied.

Once Presley, Phillips, and the others conjured the first incarnation of rock and roll, the music quickly became a model for a new mode of being that the audience could explore. Like the German "swing kids" in the thirties who apparently greeted and identified one another by whistling a nonverbal melodic phrase from Duke Ellington's "It Don't Mean a Thing (If It Ain't Got That Swing)," according to an article in the magazine *Cowboy Songs* in 1955, "the current greeting among [Memphis] teenagers is still a rhythmical line from the song ["That's All Right"]: 'Ta dee da dee dee da."[136] In both cases, there was a felt potency for young people in these rhythmic, melodic phrases, a power that many in the old guard could not seem to comprehend and that soon spread outside Memphis to the nation and the world. Like a ritual incantation, the latter phrase signified that the direction of novelty at that moment in the domain of popular culture was not in the words that Presley was singing—those were almost beside the point—but in the affect that his rhythmic physicality mediated in his audience. Thus, it could even be said that something essential to the trajectory of Western culture in the twentieth century is encapsulated in these rhythmic phrases, as there has been a growing nostalgia in modernity for the archaic, prerational modes of experience as a corrective reaction to the exclusive privileging of verbal, logical, and rational modes, perhaps culminating in the twentieth century.[137]

As suggested above, not only was Presley's music an enactment of this transformative trajectory, but Presley himself appears to have been something like a symbolic incarnation of this process. For Phillips and for the worldwide audience that gave Presley their attention, he was an agent of radical novelty not only in music, but in affective attitude and physical performativity. Phillips was not initially concerned with Presley as a "physical specimen," he asserts: "I wasn't thinking, 'Is he going to look good onstage, is he going to be a great performer?' I was just looking for something that nobody could categorize." Even to the visionary Phillips, the visual aspect of Presley's performative style came as a "revelation," an unexpected uncovering of something profoundly new.

Even Presley himself was not initially certain that the way he was performing had value for, as Moore describes it: "During the instrumental parts he would back off from the mike and be playing and shaking, and the crowd would just go wild, but he thought they were actually making fun of him."[138] Presley had spontaneously created a phenomenon that was not entirely of his volition, but that seems to have embodied an historical process searching for appropriate expression. Without understanding why, Presley discovered that he could enact certain bodily motions that would provoke a nearly unprecedented response.[139] According to Moore, Presley's "movement was a natural thing . . . but he was also very conscious of what got a reaction. He'd do something one time and then he would expand on it real quick."[140]

Presley found that he had an intrinsic gift for producing ecstasy in the primarily young people who comprised his audience. However, although this ability was instinctive, he consciously cultivated it through a process that philosopher William James describes as "radical empiricism," for he retained what worked and discarded what did not.[141]

Presley was developing a kind of gestural language to convey what could not be communicated through words for, as Bob Neal explained:

> His show developed in that sometimes if he was onstage and just through some accidental movement there would be a big scream or reaction, he would automatically remember. On the other hand, if he devised something and got a dead reaction, he would never worry about it, he would drop it and go on to something else. It was just as automatic as breathing to him.[142]

With the participation of his audience, Presley developed a profoundly novel somatic code that adeptly expressed the quality of the moment. As a performer with the exceptional capacity to read his audience's reactions and adjust his performativity accordingly, Presley seems to have been elected by that audience to mediate an impulse that was ripe for expression. Thus, the audience appears to have created Presley just as much as he created them—a co-creation in the truest sense. As Presley expressed it: "If I do something good, they let me know it. If I don't, they let me know that, too. It's a give-and-take proposition in that they give me back the inspiration. I work absolutely to them. . . . They bring it out of me: the inspiration. The ham."[143]

An analogy can be made between Presley's performative mode and a surfer riding a wave, recalling William James' "single drops which sparkle in the sun as they are flung far ahead of the advancing edge of a wave-crest"[144] of novelty's ingression into historical process. As Guralnick describes Presley's performance style, the defining characteristic is that "over and over again he stops in the midst of a practiced gesture and shrugs his shoulders, audibly exhales, rolls his eyes, *freezes*—just waiting for the wave that has been momentarily stilled to roll back over him." As with surfing, Presley does not seem to have been in control of the unconscious, elemental forces that were carrying him. Rather, his mode of eliciting reaction from his audience seems to have been a process of developing and rehearsing his gestural language, and then positioning himself correctly, both physically and in terms of the affect that he was manifesting, to catch the "wave" of inspiration or connection that was the ultimate source of his appeal. His attitude toward his performance generally seems to have been one of slyly amused looseness and receptivity, opening himself to the desire of the audience to connect with the potency for which Presley acted as a catalyst.

As discussed above, Presley had made a careful study of how physicality produces affect by watching Dean and Brando, as well as by watching and listening to his favorite singers, and by testing experimentally what produced the desired effect in the crowd. However, when he strode on stage in front of an audience, this preparation only carried him part of the way to the felt connection to which he was drawn. It seems to have been his radical receptivity to the qualitative nature of temporality, Bergsonian duration, which allowed him to induce the kind of collective feeling that he did. As one eyewitness noted: "When Elvis was performing, everyone had the same basic reaction. It was spontaneous. It reminded me of the early days, of where I was raised in East Texas and going to these 'Holy Roller' Brush Arbor meetings: seeing people get religion."[145] As this observer suggests, the similarity between Presley's performances and religious revivals does not appear to be merely a surface resemblance, but rather a manifestation of the same largely unconscious impulse toward ecstasy that had long existed on the margins of a rationalized American culture, from the Great Awakenings and religious revivals of the eighteenth and nineteenth centuries, to the performative physicality of swing music and dancing in the nineteen thirties. Indeed, as Palmer notes, the rhythmic tropes that form the palette of rock and roll "are capable of transforming an audience into participants in communal ecstasy . . . forged and tempered in hundreds of years of religious ritual, from Africa to the Caribbean to the American South."[146] Clearly, the impulse toward the return of repressed affect did not suddenly appear in 1954 *ex nihilo*, as all the precursors mentioned above presaged the heights to which the impulse embodied in rock and roll would attain, first through Presley and his contemporaries, and then through the Beatles, Dylan, and others on an even more expansive scale in the sixties.

"Like a Mirror"

The reaction that Presley produced in his audience was "mass hysteria,"[147] resembling earlier historical eruptions, but on an unprecedented scale and with a novel intensity. Eliciting "screams of anguish" and "shrieks of ecstasy," Presley appears to have been driving his audience to a frenzied state, not only through his ritualized performance, but by his very presence. For Phillips and promoter Bob Neal as they watched the show, "this was something beyond either of their wildest expectations."[148] Even the men who participated in the creation of this phenomenon could not have predicted the sheer force with which audiences would respond. With Presley as catalyst, the teenagers of America let out a collective wail, initiating the liberation of felt experience that would find its culmination in the following decade. This rupture transformed the way a whole generation thought about their most intimate selves: their bodies and minds, their sexuality, their race, and their basic mode of relating to the world. In fact, to a large degree, we still live in the space that Presley and his contemporaries cleaved into the darkness, to employ a Jamesian trope.[149]

By all accounts, Presley seems to have possessed a quality that allowed his audience to perceive themselves in a new light. As Marion Keisker describes: "He was like a mirror in a way: whatever you were looking for, you were going to find in him." Presley appears to have been a focal point for the playing out of the deepest psychological drama of his culture. He embodied the American dream for a time, the dream of profound transformation via fame and wealth, certainly, but also via the more intangible quality of "cool" explicated above. As one admirer said: "We all wanted to be like Elvis"[150] because he seemed simultaneously godlike and all-too-human. He projected the appearance of effortless confidence and equanimity, but he was also authentic and accessible, even vulnerable in his public persona, though seemingly indifferent to the expectations of rational culture, at least until his induction into the army.[151]

Presley was the great American hope at that moment in the mid-fifties, and his fans poured countless amounts of money and attention into allowing him to become a shining beacon of human aspiration. Indeed, it is striking that, in a 2009 interview for *Rolling Stone*, Bob Dylan declares that "Elvis was truly some sort of American king. His face is even on the Statue of Liberty."[152] In fact, Presley's features do bear a striking resemblance to those of "Lady Liberty," and in those brief years between the release of "That's All Right" in 1954 and Presley's induction into the army in 1958, the singer was something like the embodiment of freedom in the collective imagination, an agent of liberation from the tyranny of the past.

But most of all, it was Presley's singing, tellingly inseparable from his physical movements, that captured the attention of a generation, and the way his vocal and gestural performativity made that generation feel. Presley simply possessed a charisma that is impossible to manufacture, and this "animal magnetism" expressed itself through his vocal motivity. There was an elemental potency produced by the relationship between

Presley and his audience that Presley himself did not fully intend and that he had little control over, and which had the precise effect of driving the audience "out of their minds," one definition of ecstasy, allowing for the ritualistic surrender of rational thought to focus on the felt quality of experience. According to a review of a Memphis show in 1956, young audience members "broke from their seats, swept like a wave up to the stage. . . . Elvis pleaded with them as pleasantly as he could to sit down, but it was like Canute telling the tide to stop."[153] Although Presley certainly had some agency in his performance, there seems to have been a historical impulse manifesting as a titanic surge of psycho-sexual affect beyond the ability of any individual to predict, create, or control. Presley appears to have been just as caught in the current of historical necessity as his audience, and together they acted out the transgressive narrative that would constitute the core of the counterculture's identity over the ensuing decades.[154]

The transition between rational and affective modes of constructing experience implicit in Presley's admonition to "get real, real gone for a change" seems to suggest that rock and roll was an artistic mediation of a profound epistemological shift in the history of Western culture. However, I would suggest that, while it was necessary for the intellect-privileging modern mind to explore, for the next half-century, the deconstructive moment of rupture between "epochs" that the main forms of postmodernism represent, Presley enacted this moment only briefly before forging on.[155] Indeed, the moment of pause that Presley performs after he cuts short the first version of "Milkcow Blues Boogie," but before he starts the second version can be seen as the dramatization of an interregnum between eras before he leaps into an early, prototypical model of what would become a novel mode of constructing experience. Based on the testimonies of those who witnessed Presley's early career, as well as on the subsequent permutations of the genre that Presley largely initiated, this mode appears to be constituted in the primacy of a way of thinking that privileges neither the intuitive mode of consciousness that largely defined premodernity nor the rational mode that has generally defined modernity, but rather reconciles these two modes, recognizing that each is an indispensable heuristic tool for understanding seemingly incommensurable domains of process.

CHAPTER 2
"A CREATIVE TENSION"

What is difficult, of course, is to see both images, both truths,
simultaneously: to suppress nothing, to remain open to the
paradox, to maintain the tension of opposites. Wisdom, like
compassion, often seems to require of us that we hold multiple
realities in our consciousness at once.

Richard Tarnas, *Cosmos and Psyche*[156]

Whereas Elvis Presley bore the personas of both edgy rebel and popular performer within his character in a relatively undifferentiated unity, John Lennon and Paul McCartney polarized themselves into these roles respectively, McCartney displaying an "appetite for kitsch" similar to Presley, while Lennon shared Presley's transgressive propensities.[157] Of course, both Lennon and McCartney contained this polarity between what are roughly definable as radical and conservative impulses within themselves as well (though they were both politically progressive), but their sustained alliance over the course of the Beatles' existence appears to have anchored them, allowing each one to pull in his direction, thereby producing an emergent entity that transcended their individuality as well as their influences.

Lennon and McCartney grew up together largely through their rock and roll apprenticeship, bound together by their mutual devotion to the genre, and for the first time in rock and roll, though in some ways prefigured by the Everly Brothers, Lennon and McCartney demonstrated that strong solo personalities could work together in a group as equals. Although the unit they formed was ultimately unsustainable, McCartney allowed Lennon to become a beacon for "truth" (exemplified in Lennon's song from the *Imagine* album "Gimme Some Truth") while Lennon allowed McCartney to be a brilliant performer, composer, and promoter of both their music and the countercultural ethos that they represented, transmitting previously marginal modes of thought into popular consciousness. Together, Lennon and McCartney were able to achieve the highest level of fame by combining sublimely beautiful music with the most profound kind of authenticity.[158]

As long as they were able to keep the group together, the partners formed an unassailable axis of countercultural, transformative force. As Ian MacDonald puts it: "the two represented a classic clash between truth and beauty,"[159] and although this radical difference in Lennon's and

McCartney's approaches certainly generated friction that ultimately led to the "divorce,"[160] as Lennon would call it, this "sibling rivalry" that Lennon describes between the two men also seems to have produced the creative energy that drove the band to ever greater heights over the course of their relatively short career. As Mark Lewisohn asserts: "The fusion of their talents and personalities would change the world."[161] Indeed, it seems clear that the two young musicians made the conscious choice when they first met to combine their considerable, and considerably different talents to create something that exceeded their individual capacities. As Lennon once said: "The records are the point. Not the Beatles as individuals,"[162] emphasizing the collective nature of their endeavor, for their immense creativity was impelled by the relationality of the two young men.

"Everything Else Was Unreal"

Beginning in the mid-fifties, rock and roll not only created a soundtrack to the lives of a generation, but, more than any other factor, it provided a general cultural attitude for young people, expressed in dress, speech, a wide array of thematic concerns, and, perhaps most importantly, in the focus on bodily knowledge as a counterbalance to the rationalization of predominant sectors of postwar British and American culture.[163] As Lennon declared: "rock'n'roll was real. Everything else was unreal. It was the only thing to get through to me out of all the things that were happening when I was fifteen."[164] Thus, it was not religion or business or politics or any of the other areas of human endeavor that gave Lennon's life meaning, that had the quality of reality, which is to say that, for the young musician, rock and roll addressed the way he felt what William James describes as "the total push and pressure of the cosmos"[165] better than any other form of cultural process.

Indeed, Lennon and his bandmates' devotion to rock and roll appears to have exemplified and mediated what MacDonald describes as "the true revolution of the sixties," which, "more powerful and decisive for Western society than any of its external by-products—was an inner one of feeling and assumption: a revolution in the head" which is "readable nowhere more vividly than in The Beatles' records. In effect," he concludes, "the 'generation gap' which opened in the Fifties turned out not to be a quarrel between a particular set of parents and children but an historical chasm between one way of life and another. . . . A new way of life so persuasively and pervasively replaced an earlier one that the majority made the mental crossing between them without really noticing."[166] The project of this chapter is to trace the process by which the Beatles initially came to discover and embody this "new way of life," mediated by a focus on "feeling" that would come to characterize the sixties counterculture and its successors, liberating realms of intuitive experience that had been rendered obscure to the modern mind through Weberian rationalization, though always in negotiation with the "spirit of capitalism."

As McCartney put it in 1967: "I don't believe that it ends with our Western logical thought. . . . It can't do because that's so messed up anyway, most of it, that you have got to allow for the possibility of there being a lot more than we know about."[167] And as MacDonald aptly notes, this fundamental transformation of Western culture, enacted in large part by rock and roll, was so subtle and pervasive that the reemergence of affect into central discursive nodes seems to have occurred for many people below the threshold of conscious awareness, allowing what is perhaps the deepest shift in our culture in the last century to remain hidden in plain sight. Tim Riley concurs: "The boundaries that Presley seemed to break in his singing became metaphors for ways of thinking about life. The most aggressive rock 'n' roll is a testing of limits, a combustive enactment of the frontier spirit."[168] However, despite the depth of purpose that the genre enacted, the explicit focus of the music has always been enjoyment, for rather than being incidental to the genre's meaning, it is *because* rock and roll is enjoyable that it has been such a profound force for liberation from cultural constraint and for the development of novel experiential forms.

Thus, John Lennon was certainly not alone in feeling rock and roll to be the most significant mediator of his experience when the new genre first hit Britain on a mass scale. As Bob Spitz describes the situation, the release of "Heartbreak Hotel" in England in 1956 caused "an explosion . . . felt by teenage listeners unlike anything that had ever hit them before," impelling "an emotional groundswell" in the culture.[169] As Lennon put it: "When I heard it . . . it was the end for me."[170] These phrases directly articulate the return of affectivity repressed in modernity, for the "emotional groundswell" that Lennon experienced along with his peers on hearing "Heartbreak Hotel" seemed to him the most valuable and significant factor in his experience at that time. As Lennon declared: "Nothing really affected me until Elvis,"[171] telling Marshall McLuhan: "I heard Elvis Presley. . . . There were a lot of other things going on, but that was the conversion. I kind of dropped everything,"[172] exchanging the predominant rationalized mode of thought for the more affectively oriented mode exemplified by rock and roll.

Similarly, Lennon's childhood best friend, Pete Shotton, has said that "Heartbreak Hotel" "was the most exciting thing [we'd] ever heard. . . .

It was the spark, and then the whole world opened up for us."[173] Lennon's discovery of the genre through the figure of Presley, the individual who, more than any other, "embodied the rock 'n' roll myth," was a definitive rupture in Lennon's experience. The music produced a kind of purpose in Lennon's life that had been conspicuously lacking, perhaps due to his early abandonment by his parents, a primal wound that would continue to haunt him. For Lennon, rock and roll was the obvious vehicle for meaning-making and, although it is the rhythm that kept Lennon "mesmerized"[174] as several commentators describe it, that is, in something like a state of ecstasy, Presley was the symbolic focus for that rhythmically induced affect. As discussed above, Presley was a primary embodiment of the deepest yearnings of a generation, reflecting what his audience was feeling and thereby providing an outlet for the expression of repressed experiential modes. And Lennon is perhaps Presley's most noted devotee, the single musician with the greatest claim to being Presley's direct successor, though Lennon's embeddedness in the Beatles complicates this lineage.[175]

Even at this early stage in Lennon's development in the mid-fifties, before he met the other boys who would become the Beatles, performing seems to have come to him as naturally as breathing. As school friend Eric Griffiths remarked: "John was a born performer. . . .You could sense that when he sang. It lifted him, he was energized." According to Griffiths, Lennon possessed "a sense that you could control a crowd's emotions with your voice." He seemed "to loosen up" when performing "like a captive animal released into its natural habitat." Where Lennon felt constrained in daily life, Shotton calling Lennon "the world's worst dancer, like a stiff cardboard box," he seemed physically liberated onstage, taking on the character of a wild beast in a strikingly similar way to Presley's conscious embrace of instinctive physicality. This ability to inhabit animality, closely connected with the quality of being "energized," seems to be the factor that allowed Lennon to mediate an audience's affective experience. Although somewhat constrained by the myriad limiting assumptions and conventions of somatically repressed and rationalized mid-century modern British life, Lennon's ability to enter into what appears to be a prerational, or perhaps transrational state of consciousness granted him the ability to "control a crowd's emotions" by inducing ecstasy in himself, and increasingly in his audience. Like Presley, Lennon seems to have possessed an intrinsic charisma that drew others' attention to him and that mediated their internal processes. As Billy Preston articulated it, having gotten to know Lennon and the Beatles on a 1962 tour during which he was backing Little Richard: "You just knew he was special; genius, I suppose, stood out even then."

Although this charismatic genius can be cultivated to an extent, it seems to be a quality that is intrinsic in some characters and not others.[176]

Initially, Lennon lifted Presley to an exalted position, identifying with him, or rather his conception of him, so completely that Lennon in a sense became Presley, integrating the older singer's performative mode into his own character until it was an indelible part of him. As Shotton describes Lennon's youthful emulation: "By this time, John thought he was Elvis Presley," which seems to indicate that Lennon held an image of Presley in his mind and tried to act, think, and be exactly how he imagined his idol, from the way he dressed and moved to the way he spoke and sang. Lennon reenacted Presley's archetypal narrative, that of the young, liminal outsider who incites a revolutionary upheaval, though on an emergent level of process as, from the beginning, Lennon possessed a certain critical faculty that Presley apparently lacked.[177]

However, this lack was probably the precondition for Presley's exceptional somatic and performative genius constituted in a liberated physicality that Lennon, "a true original," could never hope truly to emulate.[178] Thus, although Lennon idolized Presley, he began to assert his independence at a young age, going as far as to mock Presley's performance in *Love Me Tender* in a 1957 scene described by Shotton: "We sat in the cinema in Lime Street and killed ourselves laughing" at Presley, as "John thought he was ridiculous." An integral part of Lennon's initiation into the mysteries of rock and roll was apparently to become critical of his idol, problematizing his exclusive identification of Presley with the genre to which he was devoted. Instinctively, he knew that although Presley had essentially created the genre and thereby brought the intuitive mode that rock and roll embodied into popular consciousness, and he could never be surpassed in this relatively pure domain, Lennon could, on a conceptual level, take the genre farther than Presley could have imagined, largely because he wrote his own songs, but also because he was simply of a more intellectually experimental temperament.[179]

Subsequently, Lennon discovered another embodiment for his aspirations in the form of Little Richard, who allowed Lennon to step outside his exclusive identification with Presley to critique the elements of his idol's character with which he did not resonate. As in the oedipal relationship between father and son, Lennon symbolically slayed Presley with his ridicule, but only to become him. And if Jonathan Gould is correct that, "in a genre of popular music that was destined to be almost entirely dominated by male stars, it fell to Little Richard to play the Queen to Presley's King,"[180] then Little Richard's flamboyant homosexuality offered the potential for a kind of oedipal consummation of Lennon's love for the genre transcending Presley alone. However, that Little Richard referred to himself as the "King *and* Queen of Rock and Roll"[181] would seem to complicate this oedipal dynamic somewhat. Nevertheless, in order to imagine himself into Presley's persona, a template through which Lennon could ultimately cultivate his own unique persona, Lennon had finally to empty that persona of mystery through his critique while simultaneously shifting his temporary allegiance to a more "feminine" figure (if we take Richard's wearing of makeup, his fluttering physical performativity, and his falsetto vocal interjections as a transgressive performance of femininity), thus rendering Presley's role accessible to himself.

In similar, though perhaps less oedipal operations, Lennon later asserted "I WAS Buddy Holly,"[182] and that Chuck Berry was "in a different class from the other performers" because "he really wrote his own stuff."[183] Indeed, these two influences, perhaps more than any others, provided the initial models for Lennon's songwriting persona. Thus, through a series of such identifications with idols and the subsequent disenchantment and psychic reconciliation with them, Lennon was able to forge his own identity, appropriating elements of different figures and combining them within the crucible of his experience into a more encompassing synthesis. And this synthesis was exemplified in the broader aesthetic range of the music created by Lennon who, like most great artists, mediated the integration of previously disparate tropes and genres within his persona, from American rock and roll and rhythm and blues to skiffle, music hall, and British comedic wit. However, Lennon's breadth of musical and conceptual scope was purchased at the expense of the narrower depth of nearly pure affective brilliance in which Presley has never been eclipsed. Ultimately, Lennon was able to return to his love for Presley, seeing him in a more balanced way, like the adult child who, after a period of rebellion, builds a more mature relationship with his father.[184]

Despite his critique of Presley, and probably because of it, Lennon was able to embody the transgressivity of rock and roll with a profound belief in its righteousness in large part because he found it affectively satisfying. Indeed, though the Cavern club in Liverpool was initially a jazz venue that allowed for some skiffle, a genre based largely on American folk, jazz, and country music popular in Britain during the same years as rock and roll's first efflorescence, Lennon flagrantly flouted the prohibition against rock and roll in a joyfully primal act of defiance. At an early show at the Cavern in 1961, the Quarry Men, who would eventually become the Beatles, began their set with an acceptable skiffle standard by Lonnie Donegan. However, for the second song,

Lennon announced "Don't Be Cruel," prompting Rod Davis, one of the early members of the band, to protest: "You can't *do* that. They'll eat you alive if you start playing rock 'n roll in the Cavern." However, oblivious to Davis' admonition, Lennon, "a boy beyond convention and control"[185] as Mark Lewisohn describes him, began the song anyway and, according to Davis: "You could tell the audience was uneasy about it, but that didn't stop John. He was just going to continue and expected us to follow."[186]

Lennon was possessed of a missionary zeal for rock and roll that impelled him to play it in the face of intense opposition. He had a penchant for loutish transgressivity aligned with the "Teddy Boys," the pseudo-Edwardian rebels who emerged just prior to rock and roll in Britain, a distinctive hybrid of Edwardian and postwar American styles of dress that Lennon temporarily adopted.[187] Like the Teds, who had a reputation for violence and destruction, he seems to have enjoyed the somewhat more subtle musical conflict at the Cavern, carrying the new genre into what was then a center of the Liverpool music scene's old order, eventually transforming the club into the primary locus of a new dispensation. Lennon implicitly understood that the jazz establishment in Britain had become a conventional orthodoxy, a music industry, which seemed to him a betrayal of the spirit of novelty that rock and roll represented at that moment. Thus, Lennon seems to have felt it to be his duty to cast those who had inexorably turned popular music into mere entertainment out of the temple, the symbolic locus of cultural authority.

"An Instant Recognition"

Paul McCartney's smooth diplomacy, his "considerable tact and social awareness,"[188] is often described as a counterbalance to Lennon's rough authenticity.[189] When Lennon and McCartney met in July 1957, "there was an instant recognition," a kind of "love at first sight"[190] based upon their mutual devotion to rock and roll. Indeed, while Lennon possessed undeniable charisma, energy, and talent, McCartney impelled Lennon to work consistently at his craft, practicing guitar and transcribing lyrics from the radio.[191] As Shotton explains: "Paul had made a huge impression on John," for, "in a way, his ability underscored all John's [musical] shortcomings."[192] McCartney, strong where Lennon was weak and weak where Lennon was strong, impelled Lennon really to become a musician or, as Lennon expressed it in his bluntly humorous way: "Paul taught me how to play properly."[193]

Whereas Lennon was direct and tactless, a large contributing factor to his fascination, McCartney had an innate feel for the subtleties of performance, for engaging the audience and holding their attention through the nuances of facial expression, movement, and pacing. Where Lennon demanded the audience's attention by smirking force of will, McCartney solicited that attention, seducing the crowd with his puppy-dog eyes and his infectious enthusiasm. Although Lennon may have been more visionary than McCartney, it also seems clear that McCartney had a greater facility for implementing that vision as a successfully propagating system, as well as simply for playing instruments.[194]

Subsequent to the "hurricane force"[195] of Lennon's and McCartney's fateful meeting, as Lennon recounts: "We spent hours just listening to the stars we admired. . . . We'd sit around and look all intent and intense and then, when the record had ended, we [sic] try and reproduce the same sort of sounds for ourselves."[196] Lennon's and McCartney's methodology for creating their sound involved close listening and attempting to reproduce what they heard, but the constraints imposed by their limited technical abilities, like Presley's rudimentary strumming, are part of what allowed them to produce novel musical forms.[197] In learning primarily by ear, it was necessary for the boys to invent their own technique and their own style, perhaps not "correct" as far as their sources, or the British musical establishment, were concerned, but highly effective nonetheless.

However, the deeper purpose of this "bashing away" seems to have been to fuse themselves into a unit so that they could act at certain moments as if they were a single mind. Their mutual immersion in an "intuitive" "rhythm"[198] suggests the mode that focuses on perceiving the qualitative nature of duration elucidated by Henri Bergson, the felt quality of the moment. Similarly, the phenomenon of "instantaneity"[199] that MacDonald describes in relation to the Beatles seems to lead inexorably back to the Bergsonian durational quality of experience, which MacDonald portrays as one of the defining factors in the cultural transformation that the Beatles did so much to mediate. Riley also evokes this intuitive approach to temporality for making music, suggesting that the tempos of the songs were determined by "feel," or even by something that exceeded the individuality of the musicians rather than by the technological precision of the metronome.[200]

In a broader sense, Gould observes that rock and roll "had a temporal as well as a visceral immediacy for" Lennon and McCartney that "seemed to be in tune with the world to come,"[201] a prophetic intimation of the emergence of a new approach to experience constituted in the dialectical reembrace of a premodern relation to temporality by the rationalized conception of time privileged in modernity. This focus on the constantly shifting quality of bodily experience, a major concern in the sixties counterculture, not only resides at the heart of great musicianship, but strongly informs the various Eastern contemplative and yogic traditions that found such favor in the West beginning in earnest during that period, in large part through the Beatles themselves, particularly George Harrison.

Indeed, adding Harrison into the group soon after Lennon and McCartney met in 1957 only increased the energetic complexity of the band. Having three guitarists in the mix impelled them to refine and "clarify" their "increasingly shapeless" arrangements, bringing an intellectual quality to the visceral physicality that was the baseline of the genre, "like cracking a code." In this kind of analytic exercise, the three young men were able to channel their exceptional intensity through the focusing structure of simplified musical arrangements, one of many moments in their trajectory when the Beatles employed the rational mode to temper the somatic drive that had been the defining characteristic of rock and roll music. Like the discipline that goes into tuning a guitar, as Spitz describes, filtering their "exuberance" through rigorous "focus" allowed their combined sonic "vibration" to attain heightened "resonance."[202] And as McCartney sums up the purpose of all this vigorous activity: "That's what I was after: *chills*," the physical recognition of novelty.[203]

"A Momentous Discovery"

In early 1958, McCartney mentioned to Lennon that he had been writing songs, playing one for him called "I Lost My Little Girl" and, according to Pete Shotton, Lennon was "floored." Through the obsessive repetition that practicing entails, an activity characteristic of rationality, the two boys worked themselves into a focused state, which seems to have formed the precondition for the emergence of inspiration, for the "momentous discovery" of songwriting. The Beatles elicited a felt epiphany that could only have been attained through rigorous commitment, Spitz hardly exaggerating when he writes that McCartney's "disclosure" of his songwriting activity "is arguably a pivotal event in modern musical history," for this discovery did in fact "set the current flowing" that would ultimately provide the impetus to mediate an integration of polarized, and seemingly incommensurable epistemologies. The Beatles' role in relation to the rationalized milieu in which they found themselves was, like Presley, to embody the repressed intuitive mode even as they did a great deal to integrate this mode with the predominant rationality of their culture. Indeed, the integration of the roles of musician and composer within the group played a large part in integrating the more somatic performative mode with the more conceptual compositional mode exemplified by Tin Pan Alley, often driven more by studious craftsmanship than pure inspiration.[204]

The Beatles transgressed the conventions of songwriting and playing, radically expanding both in the process. Their experience as performers eventually allowed them a creative freedom that can only come from spending many hours learning to connect with an audience, not primarily in an intellectual domain, but in an intuitive domain where the rules of songwriting seem conventions begging to be broken in order to make the songs more effective vehicles for the elicitation of affect. Similarly, their experience as songwriters, however intuitive, trained them in the more abstractly conceptual art of fitting words to the mathematical relations of chords, melodies, and harmonies in a pleasing and novel way, a quality that they then applied to their formal and technological musical experiments, not to mention their visual and verbal aesthetics. The Beatles formed the paradigmatic case for the rock group, in which realm they have yet to be surpassed in many ways, but particularly in the sheer number of formal and conceptual innovations that they introduced into the musical and cultural lexicons, from incorporating "modal, pentatonic, and Indian scales" and unusual instruments into rock and roll's vocabulary, to the use of tape-loops and the very idea of the "concept album." Thus, in their humorous, often lighthearted way, the Beatles catalyzed the transformation of their genre, their medium, and their culture beyond all reasonable expectation.[205]

However, before they could become avatars for the return of repressed bodily knowledge and then integrate that more fundamental mode with intellect, it was necessary for the nascent Beatles first to integrate the specific vocal and musical inflections of their influences. At the early stage of their development in 1958, the arrangements of most of the songs they played were copied directly from the records. The Beatles, as creators of a new style, found it necessary initially to emulate the styles of their predecessors, internalizing their way of approaching the world through music. By engaging in this kind of rigorous apprenticeship, they acquired the tools, the vocabulary of the genre in which they were working. Of course, original rock and roll was already an integration of disparate elements, though the Beatles took this initial synthesis and radically expanded its encompassing reach over the course of their career, as processual revolutions seem generally to consist of just this sort of consolidation of seemingly incommensurable elements.

After the Beatles' apprenticeship, there was a moment when, in order to create something genuinely new, they found it necessary to integrate the previous tropes into an emergent synthesis or, as Lennon would later put it: "Don't copy the swimming teacher, learn how to swim."[206] One might almost suspect that Lennon had read the passage from Bergson's *Creative Evolution* concerning how the act of swimming precedes intellectual understanding of what swimming entails: "Come enter the water," Bergson writes, "and when you know how to swim, you will understand how the mechanism of swimming is connected with that of walking. Swimming is an extension of walking, but walking would never have pushed you on to swimming"[207] However, what is more likely is that Lennon instinctively knew that one must thrust oneself in a leap of faith outside of what Bergson terms "the circle of the given" in order to produce genuine novelty.

Often, the discoverers of emergent modes of thought refer back to some older precedent in order to justify the audacity of their enterprise. The Beatles, revolting not only against the jazz orthodoxy of that moment in the late fifties, but against the main stream of British rock and roll exemplified by Cliff Richard and the Shadows, employed certain influences as justification for various aspects of the new and unprecedented style they were creating, one of which was the composition of their own songs. According to McCartney: "People these days take it for granted that you do" write songs, "but nobody used to then. . . . John started to write because of Buddy Holly."[208] As McCartney points out, the Beatles were the first major British group to write most of their songs and to break out of the lock-step dance moves exemplified by the Shadows. What seems commonplace now was then revolutionary, which demonstrates how quickly the revolution becomes a new orthodoxy. Like the Copernican revolutionaries who justified their Sun-centered cosmology by reference to ancient philosophers like Aristarchus, the Pythagoreans, and Heraclitus, not only Holly, but Chuck Berry, Little Richard, Carl Perkins, Smokey Robinson, Roy Orbison, Larry Williams, and Arthur Alexander all set a "precedent"[209] for, and gave "sanction"[210] to, the compositional novelty promulgated by the Beatles.

However, Holly was extremely influential on the nascent Beatles in one particular respect, for although Holly may not have been as brilliantly visceral as Presley, Berry, or Little Richard, his collaborations with the Crickets and their producer, Norman Petty, in the writing, arranging, and recording of their songs formed the early paradigm of the self-contained band that the Beatles would come to exemplify to a much greater degree. Although Holly and his band employed much the same instrumentation as Berry or Presley in his early incarnation, the Crickets, whose name would improbably inspire the greatest band of all time to identify themselves with a lowly insect, also served as the primary model for this deeply collaborative quality that would characterize the Beatles' approach to making music.[211]

In addition, Holly's relatively stiff "whiteness," in contrast to Presley's looser approach (though Cliff Richard made Holly seem positively loose-limbed), rendered him more accessible to English teenagers than perhaps any other American rock and roller for, of the Beatles' four primary influences (Holly, Berry, Presley, and Little Richard), Holly and the Crickets were the only act significantly more successful in England then they were in America. Thus, the contours of the Beatles' early style were traced by their range of influences, a spectrum stretching from the wild, unhinged physicality of Little Richard to the more polite and studiously bespectacled exuberance of Holly, whose persona created a bridge between American rock and roll and the Quarry Men's native performative influences such as Lonnie Donegan and the Goons.[212]

By all accounts, the Beatles' songwriting process is extremely reminiscent of Presley's and his band's methodless method of "acting the fool" in the Sun Studio until they stumbled upon a pragmatically viable novelty. Lennon and McCartney were drawn by a vague vision, "a general notion of where something was headed"[213] reminiscent of Whitehead's "lure for feeling," a "subjective aim" that "is not primarily intellectual."[214] All of the preexisting melodic, harmonic, rhythmic, and lyrical tropes that Lennon and McCartney were absorbing by studying the songs of others became a palette from which they could draw without analysis or premeditation, so immersed were they in the musical "tradition," to produce songs that often sounded as if they had been received fully formed, "like driftwood that had washed up onshore."[215] And this creative act was only possible because they possessed an affectively luring sense that defied the necessity, and even the possibility, of rational proof in advance, allowing them audaciously to write "Another Lennon-McCartney Original"[216] at the top of a blank page on which they would jot the lyrics to a new song. Thus, the felt "aim" of the songwriting process is not primarily a "lure" for intellectual analysis, though it is susceptible to such analysis in retrospect, but for the motive force of bodily experience. Through this process, Lennon and McCartney "created a sound," a mode of arranging sonic elements to form an irreducibly novel gestalt.

As Lennon declared: "lyrics didn't really count"[217] because, at least until their encounter with Bob Dylan, the Beatles' primary focus was on creating "hooks," whether verbal or nonverbal, that would excite their listeners, inducing the kind of self-transcendence that only a truly great refrain can. Although the Beatles were lyrically inventive, and often witty and evocative, words, as the primary medium of activity for a culturally logocentric rationality, were not the main focus of their art. Rather, it is the nonverbal elements that make the experience of the Beatles' music so affectively profound. However, contrary to Lennon's provocative statement, the words do in fact matter, but only insofar as they are sung in the overall musical context of the songs. Indeed, I would argue that the "comparative vagueness"[218] of the lyrics, the fact that they cannot be read as poetry on a page, is not a fault but a virtue, as the lyrics do exactly what they need to do in context, which is to evoke images that grant the music a conscious focus and meaning, but are not so specific or overwrought as to detract from the vital experience.[219]

"Holding a Mirror"

A large part of what allowed Lennon and McCartney to create such universally acclaimed music was their partnership, tossing the "beach ball"[220] back and forth between them. According to McCartney: "It was great . . . because instead of looking into my own mind for a song, I could see John playing—as if he was holding a mirror to what I was doing."[221] Developing their musical aesthetic face to face seems to have thrust their attention out of their own minds, allowing the two young men to feel as if they were temporarily dissolving the boundaries between their individual, egoic selves. By focusing on one another, rather than on themselves, they were apparently able to elicit from one another a polarization of their intrinsic characters, a mutual tension which allowed each of them to embody their endemic natures in a relatively pure way. It seems that they initially focused not primarily on their internal processes as Bob Dylan did, but on performing their role in the band, which allowed them to "get out of their heads" to inhabit a collective consciousness, not dissimilar to the "group mind" experienced by athletic teams or by military units, though with quite a different general orientation.[222]

While they were able to maintain their partnership, Lennon and McCartney formed a whole that seemed to surpass them individually, though the mutual partiality of their characters ultimately proved to be limiting once they split at the end of the sixties. For the duration of their immensely productive partnership, however, the two young men were able to sustain the intensity of their experience together by passing the reins back and forth between them, so to speak, rarely having to pause or hold back because one of them could always be counted on to take the lead if the other's will or inspiration began to flag. According to early bandmate Colin Hanton: "Something special was growing between them

. . . something that went past friendship as we knew it. It was as if they drew power from each other." In a very real sense, their "strangely connected" mode granted them the motive "power," which allowed them to "create an alternative reality" that ultimately became a lived reality for millions of fans, profoundly transforming popular music, and culture, in the process.

Furthermore, although verbal language was a vital aspect of their creative activity, the two young men generally "let their guitars do the talking,"[223] as Spitz puts it, for despite their markedly different personalities, they seem always to have connected most deeply in the musical domain. While words played an integral role in their partnership, their primary mode of engagement with one another and with their art was one that bypassed verbal formulation and interpretation for, as Riley writes: "The Beatles deserve to be addressed on their own terms. What's missing from most Beatles criticism is a sense of how they best expressed themselves: through instrumental and vocal interplay,"[224] through ongoing sonic conversations consisting of harmonic and instrumental punctuation, call-and-response, and other forms of musical imbrication that produced a communal, even organismic quality in their songs. As noted in relation to Presley, this primarily nonrational mode of engagement with experience is sufficient in itself, though it certainly invites the kind of analysis being performed in the present text.

However, it seems to be the case that theoretical analysis, though vitally necessary in preparing the way for creative activity or in understanding novelty after the fact, is almost always detrimental to the kind of co-creative intuitive process in which Lennon and McCartney were engaged while it is occurring. With their attention focused on the felt quality of experience, on the rhythmic and tonal resonances of their guitars and singing voices, trying to articulate what they were doing in words as they were doing it would have broken the spell, so to speak, drawing their attention away from primarily nonverbal modes and into the more rational and intellectual modes characteristic of verbal articulation. Put simply, it is nearly impossible to enact more than one mode at a time, particularly in a sustained way.

Like a car stuck between gears, the attempt to inhabit simultaneously two epistemologies generally produces a grating dissonance that is not conducive to moving toward one's destination. Thus, when the Beatles were playing, they were not talking. However, as can be witnessed so clearly in much of the recorded footage of the Beatles' banter, even their speech was often less about making rational sense than about the sound and cadence of the words, the "scouse" accent characteristic of Liverpool strikingly similar in this regard to various inflections of Southern and

Midwestern drawl in the United States, which also often seem to privilege sound over sense. Indeed, according to Gould, this playful approach to language is characteristic of the general "Lancastrian tradition of puns and deliberate malapropisms,"[225] which, aside from the focus on the sound of the words, also subverts literal meanings in favor of associative humor. "A Hard Day's Night" and "Tomorrow Never Knows" are two primary examples of this tendency, a sort of compromise formation between Presley's inarticulate somatic brilliance and the verbal obsession characteristic of the predominant British culture at that time.

Perhaps more than their verbal relationship, Lennon's and McCartney's songwriting partnership was the most tangible evidence of their rare quality. Whereas before meeting McCartney, Lennon had been something of a "rebel without a cause," his relationship with McCartney provided the context for Lennon's felt potential to manifest itself. Their mutual discovery of songwriting could be described as something like an emergent phenomenon that may not have taken form out of potentiality but for the tension of opposites that the two musicians together embodied. That is, while the qualities possessed by each of these young men alone may not have been enough to produce the kind of radical novelty that Presley created, Lennon's and McCartney's constant negotiation of their difference produced a qualitatively new style that ultimately surpassed their mentor in many ways.

Where Presley's primary role was to synthesize black and white musical and cultural tropes within himself, Lennon's and McCartney's role was to take the initial synthesis exemplified by Presley as their starting point, their thesis, and then polarize themselves along a different axis within the space that Presley had liberated, which ultimately allowed the Beatles to perform an expansive and sustained synthesis of many more novel elements than Presley had been able to absorb and recontextualize on his own. Where Presley's novelty was almost purely performative, the Beatles combined this performativity with compositional, conceptual, technological, and philosophical experimentation to produce a new whole. As is usually the case in the development of cultural process, Presley was the giant on whose shoulders the Beatles stood. Through this lineage, rock and roll appears to have been the platform for a pervasive transformation of world views that is still occurring more than a half century later and whose implications are far broader than the genre itself.

However, even in the Quarry Men's first recording in 1958, a version of Buddy Holly's "That'll Be the Day," there is an undeniable potency that exceeds Holly's influence. In the nascent Beatles' initial foray into the studio, they took Holly's song and made it their own, investing it with an intensity that Holly's version did not possess. Lennon certainly had an instinct for drawing the attention of an audience, whether onstage or in a recording, but this quality was amplified by his competitive relationship with McCartney. Although it is impossible to know how Lennon's and McCartney's music would have developed had they never met, one can catch a glimpse of this alternate reality by comparing their post-Beatles solo work to the music they made together. Though they both produced a number of great songs on their own, there is a balance and driving force granted by their partnership that is undeniably lacking in even their best solo efforts, exemplified in the harmonic blend of their voices as a sonic, physical performance of their combined characters. In this first recording of a cover song by the band that would eventually become the Beatles, the "creative tension" between Lennon and McCartney rendered the song "a minor miracle," a locus for novelty's ingression into cultural process. In making this recording, the group enacted a mode that bypassed intellect through ecstatic affect, and while they had not yet been able to evoke this kind of motivity consistently in their audience, the first step toward inducing such affect in others is apparently to induce ecstasy in oneself.[226]

"Confirmation of Their Calling"

Besides their mutual devotion to rock and roll, it is probably the death of both of their mothers when they were teenagers (McCartney at fourteen and Lennon at seventeen[227]), that cemented the bond between them. McCartney's mother had died of cancer in 1956 and, when Lennon's mother was hit by a car and instantly killed in 1958, the two boys suddenly shared a trauma that few others could understand. As McCartney would recall: "Now we were both in this, both losing our mothers. . . . This was a bond for us, something of ours, a special thing."[228] Their trajectory as musicians already determined, their mutual loss seems to have driven them into the depths of despair, which subsequently seems to have propelled them with an explosive force to emerge from those depths to bring what they had learned into the light of day. As with all of the great milestones in life, from marriage and having children to receiving a degree or losing one's parents, it is impossible to know what these things really mean until one has lived with them day after day. The effect that these experiences would have can certainly be understood on an intellectual level, but the profound changes that such events impel in one's physical being must be lived through in order to be comprehended adequately. Thus, it seems that Lennon's and McCartney's primal wounds were a primary factor in their experience that propelled them to the heights of musical achievement.

After his mother's death, which Lennon described as "the worst thing that ever happened to me," the young man descended into a period of drunken rage and self-destructive behavior, while in a balancing operation that would characterize the Beatles dynamic for the length of their career, McCartney took over temporarily as the motivating force in the group. The death of Lennon's mother seems to have given him license to explore the emotional extremes that were his inclination, but that he had until then restrained himself from fully inhabiting. This trauma produced a belief in Lennon that he had "no responsibilities to anyone now," a brutal kind of liberation, which in turn brought out McCartney's intrinsic need to succeed, and to create a musical context within which Lennon could express his anger and sadness, not only at his mother's death, but at his early abandonment by both of his parents.[229] As Lennon would scream repeatedly in the first song on his first solo album: "Mama, don't go. Daddy, come home."[230]

Emerging from his angry bender in 1959, Lennon was pulled inexorably back into the rising tide of the musical genre he would come to define, and when Lennon and McCartney went to see Eddie Cochran and Gene Vincent play in Liverpool in early 1960, they witnessed up-close a "confirmation of their calling."[231] Seeing the American musicians in action impelled them to enact the same role. In an earlier stage of their development, the distance of Elvis Presley, Little Richard, Buddy Holly, and the rest was a spur to the imaginative, exploratory discovery of rock and roll, this "ironic detachment"[232] from their primary influences granting a novel inflection to the distinctively American musical form. After this initial stage of romantic distance, however, their direct engagement with these arguably second-tier American rock and roll stars (Vincent and Cochran) seems to have done much to initiate a more focused stage in which the Beatles actually learned the specific performative techniques that allowed their heroes to induce a self-forgetting rapture in their audiences. In particular, the liberated physicality of these artists, legs splayed at precipitous angles, bodies bopping with manic abandon, seems to have provided a model for the Beatles' performative breakthrough in Hamburg later that same year.[233]

After years of honing their craft and playing in the same clubs around Liverpool, the Beatles finally embarked on their first tour in May of 1960, a nine-day jaunt through Scotland with manufactured pop idol Johnny Gentle.[234] Having dreamt for so long of being real rock and roll musicians, which generally meant going on tour, this first taste of the road seemed to them a qualitative leap forward. This was the moment when they began to be able to put into practice the role they had been imagining themselves into for years. And this role was partially constituted in producing the relentless rhythms of their music—though mediated by their sublime harmonies and clever arrangements—literally to pound the audience out of their heads and into their bodies, the crowd's rationalized cultural assumptions temporarily cast aside as the audience members were "undone by the music."

According to Gentle, Lennon and McCartney "operated on a different frequency than those around them," perhaps because their innate talent had been forged in the polarized tension between them, bonded together by their mutual pain so that they achieved a level of energetic intensity that was qualitatively different than their contemporaries. They were inhabiting what appeared to observers as a more expansive mode of engagement in which their bodies and minds were relatively unified, striving desperately, gleefully to pull their audiences up with them, out of what their milieu perceived as the static orthodoxy of rationalized postwar conformity and into the wild, creative, exploratory attitude that would come to define the sixties counterculture, though many of the counterculture's innovations were ultimately absorbed into the main streams of culture, thereby transforming those streams. Indeed, Gentle's comment that he had "never seen anything like it"[235] closely echoes Roy Orbison's statement about Presley that "there was just no reference point in the culture to compare it,"[236] both acknowledgements of the ingression of radical novelty that the two men were witnessing. Furthermore, Gentle's emphasis of their composite quality as "*Lennon and McCartney*"[237] reinforces the sense of their mutual participation in a process exceeding their individuality, fan Bernie Boyle declaring that the two young men "were so tight it was like there was a telepathy between them: on stage, they'd look at each other and know instinctively what the other was thinking."[238]

"Mach Schau!"

However, by all accounts it is the Beatles' stint in Hamburg, beginning a few months after their tour with Gentle, which truly forged them into the force for cultural transformation that they would soon become.[239] Harrison has called Hamburg "the naughtiest city in the world"[240] and indeed, the city appears to have been the ideal place for the Beatles to forego rationality and work their way into a more embodied mode. As Spitz observes: "There existed an ethos of hedonism that stretched back to the Middle Ages, when Hamburg was a member of the Hanseatic League, a free port, and therefore an essentially lawless haven." Fellow

Liverpool musician Adrian Barber has called Hamburg "kind of a Dodge City of the open seas" and, as Spitz notes, up until the early sixties when the Beatles had their first residency in the city, "the tradition was preserved as a foil to the rigid German culture, which was built around regimentation and power."[241] This rigidity of German culture had much in common with the "stiff upper-lip" of British culture (starkly contrasting with Presley's volatile upper lip, one corner twitching in his characteristic snarl), for the two great Northern European industrial powers had been primary leading forces in the rationalization of Western culture over the previous centuries, producing many of the scientific, philosophical, and technological innovations that led to the world in which the Beatles found themselves.

Although there was certainly some animosity between the two nations that had fought one another in the Second World War less than two decades previously, Hamburg was apparently home to a vigorous anglophilia, perhaps as a compensatory reaction by the generally progressive city to Germany's fascist past. Thus, the Beatles discovered a complement to their own culture in what might be described as the German equivalent of San Francisco, the permissive port town where radical ways of being come to incubate as a reaction to the predominant culture of the respective nations.[242] Indeed, it is striking that the primary side street of the Reeperbahn where the Beatles were playing was called Grosse Freiheit, which translates as "Great Freedom," as this was the ideal place for the Beatles to "find their freedom" from the constraints of British propriety. Aside from the permissive quality of Hamburg, the Beatles were liberated by the mere fact that they were strangers in an unknown city, far away from their friends and families, all of whom participated in the "reflexive debunkery of Liverpool, which blunted ambition as surely as it punctured pretension."

When they first arrived in Hamburg in August 1960, the young musicians possessed a large repertoire of songs, not only rock and roll, but skiffle and pop standards as well, though they initially failed to connect with their new audiences. Until their foray to Hamburg, the Beatles, to some extent, were scholars of rock and roll who also played— deeply devoted to the genre and extremely knowledgeable about it, but lacking the visceral intensity in their performance that the music required in order truly to move a crowd. However, the Beatles' encounter with audiences in the Reeperbahn, Hamburg's red-light district, drawn there by the area's ambiance of unmitigated instinctual activities, particularly those related to sex, drugs, and rock and roll, soon forced the Beatles to break out of their scholarly dedication to their music and into a more physical and emotive performativity largely derived from their American mentors. Simply stated, Hamburg is where the Beatles became a real rock and roll band. Or as Harrison put it: "Hamburg was really like our apprenticeship, learning how to play in front of people."[243]

Gould points out that the Beatles, by going to Hamburg, were enacting what Joseph Campbell termed the "monomyth," constituted in "a journey to a strange and distant land, in the course of which a young hero is tested by his encounters . . . and from which the hero returns . . . transformed by the experience, and possessed of some new form of strength or knowledge that has the power to change the world." This archetypal myth-form succinctly describes the Beatles' encounter with Hamburg for, just as ancient heroes such as Hercules and Odysseus found it necessary to enter Hades in order to emerge transformed, so too were the Beatles compelled to engage with the underworld quality of the Reeperbahn, which was a haven for all manner of instinctual activity associated with sinful animality and unconscious drives.[244]

However, the encounter with Hamburg's underworld tone was only the initial spur toward their transformation, for it required the concerted efforts of two geographically closer, though significantly less exalted mentors than Presley and Little Richard, or even Lonnie Donegan and Spike Milligan, to incite the Beatles to produce their collective performative style. As early manager Alan Williams notes, when the Beatles first arrived at the Indra club in Hamburg, their act was "far too deadpan," adding that the band merely "stood still and strummed." While this static performativity may have worked in some genres like folk or country music, or even skiffle to some extent, rock and roll is a type of music that generally requires movement. The essence of the genre is its rhythm, which tends to impel musicians and audiences toward physical and intuitive modes, as well as toward a more effusive performativity and Williams, intent on receiving his commission, admonished the boys to "make a show."[245]

Having grown up in Liverpool, however, the Beatles were deeply conditioned to take a skeptical, ironically humorous view of life for, as Gould observes, in Liverpool "the standard line, proudly repeated by natives to non-natives with the air of an original thought, was that life in the city was so hard that you had to be a comedian to survive there."[246] The Beatles, somewhat uncomfortable with physicality, filtered the somatic quality of the music through humor in order to mediate the absurdity of being a group of relatively inhibited young British men trying to emulate the easy instinctual physicality of musicians like Little Richard, Elvis Presley, and Chuck Berry. Indeed, as MacDonald notes, the rationalized quality of predominant sectors of English culture in the early sixties produced "an embarrassed unco-ordination of mind and body," and "even a basic sense of rhythm was rare."[247] Although the Beatles were certainly those rare British lads who had more than a basic sense of rhythm, it appears that the somatically inhibited quality of their culture at that moment still constrained their performativity to a great extent. With Williams exhorting the band to throw aside their inhibitions, Lennon particularly found the whole thing hilarious, flinging himself around the stage and parodying Chuck Berry's "duck-walk" while Williams shouted: "That's it! Make a show! Make a show!'"

Although Lennon may have initially been mocking Williams' suggestion, Lennon later declaring that "part of me would sooner have been a comedian,"[248] the band ultimately incorporated the liberated physicality that resulted from the hilarity into their repertoire, but always maintaining the ironic humor, which ultimately allowed an equally inhibited audience, particularly in Britain and America, access to their own repressed physicality. Club owner Bruno Koschmider followed Williams' lead, urging the Beatles in German to "*Mach Schau! Mach Schau!*" and the Beatles apparently found this whole scenario uproariously funny, "like the Goons doing a hilarious take on the Nazis." Humor can often constitute a profound energetic release, as what began as a parody appears to have emancipated the physically inhibited young men. The wildness of their new environment in Hamburg combined with Williams and Koschmider barking orders at them seems to have jolted the band's center of attention out of their heads, out of their analytical minds, and into their bodies.[249]

As Sigmund Freud suggests in *Jokes and Their Relation to the Unconscious*, laughter is a process which can have a cathartic effect by liberating psychosomatic content that has been repressed, and which he describes in very similar terms to the dreams that initially formed the primary textual objects for the psychoanalytic mode of interpretation. Similarly, Alfred North Whitehead is reported to have said: "Laughter is our reminder that our theories are an attempt to make existence intelligible, but necessarily only an attempt, and does not the irrational, the instinctive burst in to keep the balance true by laughter?"[250] Put simply, laughter can be a recognition of limit, the coming to consciousness of that which had been unconscious or unacknowledged, of that which exceeds our rational, theoretical formulations, a recognition often accompanied by physical disinhibition.

Thus, the effect of laughter induced by absurdist humor on the Beatles' performative mode was profound, again recalling the moment of eruption when Presley and his band created "That's All Right," the initiatory declaration of rock and roll, by "acting the fool" a half-decade earlier. Whereas before, the Beatles had been earnestly strumming their songs, focusing on their singing and playing in a rather staid and studious way that perhaps reflected their disciplined training as relatively proper English school boys, their lack of connection with the rowdier Reeperbahn audiences impelled them to try a new approach. Although the Beatles had been studying American rock and roll from afar, they had previously been embedded in the polite propriety of English rock and roll exemplified by Cliff Richard who, according to Lennon, embodied "everything we hated in pop."

Whereas Presley had grown up in the more somatically oriented African American neighborhood of Memphis, the Reeperbahn was the Beatles' first direct encounter with relatively unmediated affect on a large scale, though of a rather different kind than that encountered by Presley. Nevertheless, their tenure in Germany seems to have liberated the Beatles' emulation of African American musical tropes, Little Richard later declaring: "Man, those Beatles are fabulous! If I hadn't seen them I'd never have dreamed they were white. They have a real authentic Negro sound."[251] Through their African American heroes, the Beatles introduced many of the stylistic and performative elements often characteristic of black culture in America at that moment not only to England, but to an American public that had forgotten to some degree the pull of that musical mode in the succession of saccharine teen idols that flooded the airwaves in the early sixties. As McCartney succinctly sums up their initial orientation in the *Anthology*: "We thought we were a little R&B combo."

In Hamburg, once the band realized that the approach they had taken thus far was not efficacious in this new context, they became receptive to the admonitions of Williams and Koschmider, whose primary function, like mentors or coaches in many different areas of endeavor, was to provoke a self-overcoming in the Beatles. In this case, the band was undergoing the precise kind of transformation that they would soon mediate in larger cultural realms outside of their immediate social circles, breaking the bonds of rational propriety to act in ways that they never had onstage, though they had seen their American influences perform enough to be able to emulate their physicality with some encouragement. Thus, the knowledge of their imminent failure if they did not adapt, combined with the two men shouting at them bilingually to "make a show" seems to have elicited a release of creative vitality from the Beatles, beginning as a mockery of their mentors, but issuing into an unexpected bodily liberation.

And this liberation quickly appeared in their performances as the young men dynamically threw themselves around the stage, though always filtered through their ironic humor, transmuting their act into an exhilaratingly primal spectacle, but with an edge of satirical self-awareness. Within a very short time, this new performative style began to attract large crowds to the Indra, as this moment of transformation for the Beatles, though one of many such moments in their career, is certainly one of the most significant "changes of state" for the group that would have such a profound effect on their culture. That the transformation occurred not in an institution of higher learning or a place of religious worship, but in a seedy bar in the red-light district of Hamburg involving absurdist physical humor only adds to the remarkable quality of this metamorphosis. Although the Beatles could not have known it, the process of learning how to act with physical abandon on a small stage in an unremarkable nightclub would prove one of the most significant performances of their culture's vanguard, the maneuvers they learned here going on to influence millions of others profoundly.

Over time, the overt physicality of the Beatles' performative style would diminish significantly as they internalized the somatic liberation that they began enacting in Hamburg. However, this wilder physicality sometimes emerged in full force onstage, as can be seen in their 1965 concert at Shea Stadium when Lennon "went mad," as Starr describes it, lunging about the stage and playing the keyboard with his elbows, or in the nearly slapstick humor of their first two films, like the scene in *A Hard Day's Night* when they are running and tumbling through a field, shot from above as they whirl about in chaotic geometrical patterns, resembling nothing as much as a group of stylishly deranged hobbits. Indeed, the quality of "madness" appears, in many cases, to be coextensive with behavior that does not conform to the rationalized dictates of modern culture.[252]

"Going Down"

As a fellow Liverpool musician Johnny Byrne describes the Beatles' 1960 residency in Hamburg: "After a few weeks, you could barely move in the place, it was so jammed. . . . The heat was terrific, everyone smoked, drank. Everyone was having a blast. There was a real sense that something incredible was going down." The Beatles, through hard work and openness to phenomenological experimentation, had discovered what the audience required at that moment: a wild physicality that induced crowd ecstasy, a collective "going down" into the bodily unconscious. The ingestion of alcohol, tobacco, uppers, and other psychoactives only enhanced the feeling of somatic emancipation from the tyranny of the rational brought on by the intense rhythms and the sight of the Beatles hilariously flinging themselves around the stage. Indeed, the phrase "having a blast" recalls nothing so much as the social and psychological analogue of orgasmic sexuality. This was the Beatles' initiation into the embodied, intuitive mode that the original rock and roll had privileged, but from which early British rock and roll had shied away.

As in Presley's case, by experimenting with performative variables, the Beatles hit upon a method that created excitement in their audience. Although they would go on to produce a revolution in their art form like few others in the history of popular music, the Beatles understood that it is necessary to engage with the world as it is, not as one wishes it to be. That is, they discovered a "formula" that worked in their present context, eliciting the desired response, and so this method was pragmatically validated by the end that it produced.[253] Volume was certainly an important part of their performance, simple loudness having the effect of repressing intellect and inducing more somatic modes of experience. As evidenced in the common expression, "I can't hear myself think," rational thought seems, in large part, to be a silent speaking to oneself in words, an activity which becomes significantly more difficult when waves of immense sound are coursing through one's body.[254]

However, mere volume is not enough to induce ecstasy as anyone knows who has ever witnessed a performance by one of the many mediocre and appallingly loud bands that continue to play in rock clubs around the world. Rather, there is a subtle artistry in keeping a bar audience engaged for hours on end that involves maintaining a high level of affective intensity perhaps best described through metaphors having to do with heat or fire, for this kind of performance radiates an "energy" that seems only adequately to be describable through such tropes. However, the Beatles appear not to have been primarily focused on musical subtleties during this period, to some extent because of the limitations of their bass player and drummer, Stuart Sutcliffe and Pete Best, who played the same rudimentary, driving rhythm on nearly every song.[255] Speaking of Best, Lennon recalled: "We trained him to keep a stick going up and down four-in-the-bar, [but] he couldn't do much else." Or as musician and close friend of the Beatles Tony Sheridan put it: "Pete was a crap drummer."[256]

Nevertheless, as a result of the affect that the Beatles generated in their audiences, the group gained a reputation around Hamburg for being "crazy," with Lennon as the inevitable ring-leader, wearing a "scabby" bathing suit on stage, for instance, and "mooning" the crowd.[257] In a twenty-first century context, this behavior sounds like typical, even relatively tame adolescent escapades. However, in the context of Britain or Germany in 1960, long before the era of *Jackass* and *Punk'd*, their activity seems to have been considered somewhat more transgressive, contrary to the rational normalization of behavior. As MacDonald observes, at this moment in the early sixties, "Britain was stiff with psychic tension which was bound, sooner or later, to explode,"[258] and the Beatles in Hamburg were a paradigmatic instance of that combustive release of pressure. In fact, the Beatles and the subsequent waves of English groups that they inspired and made possible, from the Rolling Stones, the Kinks, and the Who to Led Zeppelin, Black Sabbath, and David Bowie, were perhaps the one factor that, more than any other, liberated Britain from its often inflexible militaristic conformity and class hierarchy via the somatic quality characteristic of both the music and the performativity of these groups.

Furthermore, it is clear that the Beatles were not being driven to these extreme states solely by inspiration in Hamburg, as the chemicals flowed in great abundance, particularly alcohol and uppers called Preludin, which allowed the Beatles to sustain their manic energy through their nightly marathon performances. Harrison wrote in a letter to a friend that they were "eating Prellie sandwiches"[259] not only to stay awake, but to fuel the general phenomenological tone of this period in the Beatles' narrative, which revolved around pushing pure instinct to its extreme. According to Lennon's first wife, Cynthia, when she and McCartney's girlfriend Dot arrived in Hamburg, "the pills and booze they had been stuffing into themselves had heightened their senses beyond our reason, and they overwhelmed us with their nonstop chat and frenzied excitement."[260] The substances that the Beatles were ingesting thrust their attention "beyond" "reason" and rationality, and into their "senses," their somatic selves. Indeed, this furious activity seems to have been the expression of a half-conscious impulse in the Beatles to break through into a qualitatively different mode of relating to experience, for according to Spitz, the Beatles were "on the verge of something important; everyone could feel it."[261] This felt knowledge of imminent transformation intuited by the primary actors and the community in which they were embedded remains an example of the kind of collective process that is susceptible to analysis, but that precedes rational formulation.

"An Entirely New Dimension"

For the German art school bohemians or "exis"[262] who befriended the Beatles in Hamburg, the young men were perceived as exemplars of a new way of relating to experience that implicitly incorporated ecstatic practice with the intellectual mode in which the Beatles, as former art school bohemians themselves (in the case of Lennon and Sutcliffe), were immersed, and which they made increasingly explicit in their recorded work, peaking perhaps most obviously in their mid-period "concept" albums: *Sgt. Pepper's Lonely Hearts Club Band* and *Magical Mystery Tour*. Indeed, that the Beatles essentially created the "concept" album is a testament to how much they did to integrate the mode of intuitive affectivity characteristic of rock and roll with the more rational, intellectual mode suggested by the very word "concept."

The Beatles' visual style also apparently benefitted from the physicality in which they were immersed in Hamburg. Mark Lewisohn describes the photographs taken by Astrid Kirchherr, one of the German exis who later married Stuart Sutcliffe, as having "single-handedly defined the rock band image" thereafter.[263] As had been the case for Presley, it was not only the Beatles' music that transformed culture, but their visual aesthetic and their attitude, visible evidence for the fundamental epistemological premises through which they approached their experience.[264] Indeed, as Gould writes: "These photographs struck the Beatles with the force of self-revelation,"[265] and the effortlessness with which the band "took to their new identity" testifies to the sense that the Beatles were the right people in the right place at the right time, positioned at the perfect point in their trajectory to mediate and mirror the development of their culture. Although they drew visual elements from idols like Presley, Holly, and Vincent, they also appropriated English and German stylistic tropes, from the flamboyant sneer of the Teds to the brooding seriousness—and the characteristic haircut—of the exis, synthesizing them into a novel whole for which there was "no precedent,"[266] and which "came as a complete revelation"[267] to their audience when they first exploded into popular consciousness a few years later.

Similarly, the Beatles synthesized their vocal influences with their native accents and particular vocal qualities to create their distinct singing styles, which were somatic performances of their respective identities, while their harmonies enacted the merging of those identities within the group. The Beatles' voices, both in their intrinsic physicality—the shapes and structures of mouths, lungs, noses, and throats—and in the way they sang—the various stylistic idiosyncrasies borrowed from their favorite singers or developed through experimentation—voiced their personas, the qualities that formed the characters of the singers. In enacting their complementarity, Lennon and McCartney were able to integrate their voices into a novel synthesis so that something profound emerged in their vocal relationality that neither man was able to conjure alone. However, although the direct opposition between Lennon and McCartney, while incredibly productive, could have become monotonous, Harrison added a slightly skewed perspective from outside the polarity that Lennon and McCartney had created between them, manifesting in the stylishly quirky musicality of his guitar playing, as well as in his droll voice and persona. What Harrison added complemented the others, creating the precise balance of factors from which the "Beatles' magic"[268] could manifest, the intangible combination of elements that led to an irreducible quality of affective potency.

When the Beatles returned from Germany at the end of 1960 after Harrison, McCartney, and Best were deported for various minor infractions, Mo Best, Pete's mother and proprietor of the Casbah club where the Beatles often played in Liverpool, is said to have described the band's unexpected transformation as "a revelation to behold,"[269] embodied in the dramatic coalescence of their group identity.[270] However, the revelatory transformation produced by their time in Hamburg requires no mystification to be mysterious, as it is not a combination of factors that can be reproduced through rational formulation. Rather, it is a process that more resembles the growth of an organism, so that all of the component parts are materially explicable, but the whole that arises out of the confluence of those parts seems to refuse purely material explanation in a similar way to the emergence of life from nonlife or human sentience from episodic, mammalian consciousness.

After their time in Hamburg, whereas the Beatles had until very recently seemed unexceptional to their peers, all of the factors described above had wrought in them a metamorphosis, perhaps partially ascribable to the death of Lennon's mother, and certainly mediated by their German initiation, but not reducible to these factors, producing the unprecedented phenomenon that the Beatles were in the process of enacting. At this moment in late 1960, the Beatles underwent a kind of "change of state," for although they were still playing primarily cover songs, for reasons that elude pure analysis, "suddenly everything had changed" as "they burst through an entirely new dimension."[271] The poverty and horrendous living conditions of the Reeperbahn, the ingestion of vast amounts of uppers, tobacco, and alcohol, and the sustained exposure to sex and violence that pervaded the district all contributed to forming these relatively innocent English boys into something harder, fiercer, wilder, and more willing to take risks. However, this transformation is ultimately not ascribable to these factors alone, as other talented, hardworking bands from a similar background and with similar influences underwent a similar initiation in Hamburg around the same time, though none of these others became the force for cultural change that the Beatles did.

Thus, for ultimately unknowable reasons, but seemingly driven by what Bergson describes as a "vital impulsion"[272] toward the world's self-overcoming, this felt shift constituted an initiatory moment that elevated the Beatles, and ultimately the entire musical and cultural landscape, from what they considered a conventional "feeble drone" into a visceral "excitement that bordered on anarchy," which "gave their dreams an unpredictable new lift," carrying their vision of radical transformation into the realm of the possible. However, the Beatles' time in Hamburg only "opened a small window"[273] into an experiential mode that they would enter into more completely over the course of their career, though their tenure in Hamburg and the subsequent period in Liverpool were perhaps the peak of their descent into the more purely visceral mode that Presley had exemplified. The Beatles, later known as the relatively polite and loveable "moptops" in comparison with the bands who would immediately follow them like the Rolling Stones and the Who, seem at this moment in the narrative to have been poised at the cutting edge of the descent into the underground of repressed modes performed by rock and roll. Later, in order to reach the heights of fame that they ultimately attained, it was necessary to mediate this pure affective frenzy somewhat, Lennon explaining: "Gradually, we cooled it and cooled it, and used less energy. We had a choice between dancing about, creating havoc, and playing. So we concentrated on the playing."[274]

However, at the moment of the Beatles' first homecoming from Hamburg: "I'd never seen any band look like this before," declared promoter Dave Foreshaw. "Normally," he concludes, popular Liverpool bands such as "the Remo Four or the Dominoes would come on and . . . perform in a polite, orderly way. This band's performance attacked the crowd. They [played] aggressively and with a lot less respect. They just *attacked* them!"[275] Similarly, as Pete Best describes the band's triumphant return: "We belted it out exactly as we had been doing in Hamburg, and you could physically feel the crowd gasp. It just silenced them. When we finished the first number the place just went into rapture, it just exploded."[276] And according to fellow Liverpool musician Billy Kramer: "It was just so different. . . . To act that way onstage and make that kind of sound—I was absolutely staggered." At one point, Lennon apparently admonished the crowd to "get your knickers down!" at which the crowd "screamed and raised their arms in delight." In contrast with the other Liverpool bands, the Beatles were literally wild, "a beast of a different nature" who had learned to move back into a more primal mode to produce "a state of unconscious, indiscriminate euphoria"[277] in their audience, stopping "at nothing to get a rise from the crowd."[278] For the predominant streams of British culture that so strongly privileged intellectual wit and rational propriety, the admonition toward the repressed modes that the Beatles' music and attitude embodied was profoundly transgressive, producing "a seismic shift in the landscape" of the local music scene.

After years of struggling to find their voice and their audience, the Beatles, as a result of their time in Hamburg, suddenly became the top band in Liverpool. As Johnny Byrne, guitarist for the Hurricanes, recalls: "We couldn't believe our eyes—or our ears. The sound that was coming from these guys was fantastic, it was raw and exciting, just plain rocking out, and as tight as I'd heard a band play. There was something about the way they looked, too—rough, and intense, and a little bit rebellious." According to Byrne, this band was "not anything like we remembered them from Liverpool. Once we realized who it was, Rory and I turned to each other with this shocked look on our faces and we both kind of blurted out: 'It's the *Beatles!*'"[279] The radical change that the Beatles had undergone consistently produced this quality of shock in their contemporaries.

Like Robert Johnson, who became himself in his mythic transaction with the Devil at "the crossroads" (in which he is said to have sold his soul to become a great blues man), the Beatles were likewise transformed by their immersion in the underworld ambiance of the Reeperbahn, by the encounter with "sinful," instinctual behavior. As Gould suggests, the Beatles' return to Liverpool at the Litherland ballroom on December 27, 1960 constituted a similar archetypal moment to Benny Goodman's 1935 performance at the Palomar Ballroom in Los Angeles, which produced a similarly dionysian eruption, marking the initiation of swing music as a dominant cultural force. Thus, the Beatles' return from the Reeperbahn underworld resembled not only the trajectories of ancient mythological heroes like Hercules and Odysseus, but also those of more recent musical luminaries like Johnson and Goodman.[280]

Furthermore, as with any new permutation of a genre felt to be genuinely novel by a community, the Beatles required a place with which that new dispensation could be associated. The Cavern Club in Liverpool, previously a center of the jazz orthodoxy, became the Beatles' "Mecca" for, as Adrian Barber put it: "the Cavern was a shithole—but with soul. No place was more conducive to the spirit of rock 'n roll."[281] As with the locus of many such revolutionary ruptures, the Cavern, a subterranean temple to the Id much like the clubs they had played in Hamburg, symbolized the Beatles' psychological descent into the realm of unconscious instinct. And the Beatles' following grew exponentially once they had undergone their transformation, for in bringing back what they had learned to Liverpool, the Beatles had reached a point of "phase transition," embodying the production of a qualitatively new style, which seemed to them and their audience to enact a novel way of constructing the phenomenology of the animal body.

Subsequently, this transformation attracted an audience who poured their energy and attention into the Beatles which, in turn, allowed them to carry their metamorphosis even further. This was a moment when all of the necessary factors converged so that the newly emergent demographic of "teenagers" possessed the time, money, and will to support something as intangible and ephemeral as the mass cultural phenomenon of rock and roll. The narrative trajectory of the Beatles from this point around the beginning of the sixties through the end of the sixties is one of almost continual transformation and self-overcoming, and one which explicitly led the way in the larger cultural revolution, as every novelty produced by the Beatles, whether in music, style, or attitude, produced immediate—and ever-expanding—ripples of emulation in the culture at large.[282]

Although they had a long way to go before they would become the most famous band of all time, the Beatles had finally discovered a way reliably to induce ecstasy in their audience.[283] According to manager Brian Epstein's personal assistant Alistair Taylor, in their early appearances at the Cavern club in 1961 after their return from Germany: "They could barely play . . . and they were deafening and *so* unprofessional—laughing with the girls, smoking onstage, and sipping from cokes during their act. But *absolutely magic!* The vibe they generated was just unbelievable."[284] Indeed, the seemingly "willful"[285] unprofessionalism that the Beatles displayed probably even contributed to their allure at that moment, as in the context of polished groups doing coordinated dance steps on the model of the Shadows, the Beatles' lack of conventional stagecraft was thrillingly transgressive. Although they ultimately added a more professional veneer to their act, their irreverence elicited a sense of authenticity in their audience. It was clear that they were not actors pretending to be rock and roll rebels; they were the real thing, living their lives within the collective persona that they carried onto the stage. However, regardless of whether their lack of professionalism was an asset or a liability, and it was probably some of both, the Beatles simply had *something*, a charismatic energy difficult to define verbally in a way that does not sound trivial to sophisticated ears (e.g. "magic" and "vibe"), but that is over and over again deemed affectively profound by those who witnessed the group in action.[286]

The music industry of Liverpool, such as it was, comprised largely of Brian Epstein's NEMS record stores, began to be drawn to the energetic activity radiating from the Cavern in late 1961. According to Alistair Taylor, who went to see the Beatles with fellow classical music aficionado Epstein at the Cavern for the first time in November: "We laughed at how both of us had been converted—like *that*—to the pop world." Witnessing the Beatles inducing self-overcoming in their audience, and participating in that ecstatic activity, produced a "conversion" in the two slightly older connoisseurs of classical music, schooled as they had been until then in the more intellectually mediated pleasures of the much older musical genre. They could not "understand it" because intellectual understanding was not the domain of experience in which this new music communicated, at least not initially.

Although rock and roll ultimately became such a pervasive and culturally significant phenomenon that a whole vocabulary has been developed to convey what it means and what it does, the music is first and foremost affective—Dylan's "How does it feel?" and Presley's "That don't move me" as the primary criteria for judging the genre. Indeed, we might add to this list any number of Beatles lyrics, from McCartney's booming heart in "I Saw Her Standing There," an almost aggressively simplistic evocation of attraction taken from their first album; through Lennon's initiatory statement of intent to share his felt knowledge of love's primacy with the world in the last verse of *Rubber Soul*'s "The Word"; to "I've Got a Feeling," the title of a song from *Let It Be*, the last album the Beatles released.

"To Smarten Them Up"

After seeing the Beatles a few times at the Cavern, Epstein offered to manage them, which required "a gigantic leap of faith"[287] on the part of the young businessman. The Beatles were playing a species of rock and roll that had not been heard before, not to mention that rock and roll itself was thought by many in the music industry to have been a fad that was nearly over, so throwing his lot in with the band was not a particularly rational business decision on Epstein's part. Of course, the phenomenon of the Beatles is an exemplary instance of one of the primary insights that comes from the study of rock and roll: that pure rationality is not always the most efficacious mode for making decisions, in business or otherwise. Although it has often been suggested that Epstein may have been sexually attracted to the Beatles, particularly Lennon, it is also clear that this was not the only motivating factor in his determination to manage the group. As with the phenomenon of

Beatlemania in general, it was not merely sexual desire, but a combination of many elements that produced Epstein's conversion, not least of which is the profound affective tug of genuine novelty embodied by the Beatles and their music.

While Epstein belied his stereotype as a relatively conventional businessman to follow his intuition about the Beatles, the group also demonstrated a business acumen that belied their instinctive orientation, for they knew that they needed someone with the resources and influence to usher them into the higher echelons of the music industry. Although they were certainly idealistic, the Beatles were also clear eyed about what was required to bring their ideals to concrete fulfillment, musician Frank Allen observing: "They were well aware of what they had to do to make it."[288] Unlike Tony Sheridan, their friend and mentor in Hamburg, who by all accounts was an immensely talented musician, but who had a habit of sabotaging his career through "obnoxiousness and undependability," the Beatles were learning to walk the fine line between wild, intuitive brilliance and the rational focus and consistency necessary to bring that brilliance to fruition.[289] Once the Beatles had found their mojo, so to speak, it became necessary to ally themselves with someone like Brian Epstein to negotiate a compromise between their "animalistic" tendencies, as DJ Bob Wooler put it, and the realities of the music business. According to Epstein: "I sensed something big, if it could be at once harnessed and at the same time left untamed."[290]

Epstein, who had previously dabbled in fashion design, window styling, and theater, wanted "to smarten them up,"[291] as Alistair Taylor put it, to appeal to a wider audience, the phrase acquiring an added resonance in the context of the Beatles' trajectory away from the privileging of intellect into a more embodied mode. Their descent into the Reeperbahn, primarily immersed in nonrational modes, was followed by a reentry into the dominant field of discourse, which implicitly construed these modes as hierarchically inferior to the privileged intellectual mode. In order to bring the more somatically attentive mode of experience into the main streams of culture—that is, onto radio and television, and into venues and record stores—it was necessary essentially to smuggle it in behind the veneer of tailored suits and what *The New York Times* later described as the "contagious . . . Beatle wit,"[292] consisting largely of clever insults and puns, like a postmodern Trojan Horse come to tear down the hegemony of the rational.

Furthermore, as Gould suggests, the Beatles' implicit project of integrating the instinctiveness of American rock and roll with the more rationalized quality of characteristic of modernity was deeply complicit with the "sleek, subtle, obsessively neat, and self-consciously modern" "mod" movement (short for "modernist") brought to public attention by London bands like the Who and the Small Faces a few years later, a movement which "sought not a retreat into the past, but a symbolic alliance with the future." Although the Beatles were never truly mod, but more a hybrid of mod and rocker, Starr's scripted statement in *A Hard Day's Night* ("I'm a mocker") being a drolly accurate enactment of the synthesis performed by the Beatles, they influenced the mods a great deal.

Not only in the Beatles' alliance with the mod subculture, but in their initiation into the music business via Epstein, and later George Martin, the group catalyzed the self-transcending impulse of their culture not by dropping out, but by navigating from the margins of the total discursive network toward the central nodes of cultural authority and participating in the commercial marketplace of that network, transforming it from the edge of the inside, as it were. By donning suits, the Beatles were declaring their participation in the predominant cultural streams, but that those suits were of an unusual, fashion-forward cut subtly, aesthetically pushed against the rationalized dictates of their era, allowing the Beatles to ride the crest of novelty's wave rather than floundering in the past as they had been in their sartorial allegiance to the leather-clad style of the previous decade.[293]

Ultimately, the quality that made the Beatles great was precisely what distinguished them from the tame pop-stars like Cliff Richard or the post-army Presley that Epstein apparently wanted to model their careers after: the "authenticity" discussed above, of which the mods were a new inflection. Thus, as with the tension between Lennon and McCartney within the group, there was also a similar sort of productive tension between the rebellious authenticity of the Beatles and the slick professionalism of their manager, and it is the negotiation between these two poles that allowed the Beatles to become the world historic phenomenon they ultimately became. Of course, holding this tension between art and commerce is like walking a tightrope and, in contrast to the Beatles, Presley fell rather firmly onto the side of commerce for the duration of the sixties, though he still made some great records during that time. Thus, the truly remarkable thing about the Beatles is not that they were able to capture the zeitgeist in its nascence, but that they were able to sustain the "creative tension"[294] throughout the seven or so years of fame before their break-up. Any student of popular music will recognize how rare it is to find an artist who almost never falls off the tightrope, but manages consistently to create great art while keeping a mass audience engaged and invested, both monetarily and emotionally.[295]

The historical, material precondition for the sustained brilliance of the Beatles appears to have been a confluence of economic and political factors, particularly the prosperity and liberalism of the sixties. These factors allowed young people the purchasing power to support such a sustained phenomenon as a symbolic enactment of cultural revolution, mediated by the much discussed "generation gap" characteristic of that moment. Nevertheless, it seems that the polarity of Lennon and McCartney within the larger polarity between the Beatles and Brian Epstein created a kind of buffer through multiple levels of reiteration, so that Lennon could embody authenticity while McCartney held the pole of compromise, though in the larger polarity, McCartney was firmly on the side of art in relation to Epstein, who represented commerce.

As Harrison comments in the *Anthology*: "That was the good thing about being four together, not like Elvis, you know. I always felt sorry later for Elvis 'cause he was on his own. He had his guys with him but there was only one Elvis. Nobody else knew what he felt like. But for us, we all shared the experience."[296] There was psychological strength in numbers grounded in affective sympathy, for although Lennon was initially the driving force behind the band, McCartney carried the weight of responsibility for a significant portion of their career while Lennon was distracted by immoderate drug intake, depression, and Yoko Ono. And, as can be seen in their solo work, particularly after their first few efforts, which were still riding on the momentum of the group, the Beatles were not able to sustain their epochal brilliance individually.

In Liverpool in late 1961, Epstein was busy inciting a transformation in his protégés very different than the one they had undergone in Hamburg, as aside from their dress, Epstein took issue with their unprofessionalism, their smoking, drinking, and cursing onstage, and their lack of a coherent setlist. Instead of tracing a dramatic arc in their performances, they simply played whatever they felt like playing in the moment, sometimes even stopping in the middle of a song if an audience member called out for another song. To put it colloquially, the Beatles were not yet "ready for primetime." Their stint in Hamburg had not so subtly pressed them in the direction of nonrational modes, privileging feeling over thought, which had been an absolutely necessary and profound course for them to follow in their developmental trajectory. However, it had also instilled some bad habits into them, including a lack of discipline and professionalism, which were Epstein's forte.[297]

On one hand, Andy Williams and Bruno Koschmider urging the Beatles to "*Mach Schau!*" had helped them to enter into a fuller engagement with intuitive efficacy. On the other hand, Epstein led the Beatles out of their subterranean scene centered on the Cavern, and into the rational daylight world of the marketplace dominated by what Max Weber terms the "spirit of capitalism." The Beatles' management contract with Epstein is the moment when they symbolically agreed to bring the modes that they had rediscovered in Hamburg into the rationalized world of modern commerce by negotiating with the established music business hierarchy, Epstein their adroit messenger. In Hamburg and Liverpool before Epstein's "makeover," their shows resembled bacchanalian revels, but they lacked the rational apollonian structure necessary for genuine communication: the "rhyme" and "reason," the "logical pacing." Where the Beatles were previously undisciplined, Epstein taught them how to "control the ebb and flow" of affective energy, to "work the crowd" with awareness and the hard won rigor of the rational mind to produce an orgasmic "climax" in their audience.[298]

Furthermore, Epstein convinced the Beatles to add a dramatic bow to their stage show and, though this showbiz flourish was controversial within the group, particularly with Lennon, their manager ultimately prevailed. According to McCartney: "Brian believed that would be very good for us . . . and I was also a great believer in that."[299] Both literally and metaphorically, the Beatles were bowing to convention, to the ever-shifting dictates of an industry built on the ineffable fascination of pop music. McCartney, generally the reasonable half of the Lennon-McCartney polarity, saw that they must make concessions to the rational mode, predominant even in commercial art and entertainment. McCartney's professionalism, his "Mr. Show Business" persona, allowed Lennon to carry the flame of authenticity, of primal affect, though always in a compromise formation with his more intellectual tendencies. Whereas McCartney engaged with rationality in a more practical way, Lennon was of a philosophical temperament, appearing implicitly to justify his focus on feeling as a kind of experiment in identity. On his own, this consciously adopted primitive attitude may well have prevented Lennon from achieving real commercial success, which is often the case with immensely talented and uncompromising artists. However, in the context of the group, Lennon's rebelliousness is part of what initially fueled the Beatles' intense creativity, McCartney's facile politesse mediating Lennon's often brutal candor.[300]

As with most relationships, that between Lennon and McCartney represented the meeting of two worlds, two distinct ways of participating in experience. Although the pair shared a passionate devotion to rock and roll, their inclinations often emphasized different aspects of the music, Lennon generally preferring a dissonant, horizontally melodic mode "moving up and down as little as possible," while McCartney generally wrote in a consonant, melodically vertical mode "ranging freely across the stave in scalar steps and wide intervals."[301] The "friction" caused by these fundamental differences, and impelled by their mutual ambition, "drove them to fertile middle ground." They both implicitly seemed to know that, as long as they maintained their partnership and managed to subsume their difference in the group, they possessed a combined force that rendered them unstoppable. However, the very "creative tension" that propelled the band was also the factor that ultimately made their partnership unsustainable.[302]

"We Should Have Rocked Like Mad"

Although the fans in Liverpool and Hamburg knew the Beatles possessed qualities that set them apart from the crowd, the only demonstration record the band had to play for A&R men—the only material evidence of their music aside from their live performances—was a cacophonous recording of one of their shows, which did not even remotely do justice to the excitement they generated in person. As the poor sound quality of their demo attests, although the Beatles had forged themselves into skillful performers who could elicit ecstatic excitement from their audience, they had as yet had very little opportunity to develop their skills as recording artists, which is a rather different activity than playing live in front of a crowd. Thus, their audition for Decca Records on New Year's Day 1962 was a mediocre showing that did not live up to their incredible potential, McCartney later referring to the songs that they recorded, including comedic standards like "Three Cool Cats," "Besame Mucho," and "The Sheik of Araby," as a "fairly silly repertoire."[303]

Having tied themselves to Epstein, the Beatles were attempting to bring the mode that they had developed in live performance into a conventional music industry. Thus, their song selection for the audition was based primarily on rational considerations rather than the more intuitive mode that they had been enacting. In trying to woo the established musical institutions, they had compromised some of their wilder tendencies, trading leather for suits, bowing, and writing setlists that traced a dramatic arc rather than doing whatever they felt in the moment. However, at the Decca audition, they compromised too much, making too many concessions to music business conventions, an overcompensation that essentially vitiated the spirit of their music. By suppressing their intuition in favor of the considered opinions of "experts" like Epstein and producer Mike Smith, they nearly killed their career as purveyors of radical novelty.

Listening to the audition, one is struck by the polite lack of visceral intensity characteristic of the band's earlier music. This moment in the narrative development of the Beatles shows the pendulum swinging too far toward basing their musical decisions on the hope of cultivating commercial appeal to the point that there is very little of the raucous, rebellious edge universally ascribed to the band's Hamburg period evident in these recordings. Although many of the sonic elements are present that would soon allow them to conquer the world—their voices and playing style—there is a quality of inspiration and energetic vitality that is undeniably absent in these lackluster performances. Being justly rejected by Decca is the event that seems to have broken the momentum of their trajectory back toward the rational end of the polarity represented by Epstein, and that confirmed the impulse toward the wild physicality which had drawn them to rock and roll in the first place, and which had initially attracted Epstein to them.[304]

Through this series of pendulum swings, the Beatles progressively integrated the two poles of art and commerce, generally coextensive with the polarity of novelty and habit, increasingly moving toward a type of music that was authentic to their intrinsic sense of things, always shifting and nearly impossible to define, but that was accessible to the various gatekeepers who determined whether the songs would ever be heard, as well as to the audience that must ultimately judge the music's value. The songs and performances of the Decca audition appealed to what the Beatles thought the record label would want. They had over-analyzed their song selections, choosing covers based on what had worked for others in the past, though Lennon immediately recognized that they had betrayed the more intuitive criteria that are the *sine qua non* of good music, for as he later said of the audition: "We should have rocked like mad in there and shown what we're like when we're roused."[305]

Nevertheless, it seems almost inevitable that the Beatles would have momentarily succumbed to the gravitational force of convention, for rather than being merely marginal "madmen" who had completely rejected rational thought, the band appears to have devoted their lives to what I would suggest is the primary implicit project of rock and roll music: to demonstrate that modes of experience the predominant sectors of culture often considered "mad," exemplified by the genre's reembrace of "primitive" affect, had value for the further development of that culture. Intuition, constituted primarily in attention to bodily feeling, seems to have functioned as something like a dialectical complement or antithesis to the original thesis posited, which is that humanity is defined purely by the rational mind as Descartes so starkly exhibited in his equation of thought with human being: "I think, therefore I am."

As philosophers like James, Bergson, Whitehead, and Tarnas have all argued in different inflections, the twentieth century has been the primary temporal locus for the reembrace of affectivity, a mode of engagement with process that these theorists perceive to be as valid and necessary for a sustainable and integrated culture as critical intellect. I hope I am some way toward convincingly showing that the Beatles were one of the primary cruxes upon which this discursive reunion of mind and body has turned, what MacDonald calls "the quiet inner revolution of attitude and assumption within whose consequences . . . we live today."[306] Thus, it is because the Beatles cared so deeply about being recognized by their culture that they were momentarily seduced by the "repetition" of already existent modes, perhaps the defining quality of institutions and cultural hierarchies, which are ultimately rational, based on abstract conceptual rankings, mores, and positional power relations as opposed to the more immediate relationality characteristic of bodily experience. It seems to have been necessary for the Beatles to go through this humbling experience in order to be reminded that the appropriate focus of music is not primarily rational concerns, but the irreducible felt quality of the moment.

"A Rather Unpromising Group"

Although by May of 1962 the Beatles were widely recognized as the top band in Liverpool, almost every British label had declined to sign them, due in large part to the Decca tapes, which became the demo that Epstein played for the other labels. Epstein, at his wit's end, called upon Sidney Colman, an acquaintance who hesitantly suggested Parlophone Records. Colman was hesitant because, according to George Martin, the head of A&R and a producer at the label, Parlophone was the "'poor relation' in the corporate family of EMI."[307] Colin Manley of the Remo Four, putting it even more bluntly, called the label "the bastard child of the recording industry . . . kept locked away in the clock tower and treated with disdain."[308] More specifically, Parlophone was primarily known for recordings by comedy and classical acts, not pop groups.[309] However, it just so happened that Martin had come to the conclusion that, in order to keep the label vital, he would have "to do something" with acts that had fallen "between the cracks" at the other English labels.[310] Parlophone would ultimately retain its association with comedy and classical music, though primarily in the dramatically recontextualized locus of the Beatles' records, which often incorporated comedic elements and classical instrumentation, particularly in their middle, "psychedelic" period.

In an initial meeting with Martin, Epstein attempted to sell his band to the producer with the zealousness and overinflated rhetoric of a true believer. However, Martin was not particularly impressed with the Decca recording, later admitting that he felt the Beatles were "a rather unpromising group." Based on that evidence alone, Martin justifiably felt that their selection of covers was pedestrian, and that their original songs were "very mediocre," though he heard "a certain roughness," probably in Lennon's voice, which stopped him from dismissing the group outright. Here we see the Decca audition still haunting the Beatles, nearly sabotaging their last chance to record for a label. Although the Beatles had temporarily compromised the visceral intensity that made them exceptional in their Decca audition, it seems likely that Martin sensed something of this vitality simmering below the surface. Thus, it is only Martin's vision, or perhaps his desperation, that allowed the Beatles, generally acclaimed as the greatest band in the history of popular music, to pass through the humblest side-gate of the music industry. Through this felicitous concatenation of circumstances, the Beatles, as exemplary outsiders, received one last chance to prove themselves to the guardians of the music business hierarchy.[311]

However, before Epstein secured their session for Parlophone, the Beatles returned, in April of 1962, for another stint in Hamburg. When they arrived, they learned that Stuart Sutcliffe, Lennon's best friend and their former bass player, had died of what appeared to be a brain-hemorrhage. Perhaps this tragedy created the pathos necessary to push them over the hump from being a popular local band in Hamburg and Liverpool, to being genuine recording artists, though one could also imagine a scenario in which such a tragedy could have dampened their momentum. Thus, regardless of whether this event was causally related to their continued upward trajectory, the Beatles were determined to press on, playing furiously in their residency at the Star-Club, which Adrian Barber described as "an immense, cavernous rock 'n roll cathedral," a tabernacle to the Id, to that which had been rendered unconscious in predominant discursive streams.

Their residency at the club was a phenomenal success, which certainly boosted their confidence in the musical mode they had developed as they prepared to face what amounted to their last prospect for attaining stardom in their upcoming Parlophone session.[312] This period in Hamburg seems to have cemented their status as the preeminent Liverpudlian band for, with six other bands from their hometown joining them, the shows were a definitive demonstration that a distinctive Liverpool sound—Merseybeat—had emerged.[313] A novel and distinctive style had been created by the Beatles and their contemporaries, but it still required a catalyst, one group to have a hit, which would then create a demand for the whole scene. By all accounts, the Beatles had emerged as the Liverpool band most likely to take their local milieu to the national stage. Indeed, the primary factor that set the Liverpool music scene apart from the many other English cities filled with aspiring rock and roll bands appears to have been the Beatles themselves.[314]

"I Hope We Passed the Audition"

More than simply another narrative of the Beatles' rise to fame, the aim of this chapter is to explicate, through the concrete specificity of the Beatles, the processes by which novelty is promulgated through culture, transforming the systemic networks of relation that radically new forms encounter in their development, radiating through the media that mediate the discursive trajectories of historical transformation. Indeed, this is a pattern of processual activity played out in many inflections again and again in many domains to the extent that such moments of revolution in the cultural system may seem obvious in retrospect. However, these moments of rupture are almost always surprising in both the form and timing of their occurrence. The Beatles are so close to our cultural self-conception that it can be difficult to see them objectively for the profound novelty that they embodied.[315]

Thus, it is an intrinsically problematic task in the world that the Beatles so fundamentally inform to see that, when the Beatles entered Abbey Road Studios for their session with George Martin, the situation resembled nothing so much as an instance of wild, unsophisticated primitives stepping into engagement with the cultivated technological sophistication of modernity. According to Lennon: "When we came down we were treated like provincials by the cockneys . . . looked down upon as animals. We were *hicksville*."[316] This narrative is familiar to Beatles enthusiasts, but its occluded import, the sense that this moment was the locus for a cultural bifurcation, a split that could have gone either way, is difficult to see without the rosy knowledge of what eventually occurred coloring one's perception of the event. Things are one way, and then, with relative suddenness, they are another, and no one can know where and when these moments of discontinuous transformation, the fundamental reorganization of the system's rules, will take place. However, after the fact, it generally appears that it could not have gone any other way. The situation in question, stripped of its mythical import, could be described as nothing more than a little dance band entering into a recording studio for a session, but this encounter is one of those rare moments on which the direction of history depends, allowing the Beatles to become a symbolic focus for the larger transformations of their decade.

The radical quality of the continual "revolution in the head"[317] that the Beatles underwent from the beginning of the sixties until their break-up at the end of the sixties is perfectly encapsulated in Lennon's joke at the close of their last impromptu concert on the roof of Abbey Road Studios in 1969: "I'd like to say 'thank you' on behalf of the group and ourselves, and I hope we passed the audition." The actual "audition" inside that same building less than a decade before the rooftop concert is a defining motif of the Beatles' career: from this moment on, tested again and again, they always managed to pass into wider and higher realms of culture until they had reached "the toppermost of the poppermost," and there were no more auditions left to pass, a situation that provided the context for the perfect summation of Lennon's ironic statement. On one hand, it appears the height of absurdity for the most famous and successful band of all time to express the sentiment that Lennon voiced. However, in the context of the actual lived experience of the Beatles, they were still essentially the same young men who had optimistically set out for their session less than seven years before in the summer of 1962. Indeed, one of the most appealing things about the Beatles is that they never seem to have lost their sense of humble aspiration, even when Lennon was claiming that the group was "bigger than Jesus."[318]

The Abbey Road building into which the Beatles entered on what can only be referred to as that fateful day, June 6, 1962, while "boxy" and "unpretentious," had been the site for the development of some of the most important technological innovations in recording, including "the fundamentals of stereo," "moving-coil microphones," and "large-valve tape recorders."[319] The Beatles were, thus far, almost exclusively a live band, focusing on generating frenzied excitement in audiences. Abbey Road, however, represented a rather different venue of transmission. The Beatles stepping into the studio were an effective embodiment of intuitive modes literally entering into commerce with the rational, scientific epistemology productive of recording technology.

In addition to recording innovations, EMI, the parent company of Parlophone, had been one of the primary developers of television and radar, though this period of radical innovation was over by the 1950s, and the company had retreated into a relatively static orthodoxy, with Abbey Road studios as one of the primary exemplars of this technological complacency. Like the cliché primitives entering into a center of cultural power, the Beatles were initially intimidated by the sheer magnitude of the facilities. Abbey Road, generally described as something between a scientific laboratory and a library, was starkly different from the dank, underground clubs to which the Beatles had become accustomed, the architectural and aesthetic qualities of a building profoundly informing the affective tone of the activities that occur inside.[320]

The ambiance of Abbey Road was reflective of a rational approach to making records based on fixed schedules and technical procedures. According to engineer Alan Brown, the studio practiced a "very strong engineering discipline," explaining that "we all wore white lab coats when we worked."[321] This description sounds more like a science lab than a place for recording rock and roll. The clean, rather utilitarian rooms of Abbey Road, filled with the latest in recording technology, would have, like a film set, created a certain tone, visible in the activity of technicians carefully turning knobs and flipping switches under white ceilings. This setting speaks volumes about the mentality that went into its construction, which prizes efficiency and rational structure over aesthetic concerns, and which profoundly affects the felt experience of activity, and thus the concrete products that result from that activity.

The interior of the building was blank, an orderly and brightly lit container for precise technological accomplishment. In contrast, the Cavern Club in Liverpool, the venue most associated with the Beatles' early career, had the quality of a decrepit Victorian cellar, having previously served as a produce warehouse, with narrow stairs leading down to a dimly lit room with rounded ceilings of rough-hewn stone curving steadily into walls of the same coarse material, dripping with condensation from the bodies packed within. Where Abbey Road was a neat, spacious building conducive to technical problem solving, the Cavern was a place more conducive to losing oneself in the hot, fecund press of bodies and the pounding rhythms echoing through the tight, womblike hall.[322]

This difference was only amplified by the respective environs of the buildings, the affluent St. Johns Wood area of London in which Abbey Road was situated contrasting sharply with the Matthew Street location of the Cavern Club in Liverpool, which had been the site of a produce market dotted with pubs, a decidedly more working-class locale. Thus, the distinction between these two primary loci of the Beatles' public identity could not be more stark: the site for the distribution of the produce of provincial physical labor and its accompanying after-hours ambiance of alcohol consumption juxtaposed against the posh centrality of a studio generally dedicated to technological development and the recording of high cultural classical music and verbal comedic wit.

The Beatles' seven-year inhabitation of Abbey Road produced a deconstruction of this opposition, both in concrete practical ways, and more broadly in the public imagination, culminating in the iconic photo of the long-haired, bearded, and barefoot (in McCartney's case) Beatles crossing the road on the cover of their last recorded album, named for the studio in which they produced the bulk of their music. Where there was tension in their first encounter, Abbey Road ultimately became synonymous with its provincial invaders through a sustained engagement of polarized relational modes. Although the Beatles would come to represent the return of repressed epistemologies into the predominant technological culture of commercial media, they were only able to perform this return by deeply integrating the rapidly advancing technologies into their music, from double-tracked vocals and sped-up piano solos to backwards guitars and tape-loops.[323]

The Beatles were rebellious agents of change producing transformation through their prolonged involvement with this place that so strongly epitomized the rationalization of culture, down to the music that the culture produced, which is perhaps the most accurate metric that one can hope to find for the state of a culture's soul. The Beatles, who had spent most of the last few years riling up drunken crowds of sailors, strippers, art students, and wage-workers, inhabited a different mode of relating to experience than the clean, precise quality of the studio. Again, as with the tension between Lennon and McCartney, this broader tension of opposites produced the friction necessary to generate profound novelty. Although the band's unorthodox attitude certainly made waves, so to speak, the friction between the Beatles and Abbey Road, fractally echoing the friction between Lennon and McCartney, generated an energetically charged atmosphere as the group arrived for their session.[324]

The encounter with Martin and Abbey Road Studios produced a shift equally significant to the Beatles' initiation in Hamburg, but of a radically different character. As with their epiphany at the hands of Williams and Koschmider, the Beatles willingly submitted themselves to the more professional mode exemplified by Martin and Abbey Road, particularly after the failed Decca audition.[325] The Beatles seem implicitly to have understood that the Abbey Road assessment was an initiation not into primal modes of experience, but rather into the equally profound critical and analytical faculties developed primarily in modernity. Because the Beatles had, thus far, largely focused their attention on embodying the somatic modes characteristic of early rock and roll, this encounter became one of the primary narrative enactments of the engagement between intellect and intuition that took place so dramatically in the sixties. This initiation, rather than the "baptism by fire"[326] of Hamburg, exhibited more the quality of a music school examination and, after the Beatles played their songs, Martin and his team were initially uncertain whether the band measured up.

The Beatles had developed their musicianship, and particularly their singing voices, to a relatively high degree, but their selection of material was not connecting in the studio the way it did live, and Martin justly thought the songs they had written were not of the highest quality, probably because the band's primary focus had been on performance. As Martin recalls: "They were rotten composers,"[327] asserting that "their own stuff wasn't any good."[328] Of course, this assessment is particularly striking given that the Beatles would very soon become known as among the greatest songwriters in the history of popular music. Indeed, what seems to have produced this dramatic change resembles nothing so much as an academic critique. As Martin describes the situation, he and engineer Norman Smith "laid into them for about an hour and . . . were pretty forthright" with their criticism, admonishing the young musicians for not having "suitable material,"[329] while Smith felt that they should "embellish the sound"[330] of the band.

This is a kind of critical initiation that Presley never seems to have experienced, and it appears to be these successive initiations into both the intuitive and the intellectual modes that allowed the Beatles to produce an integration of these two epistemologies, which was a step beyond the synthesis that Presley produced. By "laying into them," Martin and Smith apparently incited the Beatles' analytical faculties, which impelled the band more critically to examine all aspects of their art, Martin's professional experience granting structure and focus to the Beatles' creativity, thereby bringing the rational mode into dialogue with the more instinctive mode in which the band had been immersed, rather than dampening that mode as had been the case at the Decca audition.[331]

"The Turning Point"

However, Martin and his assistants did not share one criticism, which, as Ron Richards said to Martin, was that "Pete Best wasn't very good," telling the producer: "He's useless, we've got to change this drummer."[332] Best simply did not possess the innate subtlety of feel required to lift the Beatles' music from being merely good, to being great. The Abbey Road professionals, having worked with the best session musicians, could immediately tell that Best was holding the Beatles back, so it would be necessary to let him go, difficult though it might be to kick him out of the group. However, even aside from the as yet unspoken issue of the drummer, the withering critique was painful, but it seems to have been necessary in order to break down the band's immature and amateurish presuppositions, a process that ultimately had the desired effect of impelling the Beatles to rebuild themselves to think like professional recording artists.[333]

A lesser group might have given up in anger and despair right then and there, as critiques like the one Martin and Smith gave the Beatles are never easy to hear. After Martin's severe assessment, Smith recalls: "They didn't say a word back, not a word. They didn't even nod their heads in agreement. When he finished, George said, 'Look, I've laid into you for quite a time, you haven't responded. Is there anything you don't like?' They all looked at each other for a long while, shuffling their feet, then George Harrison took a long look at George and said, "Yeah. I don't like your tie."[334] And as Spitz describes: "The room went silent. For a split second, nobody breathed. A line had been crossed. Martin fixed George with a stern look, not certain what tack to take with this boy, when he noticed the flicker of a smile at the corner of George's mouth. A joke! He'd been making a joke! What a perfect ice-breaker. Martin's grin flashed approval ear to ear." According to Smith: "That was the turning point,"[335] the Beatles falling into the humorous banter they had developed in their many hours together. "I really think the Beatles got their recording contract because of that conversation," Smith concludes. "Let's be honest: they got that recording contract because of their enthusiasm, their presence, not because of their music. During that one conversation, we realized they were something special."[336]

Nervous about their session, wanting desperately to succeed, the Beatles had been trying to conform to how they imagined "serious musicians" comported themselves, though this impulse toward compromise was surely tempered by memories of the Decca audition. Nevertheless, in this most antithetical of environments to their usual rock and roll clubs, the Beatles' brilliant wit had temporarily been cut off from their musical personas. Harrison's joke was the moment when the two were first truly integrated within the purview of the predominant music business hierarchy, for they had encountered an authoritative mentor who saw the potential, not only, or even primarily, in their music, but in their humor. According to Martin: "I did think they had enormous talent, but it wasn't their music, it was their charisma, the fact that when I was with them they gave me a sense of well-being, of being happy. The music was almost incidental. I thought, 'If they have this effect on me, they are going to have that effect on their audiences.'"

Through their "wordplay" and "double-talk," the Beatles proved that they were "something special," though this "something" had as much to do with their personalities as it did with their playing. Harrison's

89

"crossing the line" was a moment of transgression that took belief in the rightness of their cause, but also required a sympathetic interlocutor, which it found in Martin, producing an ecstatic hilarity reminiscent of their breakthrough moment in Hamburg mediated by absurdist humor, though in an almost precisely opposite context. This was a "turning point," not only in the conversation, but in the Beatles' career, and in the trajectory of popular music itself. Had Harrison not cracked his joke, there is every possibility that Martin would have rejected the band, which would most likely have killed their last chance of recording for a label.[337]

Although the Beatles had thus far been focusing on developing their intuitive capacities, they had also been developing the verbal wit that was ultimately as important to their appeal as their music. Thus, though the Beatles spent the rest of their career effecting an integration of their two primary modes—the witty humor and the intuitive musicality—this moment, significantly orchestrated by Harrison, not Lennon or McCartney, was a primary transductive instance that turned the tide, so to speak. Though Harrison's joke might at first glance seem trivial, it is just such moments on which the bifurcations of history depend, though it seems almost inevitable that the Beatles would produce this sudden reversal in this situation. As it is said, "character is destiny," and the Beatles had been developing their characters their whole lives in preparation for this moment.

Harrison's joke appropriated the critical mode to which Martin and Richards had been subjecting the Beatles and placed it in the context of the Beatles' embodied, absurdist mode, simultaneously acknowledging and parodying the critique they had just received by reciprocally critiquing the small, seemingly trivial detail of Martin's tie, which probably did in fact offend the aesthetic sensibility of Harrison, who is perhaps the most stylish Beatle.[338] By criticizing Martin's tie, Harrison implicitly expressed recognition of the critical mode's utility but, at the same time, put that mode in its place. This quip demonstrated the absurdity that results from the exclusive focus on "negative judgment"[339] characteristic of the critical mentality, particularly in the context of rock and roll, whose primary mode of significance eludes the critical mode, appealing directly to the more fundamental somatic domain.

This episode is another instance of Whitehead's "slightest change of tone which yet makes all the difference," for nothing material changed in the encounter—the Beatles' music was the same, they were still the same people with the same characters and capacities—but the fact that Harrison's joke radically transformed Martin's attitude toward the group from negative judgment to positive affirmation is a subtle shift in affective tone that ultimately allowed the Beatles to become recording artists at all, which in turn did make a substantial difference in the culture's experience. Furthermore, it is highly significant that Harrison produced this reversal because it proves just how much the Beatles really were a group entity. Although most of the focus, particularly in the early years, was on the polarity formed by Lennon and McCartney, Harrison's wry wit, as well as his eccentrically engaging musicianship, acted as a foil to diffuse and redirect the tension endemic to the Lennon-McCartney partnership. The only thing that was missing now was the simple affability and superb feel of the drummer who would complete the Beatles' circle of nearly universal accessibility.

"Natural Feel"

In addition to all of Epstein's previous work, one of the manager's most important contributions to the group was convincing them, on George Martin's advice, to replace Pete Best with a more suitable drummer. Persuading the other Beatles does not appear to have been difficult, as they do not seem to have felt a particularly strong bond with their old drummer, a laconic loner lacking the sense of humor shared by Lennon, McCartney, and Harrison. Lennon explains: "Pete was a bit slow. He was a harmless guy but he was not quick. All of us were quick minds and he never picked up on the idiom." According to Lennon: "We were always going to dump him when we could find a decent drummer."[340] Thus, long before Martin's suggestion via Epstein, the three core Beatles had already been considering a replacement, and they knew exactly who they wanted to complete the band: their old friend Ringo Starr.[341]

According to Adrian Barber, Starr "was an excellent drummer and had a good feel,"[342] developing "some sort of rock lope,"[343] as Starr describes it, his personality and drumming uniquely suited to support the Beatles' songs. Of the four final Beatles, Starr, perhaps because of his frequent illness as a child, seems to have been the most naturally able to put aside egoic consciousness, one interviewer describing him as "less complicated and more mature than the others,"[344] which allowed him to create "grooves" that very simply felt good, that produced positive affect, which seems to be the essence of quality musicianship.[345] Where Lennon and McCartney embodied, in different ways, the fraught trajectory from the privileging of the rational mind to the integration of that mode with repressed epistemologies, Starr, the oldest member of the group, in his quietly good-natured way appears already to have found an easy center between mind and body by the time he became a Beatle. As McCartney expresses it: "He's a grown-up, Ringo—always is, always has been. I suspect when he was about three he was a grown-up."[346] Though never an intellectual, Starr had an instinctual feel for the witty repartee that characterized the Beatles' collective persona, while grounding their brilliance with his solid, distinctive drumming and loveable charm. According to Lennon: "To be so aware with so little education is rather unnerving to someone who's been to school since he was fucking two onwards."[347] Where Best had been vain and heavy-handed—"mean, moody, and magnificent"[348] as DJ Bob Wooler described him—Starr added a warm humor and steady balance that completed the group's constellation of qualities.

Displaying an instinctual feel for rhythm that exceeded verbal articulation, Starr's drumming exemplifies the dictum from William Blake's *The Marriage of Heaven and Hell*: "Energy is eternal delight." Indeed, the "natural feel" that Starr exhibited seems to be a kind of bodily knowledge that comes, paradoxically, from learning consciously to let go of mind to enter into a state similar to the one performed by Presley and his compatriots in the invention of the genre that Starr's group would come to exemplify. Thus, the drummer's playing was not the product of pure instinct, but of hard work, many hours of practice, and experimentation—the rational discipline of rehearsal producing affective potency. The verbal formulations used to describe what Starr was doing—cadence, syncopation, and so on—come after the doing, and are incidental to his mastery.

Indeed, this seems to be the case with all analysis: it is useful, even vital for understanding a creative act after the fact, for impelling one to change or refine one's approach, but in the flow of the inspired moment, intellect is generally an impediment, the unwanted intrusion of doubt into the direct engagement with experience. Put simply, intellect is appropriate for some activities and not others, for writing about music but not for playing music, at least in the moment of playing. As with the "true love"[349] that Starr felt for the drums, good musicianship is something that cannot be achieved primarily through analysis of the potential beloved's attributes and accomplishments, but rather something that one must feel.[350]

And it is precisely this subtle quality of "feel" that was the missing element in the Beatles with Best on drums. The Beatles had matured and integrated their parts until they had overcome themselves, at least in a collective, musical context. They possessed an intuitive musicality, which had a "cleverness" and "ingenuity" that can only be an indication of the more intellectual mode that analyzes and critiques, finding novel and interesting ways to frame and direct the melodic, harmonic, and rhythmic qualities that are central to playing music, giving them a "sharp, inventive twist," though "a lot of it happened without a great deal of forethought," a paradoxical operation whereby intellect and intuition seem to have been integrated in an emergent synthesis. With Starr in the group, the Beatles possessed the optimal array of qualities among them to make music that satisfied in every domain of experience, from the most visceral, somatic domain of "feel," through the domain of emotional potency, to the domain of intellectual interest, to perhaps even more intangible domains.[351] As Harrison expressed it, referring to a show in late 1961 when Starr had filled in for a sick Pete Best: "[When Ringo] sat in with us it felt *complete*. It just really happened, it felt really good."[352]

Although they had become a popular and effective group with Best, the "magic," the irreducibly numinous quality of experience, did not fully manifest until the fourth member of the quaternity entered the picture. Their playing is ultimately a reflection of their relationships with one another, and Best's status as outsider in the group, both musically and socially, had caused the band to sound and feel ultimately incoherent, with Lennon, McCartney, and Harrison inhabiting a simultaneously cleverer and more somatically nuanced sensibility than Best. It is clear that the three original Beatles did not particularly enjoy their early drummer's company, so it would have been extremely difficult to play music with him that was fully enjoyable for both themselves and their audience. Whereas Best's "unobtrusive, undistinctive" lack of subtlety flattened the sound of the band, bringing all the players down to his lowest common denominator, Starr elicited the extraordinarily distinctive feel of the band that is one of their greatest strengths but which, until then, had been unrealized potentiality.[353] As Starr put it: "I was lucky to be on their wavelength when I joined the group."[354]

"The Beautiful Balance"

However, although according to Abbey Road engineer Ron Richards, "they had their own *sound*," which "set them immediately apart"[355] from the majority of other groups, how they would be received in the national music market was still an open question. "I desperately wanted my own Cliff," George Martin explains. "I was so hidebound by Cliff Richard and the Shadows that I was looking for the one voice that would carry them."[356] Ron Richards describes an ambulatory conversation he had with Martin to determine how to promote the band: "He knew how important it was to establish their identity," Richards asserts, "so we kept walking and talked about what to call them—Paul McCartney and the Beatles, or John Lennon and the Beatles," initially attempting to fit the group into the usual template of that musical moment in which there was almost always an individual leading the group, a choice between McCartney, "the pretty boy," or Lennon, "the down-to-earth type." As Richards describes the conversation: "It went on like that, back and forth, as we continued along Oxford Street," though, "when we got to the end, we knew it was perfect the way it was,"[357] Martin later admitting: "I was being too conventional—but then I hadn't really heard anything quite like them before."[358]

As with most rational decision making, Martin and Richards were attempting to model their newly signed group on previous precedent rather than on an awareness of the rare but inevitable emergence of processual ruptures. This is a common fallacy in the music industry (and many other areas of endeavor, for that matter) as A&R representatives are notorious for trying to sign acts that look and sound like bands that have had recent success, or to mold the bands already on their label's roster on the model of previous successes, rather than working with the artists to help them develop the qualities that make them unique and novel, which seems to be the highest aim of most music, at least as far as audiences and musicians are concerned. Rendering music subservient to a rational mentality, which tends to repeat what has worked in the past, seems to have a dampening or repressive effect on the ineffable quality of musical inspiration, which is after all the factor that draws most listeners to music in the first place.[359]

Indeed, the commercialization of music, though necessary for the wide dissemination of that music, is so often decried for precisely this reason: the devouring of the primarily intuitive musical mode by the rationality of the marketplace tends to make for mediocre music. It is only at certain intervals in the history of this art form in the twentieth century that revolutions driven by novel inspiration have broken through the mediocrity of a static recording industry, visible in the emergence of bebop in the early forties as much as in the punk rock revolution of the late seventies. The advent of the Beatles is a primary moment of this kind of rupture, as the Beatles were the antidote to the "white bread" teen idols playing a tame and sanitized version of rock and roll that had risen to prominence by the early sixties.

Martin's and Richards' strolling discourse concerning how to market their new signing was a moment when the cultural guardians could have pulled the Beatles back into the gravity of the old way of being, for who knows what would have transpired if the group had been billed as "Paul McCartney and the Beatles"? Thus, it is a testament both to the vision of Martin and to the genuinely novel musical collective that the Beatles had forged that the producer ultimately decided to maintain "the beautiful balance they seemed to have found."[360] The Beatles were young and new to the music business, but Martin and his engineers, committed members of the institutional hierarchy, found it necessary to analyze their new act, critiquing the Beatles' music before they bought into it, in terms of both monetary and emotional investment.

However, it is not primarily for rational reasons that Martin decided to keep the band a group; as William James particularly understood, rationality often merely finds justification for our intuitive sense of things. Thus, it seems that Martin engaged in the analytical dialogue to satisfy himself that his decision was based on sound logic, though ultimately it is his intuitive faculty that convinced him it was "perfect the way it was." This analytic discourse by Martin and Richards presaged the public reaction to the Beatles and to the sixties counterculture in general: both ultimately succeeded in redirecting the flow of cultural process, but it was necessary for a great deal of dialogue, of "back and forth," to occur before the rebels could be elevated to an exalted cultural status.

"Please Please Me"

The Beatles were elated when their first single, "Love Me Do," was released and eventually made its way into the top 20 in the British pop charts in late 1962, Starr declaring it "*The* most momentous moment—that we had a record out," and Harrison recalling: "First hearing Love Me Do on the radio sent me shivery all over. It was the best buzz of all time."[361] However, once the initial excitement had worn off, this chart position fell short of where the Beatles needed to be in order to have the kind of career that they envisioned. Thus, it was vitally important that their next offering make a larger impact. As their second single, the Beatles released "Please Please Me" in early 1963, into which they managed to condense all the novel excitement of their live shows in a way that they had not quite been able to achieve with "Love Me Do."[362] They compressed everything they had learned into the space of one song, the long process of integrating visceral intensity with the musical inventiveness and wit that transformed rock and roll, making it exponentially more complex.[363] In this way, the Beatles rendered the ecstatic affect that they induced in their performances available on a massively wider scale so that anyone with a radio or record player could participate.

Although Martin initially found the song "very slow and rather dreary,"[364] once the band, at Martin's urging, produced the more up-tempo arrangement heard on the record, the producer's sentiment about the song underwent a radical shift. It is again a testament to Martin's exceptional intuitive capacity that, after listening to the first playback of the recording, he was able to tell the Beatles: "Gentlemen, you've just made your first number-one record."[365] Thus, the skeptical holdout and representative of the established order was now completely won over to what the Beatles were creating, perhaps because he had a hand in its creation, but also because Martin's input was the final factor that produced the record's encapsulation of profound novelty. And Martin's reversal is prophetic of the success that the song would achieve, quickly rising to number one in the British pop charts, for the record itself seems to have demanded such recognition. "Please Please Me" is one of those nearly perfect records that is undeniable, capturing a certain energetic gestalt that can reliably induce positive feeling in the listener time after time, but that cannot be manufactured or reproduced through a rationalized formula.

From the very first bass and drum hit issuing into the simultaneously breezy and exhilarating swoop of the harmonica and guitar line, listeners in 1963 would have immediately recognized the sound of "Please Please Me" as novel, viscerally driven by the eighth-note insistence of McCartney's bass part. Then the vocals come in, sounding like the Everly Brothers on amphetamines, not far from the truth, with Lennon singing the simple, nursery rhyme melody and McCartney holding a pedal-tone on the high first note. This bifurcating harmony, combined with the deliberate cadence of the words and the driving rhythm, has the effect of producing a dramatic tension that, reflecting the gist of the lyrics, evokes the primal yearning of adolescent sexuality.[366] And the hacked-out, rising bar chords over the stop in the middle of the verse only serve to punctuate this tension, as do the five individual notes, played in unison on guitar and bass at the end of the verse. However, the most thrilling moment of the record is when Lennon rasps "come on," as if imploring the world to satisfy his visceral desire for connection, continually ratcheted up by the harmonized echoes from McCartney and Harrison, emphasized by Starr's adeptly modulated drum fills, moving from the optimistically ascendant major fourth to the querulously searching minor second to the darkly menacing minor sixth and back to the hopeful major fourth, a sequence that, in concert with the words, creates a sense of intense yearning for the warmth of sexual satisfaction.

The movement from the minor second to the minor sixth creates a displaced affect of doubt and difficulty in which a weaker group could have become mired in maudlin sentimentality, but it is carried through by the rhythmic animal potency of the three voices in the "come on" bridge. And then the band drops back to the big open E root chord, the lowest and most fully resonant chord on the guitar, for the tagline, "please *please* me," which feels like a return to an original state of unity, but immensely complicated and recontextualized by having passed through the harmonic odyssey of the bridge. Thus, in the space of almost exactly one minute, the song has carried the listener from the homey docks of Liverpool evoked by the harmonica line, which reiterates and dramatically reframes the harmonica part on the simpler "Love Me Do" (which itself appropriates the harmonica introduction on the previous year's top-selling British hit, Frank Ifield's "I Remember You"[367]), into the coaxing, cajoling, and demanding "come ons" that guide the listener through the anxiously libidinal labyrinth of the bridge, and back into the wide-open, orgasmic release of the chorus, which seems musically to enact the fulfillment of the sexual reciprocity that Lennon and his bandmates appear to be seeking in the lyrics.[368] All of these tortuous twists and turns amount to a multilayered narrative complexity packed into a span of time so short as to have been previously unimaginable, a moment qualitatively similar to Presley's recording of 'That's All Right,'"[369] though on a higher level of conceptual order, a hallmark of rationality. Although the lyrics of "Please Please Me" may appear a bit trite or facile to a twenty-first century sensibility, it seems that this record is one of the primary initiatory moments of the rupture the Beatles would enact for their culture over the ensuing decade.[370]

"A Phenomenon of Some Kind"

"Please Please Me" sparked the manic conflagration that would catalyze the emerging counterculture, for as press agent Tony Barrow describes the reaction to the first show the Beatles played in London following the record's success: "Immediately . . . the kids started screaming," he says, "I'd never experienced anything like it before. The Beatles, at this time, were basically unknown. But if this bunch of kids in London had gotten as far as finding out the individual band members' names, then it was a phenomenon of some kind, which, to me, was extremely significant."[371] The Beatles, through all of their various transformations, impelled to a great extent by the need to reconcile polarized experiential domains, had discovered a relational mode which, at that moment, seems to have possessed the quality of producing ecstasy in their audience.

This ecstatic enthusiasm was often referred to as "hysteria"[372] in the press, and while it did sometimes devolve into hysterical behavior, this word is loaded with pejorative significance against women, who had for centuries been diagnosed with this supposed pathology if they exhibited inclinations counter to the prescribed feminine roles. In contrast to this reductive interpretation, according to Barrow, the audience was "genuinely excited. . . . They knew the song; they knew about the band.

It had to be spontaneous, to some extent. But if you ask me, that special Beatles mystique was already at work."[373] All of the experiential terrain that they had traversed, from the original forging of the partnership between Lennon and McCartney, through the years of hard work and obscurity, the Hamburg initiation, the failed Decca audition, the signing with Parlophone, and, finally, the recording and release of their first two singles, had forged a numinosity around the band that communicated itself to their audience by their very presence.

Even at this early stage in their career, the Beatles embodied a process perhaps best expressible by the word "phenomenon" because it exceeded the scope of conventional language. To the sophisticated London culture, they seem to have symbolized a novel incarnation of rock and roll's primal mode, though largely stripped of the racial overtones connected to Presley and his contemporaries in the previous decade. Lacking the racially transgressive connotations exemplified by American rock and roll, the Beatles produced a similar kind of reversal and integration of polarized opposites in terms of class and region, mediating what Gould calls "the birth of Northern chic."[374] It is usually the case that processual transformations originate from agents outside the systemic centers, and the cultural revolution catalyzed by the Beatles is no exception, Liverpool perfectly fulfilling this criterion in relation to the cultural dominance of London.

Impelled by the Beatles' unassailable synthesis of accessibility and novelty, not just in their music, but in their visual style and physicality, English rock and roll was suddenly a viable proposition. As one observer put it: "To those of us in England who lived for the next great American single . . . it seemed like the Beatles were the promise we'd been waiting for all our lives." If it appears as if accounts of the Beatles' rise keep ratcheting up the superlatives until it seems there is nowhere left to go, and then, again and again, transcend the limitations of what seems possible, this is precisely the affective quality that accompanied the Beatles over the course of their relatively brief existence. More than any other group, their career was a long, nearly uninterrupted series of culminations, one after another, carrying their audience higher and higher, lifting them out of the static conformity that largely characterized the predominant cultural streams of the fifties and into what many perceived as a radically new and expanded world.

Although some of the songs that the Beatles played in the early performances of their fame in 1963 were not as thrilling as their first number one single, the overall effect of their sound and their appearance catalyzed the audience. Through the many musical elements and performative techniques that they had developed over the years, they were increasingly able to induce a feeling of self-overcoming in the crowds, the audience jolted out of their rational minds and into their primal bodies. Though not individually as physically gifted as Presley, the Beatles had developed similarly effective collective techniques, though of a less sexual quality, to induce mind-displacing euphoria in their largely female devotees during live performances, particularly the head-shaking falsetto "oohs," adapted from Little Richard, which became the band's early trademark.

The effect that this presentation had on the audience is undeniable, and still thrilling to hear, for according to Colin Manley of the Remo Four, describing the show: "Just a few weeks before they'd been nothing more than mates, one of us," he recalls, "but it was clear that night they'd become stars." The "ecstatic response" from the audience created an "aura"[375] around the band, a felt quality that starkly distinguished them from their old friends, as well as from their old selves. And indeed, what came to be known as "Beatlemania" does not seem to have been merely the trivial histrionics of hysterical teenage girls ("phony Beatlemania"[376] as the Clash would call it in "London Calling" during the following decade), for according to entertainer Kenny Lynch, who witnessed the mania up-close: "The Beatles shook those crowds up, even scared them a little." The audience members were genuinely frightened by the relative extremity of the spectacle, which is a primary way of overcoming inhibition, but only "a little," just enough to allow the crowd members to express their repressed libido in a comparatively safe context, a moment that numerous observers have described as something like a "tipping point" in the cultural process.[377]

In all honesty, it may seem a bit ridiculous that every time the Beatles went through a significant experience it is described as "the turning point" in their career and in history, the moment when they became the avatars of cultural revolution. However, as mentioned above, this quality seems to have followed the Beatles wherever they went as they enacted what amounts to a transformation in consciousness for their culture.[378] In this "succession of climaxes," as Bob Wooler put it, each moment of change may not have been unique in the overall trajectory of the Beatles' career, which consisted of many such moments, though in the history of culture, and even in relation to most of their peers, each of these moments was a rare and highly significant event that elicited qualities of human experience on a mass scale that had never before emerged in quite that way.[379] In this sense, each of these epiphanic instances constituted a genuine moment of rupture in the historical process. As Lennon later commented, rather than immediately trying to act as the cultural icons that they ultimately became, "your goal is, you know, always a few yards ahead rather than right up there" in the unimaginable heights that they eventually attained. Their primary ambition was "making it big in Liverpool, then being the best in the county, you know, then being the best group in England, and then we'd go for Scotland and break them in, and things like that,"[380] which seems to be Lennon's way of saying that the Beatles were always striving to overcome their present state, but one step at a time, through the consistent and pragmatic elicitation of ecstatic affect.

The writing of "I Saw Her Standing There" can be considered another such transformative moment in the history of popular music. McCartney wrote the first few lines on the van ride home from a gig in 1962: "she was just seventeen, and she'd never been a beauty queen." However, when he played the first draft of the song for Lennon, the two boys came to the mutual conclusion that the second line was "useless,"[381] replacing it with the more off-the-cuff and evocative "you know what I mean," which McCartney declares "means *nothing*, completely nothing at all."[382] However, as with so many of the Beatles' artistic decisions, this choice for the second line of what became one of their most loved songs was in fact "a prophetic gesture," as Spitz describes it, to young people who were literally dis-affected from their somatic selves. Apparently without McCartney's awareness or consent, this phrase tacitly acknowledges that the sexual, affective qualities of experience that tend to be particularly intense in teenagers defy the necessity of verbal formulation. While the relatively conservative main streams of culture in the nineteen-fifties had served to repress this kind of knowledge in the West's technologically mediated self-conception, producing an artificial innocence that continually threatened to burst at the seams, the Beatles implicitly recognized that the juxtaposition of the girl's age with the pulsating bass line communicated more information about the tumultuous urges of youth than a descriptive couplet ever could. By starting out the song in this way, McCartney and Lennon were essentially winking at their audience, conveying in the secret code of the young a subtle indication that their moment had come, and that this moment was thrillingly visceral.

Similarly, as Epstein is reported as having described the band in the studio during the recording of their first album, accomplished almost entirely on February 11, 1963: "They just put their heads down and played,"[383] which seems figuratively to suggest that, rather than analyzing and critiquing, the Beatles, when playing music, would temporarily relegate their minds to a subordinate position in relation to more embodied modes, feeling their way through the songs as they had learned to do in the many nights spent performing in Liverpool and

Hamburg. They had developed a kind of mutual resonance by playing together so often that they were apparently able to enter into elevated states of awareness through their collective intention and their ecstasy-inducing rhythms.

Even before the release of their first album, however, the success of their second single produced yet another qualitative "leap" in the Beatles' narrative trajectory, as they were now having real, transformative effects on individuals and on the culture that these individuals comprised throughout the United Kingdom, one observer at the time declaring that "their physical appearance inspires frenzy."[384] However, it was no longer necessary for the group physically to be present to induce this activity—even their music and image were unnecessary in some cases—for their very name became a powerful word, imbued with significance, which could invoke intense affect in their fans merely by its utterance. As mediators of the return of repressed epistemologies, the Beatles fed off this increasing flood of energy and attention, for this is precisely the kind of fame that they had been envisioning through those hard years in Liverpool and Hamburg. Although they would later tire of the mania, at this early stage in the phenomenon, the Beatles embraced the rising tide of affect directed toward them. Chosen by their culture to perform the most profound yearnings of the moment, the Beatles were propelled forward by historical forces that they could not control, though they willingly accepted their election as avatars of a new dispensation.

Although slightly greater numbers of musicians have reached this initial phenomenal status, one quality that made the Beatles such an exceptional phenomenon was the consistency with which they practiced their art, regardless of the many distractions of fame. They were certainly inspired by their success, writing cascades of songs in this initial rush of notoriety.[385] However, it is the Beatles' commitment to steady productivity that set them apart, for according to Kenny Lynch, who was part of the Beatles' package tour: "They wrote every day on the coach, like clockwork" amidst the "highs and lows" of life on the road, a phrase evocative of the affective mode. This "roller-coaster" quality is characteristic of feeling, which is an indispensable mode of engagement with reality, but which requires the mediating critical distance and organizing structure of rationality, "like clockwork," to achieve its greatest effectiveness. Intellect without affect lacks meaning, but affect without intellect lacks consciousness. While the Beatles had previously been cultivating the intuitive mode in relation to a culture that often privileged rationality, they increasingly represented the integration of these two modes. The intuitive mode in which they had been immersed issued into the focused expression of their songs, for as they discovered in their critique at the hands of George Martin, simple, unmediated feeling is not sufficient to produce genuine novelty.

As agents of novelty's ingression into cultural process, the Beatles had been called into the limelight by popular demand and the assent of the gatekeepers of institutional hierarchies. Indeed, the audiences for a tour in the fall of 1963 were almost entirely composed of teenage girls, screaming and weeping in ecstatic release, acting "as if they all knew one another." According to press agent Tony Barrow, speaking of a show at the prestigious Royal Albert Hall in London: "they acted that way because they had one thing in common . . . They were Beatles fans.'" Their mutual enthusiasm for the group produced a collective quality—they were all profoundly moved by the same phenomenon. The Beatles were eliciting, in the most revered and public of British venues, an ecstatic reaction, which is as appropriate a moment as any to mark the inception of Beatlemania. The collective self-transcendence contained in this neologism had traversed from the Cavern and the provincial halls to the center of institutional sanction in England, and the country—soon the world—would ultimately be transformed by this cultural infiltration. The developmental process of the genre had reached a point at which the whole industry, indeed the whole country, began to reconfigure itself around a band that had until recently been a group of liminal outsiders with few prospects. The underdogs, with relative suddenness, had been ushered into the center of technologically mediated discourse to participate in a profound revision of the narrative at the heart of their culture.[386]

In this moment, the impulses toward cultural revolution and sexual liberation were deeply intertwined, and this multivalent return of repressed modes found one of its greatest catalysts in the Beatles, as can be witnessed in video footage of concerts from these years. "You don't have to be a genius," one psychiatrist at the time commented, "to see parallels between sexual excitement and the mounting crescendo of delighted screams through a stimulating number like 'Twist and Shout.'"[387] However, Beatlemania cannot be reduced to sexuality, Brian Epstein referring to the phenomenon as "simply a kind of mass pathology," which is often the case with the return of repressed psychic contents of many kinds, contending that the Beatles "have an extraordinary ability to satisfy a certain hunger in the country,"[388] apparently a hunger for somatic release from rational propriety.

Similarly, social critic Barbara Ehrenreich has suggested that "the attraction of the Beatles bypassed sex and went straight to the issue of power,"[389] the power to express repressed affect, including "female assertiveness, female aggression, female sexuality, and female solidarity"[390] in public. Thus, when one police officer participating in the mayhem claimed that "these people have lost the ability to think,"[391] he seems to have been correct in the sense that the sheer potency of the experience impelled the audiences' center of attention literally out of their minds and into their bodies. However, where the officer saw this impulsion as a lack, to many of those who participated, it was experienced as a plenitude: not the absence of thought, but the intentional overcoming of the hegemony of the rational.

One attendee at a concert in 1964 described the experience in elemental terms: the "screaming, weeping ecstasy . . . felt like an earthquake. . . . It would start at one end [of the arena] and continue to the other. It was incredible to do nothing but stand there, letting it wash right over you."[392] Based on the descriptions of those who experienced these concerts, as well as on the video footage, the sheer force of the collective emotion catalyzed by the Beatles is strikingly clear. As the *Daily Mail* wrote of one fan: "Screaming like an animal, and wearing almost as much leather as one, the young girl writhed and shook in some private ecstasy."[393] However, although this description evokes the visceral animality produced by Beatlemania, it is precisely public, not "private ecstasy" that characterized the phenomenon. It seems that this public ecstasy was an intentional performance, for though no individual could control the elemental force of Beatlemania, it appears that the young, screaming girls consciously participated in the phenomenon, allowing the music and presence of the Beatles to catalyze their internal process. Although the historical imperative that produced the ecstatic affect characteristic of Beatlemania had not been manufactured and could not be stopped, the participants willingly took part in this pandemonium, the spectacle providing a socially acceptable outlet for the urge toward wild physical abandon that had so long been repressed.

The tide of change that lifted the Beatles continued to rise throughout 1963 as their records monopolized the English charts in a way that no musician had ever accomplished. Similarly, witnessing the Beatles' arrival for the first time in America in February 1964 after "I Want to Hold Your Hand" had reached number one on the *Billboard* "Hot 100," one observer exclaimed that "no one, I mean *no one*, has ever seen or even remotely suspected anything like this before!"[394] Although there were many precursors to the phenomenon of Beatlemania, from religious awakenings and revivals over the centuries to the furors over Valentino, Sinatra, and Presley, this incarnation of mass ecstasy was occurring on a higher order of magnitude than those other manifestations, permeating the cultural psyche via concurrently emerging technologies in a way that nothing of this kind had ever done.

"Bemused Awareness"

As with Presley, once the Beatles started to gain notoriety, the backlash from the press was harsh and swift. In response to their era-defining appearance on *The Ed Sullivan Show*, the largest television audience to date aside from the day of President Kennedy's assassination a few months earlier, Jack Gould, the same *New York Times* critic who had panned Presley a decade before, relegated the Beatles to the status of "a fad," though he acknowledged their "bemused awareness." As Gould writes: "Televised Beatlemania . . . appeared to be a fine mass placebo," a "sedate anticlimax" to the expectation that had been built up in the press for the Beatles' first trip to America.[395] Similarly, the critic for the *Washington Post* wrote that the Beatles "seemed downright conservative . . . asexual and homely,"[396] while *Newsweek* had previously described the band's music as "High-pitched, loud beyond reason, and stupefyingly repetitive."[397] The *Herald Tribune* inexplicably declared in its front-page headline: "BEATLES BOMB ON TV," the critic claiming that the Beatles were "a magic act that owed less to Britain than to Barnum." Continuing the tirade, he writes that the Beatles "apparently could not carry a tune across the Atlantic" and that they were "75 percent publicity, 20 percent haircut, and 5 percent lilting lament."[398] These are severe appraisals, certainly, but compared to the vitriol aimed at Presley and his contemporaries, the critical response to the Beatles was somewhat restrained, portraying them not as a threat but rather as a trivial fad, which is almost a worse indictment for would-be rebels. Whereas Presley had been derided as a vulgar, dangerous animal, the Beatles were dismissed as merely insubstantial.

It is certainly a sign of progress that the press at least recognized the Beatles' "bemused awareness," visibly expressing their integration of intellectual and intuitive modes, which rendered them more palatable to the established media than their rock and roll precursors had been. However, to rephrase McCartney's lyric in "I Saw Her Standing There," the youth knew what the Beatles meant; they were in on the joke, and cranky journalistic incomprehension did absolutely nothing to abate the feverish momentum that was carrying the Beatles, and primary streams of culture along with them, into a new and distinct historical period. However, as the decade progressed, even most journalists were won over by a revolution in consciousness that left many aspects of culture transmogrified in its wake. Ultimately, what the Beatles performed for their culture, for young and old alike, was the conscious awareness characteristic of rationality brought to bear on the intuitive physicality endemic to rock and roll, an initiatory reembrace of affect by intellect.

That one reviewer compared the Beatles to a circus magic show perfectly demonstrates how close yet how far these critics were from understanding the phenomenon that was igniting the youth of Britain and America. Only one so immersed in the intellectually privileging critical mode of postwar modernity could mistake the genuine, once-in-a-generation enchantment that the Beatles were producing for a carnival sideshow. Indeed, the first lines of Richard Tarnas' *Cosmos and Psyche* speak to this very fallacy: "Skepticism is the chastity of the intellect, Santayana declared, and the metaphor is apt. The mind that seeks the deepest intellectual fulfillment does not give itself up to every passing idea. Yet what is sometimes forgotten is the larger purpose of such a virtue. For in the end," Tarnas writes, "chastity is something one preserves not for its own sake, which would be barren, but rather so that one may be fully ready for the moment of surrender to the beloved, the suitor whose aim is true."[399] The youth of America were ready for a passionate consummation of belief while the press initially remained skeptical in the face of the miraculous. However, as the decade progressed, most of these journalists were won over by the radical upheaval that left many aspects of culture transmogrified in its wake.

The Beatles, faithful in the righteousness of their mission, were apparently not discouraged by the initial negative response from the press, but took it as a challenge. As Lennon put it: "If everybody really liked us, it would be a bore. . . . It doesn't give any edge to it if everybody just falls flat on their face saying, 'You're great.'"[400] This attitude recalls the Beatles' first shows at the Cavern when Lennon took perverse pleasure in playing rock and roll in spite of the prohibitions of the jazz establishment. There was something in Lennon's character that impelled him toward such gleeful rebellion. Similarly, at an early American press conference, the Beatles applied their charming wit to full effect, converting a hostile group of journalists through their irresistibly absurd mode of relation. It was a combination of all the elements that made them exceptional—their music, their style, and their charisma—that seduced the audience. But it was primarily the Beatles' quick humor, their ability to engage in witty repartee—the stock-in-trade of much mid-twentieth century journalism—that won over the American press. Thus, the Beatles continued to demonstrate that they were an ideal vessel for the return of repressed modes of experience. By integrating these modes with the privileged rational mode in their artistic and public personas, the

Beatles ultimately provided a focus for the integration of these epistemologies in the predominant discursive domains.

"Literary Beatle"

Another significant step toward the cultural legitimation of the Beatles came in the form of Lennon's first book of poetry and sketches, *In His Own Write*. Displaying his facility with the written word, even in the rather ludicrous and childlike form of Lennon's book, gave the high cultural press a justification for elevating Lennon, enjoying his new role as the "literary Beatle," to the exalted status that he ultimately achieved. Although this endeavor was clearly a sideline for Lennon, a genre in which his gifts, judged on their own merits, were real but modest, the simple fact that a hugely famous pop singer had produced a written work gave the journalistic establishment, which generally privileged the intellectual mode of writing over the more intuitive, non-verbal musical mode, a way to place Lennon within the canonical cultural hierarchy of which they were guardians.

Indeed, it is instructive that Presley, who never produced a written work, remains largely outside the high cultural canon, while his immediate successors, Lennon and Dylan, are both generally accepted into that canon, both having produced literary volumes early in their musical careers. Lennon articulated the new movement toward embodied absurdity and intuitive humor for these often highly literate journalists, many of whom were ironically illiterate in the somatic language of popular music. For those who had not learned how to feel their way into music based on blues and country, Lennon's written performance of many of the same themes and attitudes that the Beatles exhibited musically allowed a generally older and more conservative element of the public access to the emerging counterculture of which Lennon and his bandmates were the primary British exemplars. Similarly, it gave the journalists who liked the Beatles, but were hesitant or did not have the vocabulary necessary to "defend" them in polite society, the opportunity to support the emerging phenomenon of Beatlemania on more familiar ground, favorably comparing Lennon's work to writers from Lewis Carroll and Edward Lear to James Thurber and James Joyce.[401]

To some extent, because the Beatles' wit, rendered "literary" in Lennon's book, made their music and the cultural movement that they represented accessible to the guardians of high culture, they began to receive sanction from that cultural stream in the form of awards and accolades, while the general public bought unprecedented numbers of their records. It has often been noted that, in April 1964 in the United

States, fourteen of the singles on *Billboard's* "Hot 100" chart were by the Beatles. Having emerged as emissaries from the collective unconscious, the dark caverns of Liverpool and Hamburg, into the bright lights of cultural centrality, the Beatles managed to walk the tightrope between edgy authenticity and mainstream cultural acceptability with an aplomb that belies the extremely rare nature of this feat. Indeed, to the millions of aspiring musicians who have ever dreamed of having *one* song crack the "Hot 100" chart, the Beatles' success could be described as almost "obscene" in its profligacy, though it is difficult to fault the Beatles for taking more than their share of the glory because their music was so consistently and undeniably great.[402]

By mid-1964, the group had become a primary focus of international attention, the press and public following their every move and hanging on their every utterance. As with many of the brief fads and fascinations that successively capture the interest of millions, the Beatles were elevated to the status of cultural obsession. However, unlike most of the phenomena that come to dominate the media for a few days or a few weeks, the Beatles managed to maintain a consistently central role for almost a decade, and even at various moments after they disbanded at the end of the sixties. Such a phenomenon is still largely unmatched, for the Beatles were prime movers of a cultural revolution that continues to condition many of our aesthetic, intellectual, and experiential possibilities.

"A Slightly New Sound"

Following the release of *With the Beatles* in November 1963, a large step beyond their debut album, the summer of 1964 was arguably the peak of Beatlemania, marked by the release of both the film and album *A Hard Day's Night* in July of that year. The album, their first containing all original compositions (and their only such album during their early, pre-*Rubber Soul* period) constitutes a musical and lyrical encapsulation of the integral synthesis of affective "feel" and rational "wit" that the Beatles had been developing over the previous few years. And not only were the compositions growing simultaneously in both sophistication and emotional depth, but the instrumentation was expanding the palette of rock and roll, particularly in Harrison's use of the newly produced Rickenbacker 12-string on the kinetic title song, as well as in his use of classical guitar on "And I Love Her." Similarly, the film, containing six of the album's songs and a clever screenplay written by Liverpool playwright Alun Owen full of hilarious "one-liners," puns, and malapropisms, more than anything cemented the image of the Beatles as the verbally humorous, charming lads at the eye of Beatlemania's unprecedented affective storm. Indeed, by this time, the storm had become one of truly international proportions, spreading as far as Asia and Australia where the Beatles had toured earlier in the year.

After the Beatles' deeply influential first encounter with both Bob Dylan and cannabis in August 1964, explicated in detail in the Epilogue, the group's newly charged spirit of experimentation was not limited to songwriting or to the instrumental arrangements of their songs. They also began experimenting with the medium itself, the technology of recording. In particular, the feedback at the beginning of "I Feel Fine," their "hippest single to date,"[403] recorded on October 18, 1964, can be described as a minor revelation that initiated a new aspect of musical production, and a new locus for the integration of technological rationality and somatic affect. As Harrison quips in the *Anthology*: "We invented Jimi Hendrix"[404] which, though quite a large overstatement, does acknowledge the debt that Hendrix's use of feedback owed to the Beatles.

Like the "happy accident" from which emerged Presley's "That's All Right" and, thus, rock and roll, the Beatles' first use of feedback on record was one of many novel innovations they introduced as part of their general transformative trajectory. Indeed, the image of "hitting a gusher," as Spitz describes this moment, is apt in that the Beatles were tapping a resource for which all of the elements were already present, but which had not yet been enacted consciously.[405] This sudden advance into technologically mediated sonic novelty, fueled by the influence of their peers and some new psychoactives, particularly cannabis and LSD, was expressive of the expansively inspired impulse toward change characteristic of that period. This is the moment when the Beatles began using the studio as a kind of instrument in itself, which directly prefigured the introduction of synthesizers, drum machines, and recording programs like Pro Tools and Logic that would become ubiquitous in the ensuing decades.

1964's *Beatles for Sale* was a relatively conservative record within the Beatles oeuvre, a well-crafted consolidation of the gradual growth of their first three records, though with a more pronounced leaning toward country music. 1965's *Help!* was a similarly steady progression on the elements that had won them international acclaim. Although not as revolutionary as the albums to come, *Beatles for Sale* and *Help!* showed their craft progressing so that chord changes, textures, and lyrics exhibited a subtly new attitude, exemplified in the transition from the black-and-white format of the film *A Hard Day's Night* to the color format of the *Help!* film. Although the Beatles were essentially the same band that had produced their first three records, the catalysts of Dylan and cannabis, as well as simply the onrushing tide of culture, had impelled a shift in their approach, visible in all of the stylistic elements mentioned above, but not reducible to these things. Indeed, although *Help!* is not as dramatically experimental as the albums to come over the next few years, it contained the first glimmers in the Beatles music of what would come to be referred to as "psychedelia."

"Ticket To Ride," the first single released from the album, was something different for the Beatles with its strange, loping rhythm and its chiming, raga-like guitars. As Lennon would later comment: "It was a slightly new sound at the time," quickly revising his estimation of the song as "pretty fucking heavy."[406] In fact, referring back to Whitehead's oft-quoted dictum about "that slightest change of tone," the qualities of being "slightly new" and "pretty fucking heavy" (whether Lennon is referring to the sound of the song or the gravity of the innovation) are not mutually exclusive. Examined atomistically in its constituent parts, "Ticket to Ride" does not seem particularly revolutionary, aside from a number of modest lyrical, rhythmic, and harmonic innovations. However, taken as a whole, the emergent effect of these combined innovations is radically different from anything the Beatles, or any other rock and roll group, had ever done before. Listening to the song a half-century later, one might miss the dramatic quality of this transformation precisely because radical novelty widely disseminated quickly becomes normative. However, by all accounts, the song was experienced in that moment as one of the many unprecedented transformations produced by the Beatles.

"A Saturation Point"

This series of transformations did not come without its price, though. As Lennon recalls his evolving relationship with McCartney: "We were different. We were older. . . . We knew each other on all kinds of levels that we didn't when we were teenagers." Forced to mature by the intense pressures of extraordinary fame as well as the desire to be master of one's own domain that often accompanies growing older and more successful, Lennon and McCartney both sought to expand into a fuller individuality. This natural impulse inevitably created cracks in their partnership, which had been founded upon the adolescent submersion of individuality in the group. However, this "creative tension,"[407] though at times uncomfortable and ultimately unsustainable, is a large part of what allowed the band to create what many would agree is their most fully realized music in the latter half of the sixties, though it is impossible to say if the music from their early, middle, or late period is qualitatively the greatest, as all three periods fulfilled a central role in the evolution of rock and roll as well as of historical process in general. Indeed, the Beatles are one of a very few musical groups about whom as many people proclaim a preference for their middle or late work as for their early records.[408] Nevertheless, at this stage in their development in the mid-sixties, the Beatles were still working together fully as a band, rather than as three separate singer-songwriters with backing bands as they would construe the making of *The White Album* a few years later.

The first real crack in their group unity was McCartney's "Yesterday," which he recorded and performed solo on acoustic guitar with an orchestral string accompaniment. As McCartney describes the song's inception, the melody came to him in a dream, a transmission that appeared to him to exceeded the possibility of conscious volition in the melody's composition, so much so that he felt compelled to seek out the opinions of friends to convince himself that it was not "a nick,"[409] a borrowed melody from some forgotten classic. As McCartney later explained: "It was all there . . . like an egg being laid . . . not a crack or a flaw in it. . . . It was fairly mystical."[410] Perhaps more than any song he would ever write, McCartney felt that the melody of "Yesterday" was given to him by something beyond him, preexisting and whole from some other realm of being. As McCartney's friend Bruce Welch put it: "I knew it was magic," and it is indeed striking that one of the most covered songs of all time is one that McCartney explicitly felt did not come from him, but from something that transcended him.[411]

However, while the Beatles were undergoing what they describe as a profound revolution of consciousness, the inevitable, if short-lived, backlash was occurring against them. The *Help!* film was given mostly mediocre or worse reviews by a press that had been almost unanimously laudatory since the initial knee-jerk rejection in some quarters of the press a few years before. In particular, the *NME* described the film as "unfunny" and "100 minutes of nonsense,"[412] which aside from the songs and a few good moments is fairly accurate, McCartney later recalling: "We enjoyed making *Help!* more than *A Hard Day's Night* but looking back on the two I think *A Hard Day's Night* was the better film."[413] Similarly, Lennon's second book of humorous drawings, poetry, and prose, *A Spaniard in the Works*, was generally panned by critics, the novelty of a pop star publishing a "literary" work perhaps having worn off, though the first book, written over a number of years, is generally of higher quality than the second book, written completely in 1964.

Aside from the genuinely diminished quality of Lennon's second publication and the Beatles' second film, however, Lennon felt that the negative reaction was a result of the band having reached a "saturation point" in public consciousness, which seems partially true. As he described it: "you couldn't walk down a street without having us staring at you." The rest of the group and their manager all agreed that they needed to step back from the public eye for a while in order to create a demand for the group. As Harrison put it: "We need less exposure, not more. . . . It's been Beatles, Beatles, Beatles."[414] As with their previous periods of transformation in Hamburg and following Martin's critique, it seems to have been necessary for the Beatles to undergo essentially another psychological ego death and rebirth. Not only did this death and rebirth occur in the individual domain through the catalysts of Dylan and psychoactives explored in more depth below, but also in the emergent quality of the Beatles' narrative in popular consciousness, which seems to have required something like a mild form of crucifixion by the press and fans (though they continued to buy the records) in order to impel the group toward further transformation, and to clear a space within which a further permutation of the Beatles mode could emerge.

For the year stretching from the release of *Beatles for Sale* in December 1964 through the release of *Rubber Soul* in December 1965, the Beatles, perhaps rendered temporarily complacent by the unprecedented success of the previous two years, fell behind the new groups emerging at that moment, from the Rolling Stones, the Kinks, the Who, and the Yardbirds in England to Dylan, the Byrds, and the Beach Boys in America. As McCartney observed: "Things were changing. . . . The direction was moving away from the poppy stuff, like 'Thank You Girl,' 'From Me to You,' and 'She Loves You.'"[415] Culture refuses to stand still, always pushing forward into novelty, and there is arguably no time in history when the pace of transformation was greater than in the nineteen-sixties. Whereas the Beatles had previously been a thrilling cultural phenomenon in which even many of the most hardened hipsters were caught up, grumblings had started to arise that the Beatles were merely "teeny-boppers" no longer worthy of serious consideration. Thus, the Beatles, rather than be relegated to the status of "has-beens," realized that they must integrate the new styles into their musical aesthetic if they were to continue to be relevant to the emerging counterculture. However, this change was not merely a cynical marketing move, but a natural progression induced by both the unprecedentedly strong competition and the Beatles' exceptional impulse toward novelty.

Even the younger fans, still carried along by the elemental force of Beatlemania, were growing older. The innocent mayhem of Beatlemania was inexorably shading into a darker, more violent kind of upheaval as the Beatles commenced their second U.S. tour in August 1965. Perhaps the most visible sign of the coming rupture occurred during the first show of the tour at Shea stadium, which proved to be the peak in sheer magnitude of their performing career, and the largest concert ever put on at that moment. As the *New York Times* described the audience, which had collectively commandeered the performance through their sheer wailing magnitude: "Their immature lungs produced a sound so staggering, so massive, so shrill and sustained that it quickly crossed the line from enthusiasm into hysteria and was soon in the area of the classic Greek meaning of the word pandemonium—the region of all demons."[416] The Beatles were approaching a point of crisis at which they could remain in their first incarnation as do so many musical acts, playing their role as moptopped props for the expression of repressed libido in their young fans, or they could dramatically change their approach.

However, it was not just the Beatles, but something in the culture at that moment that seemed to be impelling this crisis and transformation. Indeed, as the *Times* writer's use of the ancient concept of "pandemonium" suggests, this "region of all demons" appears to have been an enactment of the return of those aspects of human experience that had been repressed by the successively dominant systems of Christianity and scientific rationalism as demonic and sinful on the one hand, and as irrational and base on the other. Beatlemania provided a focus for a collective moment of release, though by this point, the novelty had worn off so that the Beatles, following their psychoactively mediated transformation, could no longer play the role that they had worked so hard to inhabit in good conscience. As Lennon recalled: "It was ridiculous! . . . We couldn't hear ourselves sing. . . . You can see it in the film, George and I aren't even bothering playing half the chords, and we were just messing about."[417] The phenomenon that the Beatles had mediated, though of deep cultural significance, had grown beyond their control to the point of absurdity, though it is a testament to the inertia that so often comes with success that the band kept touring for a full year after this moment.

In the midst of the mania, the Beatles took a six week break in the fall of 1965, which allowed them the kind of quiet introspection and solitude that had been impossible when they were touring, but which appears necessary for inspired creative activity. This moment of pause allowed the Beatles to maintain a healthy balance; it was a clearing moment, a time to replenish their resources in order to prepare for the further revelation that they could collectively sense just over the horizon. During this period, the phenomenon of Beatlemania was becoming increasingly less connected to the four bandmates, existing primarily in the media of recordings, film, and in popular discourse. The Beatles' individual identities, and thus the emergent entity of the Beatles, could no longer be contained within the mythological framework they had co-created with their audience. And out of this moment of meditative reflection came what most consider the Beatles' first mature work of art on the scale of an entire album: *Rubber Soul*.

"The Departure Record"

The four young men did not know precisely how their new record would sound, but they knew it would have to be something qualitatively different than anything they had produced before because both the Beatles and their culture were changing at a frantic pace. According to McCartney, the group was "bored by doing the same thing,"[418] elaborating elsewhere: "You can't be singing 15-year-old songs at 20 because you don't think 15-year-old thoughts at 20."[419] In a musical rather than a lyrical context, Harrison added: "We were suddenly hearing sounds that we weren't able to hear before." And as Starr generally recalled: "We were expanding in all areas of our lives . . . opening up to a lot of different attitudes."[420] Whereas their records up to this point in the fall of 1965 showed a general continuity of development, the Beatles sensed that their new record would be a radical leap forward, still a Beatles album with their highly distinctive voices and musicianship, but exhibiting an emergent novelty qualitatively similar to their initial breakthrough with "Please Please Me" three years before. The elements that composed the new album would not be dramatically different from the previous music they had made aside from relatively minor innovations like the sitar on "Norwegian Wood," the fuzz bass on "Think for Yourself," the French lyrics on "Michelle," and Lennon's dramatic intake of breath on "Girl," but the shift in their approach and context would reframe their previous tropes, synthesizing them in new and unexpected ways.

Where the Beatles' albums through *Help!* were clearly identifiable as essentially "pop" records, *Rubber Soul* would be something that had not been heard before precisely because the Beatles themselves were learning to hear in new ways. Impelled by the pressure of their peers and a tight self-imposed deadline to write the material for the new album, mediated through the imaginatively meaning-infused ambiance of cannabis, the Beatles were able to produce songs like "Drive My Car," "Norwegian Wood," "Nowhere Man," "The Word," "Michelle," "In My Life," and the other novel compositions that they would record. And like McCartney's experience of writing "Yesterday," "Nowhere Man" seemed to come to Lennon fully formed, "the whole damn thing" spontaneously emerging as he woke from a dream.

Although Lennon claims to have spent "five hours"[421] struggling to write something of value before dozing off, when the song came, it flowed effortlessly. Whereas some songs, like "Drive My Car" for instance, appear to be crafted consciously to produce an aesthetically pleasing piece, "Nowhere Man" has more the quality of a revelation, long hoped-for, and rather sudden and unexpected when it finally comes. In fact, "Nowhere Man" seems to be a more complete and perfect expression of the theme that Lennon had previously articulated in "I'm A Loser" from *Beatles For Sale* and "Help!" from the album of the same name. These songs were progressively circling in on Lennon's affective core, his primal wounds from his early abandonment and the tragic deaths of his mother and his best friend, Stuart Sutcliffe. By creating these songs, Lennon seems to have been performing a process of self-healing and transformation, which, concretized in these compositions, became accessible to his audience, allowing them to heal and transform themselves through the catalyst of the records, enacting the reintegration of affective attention that pervaded these songs.

Not only the lyrics, but the music itself had grown qualitatively more subtle and profound by entering more deeply into engagement with the repressed epistemologies. For instance, McCartney's bass line on "Nowhere Man" is one of the greatest masterpieces of that most humble and self-effacing of instruments, often the most difficult for non-musicians to pick out of the ensemble sound, as it is the heartbeat of the band, the deep resonant tone that affects the listener more on a somatic level than on a conscious one. McCartney's complex, propulsively wandering bass line perfectly complements the searching affect of the lyrics, the gloriously lazy cadence of the layered harmonies, and the chiming guitars, like a clarion call to self-knowledge.

Similarly, according to Harrison: "The studio itself was full of instruments: pedal harmoniums, tack pianos, a celeste, and a Hammond organ. . . . That's why we used all those different sounds on our records—because they were *there*." In particular, Starr has referred to Harrison's use of sitar on "Norwegian Wood" as "a mind-blower." As Starr remembers: "We were all open to anything when George introduced the sitar," an act which did a great deal to liberate the spirit of experimentation, after which "you could walk in with anything as long as it was going to make a musical note."[422] And furthermore, as George Martin recalls of *Rubber Soul*: "For the first time we began to think of albums as art on their own, as complete entities."[423] Not only were the Beatles radically stretching their boundaries in terms of lyrics and song construction, but also in the arrangement, instrumentation, and recording of those songs. Rather than thinking of the album as a few singles accompanied essentially by high quality filler, the Beatles were one of the first popular artists to think of the album as a work of art, a "complete entity" like a novel or a film with a narrative arc, meant to be listened to as a whole rather than merely as a collection of songs.

It may be difficult to see the fundamental transformation that this shift constituted a half-century later, for we live in a world in which this way of thinking is the norm. Even the title *Rubber Soul* apparently alludes to the stretching of identity and genre just as the cover photo was elongated, for the Beatles saw this new record partially as an elaborative expansion of the soul genre then emerging out of rhythm and blues as well as an expansion of their collective persona. The effect that this album would have on subsequent musicians and on predominant cultural streams cannot be overestimated. Indeed, though the Beatles would perhaps go on to make greater records, and certainly more mature, experimental, heavy, and portentous ones, *Rubber Soul*, along with Dylan's *Bringing It All Back Home*, was "the departure record," as Starr nominated it, performing a crucial turning point in the historical process from the postwar era to the emergent attitude of the sixties counterculture. These two records, perhaps more than any others, initiated the aesthetic possibilities that continue to inform Western culture almost a half-century later.[424]

CHAPTER 3
"LOOKING FOR THE INNER HEAT"

*Mythical consciousness is a mode of being in the world that
brings with it imaginal persons. They are given with the
imagination and are its data. Where imagination reigns,
personifying happens. We experience it nightly, spontaneously,
in dreams. Just as we do not create our dreams, but they happen
to us, so we do not invent the persons of myth and religion; they,
too, happen to us. The persons present themselves as existing
prior to any effort of ours to personify. To mythic consciousness,
the persons of the imagination are real.*

James Hillman, *Re-Visioning Psychology*[425]

The Beatles seem to invite from their biographers a journalistic
eloquence that never delves very deeply into any one character, which is
an entirely appropriate approach for a band whose defining characteristic
is that they are four equals in constant dialogue, accounts generally
focusing on the relationships between the individual Beatles and between
the Beatles and their audience. Conversely, Bob Dylan invites a kind of
interior depth that the Beatles generally do not, as Dylan's is the story of
the lone genius poet who is primarily concerned with his own internal
process and the way that process is mirrored in the world. In his memoir,
Chronicles, Dylan has written with depth and insight about a significant
portion of the period in his career that is the main focus of this chapter:
his childhood through the moment in 1965 when he "went electric," the
platform from which he would subsequently transform the genre of rock
and roll. Although Dylan tells much of this narrative in relation to his
friends and influences, he less often recounts stories about his
relationships with these people, rather giving what amount to character
sketches of the individuals that he admires and from whom he has
learned.[426]

Although Dylan is explicitly philosophical, he does not seem
particularly interested in academic philosophy of the kind referred to in
these pages, declaring "I'm not even a philosopher"[427] with his enigmatic
grin at a 1965 press conference. However, he is clearly interested in the
philosophical strains of music, literature, poetry, painting, film, history,
and any number of other subjects. For instance, Dylan writes: "Balzac
was pretty funny. His philosophy is plain and simple, says basically that
pure materialism is a recipe for madness."[428] Although Dylan seems

merely to be summarizing Balzac's philosophical orientation, Dylan hardly ever says anything innocently, rarely expressing ideas in an impartial, objective manner, but rather speaking in ways that demonstrate that he understands concepts because he has lived through them, and that those concepts are always already embodied. Thus, Dylan implicitly acknowledges here one of the primary insights traced in the preceding pages: that the almost exclusive privileging of reductive "materialism" and its accompanying rationality in modernity has produced a kind of collective "madness," describable as a mass psychosis resulting from the systemic repression of affectivity.

As with his reference to Balzac, Dylan writes in *Chronicles* about almost everything in this oblique manner. Much of the narrative is concerned with the large cast of characters that he admired and respected. He writes directly about himself less often, rather giving an impression, as in a photographic negative, of what he was thinking and feeling in relation to these other people. It seems likely, based on this evidence, that he thinks about himself and defines his character largely in this way, becoming himself by constantly projecting himself into the subjectivity of others. Whereas the Beatles maintained a conceit of critical distance from the phenomenon they were creating by means of their collective ironic humor, Dylan has maintained a similar distance through an obfuscating, mysterious, riddle-like way of speaking that often relies less on humor, though he can certainly be hilarious when he feels the urge.

In fact, Dylan's attitude reveals much of the same absurdity that the Beatles evinced in their humor and lyrics, but Dylan's mode of verbal expression is more like a Zen koan or the modern poetry by which he was explicitly influenced. The Beatles as well as their commentators expressed self-awareness more in their attitude and in their witty, cutting banter, by saying things without saying them, whereas it is rarely quite clear what Dylan is actually saying, as many of his statements are metaphorical or paradoxical, aphorisms that can be taken on different levels of discursive signification, evoking profound depths and dizzying heights with Dylan as opaque medium. As Greil Marcus describes Dylan at an early show opening for Joan Baez in 1963: "Something in his demeanor dared you to pin him down, to sum him up and write him off, and you couldn't do it."[429]

"My Place In the Universe"

Similar to both Presley's Memphis and the Liverpool of the Beatles, Hibbing, Minnesota, the place from which Dylan emerged, was liminal in relation to the culturally dominant cities like New York and London. As Dylan reflects in an irascible 2012 interview for *Rolling Stone*: "Where I grew up was as far from the cultural center as you could get. It was way out of the beaten path." Later in the same interview, he relates the marginal quality of his hometown to Liverpool: "John [Lennon] came from the northern regions of Britain. The hinterlands. Just like I did in America, so we had some kind of environmental things in common. Both places were pretty isolated. Though mine was more landlocked than his. But everything is stacked against you when you come from that."[430] Extrapolating from Thomas Kuhn's work in *The Structure of Scientific Revolutions*, it seems to be the case that revolutions, whether scientific, political, or cultural, like those mediated by Presley, the Beatles, and Dylan, almost always issue from the margins of culture, often in a literal, geographical sense, for it is apparently an intrinsic quality of process that those at the edges of cultural power are usually more open to ideas outside the cultural system whose integration into that system constitutes the engine of novelty.[431] As Tim Riley suggests, the geographical, cultural, and psychological "fringes" are the "true holy ground" of rock and roll.[432]

Dylan was a true scholar of musical history. Like the Beatles, he grew up on rock and roll, though he was closer to the source. If rivers are the arteries of a country, then highways are the nerve fibers, and Dylan felt that growing up at the North end of Highway 61, which ended in Duluth, Minnesota, the same road that had been "the main thoroughfare of the country blues," formed an abiding connection between him and that deep repository of African American experience. Similarly, growing up near the source of the Mississippi River, "the bloodstream of the blues," which he "always felt . . . was in my blood," created a profoundly durable association with the genre for Dylan. Indeed, though he explored many styles in his long career, Dylan would always return to the blues for, as he writes: "it was a counterpart to myself," a mode of relation that defined him at his very core. Whereas Presley and Little Richard and Chuck Berry and the Everly Brothers embodied the quintessence of musical achievement for the Beatles, particularly in their early years, Dylan quickly passed through these more contemporary influences to immerse himself in the archaic tradition of folk music, of which the blues were an integral part.[433]

When asked at a 1966 press conference, "Why do you sing?" Dylan answers: "Why? Just because I feel like singing."[434] Although this statement seems rather transparent, it bears unpacking. Dylan did not answer that he sang for any high-minded reasons, to change the world or to create great art, though he certainly did both of these things, but simply because he felt like it. There is no more direct evocation of the supposition that Dylan has been driven primarily by affect, though counter to the trivial connotations that this supposition might evoke in the context of a rationality privileging modernity, Dylan in many ways proves affect to be a window into the most profound mysteries of human experience in the animal body.

Bearing a strong similarity to descriptions of both Presley and Lennon, the boy who would become Bob Dylan is consistently portrayed as having possessed a quality common to artists alternately described as "awareness" or "sensitivity"; he simply seemed to see and feel more of the world than other children.[435] However, while this heightened awareness renders many artists intensely sensitive to criticism, Dylan seems not to have suffered much from this usual downside to the artistic temperament, or perhaps a compensatory toughness was ingrained into him from a young age by the harsh climate of the coal-mining town of Hibbing, as well as by the recurrent admonitions of his grandmother (whom Dylan calls "my one and only confidante") to "just let it go—let it wear itself out."[436]

Robert Shelton speculates about Dylan's childhood home: "The living room was so clean and orderly. Everything was in its place. Maybe that is what they expected of him, to be just another home appliance, to turn on and off."[437] Although by all accounts Dylan's parents were attentive and generous,[438] it seems that they were also steadfastly committed to the rationalized ethos characteristic of 1950's Midwestern modernity, for as Dylan described his childhood to Nat Hentoff in 1964: "I wasn't free. . . . I was constantly on guard. Somehow, way back then, I already knew that parents do what they do because they're up tight. They're concerned with their kids in relation to themselves. . . . They want you to be what *they* want you to be."[439] This statement suggests the imposition of restrictive conceptual mores on many in Dylan's generation by their parents' generation, which perhaps took the privileging of rationality more for granted than the generation born around the time of the Second World War when the world was at its most flagrantly irrational, the residual Enlightenment and Victorian presuppositions about the proper conduct of life coming starkly into contrast with the bestial horrors of war. Nevertheless, for no materially discernible reason given his conventionally comfortable upbringing, and as opposed to most other humans, close friend Victor Maymudes asserts that Dylan "knew he was on fire when he was eleven."[440] Or, as folksinger Pete Seeger expressed it in 1964: "Dylan may well become the country's most creative troubadour—if he doesn't explode."[441] Dylan clearly possessed an extreme intensity beyond the explanatory scope of his family background.

"Strange Countries"

As with many young men of his generation, Dylan identified deeply with Elvis Presley, though he often seems more hesitant to discuss Presley than his other influences, perhaps because the primary originator of rock and roll was so pervasive, and Dylan refused to be constrained by the usual obeisances. As he explained in 1978: "Elvis was there. He was there when there wasn't anybody there. He was Elvis and everybody knows about what Elvis did. He did it to me just like he did it to everybody else."[442] Dylan acknowledges the profound impact that Presley had on him and his generation in his initiation of rock and roll as so obvious and central to the genre and to American culture that he hardly needs to be mentioned.

Another of Dylan's primary influences, whom he heard on both radio and record from an early date, was Hank Williams.[443] As Dylan writes in *Chronicles*: "The sound of his voice went through me like an electric rod. . . . Even at a young age, I identified fully with him. I didn't have to experience anything that Hank did to know what he was singing about." Through recordings or transmissions of Williams' voice, the older singer's identity seemed to resonate with Dylan's, causing the young boy to feel intuitively drawn into identification with the man generally considered the father of country music. Dylan sensed something of Williams in himself, imaginatively becoming him just as Lennon had with Presley (though Dylan also seems to have identified with Presley in a similar way and Lennon was a Williams fan), to the point that Williams' death in 1953, when Dylan was only eleven years old, affected him profoundly: "Hearing about Hank's death caught me squarely on the shoulder. The silence of outer space never seemed so loud." Even at that young age, Dylan was apparently discerning enough to know exceptional music when he heard it, the metaphor of "outer space" as a psychologically transcendent realm a recurrent image in his narrative. Dylan recognizes that transformative artists like Williams were somehow able to go "beyond the circle," a phrase that seems to echo, whether consciously or unconsciously, Bergson's "circle of the given," to produce something radically novel, something that had never existed before though all of the material elements were extant.

Furthermore, Dylan acknowledges his debt, and by proxy, the debt of many songwriters, to Williams. The country singer's songs are indeed some of the most sublimely constructed compositions in popular music, from "Your Cheatin' Heart" and "I'm So Lonesome I Could Cry" to "Lost Highway" and "Ramblin' Man," so that they are often described as seeming received rather than composed, a quality that is often ascribed to Dylan's songs as well. As Dylan writes in *Chronicles*: "A song is like a dream, and you try to make it come true. They're like strange countries that you have to enter." By spending many hours listening to Williams' records, immersed in the affective tone of these "strange countries," Dylan seems to have "internalized" the mode that Williams enacted. Imaginatively inhabiting the internal, subjective terrain that Williams had explored and expressed through his songs apparently allowed Dylan to access that space within himself, the time spent there allowing the particular mental and physical qualities of that "high lonesome" psychosomatic experiential domain subtly to affect the development of the young boy's bodily economy, incorporating the felt identity embodied in Williams' songs into the young Bobby Zimmerman. As Dylan describes it, he seems literally to have absorbed something of Williams' affectivity into himself through the medium of recorded song, perhaps through the emulation of William's posture, breathing, tone of voice, facial expression, and so forth. Indeed, this seems to be just one instance, albeit an especially significant and intense one, of the kind of process that occurs whenever one listens to music. In a similar operation to the truism that "you are what you eat," it also seems to be the case that "you are what you listen to," though Dylan apparently possessed an especially profound receptivity to musical transmissions of affect.[444]

"A New Form of Human Existence"

However, like many in his generation, "when rock and roll emerged," David Hajdu writes, Dylan "became obsessed with the music,"[445] becoming a fan of Presley, Holly, Little Richard, and the rest.[446] Although, as Hajdu notes, Presley "had helped introduce young people to aspects of the folk sensibility,"[447] according to Dylan, by the early sixties after Presley had returned from the army, "nobody listened to him." It had only been three years since Presley had been drafted into the army in 1958, but to a twenty year old Dylan whose high school years had almost exactly coincided with the peak of original rock and roll, 1955-58, this relatively brief period must have felt like an eternity of mediocrity. In fact, it seems likely that this sense that popular music was lacking excitement and vitality, the quality of taking "songs to other planets," is probably a large part of what impelled Dylan ultimately to produce a new revolution in rock and roll, partially through a synthesis of that music with the more sophisticated and experimental mode of the beat poets, "the *On the Road, Howl* and *Gasoline* street ideologies" that Dylan found lacking in popular culture at the beginning of the sixties.[448]

The moment when Presley was inducted into the military marked the end of the era of original rock and roll. The waking beast was temporarily tamed, or at least mollified in the late fifties and early sixties. However, the impulse toward radical transformation through the embrace of repressed epistemologies reemerged with renewed vigor in the form of what would come to be called the counterculture in the sixties. As Dylan acknowledges in Scorsese's documentary, *No Direction Home*, in Hibbing in the fifties: "The music that was popular *was* 'How Much Is That Doggie in the Window?'"[449] though original rock and roll was still fresh in the young man's memory. As Dylan writes: "It wasn't that I was anti-popular culture or anything and I had no ambitions to stir things up. I just thought of mainstream culture as lame and a big trick."[450] This was the brief moment of pause between the initial revolution of the fifties and the even more transformative decade of the sixties, an interregnum when the countercultural impulse was pushed back underground into the more sophisticated and intellectual manifestations of beat poetry, folk music, and bebop (as opposed to the British jazz that the Beatles abhorred), which all carried a radical impulse similar to that of rock and roll, but which simply did not possess the same visceral drive and intensity coupled with wide accessibility as the musical genre initiated by Presley and his contemporaries.[451]

Although the folk and beat movements were certainly allies in their rejection of the predominant culture, many folkies and beats did not quite see eye to eye at this historical moment.[452] As Dylan writes: "The Beats tolerated folk music, but they really didn't like it. They listened exclusively to modern jazz, bebop."[453] However, though these three countercultural streams—folk music, beat poetry, and bebop—were relatively distinct and not yet integrated, Dylan seems to have sensed that they were bound to come together down the road, the separate streams flowing into the countercultural flood that occurred in the mid-to-late sixties, "a new form of human existence"[454] which Dylan did much to mediate, and which transformed the main streams of culture even as it was absorbed by those predominant discursive networks.

Despite the beats' "exclusive" allegiance to jazz, to which he could not entirely relate (and which he may be exaggerating somewhat for rhetorical effect), Dylan is probably the single figure who did more than anyone else to bring the two countercultural streams of beat poetry and folk music together. Although he still cared deeply about the main streams of American culture in which he was embedded, Dylan's allegiance was explicitly with the poets and the folksingers and implicitly with rock and roll, though this abiding commitment would only come to light a few years later. In this moment between revolutions, rock and roll had been temporarily coopted by the predominant commercial culture: Pat Boone had bigger hits than Little Richard with bland, sanitized versions of his songs and, most significantly, Presley had been coerced into cutting his hair and submitting to the military-industrial power structure, which would be the primary locus of dissent for the sixties protest movements, the rationalized "machine" that Mario Savio would fiercely exhort the students of Berkeley to throw their bodies upon half a decade later in 1964.

"Bumping and Grinding With a Bull on Top"

Dylan had been influenced profoundly by the beat poets as a teenager. As he explained in a 1985 interview: "I came out of the wilderness and just naturally fell in with the Beat scene, the bohemian, Be Bop crowd, it was all pretty much connected. . . . It was Jack Kerouac, Ginsberg, Corso, Ferlinghetti . . . I got in at the tail end of that and it was magic . . . it had just as big an impact on me as Elvis Presley."[455] However, Dylan's relationship with the beats was not one of simple admiration and influence for, as he writes in *Chronicles*, when he first arrived in Minneapolis, just having graduated from High School: "I suppose what I was looking for was what I read about in *On the Road* . . . for what Allen Ginsberg had called the 'hydrogen jukebox world,'" which Dylan describes as "a wasted world and totally mechanized." As Dylan recognized: "Creatively you couldn't do much with it."[456] For Dylan, the beats were primarily reacting to the materiality and commerciality of postwar America, protesting the dominance of industrial materialism that Dylan felt to be a waste of the world's creative potential, but which he intuitively saw a way out of that many of the beats perhaps did not.

Although they were extremely influential in his early development, Dylan felt that the beats, particularly Jack Kerouac, were ultimately reactionary, defining themselves by what they were against rather than what they were for. However, some of the beats certainly evolved with the emergence of the sixties counterculture, Allen Ginsberg being the most obvious example, Dylan saying that "I know only two saintly people. I know just two holy people. Allen Ginsberg is one."[457] Like many great artists, Ginsberg seems ultimately to have defined the beat movement by transcending it, much as Dylan did with various musical genres, the two domains intertwined largely through the relationship of these two men. Ultimately, whatever one thinks of Dylan's critique of the beats, it is clear that Dylan's accomplishments would not have been possible without these poets as direct precursors, whose project he extended even as he reacted against certain aspects of it.[458]

Nevertheless, in saying in relation to the beats that "even a lost cause . . . would be better than no cause," an implicit reference to James Dean's *Rebel Without a Cause*, Dylan seems to be articulating an inflection of what has often been characterized as an overcoming of the postmodern "incredulity toward metanarratives" (to employ Jean-Francois Lyotard's phrase) in favor of a more constructive kind of multivalence, a mode of engagement arguably closer to what poet Charles Olson intended in his coinage of the term "post-modern."[459] Dylan would soon write some of the most powerfully scathing indictments ever recorded of the "bourgeois conventionality" against which the beats railed. In particular, "Ballad of a Thin Man," whose "Mr. Jones" seems to be the epitome of the "man in the gray flannel suit"[460] that Dylan sees the beats reacting against, embodies such a critique of the normalized rationality of predominant postwar cultural streams.

However, the subtle but essential difference between Dylan's vision and that of the beats as he presents them is that Dylan seems to have meant this song, and others, not as a simple reaction to the predominant mode, but as a provocation to the adherents of that mode to find out exactly what is "happening" that Mr. Jones does not understand. Indeed, that Dylan, in the same mid-sixties period admonishes his audience to ask themselves "how does it feel?"[461] suggests that Dylan had discovered the affective mode as an effective countermeasure to the exclusive privileging of rationality. Instead of merely rejecting "bourgeois conventionality," which is how he perceives the primary activity of the beats, he seems to be telling the Mr. Joneses of the world to understand what is happening with the emerging counterculture by participating in that counterculture, which generally seems to have entailed paying conscious attention to one's bodily feelings through various practices, both musical and otherwise.[462]

Whereas Dylan perceived the beats as simply decrying the old order, he felt himself ready to move on to a new way of approaching the world. Although the beats' impulse was in this direction, Dylan saw their creativity as circumscribed by the mode they were reacting against, whereas Dylan did not feel much need to define himself in relation to the predominant mode after a brief adolescent rebellion, though the beats clearly created the precondition upon which Dylan could viably surpass them. Many years later in Scorsese's documentary, Ginsberg, choking up with emotion as he describes hearing Dylan for the first time, specifically "A Hard Rain's A-Gonna Fall," says that he wept "'cause it seemed that the torch had been passed to another generation from earlier bohemian or beat illumination and self-empowerment."[463] As early as 1961 when Dylan first arrived in New York, the young singer sensed that the countercultural flame of novelty was about to be handed from the beats to a new movement. Thus, though Dylan had been profoundly influenced by the beats, he began to see that movement's limitations at an early age as he immersed himself in folk music.

In 1961, Dylan began to delve deeply into the other forms of poetry that seemed to him more vital than the beats. Having carried Jack Kerouac's "'hungry for kicks' hipster vision" in *On the Road* "like a bible," "within the first few months" of Dylan's arrival in New York City, he seems completely to have integrated the aesthetic that Kerouac exemplified, the "breathless, dynamic bop poetry phrases." However, he now felt that, although the form was profound, the content was to a large extent "purposeless," an attitude derived to some extent from an existentialism that he felt "inspired idiocy,"[464] perhaps because it would often define reality as an essentially random and meaningless collection of atoms in which we must bravely make our own meaning despite all evidence to the contrary (though the beats often critiqued existentialism in a similar operation to Dylan's subsequent critique of the beats).

Dylan seems to have felt a kinship with this stream of thought up to a point, having read "everything from Sartre to the beats"[465] during his year in Minneapolis after high school, but it is the focus on the intrinsic meaninglessness of existence, or more precisely the mere rejection of the kinds of meaning posited in modernity that seems to have turned Dylan in other directions. Yes, he seems to imply through his creative activity and his often oblique utterances, recognize that meaning is constructed, but rather than believing that this recognition connotes that there is no intrinsic meaning or purpose in the world, perhaps it makes more sense to believe that the human mind participates in the creation of the world's meaning. From this perspective, because the human mind is evolved from and embedded in the cosmos, sentience can be seen as the cosmos coming to know itself, or as Richard Tarnas expresses it: "The human mind is ultimately the organ of the world's own process of self-revelation."[466] In this view, none of the material facts have changed, but this subtle shift in affective tone "yet makes all the difference" for the possibility of genuine meaning in human experience.

It seems clear that Dylan was able to create his many titanic imaginative works because he understood what Kerouac and Sartre were saying about the constructed quality of reality, but whereas they seem to have taken this recognition as a negative indication that we are merely putting window-dressings on a vast and fathomless void, Dylan, in shifting his allegiance away from Kerouac in particular, seems to have realized that the fact that experience is constructed can mean that we literally co-create the world by the products of our imaginative labors. Furthermore, Dylan's description of Kerouac's character Dean Moriarty going "through life bumping and grinding with a bull on top of him"[467] is strongly reminiscent of the Wall Street bull statue in New York, which is as good a symbol as any for one of the primary aspects of modernity, the "spirit of capitalism" and the single-minded, "bull-headed" drive toward unlimited progress and growth at any cost, leveling all in its path. Kerouac, as described by Dylan, was ultimately reactionary because he remained in the shadow of modernity, rebelling against its oppressive consistency. On the other hand, Dylan did not seem to feel particularly oppressed by anything, except perhaps by the weight of his own visions.

"The Greatest Holiest Godliest One"

The most prominent influence on Dylan's music and persona during his initial rise to fame, more than Presley or Williams or the beats, was Woody Guthrie for, as Dylan asserts in *Chronicles*: "the songs of Woody Guthrie ruled my universe,"[468] once even extolling Guthrie as "the greatest holiest godliest one in the world,"[469] and elsewhere proclaiming Guthrie a "genius genius genius genius."[470] Describing his first major encounter with Guthrie's music, most likely in 1960 during a year spent in Minneapolis, Dylan recalls listening to "about twelve double sided 78 records" by Guthrie. Although Dylan had appreciated Guthrie's music before, he "hadn't actually heard" the singer from Oklahoma in "this earth shattering kind of way." Now, the experience of hearing "all these songs together, one after another" made his "head spin" with the euphoria of discovery.

Dylan goes to great lengths to describe precisely what it was about Guthrie that struck such a resonant chord in him and, much like the other character sketches and artistic analyses that Dylan provides, this description of perhaps his greatest influence seems to reveal much about how Dylan sees himself. Like Dylan, "Guthrie had such a grip on things," a phrase that seems to indicate an acute awareness or sense of perspective evident in his compositions and performances. Both singers were able to see and express the vast complexity of experience in deeply insightful ways without reducing that complexity. Similarly, the three adjectives that Dylan uses to describe Guthrie: "poetic and tough and rhythmic," evident in songs like "Hard Travelin'," "Cumberland Gap," and "I Ain't Got No Home," also accurately describe the combination of factors that made Dylan exceptional: a verbal or intellectual fluency colored with the romantic quality usually implied by the word "poetic," integrated with the physical and intuitive "rhythmic" musicality that made the singing affectively effective, and the "toughness" that indicates a determination, drive, and potent intensity impelling and supporting the integration of the intellectual and somatic modes suggested by the other two qualities.

Guthrie's "mannerisms" and "diction," both rather subtle qualities in singing, had a titanic physical effect on the young Dylan: they "just about knocked me down," "picked me up and flung me across the room," felt "like a punch," and "tore everything . . . to pieces." This violent force of feeling that Guthrie had developed into "a perfected style of singing that it seemed like no one else had ever thought about," coupled with "the infinite sweep of humanity" in his lyrics, proved to be perhaps the single most profound influence on Dylan's own style.[471] Like Guthrie, there is a vigor in Dylan's singing, coupled with exceptional subtlety and creativity in phrasing that produces a visceral reaction in the listener.[472] Indeed, this is why it is often said of Dylan that one either loves him or hates him; his voice is confrontational, making one feel the affect that it is conveying in a particularly intense way ("Intensity, that's what he's got,"[473] proclaimed producer Tom Wilson in 1964). And this intensity, combined with the brilliance and elevated perspective of both Guthrie's and Dylan's words, produces a sense that both singers are communicating something urgent and profound for, as Robert Ray has observed: "The *sound* of Bob Dylan's voice . . . changed more people's ideas about the world than his political message did."[474] Indeed, one of the ways that Dylan integrated intellect and intuition is simply by singing complex, evocative words with multiple layers of meaning in an earthy, forceful style. Although, ultimately, Dylan's singing was deeply original, it was necessary for him to emulate Guthrie's singing in order eventually to surpass his mentor.

However, in 1960, Dylan had not yet become the epochally transformative artist that he soon would, and it is precisely through his compulsive aping of Guthrie that Dylan found a platform from which he could develop his own performative identity.[475] Dylan, in a "trance," felt that in discovering Guthrie he had somehow discovered himself, "feeling more like myself than ever before." Dylan sensed that Guthrie was expressing qualities of experience that Dylan had perceived, but did not have the specific tropes to articulate. In Guthrie, he saw "some essence of self-command,"[476] a phrase that seems to indicate, in this context, the ability to master one's own physical and mental processes by means of heightened awareness to focus one's energy in order to produce ecstasy in oneself and in one's audience, though certainly of a more introspective kind than Presley induced with his swiveling hips and baritone "uh-uh-huhs," or than the Beatles produced with their head-shaking "oohs" and searing harmonies.

Dylan found in folk music, with Guthrie its prime exemplar, a novel way of approaching the world that had precedent in an archaic mode generally repressed in modernity, as many of the rural places that Guthrie traveled through, the sources of folk music, often still saw the world through predominantly premodern modes of consciousness. As Dylan tells Scorsese: "I thought folk music was delivering me something, you know, which is the way I always felt about life, you know, and institutions, and ideology, and it was just, you know, uncovering it all."[477] Dylan understood that folk music, in both its lyrics and its somatic performativity, expressed a way of relating to the world that he had always sensed intuitively but had not possessed the verbal or musical tools to articulate, something intrinsic to human experience that had been rendered difficult even to perceive by systematic cultural rationalization. In fact, it even seems plausible that the phrase "you know," recurrently employed by Dylan, is not merely an inarticulate verbal tic, but an implicit, perhaps unconscious recognition of his interlocutor's intuitive knowledge. Appropriately, for reasons that appear to defy rational explanation, Dylan was one of the few artists able to inhabit primarily the intuitive mode, but also able still to find huge and consistent success in a largely rationalized culture, thereby mediating the intuitive mode's ingression into historical process.

"A Hard Guy to Get Past"

Believing that he was Guthrie's successor before there was any material evidence to support this supposition, Dylan found it necessary to emulate not only Guthrie's music and attitude, but all of the elements that composed his mentor's identity, even down to sometimes claiming to be from Oklahoma. Guthrie offered an alternative to the primary mode of rebellion exemplified for Dylan in that moment by the late James Dean, Elvis Presley, and the beats. However, as Dylan admits, although his discovery of Guthrie allowed him to perceive the world with new eyes, his ascension to the role of Guthrie's successor was not all confluent discovery:

> Singing Woody's songs, I could keep everything else at
> a safe distance. This fantasy was short-lived, however.
> Thinking that I was wearing the sharpest looking
> uniform and the shiniest boots around, all of a sudden I
> felt a jolt and was stopped short in my tracks. It felt like

someone had taken a chunk out of me. Jon Pankake, a folk music purist enthusiast and sometime literary teacher and film wiseman, who'd been watching me for a while on the scene, made it his business to tell me that what I was doing hadn't escaped him. "What do you think you're doing? You're singing nothing but Guthrie songs," he said, jabbing his finger into my chest like he was talking to a proper fool. Pankake was authoritative and a hard guy to get past. It was known around that Pankake had a vast collection of the real folk records and could go on and on about them. He was part of the folk police, if not the chief commissioner, wasn't impressed with any of the new talent. To him nobody possessed any great mastery—no one could succeed in laying a hand on any of the traditional stuff with any authority. Of course he was right, but Pankake didn't play or sing. It's not like he put himself in any position to be judged.[478]

As with George Martin's devastating critique of the Beatles, Pankake was an older, well-educated, and "authoritative" guardian of culture, a sort of gatekeeper, though of a more subtle kind than Martin, an English professor who played a vital role in Dylan's development by bursting his bubble of "fantasy" that he could actually become Guthrie. Indeed, the image of Pankake "jabbing his finger" into Dylan's chest is a physical enactment of the critical mode puncturing the purely intuitive mode which, without the mediating influence of intellectual analysis, appears prone to inflated delusion and self-deception of the kind Dylan initially experienced in relation to Guthrie, as belief without some moderate degree of doubt seems to preclude self-awareness.

Like the Beatles' critique by Martin, though earlier in his trajectory, this was one of Dylan's main points of initiation into the intellectual mode that he had temporarily turned away from in favor of the intuitive modes characteristic of folk music and rock and roll. As with the "police" or other authority figures, Pankake played a conservative but necessary role in Dylan's developmental process, another instance of the Hegelian negative. Though youth often justifiably rails against such cultural authorities, these authorities exist to do exactly what Pankake did for Dylan. That is, if Pankake or someone like him had not rained on Dylan's parade, so to speak, it is unlikely that Dylan would have ever outgrown his emulation of Guthrie, and our culture would be a much poorer place with an obscure Woody Guthrie clone named Bob Dylan instead of an artist of world-historic significance going by that name. Of course, just because the role that Pankake played was a necessary one does not mean that he does not also deserve some criticism as a critic who "didn't play or sing," who did not even endeavor to take artistic risks and, thus, "did not put himself in any position to be judged." As the saying goes: no risk, no glory. Pankake risked little and achieved a concomitant amount of notoriety, mostly as an anecdote in Dylan's memoir. Conversely, Dylan risked a great deal, which allowed him to act as one of the primary performers of the compensatory ingression of affect into a rationalized culture.[479]

However, it should also be emphasized that not only did Pankake's critique puncture Dylan's fantasy, but it actually liberated Dylan from a kind of repetition characteristic of a relatively naïve relation to the rational mode. Dylan had been endeavoring to produce novelty by exactly reproducing Guthrie's musical persona, though in retrospect it is obvious that lightning never strikes in the same place twice; that is, novelty can only take a particular form once, as when the new form of process has passed from potentiality into actuality, it is no longer novel, and novelty must subsequently find a different avenue for its expression. Indeed, this is a paradox at the heart of novelty's ingression into process, as well as at the core of Dylan, who is a primary avatar of that ingression. As Bergson writes in *Creative Evolution*: "*There are things that intelligence alone is able to seek, but which, by itself, it will never find. These things instinct alone could find; but it will never seek them.*"[480] Thus Dylan, in his emulation of Guthrie, a relatively unconscious relation to immediate experience, was temporarily content to dwell in the preexistent modes until Pankake's critique provided the spur to self-awareness that impelled Dylan to surpass the already existent style.

In this paradoxical operation, Dylan, without the benefit of training in critical rationality, was temporarily thwarted in his search for novelty by falling prey to the simplest kind of rational fallacy, the attempt to create something new by simply repeating what has come before. Pankake's critique apparently incited a more conscious rationality in Dylan that, in turn, further liberated Dylan into the intuitive realms that he explicitly favored. Indeed, a progression can be seen through the three artists examined in this study, for while Presley primarily enacted an initial rejection of rationality, and the Beatles enacted a relatively simple rejection and dialectical reintegration of rationality, Dylan, true to form, enacted a subtly complex imbrication of this polarity through various compromise formations such as this encounter with Pankake's intuition-liberating critique.

However, although Pankake allowed Dylan to transcend habit through the performance of analysis acting upon naive intuition, Pankake himself was not a primary agent of novelty because, at least in this context, he only embodied the critical end of the polarity, while Dylan increasingly embodied a synthesis of that polarity. As Whitehead observes, pure intellect requires "recurrence to the utmost depths of intuition for the refreshment of imagination,"[481] but intuition also requires critical analysis in order not to become trapped in blind organismic compulsion. The two modes are vitally complementary, as the eras in history when one mode has been predominantly suppressed in favor of the other seem equally to be repressive of novelty, whether through the barbaric violence of unmitigated instinct, or through the neurotic nihilism and static conformity characteristic of intellect run amok, which for most of this text's potential readers is somewhat closer to home. Indeed, some of the worst atrocities have been perpetrated by "civilized" cultures, justified by overly rationalized premises. Thus, it is neither the rational nor the affective modes that appear to be the culprit for the many manifestations of cultural dis-ease, but an imbalance of this fundamental polarity in human experience.

Much as Dylan paradoxically sought novel ways of relating to experience in the premodern past, he was liberated into a more expansive mode, having been unconstrained in the habitual emulation of his mentor, by the critical mode more often associated with "negative judgment" (by Whitehead) and repetition compulsion (by Bergson) in late modern culture. In some contexts, particularly in more conservative or religiously fundamentalist communities, or in underprivileged communities without access to quality education, critical thought is the mode that should perhaps be emphasized as a counterbalance to the tyranny of feeling, usually justified by simplistic conceptual structures.

However, the most influential streams of Western culture since the seventeenth century, taking many forms, appear to have engaged in an opposite sort of privileging operation, for as Whitehead writes: "The mentality of an epoch springs from the view of the world which is, in fact, dominant in the educated sections of the communities in question."[482] In this way, the cultural spectrum traces something like a waveform surging through historical process: even though there are many countervailing vectors mediated by fundamentally different approaches to experience in numerous compromise formations, it appears that at the moment of John Pankake's critique of Bob Dylan in 1960, the young singer was a primary embodiment of the vanguard of postmodernity in its more constructive guise. Dylan apparently brought to popular consciousness those epistemologies that had been reintroduced into discourse in the more purely academic domain earlier in the twentieth century by theorists like Bergson and Whitehead and in the more purely visceral domain by the original rock and rollers.

Dylan did not undergo an instantaneous transformation in Pankake's hands, however. Rather, it was a series of encounters between the two men that mediated this period of Dylan's self-becoming. "You're trying hard, but you'll never turn into Woody Guthrie," Pankake scolded Dylan. "Jack Elliott's already been where you are and gone." Dylan had never heard of Ramblin' Jack Elliot, so Pankake played some of his records for the young singer, to whom Elliot sounded "like Woody Guthrie, only a leaner, meaner one, not singing the same Guthrie songs, though." Dylan quickly acquiesced to Pankake's critique, for as Dylan admits: "Elliott was far beyond me." The external acknowledgement that Dylan was trying to become Guthrie cast this attempt in a new light. Whereas before, Dylan's emulation of his idol had been a pure and pleasurable activity, now it was shown to be a limitation, a step in a process of becoming himself through self-overcoming.

Indeed, Dylan's statement that "it was no fun being around Pankake" attests to the older man's loyalty to the conventional, negating mode of consciousness, as rationality alone can only analyze phenomena into their constituent elements, a myopically reductive partiality intrinsically blind to the possibility of novelty's emergence. Dylan saw the necessity of integrating this critical mode with the novel archaic mode he was exploring, but he recognized that the critical mode alone tended to be repressive of novelty, a quality often accompanied by the affect of "fun." As Dylan came implicitly to understand, while pure intellect finds its culmination in "negative judgment," pure affective novelty unmediated by intellect is ultimately hedonistic and mute. Thus, though he did not enjoy Pankake's critique, Dylan was self-aware enough to realize that he must undergo it to become what he felt he was on the path to becoming.

Nevertheless, before he could create something genuinely new, it seems to have been necessary for Dylan to "become" Elliott as well, integrating the further permutation of the role that Guthrie had previously played. However, following Pankake's critique, Dylan was momentarily at a loss in the trajectory of his self-becoming. Discovering Guthrie, he had found an already mapped corner of the world that his affectivity resonated with profoundly, but Dylan felt that it was not his fate to remain a Guthrie imitator. In a sense, Pankake killed the identity of "Woody Guthrie" that Dylan had briefly inhabited so that, for a brief period, perhaps just that one evening, Dylan "felt like the dead men walking through catacombs," a ghost of his former identity who had not yet found a new role to inhabit. At first he tried to deny Elliott's influence, "to block it out of my mind," indicating an initial resistance to the critical mode embodied in this instance by Pankake.

However, Dylan does not seem generally prone to prolonged self-deception, and the death of Dylan's Guthrie persona quickly issued into his rebirth as none other than Ramblin' Jack Elliott: "A few weeks later, Pankake heard me playing again and was quick to point out that I didn't fool him, that I used to be imitating Guthrie and now I was imitating Elliott and did I think in some way that I was equivalent to him? Pankake said that maybe I should go back to playing rock and roll, that he knew I used to do that." Again, Pankake was the critical agent that punctured Dylan's emulation of the man who had emulated Guthrie and then possibly even surpassed him in Dylan's estimation. Perhaps Pankake could somehow sense from Dylan's style and attitude that he used to play rock and roll, but his suggestion to Dylan that he return to that genre proved prophetic, for this is exactly what Dylan would do a few years later once he had established himself as the primary heir to Guthrie, effectively supplanting Elliott in that role.

But as Dylan claims, he was not trying to be deceptive, not "trying to fool anybody." Rather, he understood in retrospect that in order to move toward his felt destination, this period of emulation was a necessary stage that he must pass through, "doing what I could with what I had where I was."[483] Dylan seems to have been absorbing preexisting elements within himself, devouring Guthrie and Elliott so that he could employ their tropes to produce a novel synthesis of their styles. As all good artists know, one must pass through an apprenticeship in which one emulates and integrates one's precursors before one can surpass them. However, at the stage in his development initiated by Pankake's critique, it was necessary for Dylan to understand that although becoming Guthrie and Elliott felt like he was becoming more himself, these identities were not resting places, but stepping stones on a path that ultimately produced the artist who would play such a large role in the transformation of his culture.[484]

This section of Dylan's narrative vividly illustrates his exceptional persistence, his intrinsic will toward transformation, so that the egoic death produced by Pankake's criticism did not halt Dylan's trajectory as it might have done for many other aspiring singers, but impelled him to new heights, much as the Beatles' Decca audition impelled them radically to shift their approach. Although Dylan did not "get caught up in"[485] what people thought of him because he seems usually to have taken an experimental approach to his own identity, he does not appear to have been closed off to others until he was forced by extraordinary fame to keep most people at bay.[486] As photographer Barry Feinstein has observed: "Bob really only liked to have friends like us around him. He had an image to maintain, and he protected it."[487] Although Dylan kept to his close friends, and he was guarded even with them, he seems to have been extremely open to new ideas, particularly anything that he could use to move forward. As he tells Scorsese: "I have a habit I picked up someplace along the way: whatever works for me, not to give that away so easily."[488] Dylan incorporated many elements into his identity, drawing from numerous musical, poetic, intellectual, and performative sources, but always fiercely protecting his freedom to do and to be exactly who and what he felt like doing and being, and to form habitual ways of thinking and acting that may have seemed strange or perverse to others, but that allowed him to become himself relatively unencumbered by societal constraints.

Dylan would express this very sentiment in "Maggie's Farm" a few years later on *Bringing It All Back Home* in a line that encapsulates Dylan's search for authentic selfhood based on his affective sense ("just like I am") rather than on preconditioned, rationalized roles and mores ("just like them"). Similarly, Dylan told journalist Nat Hentoff at the session for *Another Side of Bob Dylan* in 1964: "I want to write from inside me. . . . The way I like to write is for it to come out the way I walk or talk. . . . Not that I even walk or talk yet like I'd like to. I don't carry myself the way Woody, Big Joe Williams, and Lightnin' Hopkins have carried themselves. I hope to someday, but they're older."[489] Dylan's primary drive seems always to have been this search for mature authenticity, for both his music and his physical and verbal personas to be expressions of his intrinsic and ever-changing self.[490]

As Dylan told Hentoff: "What's wrong is how few people are free. Most people walking around are tied down to something that doesn't let them really *speak*. . . . All I can do is be me."[491] In his process of becoming through the liberation of authentic selfhood, and thereby the intensification and complexification of immediate experience, Dylan felt impelled to "keep straight ahead," engaging with and dispatching the "shadowy forms that had to be dealt with in one way or another," like an "honorable knight" who must confront many trials in his pursuit of the grail.[492] For Dylan, Jack Elliott, the "King of the Folksingers," was just such a "shadowy form," the expression of a mode that Dylan was compelled to become and then to overcome. However, it would still be some time after his shedding of the Ramblin' Jack persona that Dylan would create the more novel persona which would carry him toward his initial fame.[493]

"The Age of Enlightenment"

At that moment in the early sixties in Minneapolis, Dylan apparently felt that a new order was in the process of arising out of the old, and he sensed that, by passing through the successive trials of identity which he describes, he could participate significantly in the coming revolutionary upheaval through the medium of folk music, which "transcended the immediate culture," the "songs embedded in my mind like a religion." As Dylan recognizes, the old guard, the culture of the 1950s, was constituted in the privileging of that mode of thought which intrinsically seeks to repress the eruption of novelty, "like a judge in his last days on the bench,"[494] and Dylan's devotion to folk songs was explicitly geared toward the overcoming of those present constraints. It is these very songs that became the vehicle through which Dylan embodied and catalyzed the cultural revolution that was about to take place perhaps as much as any other individual.

And it is clear that Dylan saw this cultural revolution as the pivot-point between two eras: "If you were born around this time [World War II] or were living and alive, you could feel the old world go and the new one beginning. It was like putting back the clock to when B.C. became A.D." It seems that Dylan sees the years stretching from the end of World War II to the beginning of the sixties as a moment of pause and relative stasis between two distinct historical periods.[495] Furthermore, Dylan seems to be speaking almost literally when he says that he "was still in" the "Age of Enlightenment" at the moment when he was finding his artistic voice in the early sixties, for he "could still remember and feel the light of something about it" in his reading of Voltaire, Rousseau, Locke, Montesquieu, and Luther. The mode of consciousness that the young man inhabited appears to have exhibited all the characteristic optimism, revolutionary fervor, and naiveté visible in the dominant philosophy of the eighteenth century.

This era seems to have constituted something like the adolescence of Western culture, a stage of consciousness that Dylan felt himself to be enacting in what might be described as a fractal reiteration. Instinctively, Dylan knew like most young people that he must pass through the state of mind so eloquently and completely articulated by the "visionaries" and "revolutionaries" of earlier times before he could catch up with the vanguard of consciousness in his own time and place. Dylan immersed himself in the early, more expansively inspired stage of modernity in which a whole new world was opening up to the minds of the philosophers that he mentions, a stage at which this new mode of thought had not yet become an orthodoxy repressive of subsequent modes, though it did often rail against the limitations and destructive irrationality of affect unmediated by intellect. As with Dylan's immersion in the premodern modes of archaic folk music, he also immersed himself during his first few years in New York in the intellectual efflorescence of the Enlightenment, which had become nearly as archaic as the folk traditions by that moment in the mid-twentieth century.

Dylan writes about an apartment that he stayed in with friends in New York before recording his first album that seems to symbolize for him the high culture descended from the Enlightenment in which he was so interested at that moment, which he places in direct opposition to the mentality of Dylan's place of origin exemplified for him by figures ranging from Marlon Brando, James Dean, and Marilyn Monroe to Joe DiMaggio, Earl Warren, and Fidel Castro. Dylan reels off a countervalent list of names: Tacitus, Pericles, Thucydides, Gogol, Balzac, Maupassant, Hugo, Dickens, Machiavelli, Dante, Ovid. As he writes: "I was looking for the part of my education that I never got" after dropping out of his first year of college, having rarely attended classes. Raised in the Midwest, Dylan had been immersed in a certain stream of American popular culture, in what he describes as a "passion for dumbness."

In all fairness, despite being the locus of some excellent universities and pockets of thriving artistic and intellectual communities, the predominant culture of the Midwest, particularly in its more rural permutations, has tended toward anti-intellectualism in favor of more practical and intuitive knowledge constituted in attention to the rhythms of nature and the body. This focus of attention was apparently born of necessity in the central practice of rural agriculture for that area of the country, which has been described as America's "bread basket." Thus, it seems plausible that Dylan means the term "dumb" not in the common contemporary sense of "stupid," but in its more literal meaning, which is the inability to speak, perhaps recalling the "country dumb" conceit mentioned in an earlier chapter. Thus, Dylan may be suggesting that it is not that the predominant cultural streams of the Midwest breed stupidity, but rather that they often foster an interest in nonverbal, and therefore non-intellectual modes.[496]

Dylan was raised in an area of the country that seems generally to have favored certain limited forms of the repressed epistemologies, though the full range of these modes, particularly the more ecstatic and exploratory ones, were often even more repressed here than on the coasts, perhaps to compensate for the rejection of intellect by paying homage to the rationalized quality of much of America's self-conception in the fifties, conditioned by radio and television, and exemplified in the repetitive architectural conformity of suburban developments like Levittown (though there were many subcultures that complicated this facile image of the unitary, *Leave it to Beaver* postwar plastic utopia). Although deeply grounded in the repressed modes, Dylan possessed a restless intellectual mind, perhaps partially a product of his Jewish cultural heritage, embedded within the very different mode privileged in the coal-mining town of Hibbing.[497]

This dissonance between context and inclination pulled Dylan on a pilgrimage to New York City, which for him was the cultural capital of America, "a dream of the cosmopolitan riches of the mind,"[498] not to mention the Jewish capital, where he found the high cultural works mentioned above to be a revelation.[499] However, Dylan soon recognized that he could never master it all, both "high" and "low" culture, as folk music was often considered, that he had to choose a path: "I wanted to read all these books, but I would have to have been in a rest home or something in order to do that. . . . I read the poetry books, mostly. Byron and Shelley and Longfellow and Poe."[500] Dylan had instinctively chosen the high cultural stream that perhaps most carried the impulse countervalent to the privileging of rationality and materialism: poetry, which had kept the flame of the repressed epistemologies burning through the literally heady years of the Enlightenment and the ascendance of science and rationalist philosophies in the seventeenth, eighteenth, and nineteenth centuries.

Certainly, these centuries did not exhibit a simple trajectory from affect to rationality any more than Dylan's trajectory possessed simple directionality, as this fundamental transformation of culture traversed through many regressions, reactions, side roads, and compromise formations. Indeed, as Weber shows, the larger movement toward rationalism characteristic of modernity took place within the crucible of the Protestant denominations of Christianity, which is the epitome of a compromise formation, mediating the transition from premodern religious forms to the secular rationalism that would become a predominant cultural mode by late modernity. Furthermore, the religious revivals and awakenings of the nineteenth century, as well as literary Romanticism and idealist philosophy, all presaged the further ingression of premodern epistemologies into the collective consciousness of the post-Enlightenment West, perhaps culminating, at least so far, in the massive upheavals of the nineteen sixties.[501]

Thus, Dylan was at the very crest of a wave that had swept through many cultural permutations as a countervalent impulse to the Enlightenment, though this movement was inevitably shaped by its sustained dialectical encounter with rationality. And one of the primary permutations of this impulse was poetry, which is often as interested in the rhythmic sonority of words as in their literal meaning. As Dylan writes: "I read a lot of the pages aloud and liked the sound of the words, the language," which indicates that he was drawn perhaps even more to the poetic verbal cadences than to the ideas that the words expressed. Indeed, that Dylan read these poems aloud speaks volumes about how he would use these texts as models for his expansion of song forms. Dylan's inclinations led him not toward a conventional literary calling (if such a calling can be described as conventional), but rather toward songwriting deeply informed by literature and, most especially, poetry.

"A Web Too Intricate to Understand"

Dylan was drawn to New York not only because of its association with intellect and high culture, but because many of the folksingers whom he admired resided there. Dylan's relocation to Greenwich Village was a pilgrimage to what he perceived as "the capital of the world," a journey to find the people who embodied his yearning for meaningful connection in a culture where such connection seemed increasingly difficult to locate. As discussed above, Guthrie, whom Dylan describes as "the true voice of the American spirit,"[502] had been a particular mentor for Dylan through his records and biography, and Dylan was following a deeply sensed summons to explore the place that Guthrie inhabited, and eventually even to form a close personal relationship with his idol, telling Nat Hentoff in 1964: "seeing Woody Guthrie was one of the main reasons I came East."[503]

Coming from the small town of Hibbing (via the medium-sized city of Minneapolis), Dylan must have felt liberated in New York, as the complexity of that city, "a web too intricate to understand," reflects the complex mystery usually attributed to Dylan himself. Indeed, that Dylan "wasn't going to try"[504] to understand the city seems implicitly to suggest that he was interested in analyzing neither himself nor the place in which he found himself, both literally and figuratively. Rather, he seems to have been more interested in exploring the intricacies of both the city and his own mind, bringing the things he found there to light, sharing his ideas rather than trying to explain where they came from or what their deeper meaning was. As he says in *No Direction Home*: "I can't self-analyze my own work,"[505] for as seen with both Presley and the Beatles, though in rather different inflections, the analytical mode is generally incompatible with inspired artistic creativity, at least in the moment of creation.

As noted above, in reading Dylan's memoir, one is struck by how little he talks about himself, and how much he talks about other people, the cast of characters that he admired and with whom he engaged. In fact, it seems clear from his writing that this is how Dylan thinks: he projects himself into others so that he almost becomes them, empathizing with them so deeply that he elicits the potential part of himself that is like them in the process. Perhaps even more extreme than Lennon's emulation of Presley, Dylan actually seems almost to have become the characters that he inhabited, both real and invented. As Dylan himself recognizes, particularly in these early days in New York, but to varying degrees throughout his career, he "didn't have too much of a concrete identity. . . . 'I'm a rambler—I'm a gambler. I'm a long way from home.' That pretty much summed it up."[506] Dylan was an explorer, both geographically and mentally, as well as a "musical expeditionary:"[507] He went wherever he felt like going, wherever his exceptionally attuned affective sense directed him.

The Beatles were ultimately political, one of the primary exemplars of the impulse toward putting differences aside and working as a group to create great art, integrating disparate modes in an emergent entity (as in Carol Hanisch's phrase, "the personal is political"). In contrast, Dylan had many companions, but he was always ultimately a man alone, a "true loner" experimenting with his identity, trying on radically different modes one after another at a dizzying pace, integrating these modes within himself. He expresses this quality in "Jokerman" from the 1983 album *Infidels*, "shedding" successive identities just as he shed fellow-travelers, driven by what he describes as an internal "persecutor," though this inner drive that he felt so strongly seems perhaps to have manifested in a somewhat less oppressive, more expansive form in his sixties experience. And one can see this radical experimental quality in Dylan's facial expressions: like a great method actor, he is committed completely to whatever part he is playing at that moment. He does not seem to countenance much doubt, giving himself wholly and unselfishly to his successive roles.

Thus, although Dylan was a rambler, he rambled with great ambition. As he writes: "Picasso had fractured the art world and cracked it wide open. He was revolutionary. I wanted to be like that."[508] Indeed, as Leonard Cohen and others have recognized, Picasso is perhaps the closest analogue in twentieth century visual art for the way Dylan's musical career has evolved: prolific and passing through many phases, both artists transformed their medium as well as their culture.[509] And like Picasso, Dylan was a man who let his intuition guide him, forging bravely into each new realm that opened before him on his path. Indeed,

Dylan exudes an exceptional charisma similar to that of Picasso. According to friend Happy Traum: "I've never seen anything like it in my life. From the day he arrived in the city it was like nobody could talk about anything else. It was Bobby this and Bobby that, where was Bobby, what was he going to do next. Have you seen Bobby? No matter what he did or what he didn't do," Traum asserts, "people were just obsessed with the guy. It wasn't just about the music, although that got more interesting as time went on."[510] Like Picasso or the few individuals at the pinnacle of any area of human endeavor, Dylan seems to have possessed a kind of energetic "animal magnetism," drawing multiple genres into his field of influence, leaving anything he touched transformed.

Dylan describes the Café Wha?, where he got his start in the New York scene, as "a subterranean cavern," which recalls the underground quality of the Beatles' major venue in Liverpool. When the master of ceremonies at Café Wha?, folksinger Fred Neil, told Dylan he "could play harmonica with him during his sets," Dylan "was ecstatic,"[511] which obviously indicates that Dylan was happy to have a gig. However, in light of all that is known about Dylan, this phrase also seems to refer to Dylan's relatively rare capacity to induce ecstatic affect in himself and, eventually, in others. Indeed, one gets the sense from listening to, watching, and reading about Dylan that one of his defining characteristics was that he naturally entered and inhabited this state of ecstasy with more ease than almost anyone else, though this somatic state should not be mistaken for mere happiness.

In his 2012 interview, Dylan explains that, as a musician: "The thing you have to do is make people feel their own emotions. A performer, if he's doing what he's supposed to do, doesn't feel any emotion at all. It's a certain kind of alchemy that a performer has."[512] And as Dylan recalls his childhood in a 2004 *60 Minutes* interview: "I really didn't consider myself happy or unhappy. I always knew that there was something out there that I needed to get to. And it wasn't where I was at that particular moment."[513] Thus, Dylan's whole orientation did not revolve around the polarity of happiness and unhappiness, or around emotion at all, but rather around his felt sense of destination, analyzed in greater depth below.

This sense of destination was closely related to his need to be "out of stasis," always moving and transforming. However, though he was initially elated at the novelty of having a steady gig in New York City, after having spent many hours in Café Wha?, Dylan heard "nothing that would change your view of the world," which obliquely demonstrates that the young singer was not looking for mere entertainment, but for something transformative, revelatory, something that went beyond the "madness" that results from "pure materialism," which he perceived as predominant in modernity. And as is so often the case, Dylan began looking for this "world view" changing revelation in the distant past.

When Dylan first arrived in New York, he spent a lot of time at the Folklore Center, which he describes as "the citadel of Americana folk music," "a crossroads junction" of the folk scene. The center reminded him of "an ancient chapel" possessing "an antique grace."[514] Sean Wilentz describes the places in which Dylan spent most of his early days in New York, including the Folklore Center and the Café Wha?, among others, as "Dylan's Yale College and his Harvard,"[515] and as musician John Herald observes: "It was like Dylan was in all the places all the time." The Folklore Center, which Hajdu calls "the nerve center of the Village folk community,"[516] was a treasure trove of archaic knowledge and modes of experience offering all manner of "esoteric" records and songbooks containing "sea shanties, Civil War songs, cowboy songs, songs of lament, church house songs, anti-Jim Crow songs, union songs" as well as "books of folk tales, Wobbly journals, propaganda pamphlets about everything from women's rights to the dangers of boozing," and "dulcimers, five-string banjos, kazoos, pennywhistles, acoustic guitars, mandolins."

Differing from the usual library filled with novels, historical treatises, and scientific tomes, the Folklore Center was a genuine repository of folk knowledge, of the repressed modes that railed against the evils wrought by the unbalanced dominance of rationality—racism, classism, imperialism—and that sought refuge and escape in mysterious liminal places—the sea, the wild west, old churches, children's stories, and bohemian enclaves. Indeed, the "conceptual simplification and ordering" of rationality divorced from affective knowledge can justify the most barbaric behavior, from slavery to genocide, if the appropriate premises are adopted and acted upon. Although Dylan claims to have absorbed a great deal of what passed as knowledge in the main streams of culture, this archaic folk knowledge was the sort of education in which he was primarily immersed, half-consciously searching for a way out of the constraining cage that modernity had inevitably become over the centuries of its development. And this premodern orientation deeply influenced the songs that Dylan would soon write.

As Dylan notes: "The madly complicated modern world was something I took little interest in. It had no relevancy, no weight. I wasn't seduced by it." Dylan appears not to have been particularly interested in the modes of thought that predominated in late modernity, in the concerns of his day. Rather, "what was swinging, topical and up to date for me was stuff like the *Titanic* sinking, the Galveston flood, John Henry driving steel, John Hardy shooting a man on the West Virginia line."[517] Dylan imaginatively inhabited the dim American past, dreaming himself into long gone times because that is where his inclination led him, but ultimately because this immersion in a temporally distant world is what allowed him to see his own time for the transient dream that it was, which in turn made the present appear malleable, susceptible to transformation. What Dylan seems to have been searching for through this polarity of old and new, more than anything else, was an identity, a way to perform himself in such a manner that he could convey the vast complexity of what he felt but had not yet found the form and mode to express, and he did this by delving into the deep past to find a way beyond the tyranny of the present.[518]

"The Inner Substance of the Thing"

In early 1961, Dylan was playing at various smaller folk venues, but he had his sights set on what might be described as the next rung up the ladder: the Gaslight. As with the Beatles, Dylan's immediate ambitions were always pragmatically oriented toward the next step forward rather than the heights he would ultimately attain. And like Dylan, the Gaslight was "cryptic" and "had mystique," which is perhaps why he wanted to play there. He apparently felt drawn to the venue, not only because it was a more prestigious place to play, but because he sensed that its affective tone coincided with his own, a quality that he conveys through poetic, philosophical parables. Instead of stating things directly, Dylan seems compelled to express himself in words that demand interpretation, that intimate multiple levels of meaning, which bears a strong similarity to the way he describes the quality that surrounded the Gaslight: "a closed drawn circle that an unknown couldn't break into."[519] Indeed, this metaphor is more apt for the way Dylan saw his career than the ladder metaphor: while the Beatles imagined their trajectory as rungs to be climbed successively, Dylan envisioned his path as delving into successive layers of mystery and depth, a labyrinth to be penetrated and mastered. And that Dylan saw himself in this way also draws the listener into these mysterious depths.[520]

Soon securing a place at the Gaslight, Dylan "played the folk songs that I possessed and paid attention to what was going on in the moment."[521] He "possessed" the songs that he sang, not only owning them, but imbuing them with vitality and significance, and he seems to have been able to do this because he was immersed in the present, not primarily thinking about past or future, where he had come from or where he was going, but attending fully to each durational instance. As Dylan would declare in "Mr. Tambourine Man," he was learning to put off awareness of "today," a paradoxical operation whereby Dylan more fully inhabited the present by not thinking about the present as an object for past or future contemplation, but as the atemporal locus of his bodily experience. And as Marcus observes: "His sense of time, or timelessness, only rarely failed him,"[522] a timelessness that Wilentz articulates as "his ability to crisscross through time and space. It could be 1927 or 1840 or biblical time in a Bob Dylan song, and it is always right now too."[523]

Spending time at the Gaslight, Dylan was surrounded by "all kinds of characters looking for the inner heat. I felt like I was seeing it all sitting on the crest of a cliff." As with the language used to describe the Beatles' music, Dylan recognizes that the inspiration the performers were seeking was an energetic "inner heat" that could be made to burn more brightly through attention and practice. Dylan, without inflation, recognizes that he seems to have had an exceptional capacity to produce this promethean flame, and he felt like he was witnessing this scene from an elevated perspective, again the product of his exceptionally keen awareness, his intrinsic ability to see to the heart of things. Dylan knew himself to be subtly but profoundly different from his contemporaries, and it is this difference that allowed him eventually to emerge as perhaps the greatest songwriter of all time.

As he describes it, Dylan recognized that he was different from most other performers because he instinctively knew that great performance was not about getting people to like him as a person, an egoic motivation, but "about putting the song across," which was his vehicle for exploring "the universe" from inside, "the inner substance of the thing," a phrase evocative of Bergson's "inner movement of life"[524] as opposed to the external quality of reality accessible to reductive materialism. Dylan was so fully committed to this exploration of subjectivity that his singing and guitar playing were extremely intense, less focused on virtuosity than piercing through veils of illusion to get to the core of the songs, which Dylan describes as "my preceptor and guide into some altered consciousness of reality, some different republic, some liberated republic.'"

However, as discussed above, Dylan was not only deeply rooted in the folk tradition; he had also been immersing himself in the work of poets like Byron and Coleridge. With the gifts of a prodigious memory and an ability to focus intensely for long periods, Dylan was drawn to these poets and their verbal experimentalism. He knew instinctively that he wanted to combine their way of approaching language with the folk songs in which he was also immersed. As he describes it, he literally "trained" his "mind" to think like these poets just as he was training his mind by his constant absorption in song. It seems almost inevitable that Dylan would soon feel the impulse to combine these two lyrical forms, a synthesis that came to him naturally, but that had never really been accomplished before then.[525]

"A Reality of a More Brilliant Dimension"

Whereas the beat poets seemed to Dylan to be obsessed with liberating themselves from the constraints of the prevailing order, Dylan apparently found this liberation to be a necessary, but ultimately incomplete endeavor, a mere rejection of what modernity had become without offering a viable alternative. Rather, Dylan was drawn to old songs, stories, and ways of thinking that preceded his immediate context. He saw the way out of the current stalemate that the beats decried not in a rejection of the past, but in a more complete embrace of tradition, an "archaic revival"[526] of a history so deep and mysterious that it seemed radically novel in the contemporary historical context. For Dylan, having immersed himself in profoundly different ways of seeing the world characteristic of earlier times, generally constellated around mythic "enchantment" (as opposed to the "disenchantment" characteristic of modernity posited by Weber), the folk songs that encapsulated these modes of experience really did seem to evoke a "parallel universe," "a mythical realm," and "a reality of a more brilliant dimension" that "exceeded all human understanding." Indeed, the "principles and values" that folk music portrayed were "archaic" because, in folk's general focus on liminal figures from American frontiers, the "outlaw women, super thugs, demon lovers and gospel truths," and the "Stagger Lees, Pretty Pollys and John Henrys," Dylan found a window into predominantly premodern epistemologies, persisting well into modernity in the forgotten borderlands and on the rural routes of America.

It was a mythologically oriented "invisible world" whose "archetypes" seemed more real to Dylan than the scientific knowledge of distant cities and universities. Whereas for Dylan, the late modern subject was alienated from his (for it was always "he" that was referred to) labor, his culture, and even his body, the archetypal denizens of folk songs were "filled with natural knowing and inner wisdom," precisely evocative of the epistemologies so effectively repressed by the predominance of rationality in postwar America. Indeed, while the individual in late modernity seemed small and peripheral, merely a commodified and insured sack of flesh and bone with a list of marketable skills and a net worth, the figures in folk songs seemed to Dylan to defy this reductive view of human nature by their participation in the "full spectrum" of experience that was "so more true to life than life itself," "magnified" through these other modes of being in the world, "each demanding a degree of respect."

Whereas in the late modern visions of the existentialists and the beats, the world seemed vacated of meaning, the folk tradition was the repository of a mode of thought in which the world was an epic place of profound significance inhabited by larger-than-life characters. Dylan, not just academically interested in this mode, seems to have lived his life in the light of the mysterious world view that he describes, though mitigated somewhat by the intellectual self-consciousness forged in modernity that had not yet been fully individuated in premodernity. As Dylan puts it: "I was beginning to feel like a character from within these songs, even beginning to think like one," though always with the self-awareness of one who seeks out this premodern mode as a reaction to his culture rather than being born into it without access to mediating rationality.

But certainly, as Dylan notes, at that moment in the early sixties, "there wasn't enough" of this archaic way of thinking available in the main streams of culture. The mode of consciousness exemplified in folk music had been buried so effectively, expunged from collective awareness by the predominance of rationality in the central nodes of American culture's discursive networks, that it was a titanic labor archaeologically to unearth the evidence of this repressed way of relating to experience. To be sure, the older modes were there to be found, but they were "out of date, had no proper connection to the actualities, the trends of the time," as the American ideal had long been reconstellated around an entirely different center of gravity focused on paradoxically individualistic conformity, with scientific repeatability and the efficiency of the machine as the governing metaphors. The repressed modes were "a huge story" because, as James and Whitehead explicitly suggest, they had been the primary mediators of human experience prior to the seventeenth century, as the modes of thought characteristic of science had not yet been systematically differentiated from archetypal and teleological cognizance.

However, it is a testament to the adaptability of the human mind that, only a few hundred years after the Enlightenment, the mode of constructing experience that had defined human culture for so long "was hard to come across." Dylan discovered that these were modes of explanation that could account for the vital, animate, meaning-infused quality of human experience in the animal body. If these forms of consciousness had no connection to the "trends of the time," at least those predominant in the main streams of culture, then Dylan would just have to initiate new trends and, in order to perform this transformative role, he found it necessary to cut himself off from the sovereign discursive milieu so that he "had little in common with anyone not like-minded." Dylan's intuitive revulsion at explaining himself to journalists and other gatekeepers of the principal cultural hierarchies seems to stem directly from this need to maintain consciously the new mode that was constituted in the integration of archaic modes with the critical awareness more characteristic of his time. Ultimately, Dylan was an artist, not a philosopher, and he did not have the time or energy both to concretize his world-transforming visions and to explain them to skeptics, which is probably one of the reasons why so many books have been written about him: the musical and mythological narrative he created is profound and can bear the weight of such explanation.

In pursuit of the novel archaic mode, Dylan devoured everything that crossed his path, consuming ideas, songs, and characters, both in life and in fiction, as fuel to impel his continued trajectory upward and inward. It is this intense drive to "understand things and then be free of them," to see things "all at once," that impelled Dylan toward what he felt to be increasingly higher planes of awareness where he could gain a more expansive perspective on the world. His impulse was somehow to "telescope" all the things he had been devouring into "one paragraph" or "one verse" to create a synthesis of the vast knowledge of culture, a Borgesian ambition that Dylan achieved beyond all reasonable expectation.[527]

Like most exceptional artists, Dylan had a vision of bringing together various strands that had never before been synthesized: literary and musical genres, ideas and ways of thinking from ancient Greece to Civil War-era America to nineteenth century France, and he combined these elements in such a way that they seem to have been meant to come together all along. As musician John Koerner expressed it: "He was just taking everything in—he listened to everybody, and he had an incredible ability to take things in and absorb them and turn around and put them right back out there like they had always been a part of him."[528]

"Some Kind of New Template"

For Dylan, Mike Seeger, half-brother to Pete Seeger, was the prime exemplar of that to which Dylan had been aspiring: the ultimate mastery of traditional folk forms. According to Dylan, Mike Seeger had attained the highest aim of performance, which is to make the audience forget themselves in the music, evoking one meaning of "ecstasy," drawing the listener out of egoic consciousness into complete identification with the song. Witnessing Seeger's brilliant performativity apparently made Dylan more aware of his own limitations, which in turn produced a revelation in Dylan. As with many such turning points, both personal and collective, Dylan's recognition of the futility of continuing on his current path was essentially an identity crisis that impelled him to reorganize his "inner thought patterns."

Dylan had been "closing [his] creativity down to a very narrow, controllable scale" in order to master the mechanics of musical performance, but seeing Seeger play acted for Dylan like a Kuhnian scientific anomaly which sparks the revolutionary rupture, the persistently incommensurable piece of evidence that impels a reorganization of the whole system, producing the realization that Dylan "would have to start believing in possibilities that [he] wouldn't have allowed before." This encounter with performative perfection was the shock that forced Dylan consciously to expand his identity so that he could create something that went beyond the limited realm Seeger had already conquered.

Dylan realized that, when one has become fixed in one's way of seeing the world, it is necessary to "disorientate" oneself, as Arthur Rimbaud suggested, to create something genuinely new. Dylan instinctively recognized that in order to go beyond the merely performative and interpretive mastery exemplified by Seeger, it would be necessary for him to undergo a period of turmoil during which he would have to redefine the system of his identity from a performer to a songwriter who performs. Dylan had possessed the felt sense that his apprenticeship as a folksinger was leading him toward something qualitatively different, but it is not until this encounter with Seeger that he seems to have realized that his performative focus was merely a prelude to his most important work: writing songs.

Dylan suggests here that seeing Seeger perform was a revelation which impelled him "to claim a larger part of"[529] himself, to expand his conscious identity to encompass parts of his being that had previously been unconscious, dormant potential. Dylan knew that he must, to employ Bergson's metaphor, throw himself into the water, the new medium, and learn how to swim. However, Dylan intuitively sensed that, in order to expand himself to the necessary domain of awareness, he would lose the comfort of the smaller world that he had previously inhabited: "There's only one way to change things," Dylan told Nat Hentoff in 1964," and that's to cut yourself off from all the chains. That's hard for most people to do."[530]

However, Dylan writes in *Chronicles*: "America was changing. I had a feeling of destiny and I was riding the changes." Picking up the thread of a previously employed metaphor, Dylan recognized that a wave of revolutionary artistic, political, philosophical, and social transformation was sweeping through America and he sensed that he was bound not only to swim in the new medium, but to ride the crest of that wave, like William James' "single drops flung far ahead of the advancing edge of a wave-crest."[531] Indeed, Dylan seems to believe that he possessed the capacity to feel and align himself with the ever-shifting impulses in the historical process. And, as he notes, this ability was intimately connected to a transformation and expansion of his "consciousness" that would manifest in "some kind of new template" for folk songs. In turn, he seems to suggest that this "template" is homologous with a new "philosophical identity" consciously based on this novel way of approaching experience, predicated less on normative constructs than on one's affective sense of the constantly shifting quality of temporality. This approach was geared toward sustainability, toward not "burning out," but finding a way to keep the promethean flame alive by conceiving his identity as something like an actor who takes on different roles, inhabits them almost completely, and then discards them when their shelf-life has expired, so to speak.

The singer's name change from Robert Zimmerman to Bob Dylan constitutes an early and definitive declaration of the malleability of his identity. Before he left Hibbing, his cousin Reenie questioned him concerning the various names he had been using in gigs around the area. Dylan recalls the conversation: "'Who's Elston Gunn?' she asked. 'That's not you, is it?' 'Ah,' I said, 'you'll see.'" Dylan's simple, mysterious, and evocative answer to his cousin's question, "you'll see," is characteristic of Dylan's relationship to his name and, by extension, to his sense of identity. In fact, Dylan's ability almost totally to inhabit his successive roles is one of his most clearly defining qualities, a fact that he seemed to intimate to his cousin, at least in retrospect. However, as Dylan notes: "The Elston Gunn name thing was only temporary," the first of many identities that Dylan would assume.

His second choice, Robert Allen, using his middle name as his last, was perhaps too close to his real identity to suit the young man who would become Dylan. It seems likely that it is precisely because "there was little of my identity that wasn't in it"[532] that Dylan felt the impulse to push his stage name one degree further from his original, core identity, the one his parents had given him. As Dylan tells Scorsese, when he listened to the country song "Drifting Too Far From the Shore,"[533] "the sound of the record made me feel like I was somebody else, you know, that I was maybe not even born to the right parents or something."[534] Clearly there was an intrinsic impulse in Dylan that was driving him far from anything that he could call home.

Young Bobby Zimmerman, impelled to experiment with his identity in a kind of science of selfhood, and always drawn to the distant and the mysterious, added another subtle permutation to his nominative transformation when he came across a magazine article about a saxophone player called David Allyn, the letter "y" striking him as "exotic" and "inscrutable." He seems to have possessed an innate need to know the mystery of being by himself becoming an embodiment of that mystery, a transformation that first had to be exemplified in his name. Finally, having encountered the poetry of Dylan Thomas, the young man who would become Bob Dylan pushed his name one step further from its original incarnation. As he describes his thinking, it is primarily intuitive and aesthetic criteria, carefully considered and deliberated over, that led Bobby Zimmerman to become Bob Dylan. He explicates a meticulous process, much like his songwriting, in which he considers every permutation, from the precedents for various names to the sounds of the names to the visual impact of various spellings on the page. By the time he arrived in Minneapolis, he had put so much thought into his new name that it came out "instinctively and automatically without thinking."[535]

Although it is true, as David Hajdu writes, that "the irony of Robert Zimmerman's metamorphosis into Bob Dylan lies in the application of so much elusion and artifice in the name of truth and authenticity," this paradoxical quality seems to evince a deeper kind of authenticity in the case of Dylan, who appears to possess an intrinsic drive to reveal different aspects of himself through the performance of many different personas. As singer Harry Jackson observed: "He's so goddamned real, it's unbelievable,"[536] a clear articulation of the paradox at the heart of Dylan, for the quality of being "real" is synonymous with the quality of being "believable." Thus, as seems to be the potential with paradoxes generally, Dylan pushes the oppositional duality of authenticity and artifice to such a point that they are shown to be two sides of the same coin, genuine authenticity defined as the refusal of fixed identity, as the performance of how one feels in the moment rather than how one is expected to behave based on past precedent. As Dylan asks in "Like a Rolling Stone": "How does it feel to be on your own?" a stark reminder that the freedom to live based on the mercurial impulses of one's affectivity comes at the expense of the rational certainty provided by culturally predetermined roles and mores.[537]

The self-naming described above is as good an exhibition of Dylan's creative process as any, for it is clear that in his songwriting, Dylan labors over each word, constantly rewriting verses, changing phrases to add new layers of depth and meaning, so that by the time he sings a song on stage or on record, it seems like it has always been that way. And indeed, even after he records his songs, he continues experimenting with them so that the versions of songs on *Hard Rain*, for instance, which are so different than their earlier incarnations, often seem as perfect and timeless as the originals that they drastically rewrite.

And more than just lyrics, Dylan also constantly experiments with melodies, chord changes, phrasing, rhythm, tempo, and instrumentation. Although his songs are apparently simple folk tunes, in a very real sense he is as experimental as John Cage or Cecil Taylor, though whereas these experimenters in avant garde composition and free jazz, respectively, were mostly formal explorers, Dylan is primarily an explorer of content, though he has also pushed the form in significant ways, particularly in terms of song length and in melding various genres that had never been so deeply synthesized. As has often been noted, form and content are ultimately inseparable.

Another instance that compounds the evidence for Dylan's consciousness of passing through different identities comes from *Eat the Document*, a fragmented documentary of Dylan's 1966 tour of England filmed by D.A. Pennebaker (who shot and edited *Don't Look Back*), but edited by Dylan. In the footage, which appears to be near the end of the tour, Dylan, extremely thin, androgynous, and weary looking, quips in a jittery voice: "I think I'm gonna get me a new Bob Dylan next week, get me a new Bob Dylan and *use* him. Use the new Bob Dylan; see how long he lasts."[538] Beyond expressing his exhaustion after months of heavy drug use and playing to partially hostile crowds, this statement seems to exhibit an awareness in Dylan that each successive incarnation he inhabits is a role that he plays intensely until there is nothing left for that transient being to give, then it passes away and a new Dylan emerges to take its place.[539] By creating roles that he can inhabit almost completely, but which are not perfectly coextensive with his internal sense of self, Dylan built into his "philosophical identity" an escape hatch so that he would not "burn out," that is, literally die with the death of each persona as did Hank Williams, Robert Johnson, Elvis Presley, Jim Morrison, Janis Joplin, Jimmie Hendrix, Gram Parsons, and any number of other young stars.[540] As Benjamin Hedin aptly expresses it: "Dylan was the rarest of pop culture survivors—he had managed to both burn out *and* fade away."[541]

"Some Archaic Grail to Lighten the Way"

When Dylan first saw Mike Seeger and decided to start composing songs, he was already thinking he "might want to change over" to songwriting, though he sensed that he would "have to find some cuneiform tablets—some archaic grail to lighten the way." As he writes: "I had grasped the idea of what kind of songs I wanted to write, I just didn't know how to do it yet." Dylan was searching specifically for an older text that might provide him with a direction; an archaeological unearthing of some secret, ancient writings close to the origin of civilization to illuminate his path, though Dylan was looking for the origin a little closer to home in the New World. He wanted to create something profoundly novel and so he went looking for something old and forgotten to offer a way out of the tyranny of the contemporary.

"I couldn't exactly put in words what I was looking for," he writes, "but I began searching in principle for it, over at the New York Public Library," an activity that sounds more like a scholar doing research than a songwriter seeking inspiration. Nevertheless, Dylan began scrolling through microfilms of newspapers from the Civil War era to "see what daily life was like. I wasn't so much interested in the issues," he explains, "as intrigued by the language and rhetoric of the times."[542] Dylan was not looking primarily for insight into the social and political questions that folk songs so often addressed, but rather for a buried way to use language, along with its concomitant mode of thought, that he could revive in a new context. He was searching in the distant past for a way out of the predominant modes that seemed to hold everything, including music, in their iron grip at that moment in the early sixties.

Dylan was consciously rebelling against what he perceived as the conformity of "modern ideas" in his songs, by which he seems to mean the descent of late modernity, embodied in the rationalized "semantics and labels" that "could drive you crazy." This rationalization described by Dylan produced a collective madness driven by the imbalanced focus on rendering experience measurable and categorizable, with mind and matter ultimately incommensurable.[543] This seems to be the very quality that Dylan would so often react to in his interviews a few years later, the impulse to label him as "protest singer" or "voice of his generation." These labels constituted the rational mode attempting to devour and master the intuitive and affective modes in which Dylan was primarily immersed, a lens through which these kinds of labels often seemed absurd and pointless.

"The Center of the Labyrinth"

In September 1961, Dylan met John Hammond, a producer for Columbia Records, who offered him a recording contract. Although Dylan had a vaguely defined sense of the road ahead, he had until then assumed that he would rise through the usual channels of folk music, perhaps recording for Folkways Records, which was the primary label of the milieu with which he had been engaged, releasing much of the music to which he listened. However, Folkways had already rejected Dylan, so his signing to Columbia was completely unexpected, pulling him into a large corporation that specialized in smooth jazz singers like Johnny Mathis and Tony Bennett, not spiritual sons of Woody Guthrie. Nevertheless, as Dylan attests, Hammond was a visionary and Dylan could not refuse.

Dylan initially met Hammond through Carolyn Hester, a folksinger from Texas (who was married to novelist and musician Richard Farina, who in turn would later marry Joan Baez' sister, Mimi, and die tragically young), at a rehearsal for Hester's recording session on which Dylan was to play harmonica. Hester had made some music with Buddy Holly before moving to New York, which greatly impressed Dylan. As he writes: "Buddy was royalty, and I felt like she was my connection to it, to the rock-and-roll music that I'd played earlier, to that spirit."[544] Perhaps like John Pankake, Hammond could sense that Dylan's interests transcended folk music, that his attitude and intensity had some residue of his years spent devoted to "his first love,"[545] rock and roll.

That Dylan was drawn to the woman through whom he would meet Hammond because of her connection to Buddy Holly and the "spirit" of rock and roll suggests that the genre was a hidden and implicit, but vital element in Dylan's origin story, his narrative of being "signed" to a record label. Thus, it seems clear that Dylan not only aspired to attain the level of "King of the Folksingers"[546] like Ramblin' Jack Elliot, but that he also felt a kinship with rock and roll "royalty," which he would also become a few years later, though to great initial resistance from the folk community. Even at this point when he was almost completely absorbed in the folk world, he still carried a secret flame for rock and roll.

At the rehearsal, as Dylan presents it, he seems to have been far more focused on the music and helping his friend than "getting signed," the obsession of many lesser artists. Although it might be difficult to believe in the *American Idol* era that Dylan really "didn't notice" Hammond watching him as he taught Hester a few songs she wanted to record, one gets the sense that Dylan truly did not see himself as an artist with popular potential. At this point, he apparently envisioned himself more as a potential heir apparent to Guthrie, Elliott, and Pete Seeger, the leaders of the pure folk scene who had had relatively few points of connection with the mainstream. There had never been a widely popular artist who sounded remotely like Dylan, so he simply was not looking in that direction.[547] However, Dylan does not seem to be a man who misses much, and that he says that "I wouldn't have done that," indicating that he would not have taken advantage of the situation, obliquely suggests that he did in fact notice Hammond noticing him, but that, out of a sense of loyalty and propriety, he consciously kept his focus on Hester and the music rather than on his career prospects.

As the rehearsal ended, Hammond casually asked Dylan if he was working with a label but, as Dylan describes it: "I shook my head, didn't hold my breath to hear him respond and he didn't and that was that."[548] Ultimately, it was in Dylan's interest to appear humble and above mundane concerns about recording contracts and the like, for he appears to have known intuitively that one of his primary social and musical assets was his air of mysterious authenticity, which he assiduously cultivated. Thus, it seems clear that Dylan managed not to get caught up in the desperation for fame that haunts so many artists. He truly appears not to have cared very much about such worldly concerns, seeming to have understood that if he kept his sights on the heights and the depths, the middle would align itself sooner or later.

However, Dylan, always a paradox, does seem to have cared enough about worldly success to track down perhaps the one person in the world who could most advance his career at that moment: Robert Shelton, the folk critic for the *New York Times*.[549] As Suze Rotolo observes in Scorsese's documentary: "He just knew what he wanted and he could focus. He was very astute. He could pick out somebody who was important, I mean, any musician would, but he was really good at it."[550] Thus, it was perhaps not so much that Dylan was desperate to achieve fame, but that he possessed a seemingly infallible instinct for knowing which way to go, and who to talk to, to get where he felt he was meant to be.

As a result of his befriending of Shelton, the "tidal wave"[551] that Dylan had half-consciously been preparing himself to catch finally arrived in the form of sanction by the holiest of holies in the high cultural art and music scenes, a review in the *New York Times*, surging not only in Dylan's experience, but in his milieu, soon erupting into broader cultural streams. As Epstein writes, Shelton's review "was the shot heard around the world—the folk music world at least—and no one in that competitive and incestuous community would ever quite get over it. Dylan carried the column folded up in the hip pocket of his jeans"[552] like a talisman or legal proof of his identity as the great hope of the folk community, "bursting at the seams with talent,"[553] as Shelton writes in the review.

A positive review in the *New York Times* has been for modern artists and writers what Papal approbation is for Catholics. Thus, the article anointed Dylan as the standout representative of the New York folk scene, which was itself the center of the international folk movement, so it does not seem accidental that the article was published the day before Dylan's recording session with Hester when Hammond offered Dylan a recording contract. Though certainly exhibiting some bravery and foresight on Hammond's part, it is no great surprise that Hammond wanted to sign Dylan; he read the *Times* like everyone else, though Hester claims that "Richard [Farina] and I had our own copy of it, and we took it with us to the session, and it was our copy of the review that John Hammond read. We were actually pushing it off on him."[554] However Hammond learned about Dylan, the fact is that Dylan had won over some of the most influential figures in the New York folk scene as advocates, including the *New York Times* folk critic and an artist already signed to Columbia, Carolyn Hester. Thus, it does not appear to be mere happenstance that Dylan and Hammond crossed paths, for Dylan had been unerringly moving through the ranks of the musical cognoscenti toward this meeting all along.

Following the recording session two weeks after their initial meeting, when Hammond asked Dylan if he'd like to sign a recording contract with Columbia Records, Dylan writes: "I said that, yeah, I would like to do that. I felt like my heart had leaped up to the sky, to some intergalactic star. Inside I was in a state of unstable equilibrium, but you wouldn't have known it. I couldn't believe it. It seemed too good to be true." Dylan, accustomed to holding his cards close to his chest, describes himself as having been the epitome of cool in this situation, causally acquiescing to what countless aspiring musicians have dreamed of as if he was accepting an invitation to a party, which seems plausible given his generally reserved persona. However, as only he could know, that Dylan's "heart had leaped up to the sky" shows how profoundly Hammond's acknowledgement of his music affected the young singer, perhaps giving him a felt impulsion sufficient to ride the crest of the titanic wave of transformation that surged through culture over the ensuing decade. Indeed, that Dylan uses the same metaphor he had previously employed in relation to Presley's early period, taking "songs to other planets," demonstrates that Dylan perhaps felt this moment to be an initiation in him of the kind of inspired creativity he describes in Presley.

Hammond's aristocratic background combined with his "edgy" taste in music produced the ideal gatekeeper to usher Dylan into the musical mainstream, at that time curated largely by "major" labels like Columbia. As with Sam Phillips for Presley or George Martin for the Beatles, though with Pankake playing the critical role that Martin had also played, Hammond, as a representative of one of the predominant musical institutions, initiated Dylan into the fold. If the Gaslight club had been one step further into the mystery, then Columbia Records was "the center of the labyrinth," at least as far as worldly mysteries were concerned. In a similar situation to the Beatles' signing by Parlophone, Dylan was a young, untried outsider from a historically liminal genre generally associated with small, specialized "independent" labels. Dylan himself did not even remotely fit the mold of the popular artists of that moment in the early sixties, which he characterizes as the "sanitized and pasteurized" lull between the first rock and roll explosion in the mid-fifties and the British Invasion that began in 1964. However, despite Dylan's unpolished presentation, Hammond was apparently able to sense the transformative quality in the young singer, to "feel" Dylan's "thoughts," which perhaps obliquely indicates the degree to which Dylan's intuitive capacity and his rational mind were already integrated at this early stage in his career.

After he signed with Columbia, Hammond had Dylan meet with Columbia's head publicist, Billy James, so the singer could give him background information for promotional materials. To Dylan, James, whom he describes as "dressed Ivy League like he could have come out of Yale," seems to have represented the privileging of rationality in the predominant commercial and academic culture of mid-twentieth century modernity, a clean-cut mode divorced from intuitive and somatic knowledge. As Dylan narrates the situation, James, who "looked like he'd never been stoned a day in his life," wanted Dylan "to cough up some facts . . . straight and square." As noted above, the description "straight and square" is not merely metaphorical, but actually seems to describe the affect performed by those firmly embedded in the predominant ethos of the fifties and early sixties: rigid, both physically and mentally, "by the book," following well-trodden paths through marriage, career, family, sexuality, and many other aspects of experience, at least on the surface.

By contrast, the emerging counterculture distinctly grooved and slouched, moving in more circular or labyrinthine ways, both physically and mentally. Indeed, this more organismic performativity can be seen in Dylan's constant experimentation with his physicality as much as in his words and music. Whereas Billy James was straight-backed, crisp, stiff, and short-haired, like a taut vertical line between heaven and hell looking straight ahead toward the myth of unbounded American progress, Dylan was constantly leaning like James Dean, head slyly cocked, leg shaking, bouncing on the balls of his feet, hands flittering and gesticulating in fractured motion, like a kind of Dadaist dance. It is clear that Dylan was a profoundly interesting thinker, but a fact that is not often explicitly mentioned is that this interest was constantly being performed in his body.

Where James wanted Dylan to give him straight answers to straight questions, Dylan instinctively rebelled against participating in this linear, factual, demystifying mode of discourse. Rather, the whole thrust of the young singer's inclination impelled him to misdirect and obfuscate, to conjure mystery and uncertainty within which he could abide in the archaic, mythical mode of consciousness. Dylan seems to imply that James, like most of the journalists with whom Dylan developed an increasingly contentious relationship, was attempting to pull the young singer into the gravity of the prevalent way of being, the literalist, materialist mode characteristic of science and industrial capitalism. As Dylan writes: "I didn't feel like answering his questions, didn't feel the need to explain anything to anybody." His affective sense implicitly rejected the ethos that Billy James represented, which privileged rational explanation over attunement to the felt quality of experience in which Dylan was primarily interested.

"Maybe a Thousand Songs"

Dylan describes an evening after he had been signed to Columbia by Hammond but before recording his first album that provides a window into his creative process. He was in the office of music publisher Lou Levy, who was producing demos of Dylan singing songs that he was composing "on the spot, rearranging verses to old blues ballads, adding an original line here or there, anything that came into my mind—slapping a title on it." However, Dylan writes: "Nothing would have convinced me that I was actually a songwriter and I wasn't, not in the conventional songwriter sense of the word."[555] Even though the music industry, embodied in Hammond and Levy, had acknowledged Dylan as a songwriter, he still resisted the label because he did not want to be confined to a certain idea of what that label meant. His ability to produce songs "on the spot" by synthesizing other songs is an extremely rare gift that allowed him to forego craft almost entirely. Dylan did not have to think about writing songs, as this activity appears to have come to him intuitively. Indeed, part of the reason Dylan was able to create such profoundly novel compositions is that he refused to be categorized, an intrinsic drive toward freedom from constraint that would characterize all aspects of his life and career.[556]

What Dylan emphasizes in this snapshot of his songwriting process is that he consciously eschewed rational thought in favor of intuitive creativity for, as he writes: "There was little head work involved. What I usually did was start out with something, some kind of line written in stone and then turn it with another line—make it add up to something else than it originally did. It's not like I ever practiced it and it wasn't too thought consuming."[557] Dylan is here describing the time-honored process of learning a craft by emulating and appropriating the work of others, taking elements from the vast catalogue of songs that he had at his disposal and recombining them into something new. In fact, though Dylan did not perceive what he was doing as practicing, it seems clear that his constant playing and thinking about songs, half-consciously shuffling and reordering them in his head, constitutes a kind of practice, though it must have felt so natural and so pleasurable that it did not seem like work to Dylan.

It has been suggested that true "geniuses," not so much in IQ, but in creative accomplishment, are forged by thousands of hours of practice, whether they consider it practice or not, and Dylan fits this description, saying in a 1968 interview: "I certainly spent a lot of hours just trying to do what other people had been doing."[558] Similarly, Dylan writes in *Chronicles*: "I played morning, noon and night. That's all I did, usually fell asleep with the guitar in my hands." It is clear that Dylan was consumed by songs from a very young age, so that by the time he made these demos for Levy in 1961, creating new compositions out of existing elements seemed like the easiest thing in the world, though it is something that very few songwriters can do well, particularly "on the spot" as Dylan claims. And he was able to accomplish this feat, in part, because he had immersed himself so completely in the songs of others that they formed a large proportion of the texture of his daily experience. Perhaps even more than spoken language, verbal and musical song tropes were the vocabulary through which Dylan most related to the world around him. Thus, whereas writing a song seems like a difficult task for most people, Dylan seems instinctively to have constructed his experience in such a way that writing a song was as effortless an activity as expounding on some esoteric subject might be for a scholar.

However, Dylan's first song "of any substantial importance," "Song to Woody," was "an homage in lyric and melody" to Guthrie, who had become a friend and a mentor. It is completely characteristic of Dylan that what he considers "the first of maybe a thousand songs" he would compose was written as an acknowledgement of his most prominent influence, his debt to the past, for Dylan was able to be so consistently and profoundly transformative in part because he was so deeply grounded in the history and tradition of folk music. This rootedness gave the startlingly new compositions that would flow from his typewriter over the ensuing years a gravitas and authority often lacking in popular music.

It seems that Dylan judged his own songs to some extent by how meaningful they were to him personally, which indicates that Dylan's focus was not so much on the craft and mechanics of songwriting, on the borrowing of concrete lyrics, melodies, and structural elements from existing songs, in the case of "Song to Woody," taking the melody from Guthrie's "1913 Massacre." Rather, Dylan's focus was on the layers of meaning that lay behind and within the songs. He knew that if he could summon the appropriate affect, the structure of the composition would flow from him without effort or analysis. He understood that if the song was not meaningful to him, if it did not seem to part the "misty curtain" to the "invisible world" that he describes, it would probably not connect very deeply with his audience.

Judging by his profound reverence for his influences, there is no more meaningful subject for Dylan than Guthrie, whom Dylan repeatedly insists "pointed out the starting place for my identity and destiny." And the fact that Dylan wrote what he considers his first substantial song as "homage" to Guthrie rather than in a conscious attempt to establish himself as a songwriter only reinforces this hypothesis. Dylan does not seem to have thought of himself as a professional songwriter, but merely as someone with a deep and abiding passion for songs and those who create them; a subtle difference, but an important one in allowing Dylan to do what he did. Instead of choosing to become a songwriter for rational reasons, Dylan simply felt impelled by his own nature in relation to the world to create, an approach that he seems to have cultivated carefully and protected assiduously.[559]

"Hammond's Folly"

Dylan's first, self-titled album, *Bob Dylan*, released in March of 1962, and composed of primarily traditional songs, was initially deemed a commercial failure, selling less than 5,000 copies in its first pressing.[560] Hammond, undaunted, appears to have retained his confidence in Dylan, whom his colleagues at Columbia were starting to call "Hammond's Folly." Indeed, as Clinton Heylin observes of Dylan: "The failure of *Bob Dylan* would convince him that he should have more faith in his own instincts and less in others."[561] Thus, rather like the Beatles at their Decca audition, which had taken place less than three months before, though at a somewhat different point in his career, the lukewarm reception of Dylan's first album impelled in him the realization that he should trust his own intuition rather than trying to satisfy the rational expectations of others.

As Dylan told Scorsese: "Part of me was just sayin' that I didn't wanna record that record anyway, that I just did it. I didn't want to give away anything that was really, you know, dear to me or something."[562] It seems to have been necessary for Dylan, relatively new to recording, to make an uncertain album, an album on which he held himself back from revealing too much. Indeed, this impulse seems to be coextensive with his need to create a persona shrouded in mystery and depth. However, whereas this tactic of holding his best cards close to his chest seems to have been effective in his prolonged relationship with the other members of the folk community, Dylan seems to have realized immediately upon hearing his first record that making an album is quite a different mode of communication than performing in the folk clubs every night, as an album is a brief chance to convey the very best of oneself to a much larger audience. Dylan did not make the same mistake twice, the mediocre quality of his first record relative to his later work impelling him to begin writing songs in earnest, which would be the key to unlocking Dylan's immense felt potential.[563]

"Kissed Awake By the Prince of Folk Music"

At the Newport Folk Festival in 1959, Dylan's future manager, Albert Grossman, had declared that "the American public is like Sleeping Beauty waiting to be kissed awake by the prince of folk music." This proclamation proved prophetic, as four years later in 1963, Dylan was the undisputed "prince of folk music," smooching the movement, and the wider culture, from its slumber. As Epstein writes: "1962 was Dylan's pivotal year artistically, just as 1963 was his annus mirabilis in career terms."[564] He recorded *The Freewheelin' Bob Dylan*, the album that would catapult him to fame, fortune, and acclaim, in a series of sessions from July to December 1962, and these songs are a qualitative leap forward from the primarily cover songs he had played on his first record. In particular, "Blowin' in the Wind," "Girl From the North Country," "Masters of War," "A Hard Rain's A-Gonna Fall," and "Don't Think Twice, It's All Right" catalyzed the folk movement in a way that nothing else could have.

These new songs by Dylan are indisputably as great, or greater, than any of the traditional songs Dylan had been singing, but they were also radically new. Even before Dylan went electric, these songs integrated the folk idiom that was their immediate precursor with an attitude and sensibility characteristic of both rock and roll and the beats. And it certainly did not hurt that the songs were sung by a fascinating looking young man with an ancient-sounding voice. Indeed, in 1963, Dylan shed his baby fat, from which emerged the gaunt, angular visage that would become iconic in the ensuing years, suddenly appearing less like a pudgy ragamuffin and more like a Jewish Woody Guthrie or James Dean. And certainly, Dylan's intuition a few years earlier that he was bound to sing with Joan Baez was borne out by the actual course of events as he began his storied relationship with the "Queen of Folk Music," which played a great role in elevating Dylan to the status of "King."[565]

Furthermore, the success that Peter, Paul, and Mary achieved with Dylan's "Blowin' in the Wind" was the kind of success that folk musicians had rarely experienced, and only "folk pop" artists like the Kingston Trio and Harry Belafonte. Thus, it was somewhat unprecedented for a hard-core folk singer like Dylan (the subtle poetic and musical differences from traditional folk music mentioned above notwithstanding) to have a song at the top of the national charts, even performed by a more commercial sounding group. This success primed the folk community for an equally unprecedented phenomenon at the 1963 Newport Folk Festival, "the ultimate bastion of folk purity,"[566] which, as Epstein writes, was "a virtual coronation of Bob Dylan as the prince of folksingers, heir apparent to the legendary Pete Seeger."[567]

Seeger, who had played with Woody Guthrie, had arguably neither attained the level of artistry achieved by his predecessor nor the level of fame and artistry that would be achieved by his successor. Thus, Seeger acted as something like a bridge between the old dispensation and the new, a modest patriarch devoted primarily to the folk tradition and its political causes. Although Seeger wrote or co-wrote a number of classic songs, including "If I Had a Hammer," "Where Have All the Flowers Gone?" and "Turn, Turn, Turn," Dylan, still a very young man, had already produced the kinds of songs that Seeger never would, songs that energized the folk movement with a novel intensity, mirroring the affectivity of a new generation of believers.

And that Dylan and Baez were a couple was the icing on the cake, so to speak. Dylan seemed to be the leader that the folk movement had been waiting for, and he reveled in the adoration in the way only a twenty-two-year-old can, in part by carrying a bullwhip with him for the three days of the festival, cracking it periodically in a strikingly overt assertion of authority. In singer Theodore Bikel's assessment, the 1963 Newport Folk Festival was "the apogee of the folk movement," and although folk had long been perceived as outsider music, in that moment, folk had actually emerged as one of the most commercially successful genres, Dylan its prime exemplar.[568]

"The Crystal Cracked"

Dylan's life in 1963 was not all easy, confluent ascension, however. Amidst all of the public acclaim and inspired creativity, Dylan was in the process of breaking up with his first love, Suze Rotolo, who had accidentally become pregnant with his child but had miscarried. Adding insult to injury, a *Newsweek* article by Andrea Svedberg was published on November 4, 1963, the day before he played a sold-out concert at Carnegie hall, unmasking Dylan as Bobby Zimmerman, a "middle-class Jewish boy with a hobo costume and a fake accent," seemingly a death-blow to Dylan's carefully cultivated image. By all accounts, Dylan was devastated by the expose, which seems to have marked the beginning of his notoriously contentious attitude toward the press, recalling in 2012: "People have tried to stop me every inch of the way. They've always had bad stuff to say about me. *Newsweek* magazine lit the fuse way back when."[569] Thus, the initial persona that Dylan had constructed, and on the back of which he had risen to fame, did not die of natural causes, but was brutally murdered by Ms. Svedberg, an ego-death that probably would have ended the career of a lesser artist. The article seemed to reveal Dylan as a liar and a charlatan, a betrayer of the "authenticity" so prized by the folk community.

However, with characteristic aplomb, Dylan managed to turn this momentary defeat into a triumph, adroitly incorporating the description "chameleon-like" into his mythology. As Dave Van Ronk recalled: "All of us were reinventing ourselves to some extent, and if this guy wanted to carry it a step or two further, who were we to quibble?" And as Epstein asserts: "When the folksingers discovered that Dylan's oral history was a clever fiction, it didn't much affect their opinion of him. Shape-shifting was part of a tradition one could trace to Jack Elliot, Marilyn Monroe, Al Jolson, and countless actors and singers who made up stories about themselves."[570] Rather than apologizing for his perceived betrayal of the folk ideal, Dylan instead transmuted what seemed to be his greatest weakness into his greatest strength by embracing the "shape-shifting" tradition, not only of Elliot, Monroe, and Jolson, but also of what singer Liam Clancy refers to as "Shape-changers:" "In old Irish mythology, they talk about the Shape-changers.

He changed voices, he changed images. It wasn't necessary for him to be a definitive person. He was a receiver, he was possessed, and he articulated what the rest of us wanted to say but couldn't say."[571]

Certainly, this Irish shape-changing mythology had found its way into various strands of the American folk tradition in which Dylan had immersed himself, the evolving expression of an archetypal potentiality. Whereas the rationalist, literalist form of consciousness, embodied in this case by Svedberg, interpreted Dylan's obfuscating tendencies as merely lying, the emergent mode of consciousness that Dylan primarily inhabited interpreted these tendencies as an embodiment of the trickster archetype, a role pervasive in the premodern cultural mythologies in which Dylan was so interested. For the neo-archaic mode, Dylan's proclivity for myth-making was not a sign of his lack of authenticity, but rather the manifestation of a deeper kind of authenticity. As seen time and again, Dylan did what he felt in each moment, acting as a medium or "receiver" for the expression of the ever-shifting quality of temporal becoming. Through this attunement to the qualitative nature of time, Dylan enacted a kind of "truth" that exceeds the comprehension of a purely rationalist epistemology.

Nevertheless, the largely rationalized cultural milieu into which Dylan was emerging as he was ushered onto the national stage still generally perceived the situation in the conventional way so that Dylan, exhibiting exceptional fortitude in his rejection of an easily locatable identity, did a great deal to mediate the return of repressed modes into his culture by clearing an imaginal space in collective awareness where those archaic epistemologies could take root. Dylan's mythogenetic instinct seems to have been motivated not by fear, but by the need to "carry it a step or two further" than his contemporaries, taking risks with his identity that no one else was willing or able to take. As Woody Guthrie's daughter Nora has said of Dylan: "I think he's very much an experimentalist, looking into himself all the time, saying what do *I* want to do now. And that's awfully brave. He's experimenting with his own soul. That's incredible, I think. I mean, he's taken *chances*, with his soul."[572] The quality that some in the predominant cultural streams initially saw as Dylan's greatest sin, his mercurial, changeable nature, appears from this re-enchanted perspective to be profoundly courageous and valuable.

However, it was not just Dylan undergoing a traumatic moment of crisis in 1963, but American culture and its counterculture that Dylan increasingly seemed to exemplify. According to Eric Andersen: "The whole thing burst apart when Kennedy got killed. . . . This sort of cozy little womblike existence as a singer-songwriter—things changed. The

Beatles came over. The crystal cracked or something." Although segregation, the Vietnam War, unprecedented affluence, and many other factors formed preconditions for the countercultural explosion of the later sixties, Kennedy's assassination in November 1963 was the event that constituted the crucial turning point of this generation's trajectory, a trauma that catalyzed the nation's youth, while the British Invasion in 1964 would grant a more positive outlet for the heightened affective intensity that accompanied that trauma. Indeed, like the deaths of John Lennon's and Paul McCartney's mothers, though on a collective scale, Kennedy's death constituted the archetypal loss of a beloved parental figure, "the preeminent leading man of television in his day,"[573] which seems to have impelled something like a collective rebirth from the "cozy little womblike existence" of the fifties and early sixties, though the culture already seems to have been primed for this new revolution, "ready for change," as Andersen puts it.

Although Dylan does not appear to have intended to lead the emerging counterculture at this crucial moment in his nation's development, he seems to have presaged the looming crisis in his creative output with striking clarity, having presciently written "A Hard Rain's A-Gonna Fall" about six weeks prior to the Cuban Missile Crisis in 1962 and "The Times They Are A-Changin'" about six weeks prior to Kennedy's assassination in 1963, though both songs were widely assumed to have been written about those events. Dylan seems to have possessed an extraordinary capacity to sense the direction of process and to express the qualitative nature of time before most people were aware of these subtle processual shifts, a capacity traced in more depth below. He did not choose to be a leader, but he appears to have been chosen by something that exceeded him, by the necessity of his character, his ability to see and articulate what others could not.[574]

Dylan's third album, *The Times They Are A-Changin'*, might as well have been *Freewheelin' Part II*, as it consolidated the strengths of that previous album in songs like "With God on Our Side," "Only a Pawn in their Game," "Boots of Spanish Leather," "The Lonesome Death of Hattie Carroll," and the title song. Dylan's fourth offering, *Another Side of Bob Dylan*, his second of 1964, was the first album he had recorded since Kennedy's death, and it took a somewhat more personal tone than Dylan's first three albums, though the difference is perhaps not as stark as it has often been portrayed, particularly in light of Dylan's later work. Nevertheless, the generally more apolitical and emotionally revealing quality of the compositions on this record seem to have connected with many fans in a more intimate manner than his previous two records, which had consisted primarily of social commentary and abstract, archetypal narrative, both wistful and absurd.

Whereas there were two obviously personal songs on both *Freewheelin'* ("Girl From the North Country," "Don't Think Twice, It's All Right") and *The Times They Are A-Changin'* ("One Too Many Mornings," "Boots of Spanish Leather"), there are four such songs on *Another Side* ("All I Really Wanna Do," "I Don't Believe You," "Ballad in Plain D," "It Ain't Me Babe"), which tip the balance of subject matter significantly toward intimate relationships, a change that probably had a lot to do with the fact that Dylan was in the midst of a painful breakup with Suze Rotolo. Perhaps even more significantly, however, as Dylan told the *New Yorker*: "There aren't any finger-pointin' songs"[575] on the record like "Masters of War" or "With God on Our Side," though "Chimes of Freedom" and "Motorpsycho Nightmare" do seem to gesture toward issues of social justice, albeit in less overt ways than the earlier songs. Thus, although the changes may not have been as dramatic as the transformation enacted the following year in *Bringing It All Back Home*, *Another Side* made it clear that Dylan was moving away from the political subjects which had elevated him to the folk monarchy, and moving toward the more internal, symbolic mode that had until then been overshadowed by his "protest" songs.

Not only did Dylan's music and lyrics take a turn in 1964, but so did his persona. Dylan's transformation from the scruffy, chubby-cheeked young folksinger to the hard-edged king of the hipster cognoscenti, mediated through the brief "prince of folk music" persona, seems to have been a change born of necessity, as the more personal quality of his fourth album attracted a more intrusively personal kind of attention from fans. D.A. Pennebaker speculates: "I figured that Bob had grown up in a place that treated him fairly gently. The people around were probably the kind of people I had known in Chicago—not high-speed people. They were gentle people. Later, when I heard Bob's 'Girl from the North Country' I realized it was for somebody he had lost, who was that gentle kind of person," Pennebaker concludes, "and now the people he was dealing with were hard because they expected something more." Well before he went electric, the way Dylan's image was used by his audience began to make the transition from constructing him as leader of the folk protest movement to idol of a more intimate kind, many coming to see him as a kind of personal savior. As with the many mutations Dylan underwent, his transitions from Hibbing to Minneapolis to New York certainly produced a hardening and sharpening in the young singer, both physically and psychologically.

However, perhaps the greatest hardening occurred after Dylan had become famous when fans started desperately looking to him for answers that he did not possess. According to folksinger David Cohen: "Dylan was very hostile, a mean cat, cruel to people" at this stage in his trajectory in the mid-sixties, though this cruelty was apparently a defense mechanism against the massive expectations and projections directed toward him, Cohen explaining that "it was just too heavy for him, being the center of attention."[576] For instance, witnessing Dylan's cruelty to Joan Baez in *Don't Look Back* could easily turn one off of Dylan, so to speak, until one realizes that he was still a very young man trying the best he could to deal with the unbelievable pressure of incredible fame and adulation into which he had suddenly been thrust.

In 2012, Dylan summed up his experience of that period centered around 1965: " I don't really have a warm feeling for that period of time. Why would I? Those days were cruel."[577] As Dylan phrases it, his cruelty from that period was a reaction to, or simply a manifestation of the general affective tone of that historical moment. However, in a somewhat more benevolent 1978 interview, Dylan expressed understanding for his audience's projections onto him, saying: "If I wasn't Bob Dylan, I'd probably think that Bob Dylan has a lot of answers myself."[578] Thus, it is apparent that Dylan could see himself and his past in strikingly different ways through the constantly shifting lenses of qualitative temporality to which he was so intensely attuned.

Dylan was increasingly becoming a primary focus of attention for the counterculture, but it was only those in the "musical community" who, in Dylan's view, really seemed to understand where he was coming from. As Dylan tells Scorsese:

> At a certain point, people seemed to have a distorted, warped view of me for some reason and, uh, those people were usually outside the musical community. "The Spokesman of a Generation," "The Conscience of This, That, and the Other," I mean, that I could not relate to. I just couldn't relate to it. . . . As long as I could continue doing what it is I love to do, I didn't care what kinda labels were put on me or how I was perceived in the press because I was playing to people every night.[579]

Dylan was simply a musician and songwriter who, seemingly without his intention or consent, had been elevated by the collective to a position that exceeded the role of mere entertainer. Something in him, and in his moment, seems to have demanded this elevation, though Dylan, who has an apparently intrinsic need to defy any label, refused to accept a fixed identity, no matter how exalted.

Certainly, this refusal is a large part of what allowed him to keep moving forward and transforming himself and, as a result, to perform the transformation of his culture. Indeed, in a 2012 interview, Dylan even refuses what the interviewer describes as a "perception of you as somebody with a lot of phases and identities," as someone impossible to pin down. True to the end, Dylan replies: "I don't see myself that way. But what does it matter?" refusing even the label of one who refuses labels.[580] Nevertheless, his extraordinary fame does seem to have forced Dylan to choose between being open and gentle and probably being destroyed by the pressure of expectation on the one hand, and cultivating a distant, hostile, obfuscating persona that allowed him to thrive and create.

As Epstein writes of what has been referred to as Dylan's "theatre of cruelty" period in the mid-sixties: "Such scenes would be of less interest if they didn't coincide with a dazzling productivity." Indeed, watching a young man pick fights with journalists and girlfriends, however cleverly worded, is not particularly interesting until one hears the gloriously vitriolic songs Dylan produced during this period, from "It Ain't Me Babe" and "Ballad in Plain D" to "Positively Fourth Street," "Like a Rolling Stone," and "Ballad of a Thin Man." By the time Dylan sang "Visions of Johanna" and "Just Like a Woman" on 1966's *Blonde on Blonde*, both apparently written about Joan Baez, one gets the sense that he was already becoming wistful, even sentimental for the days prior to his "pitiless period" when his lyrics were "full of strife, rancor, and vengeance." It seems to have been a stage that Dylan had to pass through, a reaction to the extreme affect directed toward him, both positive and negative. This period was also perhaps a result of Dylan's instinctive knowledge that, in order to bring the folk audience with him into uncharted waters, he would first have to puncture the naïve pretensions, the "Kumbaya" bubble that surrounded the folk movement, playing a role similar to the one John Pankake had played for Dylan a few years before, though in a dramatically different context and on a collective scale.

"A Prismatic Effect"

Although Dylan was still the "King of Folk," the tension started to show at Newport 1964. Dylan was reaching toward other genres and modes to escape from the straightjacket that folk music, once so liberating, had started to resemble for him. But even this small change relative to what was soon to come was deeply challenging to his fans. Many of the audience members at the festival were apparently frustrated by Dylan's turn away from political songs toward more personal material. As Andersen observes: "Remember, things had gotten fragmented. When Johnson came in, the winds were shifting, you might say, politically. So I think he [Dylan] got fragmented, too. The glass developed a crack, and it became a prismatic effect." Certainly, if Dylan was a mirror for his culture, then not only the traumatic quality of Kennedy's assassination, but perhaps even more significantly, the effects of cannabis and LSD, which were both just starting to become widely popular among the hipster cognoscenti at this moment, served to amplify and catalyze the collective psyche in unexpected ways, like the fun-house mirror that Andersen's metaphor suggests. Indeed, as with an individual psychedelic experience, the things that had been repressed in the predominant cultural streams were coming to the surface, and the normative assumptions that had long been taken for granted were being brought into question by the cultural deconditioning agent of music and the psychoactive substances that fueled it.[581]

Like both Presley and the Beatles, Dylan received some scathing and dismissive reviews, a phenomenon that seems to have come with the territory. For instance, Irwin Silber, the editor of *Sing Out!* magazine and previous champion of Dylan, wrote an apparently well-meaning "open letter" expressing what Silber terms "love and deep concern" at Dylan's new direction evinced at Newport 1964. But the letter is ultimately conservative, not only mourning the loss of Dylan's earlier incarnation at the previous year's festival, but attempting to stifle Dylan's search for novel experiential modes. Silber writes:

> You seem to be in a different kind of bag now, Bob— and I'm worried about it. I saw at Newport how you had somehow lost contact with people. It seemed to me that some of the paraphernalia of fame were getting in your way. You travel with an entourage now—with good buddies who are going to laugh when you need laughing and drink wine with you and insure your privacy—and never challenge you to face everyone else's reality again. . . . Your new songs seem to be all inner-directed now, innerprobing, self-conscious—maybe even a little maudlin or a little cruel on occasion. And it's happening on stage, too. You seem to be relating to a handful of cronies behind the scenes now—rather than to the rest of us out front. Now, that's all okay—if that's the way you

want it, Bob. But then you're a different Bob Dylan from the one we knew. The old one never wasted our precious time.[582]

However, Dylan does not seem to have been particularly upset by Silber's letter, writing: "I like Irwin, but I couldn't relate to it." Even before Dylan "went electric," though, the folk establishment, exemplified by Silber, felt betrayed by Dylan, whom they thought had responsibility to the movement that wedded traditional folk music and political activism.

Silber's admonition is all the more ironic as he chides Dylan for apparently being corrupted by the "establishment," the "system" to which the pure folk movement, itself an established system, was the antidote in Silber's view. However, Dylan knew intuitively that as soon as an artist capitulates to what his or her audience or critics want, the art is dead in the water. Silber, whom Dylan describes as acting like he possessed "the keys to the real world," does not seem to have had the capacity to comprehend Dylan's artistic nature, which impelled him toward ever greater and more encompassing visions of that "real world" to create "something different that had not been heard before."[583]

However, aside from the conservative reactions from the politically progressive folk community, Newport 1964 was also where Dylan first met Johnny Cash, who seems to have played a large part in lending Dylan the courage to explore both the country and rock and roll of which Cash exemplified the synthesis. As Dylan tells Scorsese: "Johnny Cash was more like a religious figure to me. And there he was at Newport, you know, standing side by side. Meeting him was the high thrill of a lifetime." Furthermore, as Tony Glover describes a visit from Cash and his wife, June Carter: "Johnny called him out in the hall, and Bob came back in a few minutes later holding this guitar and he says, 'he gave me his guitar.' Neuwrith was saying, 'wow, that's an old country tradition. If somebody gives you a guitar, that's a big honor, you know?'" Having this monolith of a man, a singer whom Dylan had idolized since he was a teenager in Hibbing, sing one of his songs and essentially acknowledge Dylan as his successor seems to have liberated Dylan perhaps more than any other factor from being exclusively the heir of Woody Guthrie and Pete Seeger.[584]

Anointed by Cash, Dylan was in a position to bring together the adjacent, but clearly demarcated kingdoms of folk, country, and rock and roll into one encompassing empire. Once Cash had given him his blessing, there was indeed no looking back for Dylan, as the world seemed to him to be acknowledging through the benediction of this monumental figure that Dylan was bound to play a primary role in creating an emergent genre out of the synthesis of previously existing styles, a genre initially known as "folk-rock" (a label that Dylan detested), and subsequently as simply "rock." Indeed, the following year of Dylan's life, from Newport 1964 to Newport 1965, is the period when the new form of the genre, and the larger countercultural movement that it accompanied, was truly born, in large part through the recording of *Bringing It All Back Home* and "Like a Rolling Stone," the filming of *Don't Look Back*, and the performance at Newport 1965 when Dylan "went electric," described above.

"Just an Interruption"

Ultimately, Dylan's ascendancy as the "King of Folk" in 1963-64 was merely a step toward his more profound transformation synthesizing folk music with rock and roll a year or two later, a transformation presaged in Dylan's early love for the rock and roll genre, in the role his admiration for Buddy Holly played in his signing to Columbia, and in the sensibility that increasingly permeated his acoustically performed songs. However, there is one little-known circumstance that prefigures Dylan's most famous transformation, his "going electric," in a particularly striking way: On October 26 and November 1, 1962, during the recording sessions for *Freewheelin'*, Dylan and five studio musicians (including Bruce Langhorne, who would play guitar on *Bringing It All Back Home* three years later) had cut six takes of Elvis Presley's version of "That's All Right."[585]

Listening to the second take, if one did not know when the song was recorded, one might guess that the recording had taken place during the sessions for *Bringing It All Back Home*, not *Freewheelin'*. Although some of Dylan's subtle vocal inflections are clearly more characteristic of his early folk period, the style and feel of the song is much closer to Dylan's music after he went electric in 1965. In fact, aside from the obvious connection that Langhorne's distinctive guitar provides to songs like "Subterranean Homesick Blues" and "Maggie's Farm" on *Bringing It All Back Home*, and the somewhat less mature tenor of Dylan's voice, the song sounds perhaps most of all like one of the numerous covers that Dylan played with the Band collected on *The Genuine Basement Tapes*, recorded in Woodstock in 1967. These subtle clues notwithstanding, this recording (along with "Mixed-Up Confusion") makes the years of Dylan's first six great albums (after the relatively conventional *Bob Dylan*), 1962-1966, seem like a long, strange dream.

That Dylan recorded for his first album of mostly original material what is generally considered the first true rock and roll song even though he had been working as a solo folksinger for the previous few years attests to Dylan's abiding commitment to rock and roll. Although when Dylan went electric in 1965 it seemed to be a radical break from his performative identity, which was intimately bound up with the folk movement at that time, this moment can be viewed more accurately as a return to the rock and roll that had always been implicitly at the core of Dylan's music. As he bluntly expressed it in a 1978 interview: "It had to go that way for me. Because that's where I started and eventually it just got back to that. I couldn't go on being the lone folkie out there, you know, strumming 'Blowin' in the Wind' for three hours every night."[586] In fact, this seems to be precisely the point Dylan sought to convey by naming his first electric album "*Bringing It All Back Home*": that blues, country, and rock and roll were Dylan's starting point, the music of his youth, and the implicit basis for everything he had done and would do. Dylan was apparently always a rock and roller who had taken a detour into the folk idiom for, as Dylan told an audience at the Royal Albert Hall in London at the end of his 1966 British tour with the Hawks (later the Band): "Folk music was just an interruption and very useful."[587] His tenure as a folk musician appears always to have been inevitably leading to his rock and roll rebirth.

Based on Dylan's statement above, it might be construed that he cynically donned the trappings of folk music in order to use the genre's popularity in the early sixties as a launching pad for his own career. Indeed, as Dylan asserted soon after going electric:

> I have not arrived at where I am now. . . . I have just returned to where I am now. I never considered myself a folksinger. They called me that if they wanted to. I don't care. I latched on, when I got to New York City, because I saw [what] a huge audience there was. I knew I wasn't going to stay there. I knew it wasn't my thing. I knew that Woody did this kind of thing and Woody was famous, and I used it.

While this explanation does seem to express a partial truth, as Dylan has always been adept at finding the pragmatic way forward, it is also clear, as demonstrated amply above, that he was genuinely devoted to folk music. Indeed, this diatribe seems to be a kind of historical revisionism characteristic of an artist who had recently rejected his previous identity and milieu, and who wanted to justify this rejection in absolute terms.

Summing up his complete denial of his former self, Dylan provocatively ranted that "folk music . . . is a bunch of fat people."[588] However, it should be apparent by now that Dylan was in fact profoundly committed to the folk tradition, embodied most of all in his love for Woody Guthrie.

Thus, rather than being an either/or proposition, it appears Dylan fundamentally understood that folk and rock and roll were really just two different forms of a larger definition of "folk music" in the sense that the two genres sprang from the same deep wells of American musical experience, Dylan telling an interviewer nearly fifty years later: "I've got too much rock & roll in my blood to call myself a blues singer. Country blues, folk music and rock & roll make up the kind of music that I play."[589] Thus, folk and rock and roll's temporary polarization into "head music" and "body music" appears to have been a fantasy, a conceit acted out half-consciously in the culture to perform the reintegration of intellect, exemplified at that moment in the mid-sixties by the "highbrow" folk movement, and affect, embodied at that moment in "lowbrow" rock and roll.

Like Cain and Abel, rock and folk were sibling genres that, in Bob Dylan's mythical performativity, were ultimately reconciled through the act of Dylan infiltrating the folk movement, becoming its primary exponent, and then symbolically slaying it at the 1965 Newport Folk Festival by playing visceral electric music. In this sense, Dylan really was a kind of "Judas," as one audience member shouted at a concert Dylan played with the Band in 1966, though if one follows this archetypal analogy to its logical conclusion, Dylan was also a Christ figure for, like Judas, he performed the betrayal of the true folk believers, but only to become a martyr enacting the death and rebirth of folk as part of something far greater in the ensuing decades.[590]

"As Long As You Know"

In the final paragraph of the first volume of his memoir, Dylan writes that "the folk music scene had been like a paradise that I had to leave, like Adam had to leave the garden." And not only Dylan, but the culture that he exemplified for many of its participants, was being collectively expelled in the inexorable onward march of temporal process from the artificial edenic innocence of the fifties into the search for self-knowledge that characterized much of the sixties. All of the phenomena taking place that Dylan alludes to—feminism, the Vietnam War, the draft, and the sexual revolution—as well as the events traced above, from the adulation directed toward Dylan to the assassination of Kennedy to the British Invasion to Dylan's meeting with Cash to the prevalence of psychoactives, are all material factors that Dylan seems to imply were constellated around an underlying impulse toward profound transformation at work in the culture during this period. As Dylan writes, he "went straight into" the chaos, the "thunderhead of a world," which, like the expulsion from the womb, is both extremely "treacherous" because it is so profoundly new and unknown, but also "wide open," a vastly expanded vista ripe for exploration and for the creation of novelty.[591]

Amidst all of the turmoil, Dylan recorded *Bringing It All Back Home*, the album that, along with the Beatles' *Rubber Soul* and perhaps a few other records from this period, would transform popular music in fundamental ways. Although Dylan had played with bands before, this was the first time he had made a record with a band as a mature, world-famous artist, and this simple shift is another instance of "that slightest change of tone which yet makes all the difference." Amidst all of the angst and strife in the culture—and in Dylan's personal life—the first adjective that guitarist Bruce Langhorne uses to describe the session is "fun," which, as discussed above, is an apparently trivial word that actually nominates a significant aspect of the epochal transition taking place at that moment. Where Dylan's audience was accustomed to sitting quietly in rapt attention to the subtle nuances of the folk singer's vocal phrasing and lyrics, the addition of a band lifted Dylan's music from that of a lone poet to that of a howling madman inciting the world to ecstatic self-transformation.

And that Langhorne describes the recording session as "this sort of spontaneous telepathic thing" suggests that, rather than focusing on the lyrics, which were still just as complex and interesting as those on Dylan's earlier records, or perfecting the arrangements based on rational "mandates" and methodically laid out "charts," as Langhorne puts it, the band was primarily focused on the affective feel of the music, simply "jamming," bringing their energetic "vibes" into resonance in order to create what sounds like nothing so much as a higher order emergent entity with Dylan as egoic consciousness and the band as different somatic domains.[592] This transformation from folk to a new kind of rock and roll enacted the coming into embodiment of something like the disembodied consciousness of the emerging counterculture's poet laureate, a naked, ancient-sounding voice accompanied only by Dylan's fitful strumming and his strident harmonica. That Dylan only performed a total of fifty-five solo concerts before he went electric (not counting his many performances in smaller clubs before he was signed to Columbia) is a striking illustration that this relatively disembodied musical mode was simply unsustainable for the young singer.[593]

A conversation that Dylan has with a teenage fan in *Don't Look Back* is instructive in this regard. The girl asks if he is going to play "The Times They Are A-Changin'," and he asks, while signing an autograph: "You really like that song? What do you like about it?" She replies: "I don't know. I don't care for 'Subterranean Homesick Blues.'" Dylan responds: "You're that kind of girl, I understand right now," to which the girl boldly rejoins: "It doesn't sound like you at all," which is true enough, as until that moment, his public sound and identity had been relatively constant. Dylan, in a weary and patronizing tone, responds: "My friends were playing with me on that song. I have to give some work to my friends. You don't mind that, right? Huh? You don't mind them playing with me if they play their guitar, drums, and all that kind of stuff, right?" to which the girl answers: "It doesn't sound like you at all. Sounds like you're having a good old laugh." "What's wrong with that?" he responds. "Don't you like me to have a good old laugh every once in a while?" a statement which suggests the value of "fun," of visceral enjoyment.

The girl responds: "People might not take you seriously," a statement that demonstrates anxiety about collective judgment for stepping outside the bounds of conventional genre structures, an anxiety to which Dylan seems to have been generally immune. The singer answers: "Yeah, well, you're no different though, right? As long as you know you don't have to worry about anyone else. People take care of themselves,"[594] a declaration which may at first seem cold or lacking compassion. However, upon further reflection, it appears that what Dylan is suggesting to this young fan is that "as long as you know" that what you are doing feels authentic and satisfying, there is no reason to "worry" about what anyone else will think about you. If one feels that what one is doing has value and does not hurt anyone, then fear about the reactions of others is pointless and unproductive.

Ultimately, Dylan seems to suggest, everyone is responsible for their own thoughts and emotions, though this recognition certainly does not preclude generosity, charity, and care for others, for as he would declare in his 2012 *Rolling Stone* interview: "If we're responsible to ourselves, then we can be responsible for other people, too. But we have to know ourselves first. People listen to my songs and they must think I'm a certain type of way, and maybe I am. But there's more to it than that. I think they can listen to my songs and figure out who they are, too."[595] What Dylan seems to have understood implicitly talking to the young fan in 1966, but which has perhaps become clearer with a half century of maturity, is that worry is an emotion that gratifies some need in the worrier, not in the person who is the object of worry, which is a liberating realization, certainly, but one that is difficult for most people to put consistently into practice. Once Dylan was able to take responsibility for himself, the implication is that he was able to take responsibility for the transformation of his audience through the incitement to self-knowledge mediated by the depth of his songs. However, at that moment in the mid-sixties, Bob Dylan simply felt like playing with a band, and so he did, and this act of doing what he felt in the moment, despite the massive resistance that greeted him at every turn, seems to have enacted a profound transition in music and culture.

Langhorne describes the musicians who played on the *Bringing It All Back Home* sessions as "really funky" and having "great time," both of which could seem like trivial descriptions to non-musicians or those who have not spent many hours listening closely to music and, consequently, have not experienced the affective profundity of the qualities that these phrases describe.[596] "Funkiness" is not merely the caricature of Funkadelic and Sly Stone (though these artists are more musically subtle than they are often given credit for). Rather, it is a quality of timing in which the musicians play slightly ahead or behind the beat and incorporate hints of syncopation and polyrhythms into their phrasing to give the music a more complex and nuanced affective tone. This subtle quality, evident in so much of the best music from the late sixties and seventies, is clearly related to having "great time," though this phrase more specifically connotes a steadiness of tempo that allows one consciously to play around the beat. And these two related concepts are directly evocative of the qualitative nature of temporality. It seems that by enrolling these exceptional musicians to play on his record, Dylan was in some sense teaching his audience to shift the focus of their attention from primarily verbal meaning to a broader kind of attention that focuses simultaneously on the lyrics and on the temporally shifting feel of the music, a thrillingly complex integration that Dylan could not have achieved on his own.

II. "YOU REALLY DON'T KNOW UNTIL YOU STEP INSIDE"

CHAPTER 4
"A REVELATION TO BEHOLD"

Religion, in her fullest exercise of function, is not a mere
illumination of facts already elsewhere given, not a mere
passion, like love, which views things in a rosier light. It is
indeed that, as we have seen abundantly. But it is something
more, namely a postulator of new facts as well. The world
interpreted religiously is not the materialistic world over again,
with an altered expression; it must have, over and above the
altered expression, a natural constitution different at some point
from that which a materialistic world would have. It must be
such that different events can be expected in it, different conduct
must be required.

William James, *The Varieties of Religious Experience*[597]

One of the most striking qualities of the collective narrative told about the Beatles is the consistent use of language describing their discovery of American rock and roll as a mystical revelation, their commitment to rehearsing this genre of music as a devotional spiritual practice, and their concerts as ecstatic religious rituals. Though often mediated by a distancing ironic humor, these rhetorical tropes examined *en masse* seem to be more than mere metaphor, pointing to a profound convergence between rock and roll and religion in the experience of many of those who participated in the Beatles phenomenon. In *Beyond Belief*, Robert Bellah defines religion as "a set of symbolic forms and acts that relate man to the ultimate conditions of his existence,"[598] and this definition seems to be fundamentally true of the Beatles and their audience.[599] Indeed, it was not school or work or science or institutional religion, but rock and roll that seemed to express the deepest yearnings and intuitions of the Beatles and many in their generation, evident in their lives as much as in the "spiritual longing"[600] of their music.[601]

"The Messiah Had Arrived"

Lennon explicitly described his discovery of Presley as "the conversion,"[602] declaring that "Elvis was bigger than religion in my life."[603] And Lennon's encounter with "the spirit of [Presley's] performance"[604] does in fact appear to bear all the signs of religious conversion explicated by James in *The Varieties of Religious Experience*:

> To be converted, to be regenerated, to receive grace, to experience religion, to gain an assurance, are so many phrases which denote the process, gradual or sudden, by which a self hitherto divided, and consciously wrong inferior and unhappy, becomes unified and consciously right superior and happy, in consequence of its firmer hold upon religious realities.[605]

Lennon's conversion to rock and roll through the figure of Elvis Presley defined his relation to "the ultimate conditions of his existence" more than any other factor, for his "self hitherto divided" found in rock and roll a mode and model for relating to his most intimate bodily experience that rendered him "unified and consciously right superior and happy" in his devotion to the genre. Of course Lennon was not a deliriously happy individual from that moment forward, but this does not appear to be the meaning of happiness that James intends. Rather, in context, James seems to suggest that such conversion produces an affect of felicitous and confluent unity of purpose, a higher kind of happiness grounded in a profound sense of meaning and destination, a set of felt qualities that seem to have characterized much of Lennon's experience from this point onward.

McCartney expresses this religious quality just as directly, though always with an ironic twist, describing their early sessions listening to rock and roll records as "worshipping,"[606] and nominating Presley as "the guru we'd been waiting for. The Messiah had arrived."[607] To be precise, the irony generally employed by the Beatles is a double irony, for they often ironically negate with their tone what they are literally asserting, only to negate the negation by communicating, also through subtle tonal inflections as well as facial and gestural cues, that they do in fact mean what they say, which performs a critical self-awareness, demonstrating that they are holding the skeptical pole within their encompassing belief. As Gould aptly notes, it is a testament to their genuine veneration of Presley that, although the Beatles would cover a number of his songs live, Presley was the only one of their primary initial heroes whose songs never made their way onto a Beatles record, "almost as if he were indeed the reigning deity and they a group of novitiates, proscribed from speaking his name."[608] Or as Mark Lewisohn puts it: "Elvis Presley was God, it was as simple as that."[609]

Indeed, the Beatles' biographers generally employ such religious rhetoric with a similar irony to that employed by the Beatles themselves. Although Bob Spitz writing that "like an earnest disciple, John reacted with missionary devotion"[610] to his discovery of rock and roll, or

Lewisohn declaring that when skiffle devotees like the Beatles "heard 'That'll Be the Day,' those eternally uplifting two minutes, they were *converted*"[611] may appear merely metaphorical to casual reading, the overwhelming prevalence of such rhetoric in relation to the group from numerous sources suggests that these tropes are an acknowledgement of a truth hidden in plain sight: Lennon and McCartney really were disciples of Presley, and they really were missionaries for the return of affective intuition that rock and roll mediated. Similarly, Gould writes: "from the start of the Beatle phenomenon, the press had harped on the analogy between the zeal of Beatlemaniacs and that of religious devotees."[612] Although Gould never directly confutes the literal meaning of this statement, his rhetoric creates an ironic distance from such belief: "harped," "zeal," and "Beatlemaniacs" are all drolly overinflated terms, apparently meant indirectly to communicate an elevated critical perspective in relation to the implied credulity of "the press," a phrase which, in context, conveys a slight condescension often employed by members of the cultural elite when speaking of "the public." Thus, rather than contradicting the idea that the Beatles were essentially a religious phenomenon, Gould seems almost to find it slightly distasteful to admit the plain truth of this supposition, a rhetorical operation that encapsulates the often trivializing attitude characteristic of modern sophistication. However, minor cynicism notwithstanding, that the Beatles stayed "faithful to the sounds they loved" is a primary condition for the musical and cultural transformation that they enacted.[613]

On one hand, it is a mistake to be overly reverential about the Beatles, as one of their most attractive qualities is the self-aware levity with which they approached everything, both themselves and others, George Martin observing: "they don't take themselves too seriously."[614] On the other hand, however, once the realization has been achieved, it becomes difficult to ignore the overwhelming prevalence of religious rhetoric describing the Beatles' devotion to their music, though always with an irony endemic partially to their Liverpudlian roots and partially to their historical moment. The critical distance that this ironic stance afforded was a significant factor in allowing the Beatles to take up the promethean torch from Presley and the other original rock and rollers to move the genre toward greater self-consciousness and complexity.

Presley was not really grappling with questions; to a great extent, he was what he was and he did what he did in a generally uncritical mode. But the numinous vocabulary used to describe the Beatles again and again, thinly masquerading as metaphor or conceit, suggests that the Beatles and their milieu conceived of the phenomenon in which they were participating as something approximating a spiritual practice, while the ironic distancing allowed these themes to sit with relative ease in the container of a disenchanted modernity. Ultimately "the secular somehow becomes holy"[615] in the music of the Beatles, the wine of daily life transubstantiated into something sacred.

"An Exalted Magic"

As discussed above, agents of radical cultural transformation often emerge from liminal locations, whether geographical or social, or both as in the cases of Presley and the Beatles (who were basically working class), and Dylan (who was Jewish). Thus, like the paradigmatic birth in a provincial manger, Liverpool from whence the Beatles came was a cultural frontier as far as those who largely controlled English culture in London were concerned, which gave the Beatles' "common kinship an exalted magic, in much the way that Ozark Mountain dwellers"[616] seem to possess a certain numinosity for American city-folk. Like Presley, raised in marginal corners of the American South, the Beatles issued from the similarly "magical" Northern England. In fact, Spitz, like numerous other commentators, does not appear to employ the word "magic" arbitrarily, as in a profound sense, these liminal places have carried the countervalent impulse to the disenchanted world view, in this case exemplified by the rational techno-capitalism prevalent in postwar London.

As Harrison declared in 1966: "To me it seems that Western philosophy is very prejudiced because they look upon mysticism as a magical 'something else,' you know? But after everything the greatest Western philosophers have said, to me it all boils down to the fact that they still haven't hit upon what the Eastern people have."[617] Harrison astutely suggests that the predominant Western culture of modernity, including many of its most influential philosophers, has privileged the epistemology implicit in science, which is itself based upon the privileging of material and efficient causation, while "mysticism" and "magic" constitute radically different modes of approaching experience, which have generally been developed to a higher degree in Eastern, globally Southern, and indigenous cultures, based primarily on formal and final causation.

To give some background, near the beginning of the philosophical enterprise, Aristotle delineated four types of causation, which can be divided into two groups of two: *material causation* is the fact that material, physical objects exist at all, which is the precondition for *efficient causation*, which has generally come to mean material objects acting on other material objects, from subatomic processes to the movements of the planets. Since these two types of causation imply one another, one can perhaps refer to *material-efficient causation*, which is what we generally think of in the early twenty-first century when we use the word "cause." However, Aristotle also posited two other intertwined types of causation: *formal causation*, which is the idea that there are implicit potentialities inherent in the nature of being known as forms, archetypes, or universals that manifest in all things, while *final causation* is the telos, goal, or purpose of these formal potentialities when they are realized.

The classic example that Aristotle gives of formal and final causation is the acorn that becomes the oak tree: the oak is implicit in the acorn, but it must go through the process of development and growth in a temporal trajectory of becoming before the specific shape of the oak can be seen. Thus, although the oak is the final cause of the acorn just as one's life's work may be the final cause of one's birth, this view does not preclude free will, as there is freedom in the road toward one's destination, or even in the possibility of rejecting that destination. Experiential domains having to do with religious experience, mysticism, magic, alchemy, and teleology, which are closely connected to the lived experience of rock and roll, and to most modern countercultural streams, all generally seem to be explicable through a mode of thought based on formal-final causation rather than the material-efficient causation privileged in the predominant modern world view. And the affective, intuitive, and somatic epistemologies traced in the previous chapters appear ultimately to be doorways into these complementary causal modes delineated by the father of science, as Aristotle is generally considered.

During the Beatles' early years, the repressed affective epistemologies within the collective English psyche, deeply related to Aristotelian formal and final causation in ways that will become clear in the following pages, were apparently carried and embodied to a great extent by the English North, though it should be noted that this pole of the dialectic was also exemplified by the "underground" subcultures in London itself from which emerged such bands as the Rolling Stones, the Yardbirds, and the Who, all catalyzed by the initial success of the Beatles. As DJ Bob Wooler recalls, the Beatles "had such a magical influence on people."[618] Indeed, as Gould observes: "Whatever magic the Beatles possessed lay dormant in the soul of every English boy,"[619] and this repressed numinosity only required the Beatles to show the way, to open the floodgates of the deeply creative vitality simmering below the surface of a largely rationalized British, and ultimately Western, culture.[620]

"The Music's Alchemy"

Lennon, explicitly seeking an explanation for his feeling of difference from others, experienced the discovery of rock and roll on Radio Luxembourg as a miraculous epiphany which "gave you plenty to dream about," as one of his contemporaries put it. However, whereas dreaming is often associated with unfocused, undisciplined thinking, Lennon, McCartney, and Starr "observed the [rock and roll] radio broadcast faithfully" as a kind of spiritual discipline. Even Harrison, who was initially too young to listen to the broadcast, found a way to participate through the second-hand descriptions of a friend, which demonstrates early commitment to what would ultimately be his life's work. McCartney described it as "a revelation"[621] and, for Lennon, "the broadcast was some kind of personal blessing, like a call from a ministering spirit," for according to Pete Shotton, Lennon "regarded it like scripture." This compounding of religious language from McCartney, Lennon's close childhood friend, and one of the Beatles' primary biographers exceeds the appropriate reach of mere metaphor, suggesting that the Beatles and their associates understood what was occurring to them as an essentially religious phenomenon in its broadest sense: "revelation," "personal blessing," "ministering spirit," and regarding the broadcast "like scripture" all suggest spiritual devotion.

Indeed, that Shotton described Lennon as having "behaved distractedly" before the broadcasts recalls the passage from Mircea Eliade's *Shamanism: Archaic Techniques of Ecstasy* in which the initiate "becomes absent-minded and dreamy, loves solitude, and has prophetic visions."[622] And Lennon certainly possessed a quality that can accurately be described as "vision," as according to an art school-mate: "John had a fantastic imagination that enabled him to see things for what they really were . . . and then jumble them up in a hilarious, thought-provoking way."[623] Lennon possessed the innate ability to perceive reality by means of "imagination," to penetrate to the heart of things and see connections that others could not, and to express the things that he saw in an engaging way, all qualities that those who saw the phenomenon from the inside often describe explicitly in terms of a spiritual or mystical calling. To apply Occam's razor, it seems that the most straightforward explanation for the phenomenon in question is that John Lennon, his friends, and their influences and followers were engaging in what they experienced as a kind of religious practice through their disciplined engagement with rock and roll music and culture.[624]

Furthermore, it is clear that all of the Beatles, and Lennon in particular, had a powerful sense of calling in relation to rock and roll;

they felt compelled, sensing something that seemed to demand expression through them, something beyond their volition, later experiencing a "confirmation of their calling" at the 1960 concert by Gene Vincent and Eddie Cochran mentioned above. However, even in Lennon's earliest experiences with a band in the mid-fifties, his bandmates, having never witnessed a live skiffle group, "were obliged by John's special knowledge, unaware that his know-how was for the most part intuitive." While Spitz implies that the fact that Lennon's "special knowledge" was "intuitive" somehow deceived the other boys, just below this level of interpretation, the vocabulary that he employs almost begs for a different explanation.

It is as if Spitz is making understandable concessions to the predominant ethos which regards intuitive knowledge as hierarchically less valuable and valid than rationally acquired knowledge, but the surrounding rhetoric, and the biographer's general orientation, belies this implication, suggesting that the members of this group perceived Lennon as the recipient of an intrinsic gift that "effortlessly" produced awe in his compatriots. And this subtle, though perhaps unintentional rhetorical operation perfectly expresses the larger cultural significance of the Beatles as a postmodern Trojan Horse for the return of affective knowledge. According to childhood friend Nigel Wally, Lennon "just *knew* what to do, it was right at his fingertips. . . . It wasn't this concept he'd worked out; it came naturally to him."

And McCartney was no less devoted to rock and roll. After his mother died, he desperately clung to this music in the same way that many find solace in religion during difficult times. As Spitz describes in a passage that seems to demand the thesis of the present chapter, for McCartney, listening to rock and roll and dreaming himself into the imaginal world created by the music was akin to a meditative practice, "a kind of reverie," in which he would float in a womb-like prerational state of consciousness, "not even thinking," immersed in the "alchemical" quality summoned by the music.[625] Again, these words, thrown out casually, point inexorably to the deeper meaning of what is, on the surface, an adolescent boy listening to pop music, but in fact appears to be the spontaneous development of a transrational spiritual discipline by an individual who lived in a disenchanted culture, but who felt viscerally drawn to spiritual activity. Indeed, this activity appears to be a basic human need and capacity that can never be completely extinguished.[626]

The similar claim that McCartney's "talent was at the service of some hidden energy" [627] is characteristic of the language used to describe the Beatles, and rock and roll in general, as what many accounts of this genre's genesis imply is that the great rock and roll singers like Presley,

Lennon, and McCartney were vessels for the will of a higher power or an animating force—"whatever they may consider the divine,"[628] to borrow William James' phrase. All of the religious, mystical, and alchemical metaphors used to describe these men's relationship to their music are clear indications that these founding fathers of rock and roll implicitly saw the genre as a kind of spiritual practice, but perhaps less dogmatic, more expansive and encompassing, more epistemologically flexible than the traditional religions, like a spontaneously reemerging, postmodern form of shamanism, the primal, nearly universal spiritual practice of humanity.

To the two young men, rock and roll records were essentially religious texts, Spitz in one case comparing them to the Jewish Talmud, though the Beatles' religion generally privileged "the physical tug" of affective experience as opposed to the verbal facility often prized by "the people of the book." Furthermore, as mentioned above, the Beatles' initiation in Hamburg has been described as a "baptism by fire," while the Star-Club where they played has been described as a "cavernous rock 'n roll cathedral," specifically built for the inducement of collective ecstasy. Indeed, that commentators feel compelled to refer to many different religious traditions in describing the Beatles' activities attests to the sense that the boys were engaging in something that transcended the traditional religions, mediated as it was by the long developmental process of modernity.[629]

"A Gigantic Leap of Faith"

That there is a tendency toward ironic distancing suggests the collective recognition that these sorts of revelations, both mystical and musical, are not really about the figures who produced them as is usually assumed for ancient prophets and messiahs. Rather, for many twentieth century devotees of rock and roll, while the experience has certainly been mediated through the "rock star" figure, it is the revelation itself, the music itself, or the ecstatic affect that the music evokes in the listener that becomes the primary focus of attention. Thus, while Lennon would toy with the idea that he was a messianic figure, it seems that Lennon and his fans self-consciously reenacted the role that Christ and his followers played in culture, from claiming that "we're more popular than Jesus now" in a 1966 interview and singing "the way things are going, they're gonna crucify me" in the "The Ballad of John and Yoko," to devoting his life to spreading a gospel of peace and love and being tragically martyred by one of his most devoted and troubled disciples.

As Lennon declared in 1968: "If this scene is [around] in 2012 . . . the masses will be where I am today and I should be as groovy as Jesus by then,"[630] which seems to indicate his explicit understanding that messianic figures like Christ are perhaps not fundamentally different beings than their followers, but simply far ahead of their time, a role which Lennon seems to have at least temporarily saw himself as fulfilling. However, Lennon also rejected such suppositions at various points, most notably on "God" from his first solo record, *Plastic Ono Band*, where he expresses his disbelief not only in "God," "Jesus," and "Buddha," but also in "Elvis," "Zimmerman," and "Beatles," as well as on "Imagine" from the album of the same name where he expresses disbelief in "religion" in general. The spiritual aspiration and sense of election Lennon clearly felt was also apparently problematic for him, which seems to have been a product of being an exceptionally aware and visionary individual in a largely disenchanted culture. The Beatles narrative is a constant negotiation between spiritual intuition and rational skepticism, between belief and doubt.

Thus, impelling their productive conflict, Lennon and McCartney shared a fundamental understanding of the necessity of faith or intention in producing something culturally significant; not faith confined by religious dogma, but faith in the righteousness of their mission and the inspired quality of their music. As McCartney describes the band's approach when they were still struggling in Liverpool: "We had this way of getting over problems—someone would say, 'Well, what are we going to do now?' and we'd say, 'Well, something'll happen,' and the four of us believed that. . . . There was this, like, *faith*." Lennon expressed a similar sentiment, recalling: "We dreamed of being the British Elvis Presleys, and we believed it," elsewhere declaring: "We were the best fucking group in the goddamn world . . . and believing that is what made us what we were."[631] It is this quality of intention that carried the Beatles through their numerous transformations, including the shamanic Reeperbahn ordeal that produced what Mo Best called "a revelation to behold."[632]

This "will to believe" is also evinced in a humorous call-and-response that the Beatles would enact when their energy began to flag: "Where are we going, boys?'" Lennon would prompt his bandmates, to which they would respond: "To the top, Johnny! To the top!" "And where is the top?" he would ask, to which the others would reply: "The toppermost of the poppermost!"[633] This incantation, while certainly a parody of the music business circus, also expressed a profound insight articulated by William James in *Pragmatism*: "The truth of an idea is not a stagnant property inherent in it. Truth *happens* to an idea. It *becomes* true, is *made* true by events. Its verity *is* in fact an event, a process: the process namely of its verifying itself, its veri-*fication*. Its validity is the process of its valid-*ation*."[634] In this case, the truth that the Beatles were validating, though always through the distancing medium of humor, was that they were headed for great things. As James understood, in order to achieve something, one must believe that it is possible, even probable that one will achieve that thing. Although on one level of signification the Beatles performed this scenario as an ironic parody, on a deeper level, the humor allowed them to express their profound belief that they would be commercially and artistically successful while simultaneously allowing them a deflection from what they perceived as overly sentimental sincerity. In this subtle operation, they could express their feeling of teleological destination without explicitly asserting it.[635]

In a purely materialist reading, such a supposition would have seemed absurd, for the precedent of external circumstance in the months leading up to their Parlophone session in 1962 seemed to suggest that the Beatles would *not* be successful just as they had been unsuccessful in obtaining a recording contract until that point. Indeed, although Brian Epstein had taken "a gigantic leap of faith" to believe in the young group, later declaring "I knew they would be bigger than Elvis,"[636] he also acknowledged that, "from all evidence so far, the Beatles had nothing going for them." The Beatles and their manager felt that they were destined for greatness, but the only available recording, which Epstein used as a demo when shopping for a label for the group, was simply not very good. However, the Beatles' unshakable intuitive sense that they had something new and meaningful to offer impelled them to persevere, a faith that was justified copiously in due course.

And certainly, it was not just the Beatles and Epstein who possessed this sense of destination, as the milieu in which they were embedded was ripe for such an emergent phenomenon, lifting the Beatles out of the crowd when it became clear that they were the local band most likely to succeed. As DJ Bob Wooler announced one evening at the Cavern in 1962: "Hey, listen, Cavernites. . . . The next time the Beatles appear on this stage they'll be wearing their *brand-new suits*. Now, this is going to be a *revelation!*" In this proclamation we see the mythogenetic machinery gearing up, making anything that the Beatles did part of their mystique. Although there is a sense in which this announcement by Wooler was a cynical marketing move—Wooler himself admitting that "there was a touch of Barnum and Bailey in this"—it seems to have been experienced by the crowd as exactly what Wooler said it would be: a revelation.[637]

Indeed, many actions taken by the Beatles could be interpreted accurately in this double way: as evidence of a profoundly significant, essentially religious phenomenon or of merely a trivial pop-culture fad driven by the cynical desire for money and fame. It is one of the main points of Jamesian pragmatism that rationality can find valid and convincing logical arguments for seemingly incommensurable interpretations, the enchanted or the disenchanted in this case, so the difference really comes down to what the participants in the process decide to believe based primarily on their intuitive sense of the situation, their "individual way of just seeing and feeling the total push and pressure of the cosmos."[638] In the case of the Beatles, all of the elements came together to allow them to play a primary role in the radical shift in attitude of a significant portion of their generation, to provide the conditions under which their audience could choose to believe in what is often described in terms of the spiritual efficacy of the Beatles.

Of course, this belief was only possible because people were hungry for something to believe in, but this fact does not lessen the significance of the belief. It is the Beatles' faith in their mission that allowed the audience to believe and, in turn it is the audience's faith in the Beatles that spurred the band on to ever greater heights of creativity in a kind of feedback loop of energy and intention. As with all belief, this is an exemplary case of Whitehead's "slightest change of tone," and it certainly did make "all the difference,"[639] soon mediating the emergence of culture from a black and white world into the full psychedelic Technicolor that still largely defines the aesthetic possibilities of that culture a half-century later. To satisfy the dictates of the rational modern mind, it was important that what was believed about the band was at least plausible. However, the phenomenon of the Beatles attests to the value in itself of belief in something that transcends individuality, evident in the fruits that this kind of belief can bear for lived experience, especially when balanced by a moderate, healthy dose of skeptical rigor.

Brian Epstein describes the band as having "actually glowed" in their new suits, which recalls the halos often depicted around Christian saints or Buddhas. Whether the Beatles were physically emitting light or not seems beside the point, for judging by Epstein's statement, the witnesses to this revelatory instance experienced the moment "as if" the four boys were glowing, and this was what mattered to them, as this perception had a real effect on the crowd's affective state. Whether the Beatles were actually emitting light or whether this is only a metaphor for something harder to define is something for scientists and skeptics to consider after the fact, just as they have done with the purported miracles of messiahs, mystics, and shamans for millennia. Ultimately, there does not appear to be an iron-clad scientific way of knowing if these kinds of phenomena are literally true or not, for it often seems to be the case that the act of measuring the numinous disrupts the collective energetic quality, the "magic" that participants in all kinds of spiritual or mystical phenomena consistently describe.

The cogent point is that the crowd's focus of attention was not on critiquing, but on allowing the genuinely "miraculous" quality of the moment to produce the kind of positive affect, which in turn produces measurable benefits for health and happiness, that James describes in *The Varieties of Religious Experience*. However, this is not to say that the question of whether the "glowing" quality of the Beatles actually consisted of the emission of photons is not a valid one, just as the question of how many angels can fit on the head of a pin was a valid question to the medieval Christian scholastics. But it is not the correct question if one hopes to understand the experience of the people who participated in this phenomenon on their own terms, rather than imposing the rational, scientific mode on them as academia, and modernity generally, has so often done with groups projectively identified as "other," from ancient and primal cultures, to racially or socio-culturally marginalized groups in contemporary society.

However, as opposed to the relatively naive quality of most prerational religious belief, the Beatles and their audience generally maintained an essential distance from the mythogenetic narrativizing. For the fact that the Beatles are described as having been "slightly embarrassed" in the miraculous moment when their new suits were revealed demonstrates that they were still holding the pole of doubt within their circle of belief, which is a necessary corrective to the many evils that have been perpetrated in the name of unquestioned religious certainty over the centuries. As suggested above, collective human experience was bodying forth, through the catalyst of the Beatles, what appears to have been the beginnings of an integration between intuitive belief and rational skepticism. Although there were certainly philosophical precursors to this reconciliation, the sixties, as the temporal container for the Beatles phenomenon, was a primary moment in the emergence of this synthesis into collective awareness.[640]

Whereas the predominant modern cultural streams had come to construct this polarity as a choice between belief and skepticism, or between religion and science, the Beatles and many in their generation implicitly understood that these two qualities are not mutually exclusive, but complementary and deeply imbricated poles in a profound dialectical process. Academia, which might accurately be described as something like the secular priesthood of modernity in reaction to the previous priesthoods of premodernity, is only now beginning to become conscious of this knowledge that many outside the halls of institutional power have been articulating for decades, if not centuries. However, this is not to fault academia, but merely to recognize that an emergent world view cannot become explicit in a culture until the institutional guardians of that culture's highest knowledge are able to create forms of language that can viably articulate the new mode of thought, in this case what anyone who has ever enjoyed the ecstatic revelation of rock and roll knows intuitively.

Indeed, it seems that academics or priests, as the keepers of the deepest beliefs of their cultures, are usually among the last to be convinced of a new way of conceiving experience but that, when a sufficient number of these cultural guardians have been converted to a new mode of thought, a qualitatively novel epoch of human history has generally resulted, visible in the transition from the classical era to the Christian era as much as in the transition from the medieval to the modern. And at the core of these transitions, a mythic narrative invariably expresses the character of the transformation, in the stories of Jesus and his disciples as much as in the stories of Copernicus, Kepler, Galileo, Descartes, and Newton. It seems plausible to suggest that the Beatles will be considered by posterity as one of the primary characters in the transformational narrative currently in the process of composition.

Participating in the enactment of the Beatles' mythogenetic process in 1961, the newly formed *Mersey Beat* newspaper included an absurd story by Lennon entitled "A Short Diversion on the Dubious Origins of the Beatles"[641] in which a man descends on a "flaming pie" and pronounces that they shall be called "Beatles—*with an a*."[642] This pseudo-religious origin story is a parody of divine revelation that lets the audience in on the joke. The story seems to suggest that the Beatles are a genuinely religious phenomenon, but that one should not let on that one actually believes this, at least not without a wink and an enigmatic grin. This kind of double irony is what allowed the Beatles and their fans to walk the tightrope between belief and skepticism, a subtle layer of meaning that many in the old guard, having participated in the later stages of the necessary individuation of human intellect, were not equipped to comprehend. It was an inside joke for the young and the hip; a new kind of revelation which, like a gestalt picture or a "magic eye" 3-D image, one can only perceive if one looks in just the right way, not focusing too much on any one detail, but softening one's gaze to take in the whole picture, allowing what is genuinely present, though hidden in plain sight, to emerge.

Although new modes of thought are almost always criticized for this kind of "fuzzy logic," it is apparent that the specifics of an established cultural milieu are deeply informed by the beliefs that have been predominant for generations, while new modes have not yet had time to develop the particulars.[643] As mentioned above, "foolishness" appears to be an intrinsic component of novelty. Thus, a leap of faith is always required to enter into a new way of approaching reality. Copernicus, Kepler, and Galileo experienced a similar sort of resistance and condemnation in the sixteenth and seventeenth centuries to that experienced by Presley, the Beatles, and Dylan in the twentieth. The old paradigm, whatever it may be in whatever domain of activity, has always had a great deal of time explicitly to articulate the finer points of its approach, while the emerging mode must stumble in the dark, mapping out radically new territory and making things up as it goes. Thus, while many members of the generation that first thought of themselves in terms of a "counterculture" learned not to become anti-intellectual, but to put intellect aside when the intuitive mode is more appropriate to the particular needs of the situation, this mode of relation is still in the process of coming to consciousness in our cultural discourse, and particularly in academia.

As catalysts for this kind of fundamental cultural transformation, the Beatles were not content merely to conquer Britain; they felt that they were bound for international recognition. Once the group found success in England, they turned their sights to America, which they saw as a kind of "Promised Land." It is hardly necessary at this stage in the analysis to point out the religious imagery, which contains within it a yearning for the origin of the genre to which they were devoted. Having been so profoundly influenced by American rock and roll, it was the Beatles' explicit intention to bring their version of the music back to its place of inception, thereby performing a dialectical synthesis of the genre with its original incarnation. Epstein, having been "converted" by witnessing the Beatles at the Cavern, "shared their dream and persisted in his belief that an American tour should happen without delay,"[644] a passage that unintentionally provides a rather good definition of religion: the "persistence of belief" based on a shared "dream" or vision of reality. And, once they made it to America in 1964, as Gould writes of their performance on *The Ed Sullivan Show*, it was "a complete revelation,"[645] suggesting an initiatory fulfillment of the persistent belief of the Beatles, their manager, and their devotees.

"A Religion in Fact"

Of course, this persistence did not come without struggle, for on a three week tour with Roy Orbison in 1963, the Beatles relied on amphetamines to maintain their stamina, a stimulant to which the older American singer was similarly "devoted."[646] Although this reference to devotion by Orbison's biographer appears to be humorous, there seems to be an implicit subtext that the use of pills and other psychoactive substances by rock and roll musicians is often seen by the participants in the phenomenon as literally akin to the ritual ingestion of sacred medicines in many primal cultures, of which the Catholic sacrament is a distant echo. However, that these psychoactives took the form of little white pills, that is, distilled and concentrated, is more than a little problematic, as can be observed clearly in the case of Presley who was ultimately undone by addiction to prescription sedatives, amphetamines, and narcotics.

One effect of the Beatles' marginal outsider status is that their success transformed the North of England from a provincial backwater into what is consistently described as something like a holy place, a "Mecca" "conducive to the spirit of rock 'n roll." Indeed, the bare suggestion that "suddenly teenagers across the kingdom made a pilgrimage to the Cavern" could easily be taken from a medieval account of a saint or martyr, except for the fact that the concept of the "teenager" is a twentieth century invention. "It was 'Music City,' 'the Nashville of the North,' even '*Nashpool*,'" Spitz writes. And indeed, as with Nashville for country music, Liverpool had been collectively ordained as the new locus for the wave of cultural revolution that seemed to spring up, decade after decade, from city to city, back to the jazz of New Orleans, Harlem, and Kansas City, through the blues of Tupelo and Chicago, the country music of Bristol and Nashville, the rock and roll of Memphis, and the folk music of Greenwich Village. The qualities of these places pervade the musical styles that have emerged from them and provide a focus of attention for people endlessly hungry for revelation, for a physical person or group, as well as a physical place, on which to hang their yearnings for transcendence. In a sense, each of these cities, and the many more both before and after, were somehow designated, for reasons that remain opaque, as the focus of collective attention. Vienna at the turn of the twentieth century was a focus for psychoanalysis just as Seattle was the focus of grunge nearly a century later.[647]

Thus, although the Beatles were a primary catalyst in the metamorphosis of their culture, they did not seem to be causing the rising tide that lifted all ships. In the first meeting between the Beatles and the

Rolling Stones in 1963: "There were already signs of a musical undertow that was pulling uniquely talented and expressive youths into the onrushing tide of change."[648] Like a tea-kettle that climaxes in a change of state as it comes to a boiling point, or like the crest of a wave, the Beatles and the Stones were carried by a vital impulse toward novelty, a quality of the moment that these young men embodied in a way that seems to have come from something surpassing their individuality. Yet again, through rhetorical analysis, one can discern agency assigned not to the primary actors in the process, but to the process itself. In the most spontaneous of manners, a profound transformation of culture was occurring through the Beatles and their contemporaries. And as the momentum built, their exponentially expanding audience directed an unprecedented amount of energy and attention toward the band. For the "fanatics" who merely wanted to touch them or be in their presence, the Beatles radiated an undeniable numinosity. The mostly female Beatles fans who came to scream at their concerts "were engaged primarily in an act of ritualistic confirmation," suggesting a spontaneous mass participatory religious rite with the capacity to produce ecstatic transformation through belief in the numinous power of these four young men.

As in the conversion experiences that James describes in *The Varieties of Religious Experience*, though on a collective scale, "in the miraculous year"[649] of 1963, strikingly echoing what Daniel Mark Epstein refers to as Dylan's "annus mirabilis"[650] during that same year: "Suddenly everything the Beatles did resonated with meaning."[651] The surging mass belief in the spiritual significance of the Beatles impelled the renewal of the world that they inhabited as surely as if they were the embodiment of a new force of nature not yet described by physics. Indeed, this suggestion may not be far from the truth for, as Bergson understood, the vital impulse toward novelty appears to constitute a teleological trajectory intrinsic to the nature of process, which exceeds the ability of physical science, as it has predominately been conceived in the twentieth century, to comprehend: "At a certain moment, in certain points of space, a visible current has taken rise; this current of life, traversing the bodies it has organized one after another, passing from generation to generation, has become divided amongst species and distributed amongst individuals without losing anything of its force, rather intensifying in proportion to its advance."[652] Indeed, this last word suggests Whitehead's related statement that "'becoming' is a creative advance into novelty."[653] As discussed above, the response to the Beatles, particularly in their unprecedentedly massive live performances in the mid-sixties, was often described as a titanic force of nature surging through the host of humanity participating in the phenomenon of Beatlemania. In light of the insight articulated in different inflections by Bergson and Whitehead, these descriptions appear to reach beyond mere metaphor to express the coming to awareness of a previously concealed quality of reality.

Ultimately, the Beatles were enacting a narrative that was experienced by many who participated in it, particularly the Beatles themselves, as an autonomous process impelling them to ever greater heights of both artistic achievement and mania. According to one journalist: "It was *exactly* the story we'd been waiting for." And according to another journalist writing in mid-1964: "They have become a religion in fact. The days of their ministry on earth seem to be over— they don't seem to perform so much—and they have been taken up into heaven preferring to conserve the Holy Quaternity in a delicious incommunicado. All over the place though there are icons, devotional photos and illuminated missals which keep the tiny earthbound fans in touch with the provocatively absconded deities."[654] As if in expectation of a messianic dispensation, the press and audience, their genuinely religious passion overflowing the capability of ironic containment, were searching for someone to embody and express their deepest yearnings for revelation.

The descriptive language consistently employed in describing Beatlemania, encapsulated in a phrase like "pandemonium on the sidewalk,"[655] evokes religious passion at its wildest and most extreme, not least recalling the maenads of the Dionysian cult in ancient Greece, female fanatics who would achieve ecstasy through intoxication and dancing and, in the case of Euripides' *Bacchae*, hunting down and killing a king in their divine frenzy. The Beatles had little agency in the process occurring around them, as Beatlemania appears to have emerged of its own volition, no single person or group possessing the power to manufacture such a response. Rather, this phenomenon seems to have been the spontaneous expression of a new way of feeling and acting within the ritualized setting of the Beatles' concerts so that, in an incredibly short time, the transgressively ecstatic behavior became the norm.

At a 1964 concert in the UK after their return from America, according to *Melody Maker*: "A move by any Beatle in any direction induced renewed and more piercing cries,"[656] while according to the *New York Times*, Lennon, at one point so frustrated with the impossibility of anyone hearing the actual music, "looked the audience sternly in the mouth and yelled, 'Shut up!'"[657] However, this admonition did nothing to contain the crowd's enthusiasm. The Beatles and their audience were seemingly being carried by a momentum that transcended any individual participant so that the four young men from Liverpool found it necessary either to ride the wave or get off, so to speak. The Beatles were catalysts for the unconscious drive of their audience to undergo a self-transformation in the fundamental way they were relating to experience.

The "exhilarating," unstoppable "spiritual anarchy" of the shows impelled the eruption of ecstatic affect on a scale never before achieved, and the Beatles' music was the catalyst for this mass coming to consciousness of that which had been rendered discursively unconscious. Despite the Beatles' inability to control the phenomenon of which they were the focus, as the momentum grew, there was increasingly a sense that they possessed the kind of spiritual force usually attributed to prophets, saints, and shamans, "as if they gave off some special juju, as if they would make everything all right, which, in a sense, they actually did." Here Spitz implicitly recognizes that even though there is an ironic, "as if" quality to the essentially religious adoration, the actual effect that the Beatles had on their audience, and on the culture at large, appears by many accounts to have been experienced as psychologically healing, enacting a reintegration of modernity's primal wound, the split between subject and object, and between mind and body.

"Some Non-Congregational Opinions"

Although this reconciliation resulted in the collective emergence of something potent and numinous, the Beatles maintained their ironic posture even, or especially toward their own fame. This holding the pole of doubt within their encompassing belief, "tarrying with the negative" as Hegel articulated it, is what allowed the Beatles to work concretely, on a daily basis, "to keep the fantasy alive."[658] Although "fantasy" is a word, like "myth" or "magic," often trivialized in our era, the word itself does not contain this derogatory sense. Rather, "fantasy" etymologically means to "make visible" that which is invisible, which is strikingly close to the meaning of "revelation."[659] Indeed, there is no clearer evidence of the pervasive repression of formal and final causation in modern discourse than that the most basic words associated with these causal modes have taken on a veneer of triviality over the centuries of their use.

Nevertheless, the knowledge that the kind of revelatory "fantasy" in which the Beatles and their audience were immersed can disappear as suddenly as it appears impressed upon these young men the necessity of making the most of the moment, for as the title song of Harrison's first solo album declares: "All things must pass." Although the Beatles were fully engaged in the illuminating efflorescence of their own "sunrise," they instinctively knew that it could not last forever, and this knowledge is paradoxically what impelled them to create a narrative through their lives and their music that has, in fact, lasted for more than half a century and shows no sign of abating. If anything, perhaps aside from a brief backlash associated with punk rock in the late seventies and early eighties, the mythos of the Beatles seems to grow in stature every year.

Furthermore, as with any religion worthy of the name, the Beatles have their dissident devotees. In a passage that obliquely demonstrates the veracity of the phenomenon, Ian MacDonald writes: "As for the American mainstream audience, in both its published commentaries and fan effusion The Beatles are worshipped and every fragment of their output treated as sacred." He continues: "Some American 'Beatleologists' sustain lifetime careers based on minute scrutinies of The Work," including "biblical concordances of the group's lyrics, syllable by syllable. In as much as *Revolution in the Head* voices some non-congregational opinions, such pietists may deem it blasphemously iconoclastic." By parodying the spiritual quality so often attributed to the group about which he cared enough to write a rather good book, MacDonald backhandedly bolsters the notion that the Beatles really were an essentially religious phenomenon, his sardonic diatribe reminiscent of screeds by atheists who feel so strongly about the religion they are rejecting that they are compelled to devote their life to its dismantling, but which ultimately serve to underscore the religion's continuing vitality. Of course, MacDonald is not in fact an atheist of the Beatle religion, but a "protestant" reformer. Indeed, referring to the phenomenon he calls "instantaneity," which seems to be a negative inflection of Bergsonian duration, MacDonald derides "the chanting of" the "magic word" "NOW" "at demonstrations" in the sixties. Nevertheless, MacDonald recognizes that "The Beatles' faith in instantaneity produced marvelous (if occasionally monstrous) results,"[660] grudgingly admitting that the Beatles' belief in the mode that consciously attends to the felt quality of temporal experience was a primary precondition for the creation of their art, of which he is clearly a great admirer.

"A Separate Society"

By 1964, the group had become a primary focus of international attention so that, as with many of the brief fads and fascinations that successively capture the interest of the public, the Beatles were elevated to the status of cultural obsession. However, unlike most of the phenomena that come to dominate the media for a few days or a few weeks, the Beatles managed to maintain a consistently central role for the better part of a decade, and even at various moments after they disbanded at the end of the sixties. Such a phenomenon is still largely unmatched, as the Beatles were prime exemplars of a revolution in consciousness that continues to condition many of our aesthetic, intellectual, and experiential possibilities in the twenty-first century. And according to Spitz, the Beatles were "connected to a growing disenchantment with the establishment," his employment of the term "disenchantment" echoing Max Weber's, though in the precisely opposite context. Where modernity had been a long process of epistemological disenchantment, the countercultural rebellion of the sixties embodied a disenchantment with the very disenchanted epistemology that had resulted from the privileging of intellect since the Enlightenment. Much like the phenomenon of double irony, this "double disenchantment" produced not merely a return to premodern enchantment, but rather a dialectical reembrace of formal and final causation by rational materialism.[661]

And there was no greater exemplar of the counterculture than the Beatles. According to journalist Nik Cohn, writing about the band's influence on fashion, which, along with music, is one of the most affectively motivated human endeavors: "I can't overpitch this. . . . The Beatles changed everything. Before them, all teenage life and, therefore, fashion, existed in spasms; after them, it was an entity, a separate society."[662] The language that Cohn employs here sounds like nothing so much as the vocabulary of birth: the "spasms" issuing into "an entity, a separate society," an emergent organism. Similarly, Mark Lewisohn describes the Beatles' break with early promoter Sam Leach after the release of "Love Me Do" as "symbolic of severing an umbilical cord."[663] In this context, Richard Tarnas' articulation of the dialectical evolution of process as an archetypal reiteration of birth, "itself an expression of a larger underlying archetypal process that can manifest in many dimensions," is profoundly illuminating. In the case of the sixties counterculture, largely consisting of young people, the Beatles mediated the birth of a new form of being in a process that seems to be a fractal reiteration of the same archetypal process that manifests in biological birth. Like birth, the physical and material circumstances of culture brought forth the emergence of a new form of consciousness, still nascent, but not reducible to the physical elements by which it can retroactively be analyzed. In a very real sense, then, the Beatles were midwives to the nascence of an emergent mode of being in the world, one that integrated two modes, roughly the premodern and the modern, that had previously been opposed and apparently incommensurable, in a *hieros gamos*, or "sacred marriage."[664]

Although the specific manifestation of the sixties counterculture would subsequently undergo a trivializing reaction, partially justified because of the intrinsic "foolishness" of "new ideas . . . when they are first produced," it seems that the sixties perhaps marked the first flowering of a novel epoch of human history, bringing to popular consciousness a qualitatively new mode of relation. Whitehead suggests that William James produced an initiatory declaration for this emerging mode of thought in the early twentieth century just as Rene Descartes had in the seventeenth century for the novel mode that would come to be called "modernity." It seems, then, that the nineteen sixties were the moment when the neo-archaic mode of approaching experience variously articulated in romanticism, idealism, pragmatism, radical empiricism, process philosophy, depth psychology, and other related schools of thought, achieved its first success on a mass scale, though still in a relatively naïve, unconscious way. And the birth of this new world view was enacted and embodied for many millions of people by the Beatles.[665]

CHAPTER 5
"AN EXTREME SENSE OF DESTINY"

Finalism is not, like mechanism, a doctrine with fixed rigid outlines. It admits of as many inflections as we like. The mechanistic philosophy is to be taken or left; it must be left if the least grain of dust, by straying from the path foreseen by mechanics should show the slightest trace of spontaneity. The doctrine of final causes, on the contrary, will never be definitively refuted. If one form of it be put aside, it will take another. Its principle, which is essentially psychological, is very flexible. It is so extensible, and thereby so comprehensive, that one accepts something of it as soon as one rejects pure mechanism.

Henri Bergson, *Creative Evolution*[666]

Both in the first volume of his memoir, *Chronicles,* and in interviews, Bob Dylan often refers to what he called, in 2001, "an extreme sense of destiny."[667] It is a fact not often explicitly acknowledged about Dylan that this teleological affect has been one of the primary driving impulses behind his music and the narratological trajectory it has performed. Dylan tried to do what he felt in each moment or, as he told Martin Scorsese in *No Direction Home*: "I couldn't relate to anything other than what I was doing at the present time,"[668] an approach that paradoxically allowed Dylan, in his conception, to sense the contours of what was to come, a capacity explicable through Aristotelian final causation. The way Dylan appears to have aligned himself with what he describes in numerous instances as "destiny" was to be present to the felt quality of experience, engaging in an activity that closely resembles the Zen Buddhist conception of "no mind" or other similar ecstatic mystical, contemplative, or yogic practices. As Dylan suggests in numerous instances, this focus on affective immediacy as a mode of teleological cognizance was his way of participating in something that seemed to him to exceed his volition.

"Something Metaphysical from a Bygone Era"

Dylan writes in *Chronicles* that poet Archibald MacLeish, who had served as Librarian of Congress during World War II, told Dylan that he had "seemingly inherited something metaphysical from a bygone era."

197

According to Dylan, MacLeish informed him that his "work would be a touchstone for generations after" him. Dylan recounts this conversation with the utterly unique humility of one who has been told since he was in his early twenties that he was the voice of his generation, a prophet, or even the messiah. This is an idea that Dylan has lived with for most of his life, and which he has explicitly denied many times, but which seems to keep surfacing in relation to him. Dylan, in his return to metaphysics such as those described by James, Jung, Bergson, and Whitehead, does in fact seem to be perceived by many as reenacting a role similar to those of ancient prophets, though apparently not by choice. Dylan writes:

> Eventually different anachronisms were thrust upon me—anachronisms of lesser dilemma—though they might seem bigger. Legend, Icon, Enigma (Buddha in European Clothes was my favorite)—stuff like that, but that was all right. These titles were placid and harmless, threadbare, easy to get around with them. Prophet, Messiah, Savior—those are tough ones.[669]

Nevertheless, as Daniel Mark Epstein describes a Dylan concert that he attended in 1963, Dylan "had made the prophecy, and we sealed the pact with our applause."[670] Whether Dylan liked it or not, his music was perceived as prophetic by a large portion of his audience—that is, there was something in his songs that seemed to point the way toward what was to come. Thus, it does not seem to be the case that Dylan had an explicit ambition to be a prophetic figure; his ambition was to be a musician, though he was certainly ambitious in this regard. However, there seems to have been something intrinsic in his character that has often been interpreted as prophetic, something transcending of him that seemed to be coursing through him beyond his control, forces of nature pushing for expression by means of his individuality.

Dylan and his associates seem to have understood what he was creating as an enactment of a mode of being that was not so much oriented toward who he was as a private person, but was the product of something beyond him searching for expression that he felt a duty to communicate to the world. As Bob Johnston, who produced *Highway 61 Revisited, Blonde on Blonde, John Wesley Harding, Nashville Skyline, Self Portrait,* and *New Morning,* exclaims in his jovial southern accent in Scorsese's documentary: "I believe in giving credit where credit's due. I don't think Dylan had a lot to do with it. I think, uh, God, instead of touching him on the shoulder, he kicked him in the ass. Really, and that's where all that came from. He can't help what he's doin'! I mean, he's got the Holy Spirit about him. You can look at him and tell that."[671] Johnston does not seem to be speaking metaphorically. Rather, he appears to be articulating a way of seeing the world that can be expressed in more or less subtle inflections, in this case in the somewhat conventional language of Southern, American Christianity. Although Johnston's is perhaps a more straightforwardly religious interpretation than some Dylan aficionados might prefer, it seems apparent that many participants in the phenomenon felt that Bob Dylan was driven to create by "whatever they may consider the divine."[672] As Dylan explicitly claims in "I and I" from 1984's *Infidels*, driven primarily by affect, an experiential domain generally associated with the "heart," Dylan felt that something other than himself was communicating through him.

At a press conference in December 1965, when asked, after first demurring: "You really have no thoughts on why you're popular?" Dylan answers: "I just haven't really struggled for that. I don't . . . it happened, you know? It happened like anything else happens."[673] Dylan's answer indicates that he did not feel that he ever intentionally sought fame, but rather that he simply did what he felt was right in each moment and was lifted to a place of cultural prominence by necessity. According to this view (perhaps expressed most succinctly by Bob Marley in a six-word aphorism in the last verse of "I Shot the Sheriff"), whatever happens is what was meant to happen because it is ultimately what happened, and to believe that something else might have taken place in the past is simply a delusion ungrounded in what actually occurred, for the world is driven by what is, not by what hypothetically might have been.

As in several instances above, though Dylan's statement might at first appear trivial, it contains the profound implication that he was not driven primarily by egoic concerns, but by the sense that something in the nature of process was directing him. Although one might suspect that Dylan's claim that he did not struggle for fame and fortune is a conceit, I am inclined to take him at his word, as it appears that the very quality which has set Dylan apart from others is that his ambitions were less worldly than spiritual, but that he somehow managed to attain the highest level of worldly success. Expressed another way, one of the primary reasons why Dylan was able to achieve what very few artists ever have is that his worldly ambitions were secondary to his more intangible aspirations, the instrumentality of material and efficient causation in service to his teleological visions explicable through final causation. Dylan certainly possessed an instinctual genius for social politics and power dynamics, knowing who to talk to, and how to talk to them, in order to facilitate his upward trajectory, but his explicit focus was predominantly on being somatically present to his affective "sense of destiny."

In an interview in Scorsese's documentary four decades after the 1965 press conference in San Francisco, Dylan is still thinking along the same lines, stating matter-of-factly that "I didn't really feel like I was taking a step forward anywhere. Things were taking its natural course."[674] Dylan felt that he was driven by necessity, letting his telos determine his path, which just happened to be exceptional. And in a similar vein, Dylan writes in *Chronicles* that even during a period when there was "a lot of halting and waiting, little acknowledgement, little affirmation . . . sometimes all it takes is a wink or a nod from some unexpected place to vary the tedium of a baffling existence,"[675] by which he seems to imply that, even through difficult times which have the affective quality of interminability, of being stuck or becalmed, the world gives subtle hints and signs to those who are receptive to such forms of communication indicating which direction one might go. Dylan seems to imply that the most pragmatic way to approach experience is to do all one can to elicit the desired reaction from circumstances, but to know that it is ultimately impossible to force the world to give what it is not prepared to manifest.

Dylan apparently believes that it is more efficacious to arrange oneself in preparation for a wave of novelty or inspiration should one come, and the world will either encourage one in the direction that one wishes to go or continually block one's aspirations, subtly and inexorably guiding one onto an alternate path. This is a similar sentiment to that expressed by Mick Jagger in the chorus of "You Can't Always Get What You Want,"[676] necessity often eclipsing desire. Dylan seems to have understood this insight on a profound level so that he was almost always prepared to heed the call when it arrived. However, it cannot be discounted that the call Dylan ultimately heard was a summons with which only a very few in any generation are privileged. As Dylan rather incongruously told *TV Guide* in 1976: "There's a mystic in all of us. . . . Some of us are shown more than others. Or maybe we're all shown the same things, but some make more use of it."[677] Thus, Dylan suggests that perhaps everyone receives what can be interpreted validly as synchronistic intimations from the cosmos (Jung's concept of synchronicity a modern inflection of formal causation), but that only a few are equipped with the intensity and subtlety of awareness to be able to perceive these signs amidst the din of life, and fewer still possess the perfect constellation of qualities, courage and persistence first among them, to bring these signs into collective consciousness.

"Making It Come Alive"

Whatever the ontological status of these signs, Dylan began to perceive them at a young age. In *Chronicles*, he describes a scene from his youth in Hibbing that is a primary example of the relational mode that Dylan would consistently enact throughout his life. A famous wrestler named Gorgeous George had a match in Hibbing when Dylan was still in High School, and Dylan had somehow convinced the organizers to let him play some songs in the lobby of the Veterans Memorial Building where the match was taking place. Dylan was strumming and singing on a small stage as "the doors burst open and in came Gorgeous George himself." As Dylan describes it, the wrestler "roared in like the storm, didn't go through the backstage area, he came right through the lobby of the building and he seemed like forty men. It was Gorgeous George, in all his magnificent glory with all the lightning and vitality you'd expect." Dylan continued to play as "George brushed by the makeshift stage and glanced toward the sound of the music. He didn't break stride, but he looked at me, eyes flashing with moonshine. He winked and seemed to mouth the phrase 'You're making it come alive,'" though Dylan could not be sure.

However, Dylan explains: "Whether he really said it or not, it didn't matter. It's what I thought I heard him say that mattered, and I never forgot it." The young Dylan, not focused on fame or fortune, but on "doing the thing for the thing's sake," felt that Gorgeous George, a man whom he clearly admired, "a mighty spirit" who seemed to radiate a powerful, elemental energy and charisma, had somehow given the young singer his benediction in that moment. Though working in very different performative realms, Dylan apparently felt that George and he were two of a kind, both men who had a particular gift for feeling the affective tone of a room and amplifying that felt intensity through their performance, or by their very presence.

A teenager at the time of this encounter, Dylan was still in the process of finding his artistic voice and developing his skill as a performer. Even though "no one was paying much attention" to Dylan, or at least it seemed that way to the young singer, George appears immediately to have recognized where the perhaps implicit focus of attention in the room was, saying just the right thing to bring the young singer on the makeshift stage into George's realm of influence, lifting Dylan out of his current milieu. As Dylan seems to have experienced it, George was giving him affirmation that the aspiring singer could participate in loftier realms of culture than those to which he was accustomed. Although Dylan is uncertain whether George actually said that he was "making it come alive," it did not matter to him because this phrase captures the affective tone of what George seemed to be communicating by his very presence: vitality, confidence, optimism.

The precise words that George said to Dylan seem to him beside the point because George simply noticing Dylan, turning the attention of his enchanted "moonshine" eyes toward the singer communicated volumes to the young man hungry for validation from someone that he admired. As with Brian Epstein's claim that the Beatles "actually glowed," from Dylan's perspective, it is not particularly important whether he had interpreted George's words correctly, or even if George intended anything at all toward Dylan. The significant fact is that a man who had apparently developed his intuitive faculties to a high degree recognized Dylan in a crowded room enough to turn his attention toward him for a brief moment, and Dylan interpreted this as "all the recognition and encouragement I would need for years to come."[678] Had Dylan been of a different disposition, he might have interpreted George's look as simply a meaningless glance or even as a disapproving glare, but there was something in Dylan that elicited positive signs and portents from his experience, and the only evidence required of the reality of these portentous intimations is that they presaged what ultimately came to pass.

As William James writes in *The Will to Believe*: "Often enough our faith beforehand in an uncertified result *is the only thing that makes the result come true*. . . . Faith creates its own verification."[679] In a 1978 interview, Dylan corroborates James' view, recognizing that "faith" is the result of affect: "People will always believe in something if they feel it to be true. Just knowing it's true is not enough. If you feel in your gut that it's true, well, then, you can be pretty much assured that it's true."[680] However, this "gut feel" has always apparently been mediated by Dylan's intrinsic skepticism, no less a commentator than President Barack Obama having once pointed out this quality in Dylan, saying: "That's how you want Bob Dylan, right? . . . You don't want him to be all cheesin' and grinnin' with you. You want him to be a little skeptical about the whole enterprise."[681] Nevertheless, Dylan seems to be skeptical only in relation to activities and interpretations that would lead him away from what he perceives as his teleological trajectory. Had Dylan not consistently interpreted events based on this felt sense of destiny, he probably would not have been able to make such great music, as this mentality has always apparently been central to Dylan's approach to his art.

"Guthrie's Greatest Disciple"

As a child, Dylan, like the Beatles, related to the radio as gospel, as an explicitly spiritual medium. He writes: "back then when something was wrong the radio could lay hands on you and you'd be all right."[682] Like the revivalist preacher that this passage evokes, radio itself seems to have had a healing and transformative effect on Dylan. That Dylan here briefly ascribes agency to the medium rather than the disc jockey, or even to the recording artists (though he would do this to a far greater extent), perhaps suggests an implicit recognition that technologies, to use a somewhat antiquated phrase from Marshall McLuhan, constitute "the extensions of man,"[683] so that the very medium of radio has the potential to be psychologically healing.

However, perhaps contrary to McLuhan's conception of media, this healing capacity seems to depend largely on the content that the radio conveys, both "medium" and "message" playing equally important roles in the propagation of meaning. Regardless, Dylan goes to great lengths in articulating his debt to the artists who primarily formed the mythical pantheon of his youth. And not only was the radio healing, but, as Epstein writes: "Beyond the golden glow of the radio dial, a boy on the edge of dreams could envision all of America, all of history, and glimpse something of the future."[684] Indeed, Dylan's deep engagement with radio was a primary meditative technique through which Dylan developed what many commentators apparently consider to be a genuinely prophetic capacity.

During Dylan's effusive and insightful account of his discovery of Guthrie, in two successive sentences, almost in the same breath, Dylan declares that he "decided" to sing only Guthrie songs and then claims that "it's almost like I didn't have any choice," two seemingly contradictory statements that perfectly encapsulate the paradoxical complexity of final causation. In the affective and intuitive domains of his experience, Dylan felt compelled by something that exceeded his individuality, something in the nature of process, temporarily to become Guthrie, though in the domain of intellectual, egoic consciousness, Dylan chose to follow this compulsion, consciously aligning the different domains of his experience in order to allow what might be described as the self-transcending vital impulse of being to work through him.

However, he could have reasonably denied this impulse, producing in himself a divided consciousness that most likely would have paralyzed him in neurosis, or at least kept him from creating the music that he did. However, though this denial of affective knowledge is a common enough pathology, it is a testament to Dylan's exceptional character that he only rarely seems to have fallen into such cognitive dissonance, at least during his more productive periods. And indeed, by becoming "Guthrie's greatest disciple," as he puts it, Dylan chose the older singer as a mentor through whose "compositions my view of the world was coming sharply into focus," an emergent mode of consciousness perhaps definable by the integration of disparate epistemologies.

Guthrie's most famous song, for instance, "This Land is Your Land," expresses the sentiment that America is a place where many different ways of seeing the world can coexist in harmony, embodied in the juxtaposition of geographical and spatial opposites ("the New York island" and "the redwood forests," "the ribbon of highway" and the "endless skyway"), all permeated by "a voice," which suggests a volitional impulse in the nature of being toward the increasing unity of opposites. That Dylan felt "related to him," and that Guthrie "looked not unlike" Dylan's father suggests Dylan's almost complete identification with the older singer as a means of incorporating the mode that Guthrie had embodied into Dylan's own persona. Dylan seems to have sensed himself being lured toward becoming Guthrie's successor, for he "felt like Guthrie was saying, 'I'll be going away, but I'm leaving this job in your hands. I know I can count on you.'"[685] Of course, Dylan did in fact turn out to be Guthrie's heir, even developing a close personal relationship with his mentor as Guthrie lay dying of Huntington's disease in a psychiatric hospital in New Jersey. Thus, whether real prophecy or self-fulfilling prophecy, the prophecy was fulfilled, and that Dylan felt this trajectory as a kind of compulsion, as exceeding his conscious will, perhaps suggests that this "pinch of destiny" (to employ William James' phrase) was more than mere wish-fulfillment. Dylan certainly appears to have seen it this way.

A comment that Allen Ginsberg once made about prophecy seems to resonate with Dylan's view of the subject: "What prophecy actually is, is not knowing whether the bomb will fall in 1942. It's knowing and feeling something which someone knows and feels in a hundred years and maybe articulating it in a hint that they will pick up on in a hundred years."[686] Thus, prophecy and final causation are intimately connected, as prophecy is the concrete expression of a "sense of destiny," of a feeling for what is to come. Although it was only a decade or two between the peak of Guthrie's career and the beginning of Dylan's, Ginsberg's formulation seems precisely applicable to the way Dylan describes the relationship between his music and Guthrie's. One might even suspect that, as close friends, Dylan and Ginsberg may have discussed the subject, which seems to have held a powerful fascination for them both. Thus, not only did Dylan feel that he was destined to become Guthrie's successor, but that Guthrie's songs themselves were prophetic, for although "a lot of folks might have thought of Woody's songs as backdated, . . . I felt they were totally in the moment, current and even forecasted things to come."

As demonstrated above, Dylan saw folk music as the repository of premodern modes of consciousness, but these modes are not limited to attention to intuitive bodily experience, as affective awareness appears to provide access to the even more deeply repressed modes of thought characteristic of formal and final causation. Dylan's statement that "with Guthrie's songs my heart and mind had been sent into another cosmological place of that culture entirely" suggests that Dylan sees the shift which, for him, was exemplified in Guthrie's music, and more generally in folk music, as a literal shift in his cosmology, a shift that occurred in both "heart and mind," both affectively and intellectually. It appears Dylan felt that Guthrie's songs "forecasted things to come," including an epochal shift in consciousness accompanied by an equally epochal cosmological shift, implicitly constituted in the reembrace of formal and final causation alongside material and efficient causation, partially embodied in Dylan's own succession to the archetypal role previously inhabited by Guthrie, whose songs made Dylan feel personally lifted to the status of "honorable knight," a holy warrior of a new dispensation.[687]

Perhaps this sense of election partially resulted from Dylan discovering in Guthrie a singing model that suited his particular vocal peculiarities, as Dylan and Guthrie certainly had similar sounding voices, though Dylan seems to believe that Guthrie implicitly prophesied the coming of a successor who would carry his message to the world. As William James understood, any mode of thought presupposes certain premises, and these premises constitute the "over-beliefs" that James says are "the most interesting and valuable things about a man."[688] Dylan's over-belief, in this case, is his intrinsic feeling that Guthrie's music was prophetic of Dylan's own rise, and it is hard to argue with genuine greatness, for only a very few people know how far outside of conventional ways of thinking it has been necessary for Dylan to venture in order to create music that is almost universally acclaimed, and that ultimately fulfilled Dylan's intimation of his future self.

As James, Bergson, and Whitehead all suggest in different inflections, there is nothing in science that precludes the validity of belief in final causation. Rather, science itself is another kind of over-belief—the ultimately irrational, and circular, privileging of rationality, often to the denigration of other modes of explanation—that formed the background against which a young Jewish boy from Hibbing, Minnesota became one of the greatest artists of all time, a man who it does not seem strange to mention in the same breath as Homer, Dante, and Shakespeare, all of who seem to have given credence to final causation in some form.

"Somebody Holds the Mirror Up"

During his early days in New York, Dylan was drawn toward the Gaslight, the most prestigious of New York folk clubs. Indeed, as he describes the situation, it was not particularly a matter of desire for, in a similar operation to the passage explicated above, he uses the word "want" only to correct himself, saying that he "needed" to play and that he "had no choice." Dylan at this moment seems to have felt as if he was in the grip of a force beyond his control. His individual needs and will were of a secondary nature, though it is characteristic of Dylan that his personal desire and the impersonal necessity that he felt driving him were closely aligned during this period. [689]

Similarly, it seems to be no accident that Dylan's character in the 2003 film, *Masked and Anonymous*, which Dylan both wrote and starred in, is named "Jack Fate." As with nearly all of his utterances, there are layers of complex significance that seem to have led Dylan to this name. Starting with *Love and Theft* in 2001, Dylan began to produce his own albums under the alias "Jack Frost," a direct reference to Santa Claus, whom Dylan, at the end of the 2009 video for "Must Be Santa,"[690] stands next to in a Santa hat with a barely discernible smirk as if to indicate that Bob Dylan is just as mythical a being as old Saint Nick.

Indeed, as Clinton Heylin relates in his biography of Dylan: "At a 1986 press conference a middle-aged, slightly wizened rock 'n' roller insisted, 'I'm only Bob Dylan when I have to be.' Asked who he was the rest of the time, he replied, 'Myself.'"[691] Dylan implicitly seems to recognize that his "fate"[692] is to be a focus for the evolutionary movement of his culture. Indeed, his perception of this situation as fate, rather than anything intrinsically wonderful about him, demonstrates Dylan's understanding that the vast amount of attention focused on him is not primarily concerned with who he is when he is at home, so to speak, but about the role that he plays in the larger culture. As Dylan makes clear, this fate has proven both a blessing and a curse.

In 1961, further confirmation of Dylan's election seemed to come when he was called upon to play at a recording session for Harry Belafonte's *Midnight Special*. In a similar situation to Dylan's encounter with Gorgeous George, though perhaps with rather more justification, Dylan interpreted being chosen to play with Belafonte as the famous folksinger having "anointed" him. Like the aspiring mystic he seems to have explicitly seen himself as, Dylan required the occasional blessings of mentors to help elevate him to the role toward which he felt teleologically drawn. And similarly to his experience with the wrestler a few years earlier, Dylan felt that Belafonte's titanic "greatness" would "rub off" on him. Judging by the results, Dylan may have been correct.[693]

Searching for a way to express the "more brilliant dimension" that "lies behind the misty curtain," Dylan seems to have felt that a qualitatively new way of approaching experience was pushing for expression of its own volition through him. In a passage that is essentially and profoundly philosophical, Dylan explains that he could "feel" that things were "going to change" at that moment in the early sixties, though he did not "know it in a purposeful way," which seems to indicate that he was not fully conscious of the thing he felt emerging, that he did not intend to mediate it. The emergent entity seems to have chosen him as a medium, the teleological "purpose" originating from something outside him rather than from his personal intentionality.

As in Dylan's encounter with Gorgeous George, "little things foreshadow what's coming but you may not recognize them," which is to say that one must possess an exceptional awareness and receptivity to what amount to signs and portents, as Dylan did, to perceive them and thus help bring them to fruition. And as Dylan understood, this foreshadowing leads inevitably to a radical "jump" into "another world," an "unknown" world in which "you're set free," the moment of liberating rupture that many yearn for, the release exemplified in conversion, revolution, revelation, epiphany, and the relatively sudden shift between historical eras. Whitehead appears to be describing the same kind of rupture as Dylan when he writes in a previously employed passage: "New epochs emerge with comparative suddenness."[694]

However, as Dylan also recognizes, although such turning points seem sudden, "like magic" in comparison to the relatively vast temporal spans of linear, continuous equilibrium that they punctuate, one inflection of which Thomas Kuhn refers to as "normal science,"[695] these changes of state actually happen much like sunrise or sunset, or the changing of the seasons, or the beginning of a rainstorm, or the boiling or freezing of water. The change is quick; it feels immediate in relation to the quality of time that surrounds it, but it is in fact a gradual and inexorable natural phenomenon. It is a radical compaction of temporality, the eye of the needle. And although these kinds of transformations seem to be an inevitable part of process, Dylan also understands that they are almost always set off by some catalyst; a primed system reaches a tipping point and the whole pattern reorganizes itself on an emergent systemic level, as in the "scientific revolutions" that form the complement to Kuhn's "normal science."

As Dylan describes what seems to be a personal revolution in consciousness that "reflects" a collective revolution occurring at that moment: "Somebody holds the mirror up, unlocks the door—something jerks it open and you're shoved in and your head has to go into a different place."[696] It is not a matter of volition: Something occurs, either subtle or overt, that forces one to become conscious of something that had previously been unconscious, or opens a path that had previously been blocked. And Dylan is certainly one of the most qualified people to talk about this kind of transformative experience because he seems to have undergone it so intensely and completely, and in such a public way, more than just about anyone else now living.

Dylan appears to have known that in order to undergo such dramatic transformations, as when witnessing Mike Seeger performing impelled Dylan to start writing songs in earnest, he would have to give up the comfort of a "normal" life and the stability of a relatively fixed identity. In his 2004 interview for *60 Minutes,* Dylan describes this trade-off as a deal with the divine: "It goes back to that destiny thing. I made the bargain with it a long time ago and I'm holding up my end." When asked who he made the bargain with, Dylan replies, with "the chief commander . . . on this earth and in the world we can't see."[697] Dylan knew that in order to create something profoundly new, he would have to remove himself further from the normative existence exemplified by his parents, and even from the life of his contemporaries in the folk community, a life that he would seem to yearn for periodically over the ensuing decades. Somehow, perhaps only in retrospect, he understood that submitting to his destiny as a songwriter would make it impossible for him ever to go back to being merely a face in the crowd. Even then, he apparently recognized that by submitting to his felt telos, he was accepting the election of forces that exceeded him, an apparently exalted role, but one that also carried a great burden, the paradoxical weight of complete freedom "from all the chains."[698]

"You Have to Believe"

As Dylan describes the moment just before he recorded his first album when he was completely immersed in the folk music scene in Greenwich Village, he saw his future spread out before him, "heading for the fantastic lights. No doubt about it." A kernel of skepticism entered into his mind, but it was quickly banished because he knew that he was not one prone to being deluded, and what would be the point of entertaining such doubt anyway? It could only have inhibited his momentum. He had "no false hope," as he puts it, but he felt that "destiny was about to manifest itself." Thus, Dylan is one of those extremely rare visionaries who can not only see the way things must go, but is also deeply in touch with the way things are and have been. With exceptional self-awareness, he was betting that it was "not likely" that he was imagining his grand destiny, for he could see it: he felt it "looking right at me and nobody else," which indicates an affective knowledge that he was chosen for great things by something volitional in the nature of process.[699]

As Dylan explains in his 2012 *Rolling Stone* interview:

> Some people are called to be a good sailor. Some people have a calling to be a good tiller of the land. Some people are called to be a good friend. You have to be the best at whatever you are called at. Whatever you do. You ought to be the best at it—highly skilled. It's about confidence, not arrogance. You have to know that you're the best whether anybody else tells you that or not. And that you'll be around, in one way or another, longer than anybody else. Somewhere inside of you, you have to believe that.[700]

However, as Dylan implies on numerous occasions, this belief cannot result solely from the desire to believe or from making a conscious decision to believe. Rather, one's destiny and one's belief are apparently coextensive, for it is impossible willfully to produce belief in one's destination, though one can perhaps seek out experiences that transform one's belief. But then one's destiny is to seek out those transformative experiences, which again leads inexorably to the conclusion that one cannot control the wave of one's telos, only ride that wave with varying degrees of skill and awareness. As mentioned in an earlier chapter, Dylan writes: "I had a feeling of destiny and I was riding the changes," which seems to indicate that submitting to one's felt trajectory, the qualitative impulse flowing through temporality that exceeds conscious volition, allows one to become identical with that felt impulsion at the core of one's being, to "become one with the wave" as only the best surfers do.

As Dylan found his songwriting voice, even before he became a recording artist, he began to turn his sights on the next character in his narrative trajectory. As he writes, if Ramblin' Jack Elliott was the "King of the Folksingers," the "Queen of Folksingers" was Joan Baez. In retrospect, Dylan can see that his and Baez's "futures would be linked," though there was no material evidence for this "preposterous" supposition when Dylan was still an unsigned and unrecorded aspiring folksinger. Nevertheless, in the ecstatic experience of seeing Baez perform on television, which Dylan claims made him "high," he felt compelled to watch her "like a religious icon" drawing Dylan toward what he perceived as his parallel destiny to his female "counterpart." Although logically, the fact that they were the same age and that she was successful while he toiled in obscurity "almost made [Dylan] feel useless," "something" "illogical" "told" Dylan that, despite "nothing but distance and worlds and big divides between" them, they "would inevitably meet up."

Yet again, Dylan intuitively received a communication that seemed to originate externally to his own egoic consciousness informing him that he and Baez were destined to "find perfect harmony," which proved to be an accurate vision of the future.[701] Dylan chose of his own free will to accept the reality of this feeling, which allowed him to participate in the events that he sensed just over the temporal horizon. Thus, it should be emphasized that this is not a fatalistic view, in the sense that it precludes free will, for Dylan could just as easily have decided to ignore this intimation. As he asserts in his 2012 interview: "Some people never really develop into who they're supposed to be. They get cut off. They go off another way. It happens a lot."[702] Thus, the kind of destiny that Dylan seems to entertain is one in which final causation and free will co-creatively enact the ingression of novelty into actuality. And as he notes, this co-creation requires credence, for "you have to believe. Folk music, if nothing else, makes a believer out of you."[703]

"Goin' Home Somewhere"

As Dylan describes his process of becoming, one gets the sense that he did not merely encounter artists and musical styles that he loved, learning these styles and incorporating them into his own style, which is the normal mode of explanation based on efficient causation. Although this explanatory mode is partially accurate, it does not acknowledge the fact that Dylan was drawn to these musical elements in the first place because he felt they embodied a submerged part of himself that could be opened up through deep engagement with these forms of music. Thus, not only was Dylan pushed from behind, but he seems to have felt even more strongly that he was drawn toward his future self by following his intuitive sense of what belonged to him, like the child who demonstrates that he is the new Dalai Lama by intuitively choosing the sacred objects possessed by his previous incarnation. As with this child, Dylan was in the process of acquiring the tools to bring his intrinsic potentiality to full manifestation.

The self that Dylan sensed ahead of him constituted the final cause for his trajectory through temporality. From this perspective, Dylan was impelled forward by his future perhaps even more than his past, for as he says at the beginning of Scorsese's documentary:

> I had ambitions to set out and find, like an odyssey, goin' home somewhere, I'm set out to find this home that I'd left a while back and couldn't remember exactly where it was but I was on my way there. And encountering what I encountered on the way was how I envisioned it all. I didn't really have any ambition at all. . . . I was born very far from where I was supposed to be, so I'm on my way home, you know.[704]

Like Odysseus, Dylan was impelled by forces that transcended him to embark on a vast and far-reaching journey to the limits of human experience, "encountering" many perils along the way, including the outwitting of many adversaries and the descent into the underworld of repressed epistemologies. But he felt that his ultimate trajectory was to undergo all of these experiences in order to return "home" transformed, to enact a dialectical process of becoming in order to create a mythic narrative with the power to sustain subsequent generations. In this sense, Dylan was both Odysseus and Homer, the bard singing of his own internal adventures into the heights and depths of being, driven by necessity more than ambition.

As Dylan explains in his *60 Minutes* interview, destiny is "a feeling you have that you know something about yourself. Nobody else does. The picture you have in your mind of what you're about will come true. It's kind of a thing you kind of have to keep to your own self, because it's a fragile feeling. And if you put it out there, somebody will kill it. So, it's best to keep that all inside."[705] Ultimately, only individuals can know if they feel the pull of final causation, and certainly many do not, at least consciously. However, for those that do feel this pull, Dylan thinks that it is necessary to protect and cultivate this affective knowledge if one wants to act upon its domain of validity. That Dylan felt "an extreme sense of destiny," and that this feeling was fulfilled again and again, suggests that he has engaged in a phenomenological empiricism radically open to all modes of explanation without preconceived assumptions about the nature of being in the world. This radical empiricism led Dylan to embrace an emergent way of relating to experience that consciously decides, based on the rational modes characteristic of material and efficient causation, temporarily to put mind aside to enter deeply into the intuitive modes characteristic of premodernity, which seem to offer access to the direct perception of formal and final causation.

Ruminating on Robert Johnson, one of his most prominent influences, Dylan discusses the confluence of factors apparently pushed by a processual impulse toward synthesis within the young folksinger. In this passage, Dylan's reference to the "strange . . . way circles hook up with themselves" seems closely related to the issues of causation and qualitative temporality that appear to form the core of his internal process. And for Dylan, the uncanny quality that he perceives in Johnson is somehow connected to Arthur Rimbaud's phrase, "Je est un autre," translated by Dylan as "I is someone else," which "made perfect sense" to him.[706] The explanation for Dylan's art seems to have lain for him in both future and past, both final and efficient causation. In his experience, one thing led to another, but events were led by "an other," Dylan's future self, as a more literal translation of Rimbaud's phrase is "I is an other," which suggests that Dylan is never quite identical with himself, that his true identity is somewhere out there in the hazy distance and he is passing through many partial incarnations eventually to become the fullness of the potentiality implicit in the concrescence that calls itself Bob Dylan.

As he would definitively declare in 1978: "In order to free himself, to be reborn," a man "has to go outside himself." And, as Dylan describes it, rock and roll is an ideal vehicle for this self-transcending rebirth, which, like a mirror, allows one to see oneself from the outside. When asked what it means when a character from Dylan's 1978 film, *Renaldo and Clara*, declares that "Rock 'n' roll is the answer," Dylan replies: "He's speaking of the sound and the rhythm. The drums and the rhythm are the answer. Get into the rhythm of it and you will lose yourself; you will forget about the brutality of it all. Then you will lose your identity."[707] For Dylan, this liberating movement outside oneself, this becoming other than oneself, is achieved through ecstatic affect.

"The New Worldview"

According to Dylan and those close to him, the qualities of radical difference and foresight through ecstatic experience are characteristic of the primal shamans whose mode of thought Dylan seems spontaneously to have reenacted. Unlike many in the culture that had implicitly privileged intellect over affect, Dylan possessed an exceptional intrinsic capacity, which he cultivated, to have his thoughts and words coincide in each moment with how he felt, an ability described by Allen Ginsburg:

> What struck me was that he was at one, or he became identical with his breath. And Dylan had become a column of air, so to speak, at certain moments where his total physical and mental focus was this single breath coming out of his body. He had found a way in public to be almost like a shaman, with all of his intelligence and consciousness focused on his breath.[708]

What Ginsberg is describing here closely resembles the ecstatic shamanic techniques, brought to modern awareness by Mircea Eliade and others, of attuning oneself completely to the moment through drumming and focus on breath, consciously transcending egoic consciousness to become a vessel for "spirit," thereby mediating the felt quality of experience for others.

As Ginsberg no doubt understood, in numerous languages, the word for "breath" is the same as the word for "spirit." Thus, the English words "inspiration" (literally the coming-in of spirit) and "respiration" are both etymologically derived from the Latin word "spirare," while the Chinese word *Ch'i*, the Japanese word *Ki*, the Arabic word *rouh*, the Hebrew word *ruach*, and the Greek word *pneuma* all possess a similar etymological multivalence. The dual meanings of "breath" and "spirit" for each of these words are a fundamental example of the domains to which material-efficient causation and formal-final causation provide access, the physical, material act of breathing complexly imbricated with the experience of spirit in all its guises, as both informing potentiality and lure toward becoming. Indeed, it is no accident that "breathing" is synonymous with meditation in various forms of Buddhism.

Suze Rotolo, who probably knew Dylan better than anyone in his early years in New York, wrote that "he could go inside himself so thoroughly and completely that there was nothing else around but the music he was hearing in his head or the thoughts crossing his mind. He just disappeared for a spell."[709] Like contemplatives, shamans, and mystics of many traditions, Dylan was able intentionally to focus his breath or spirit almost purely in the moment, leaving his egoic mind to go "completely" "inside himself," one way of describing ecstasy, to see the world as it really was and as it could be, visions that he could then communicate to those around him through his music.

As philosopher Terence McKenna explains in *The Evolutionary Mind*, the transcription of a "trialogue" with biologist Rupert Sheldrake and mathematician Karl Abraham:

> At the high Paleolithic stage, the shaman is essentially a kind of sanctioned psychotic. In other words, shamans are able to move into states of mind so extreme that their immediate social efficacy is arguable. What I mean is that the shaman is a person, a designated member of the social group, who can mentally change into an animal. The shaman can become so animal-like that other members of the social group are appalled and draw back.[710]

Thus, it seems clear that Dylan, like Presley and Lennon, enacted and embodied the reemergence of the epistemologies associated with animality, though in a more intellectually mediated way than Presley, and perhaps even Lennon, spontaneously recreating shamanic practice in a culture in which such activity had been almost completely repressed and expunged from the armamentarium of acceptable behavior.

Dylan himself mentions shamanism on several occasions in his memoir. Although he employs the phrase "consciousness craze," perhaps to provides an ironic distance from the particular religious practice portrayed by Carlos Castaneda, like many others in his generation and those following, Dylan appears to have seen immense significance in the "archaic techniques of ecstasy" exemplified at that moment by Castaneda's fictional character Don Juan, an Amazonian shaman. And Dylan presents this collective shamanic awakening as having been deeply connected to the prevalence of LSD in the counterculture beginning in the sixties. As Dylan suggests, both of these chemically mediated practices "brought a new level of awareness or life force" and gave "people the right attitude," as one of the primary effects of "mind-manifesting" psychedelics like ayahuasca and LSD is that they seem to bring attention inexorably to the profound complexities of bodily experience, thereby acting as cultural deconditioning agents, revealing the assumptions of cultural rationalization as constructs of consensus reality.[711]

Although Dylan often claims not to have felt like a part of his generation, writing that "I had very little in common with and knew even less about a generation that I was supposed to be the voice of," he has clearly been influenced by the widespread interest in archaic religious practice, which he sees as part of a "new worldview" moving culture in a positive direction. As he asserts in the section of *Chronicles* about his recording of *Oh Mercy* with producer Daniel Lanois in the late eighties, the producer "would have to be a shaman to make this work," a phrase constituting explicit recognition that the archaic religious mode has been central to Dylan's art. Summed up in a few words, the "right attitude" characteristic of the "new worldview" to which Dylan is referring appears to be based on the repressed epistemologies and modes of causation, for formal and final causation, as well as affect and intuition, are intimately bound up with both archaic religion and psychedelic experience.

Furthermore, Dylan's self-descriptions suggest that he explicitly saw himself as having a great deal in common with primal shamans. Dylan states in a matter of fact way that he was a "visionary" with a "heightened sense of awareness" who could "transcend the limitations," not quite of this world but apart from it, "impractical," with an exceptional memory for the songs that mediate the affective experience of others, and an intrinsic faith in the righteousness of his trajectory requiring very little validation from outside himself. Given all this evidence, it seems clear that Dylan understands himself as having performed a role for his culture very similar to those of archaic shamans, ancient prophets, and spiritual leaders of all eras, though integrated with, and mediated by the rationality characteristic of modernity.[712]

"Transfiguration"

Dylan appears to have been undergoing a kind of prolonged death and rebirth initiation throughout the mid-sixties, similar to those experienced by shamans in numerous cultures around the world, which seems to have allowed him to act as a catalyst for the transformation of his culture. According to folksinger David Cohen: "His power, his mystique, just affected people in crazy ways," many in his audience sensing that "this guy *knows*, this guy *feels*, and you want to be with him." Or as Eric Andersen put it: "He's got the heaviest vibes I've ever felt on anyone," apparently a common perception by those who knew Dylan. By the mid-sixties, Dylan seems to have developed his intrinsic ability to embody the affective quality of the moment to such a high degree that he "found himself at the pole of a magnetic field" for people's deepest desires and aspirations, similar to Presley's role in his cultural moment, but at a more complex order of magnitude.[713]

Concluding the section about his self-naming explicated above, Dylan writes:

> As far as Bobby Zimmerman goes, I'm going to give
> this to you right straight and you can check it out. One of
> the early presidents of the San Bernardino [Hell's]
> Angels was Bobby Zimmerman, and he was killed in
> 1964 on the Bass Lake run. The muffler fell off his bike,
> he made a U-turn to retrieve it in front of the pack and
> was instantly killed. That person is gone. That was the
> end of him.[714]

What Dylan seems to be implying is that the fact that there was another
man named Bobby Zimmerman who died in a motorcycle wreck in 1964
(actually 1961, though this discrepancy does not seem negatively to
affect Dylan's point) is a meaningful coincidence (the definition of
Jungian synchronicity) that symbolically mirrored and enacted the death
of Dylan's old identity. This is an idea the validity of which it would be
impossible for a purely materialist mode of thought to accept, at least
outside of a novel or a film, but Dylan believes that the world does
indeed work in mysterious ways. The name coincidence combined with
the manner of the other Zimmerman's death, which pre-iterates one of
the primary images in Dylan's mythology, the motorcycle crash of 1966,
seems to suggest to Dylan a kind of cosmic orchestration in which events
are somehow pulled into his wake of significance.

In his 2012 *Rolling Stone* interview, Dylan expands on the subject of
the two Bobby Zimmermans, declaring: "You know what this is called?
It's called transfiguration. Have you ever heard of it?" "Yes," the
interviewer responds. "Well, you're looking at somebody," Dylan
declares. "That . . . has been transfigured?" comes the hesitant rejoinder.
"Yeah, absolutely," Dylan asserts:

> I'm not like you, am I? I'm not like him, either. I'm not
> like too many others. I'm only like another person who's
> been transfigured. How many people like that or like me
> do you know? . . . Transfiguration: You can go and learn
> about it from the Catholic Church, you can learn about it
> in some old mystical books, but it's a real concept. It's
> happened throughout the ages. . . . It's not like
> something you can dream up and think. It's not like
> conjuring up a reality or like reincarnation – or like
> when you might think you're somebody from the past
> but have no proof. It's not anything to do with the past
> or the future. So when you ask some of your questions,
> you're asking them to a person who's long dead. You're

asking them to a person that doesn't exist. But people make that mistake about me all the time. I've lived through a lot. . . . Transfiguration is what allows you to crawl out from under the chaos and fly above it. That's how I can still do what I do and write the songs I sing and just keep on moving. . . . I couldn't go back and find Bobby in a million years. Neither could you or anybody else on the face of the Earth. He's gone. If I could, I would go back. I'd like to go back. At this point in time, I would love to go back and find him, put out my hand. And tell him he's got a friend. But I can't. He's gone. He doesn't exist. . . . I'd always been different than other people, but this book [about the other Bobby Zimmerman, written by Ralph Barger along with Keith and Kent Zimmerman (who bear no immediately apparent relation to either of the Bobby Zimmermans)] told me why. Like certain people are set apart. . . . I didn't know who I was before I read the Barger book.[715]

A 71-year-old Dylan, in a simultaneously more open and more cantankerous mood than usual, declares unequivocally that he was fundamentally transformed in his twenties, that he died and was reborn through something like the Christian process of transfiguration, the recipient of which becomes spiritually exalted, taking on an aspect of divinity, a process that bears a striking similarity to shamanic initiation.

The Transfiguration of Christ, which St. Thomas Aquinas referred to as "the greatest miracle," is when Jesus shined radiantly upon a mountain (perhaps like the Beatles on the Cavern stage) and became mysteriously connected to the Hebrew prophets Elijah and Moses who appeared beside him. In the New Testament, Paul refers to the believers being "changed into the same image" through "beholding as in a glass the glory of the Lord," which suggests that the witnessing of the transfigured individual can mediate a similar transformation in those who believe in that transfiguration, acting as a mirror for the collective. Ultimately, the paradigmatic Transfiguration appears to have been fulfilled in the death and rebirth of Christ, which seems to be a kind of fractal reiteration of the archetypal death and rebirth of the shamanic initiation that Dylan appears to have experienced.

As Dylan asserts, those few who are fundamentally transformed through this kind of process, by various accounts including primal shamans, ancient mythological heroes, and religious figures from numerous traditions, are reborn as fundamentally new people, which separates them from the majority of humanity who have not undergone such a transformation. According to Dylan, this transfiguration is not something that one can "dream up and think" in a hypothetical, conceptual way, but something that one either experiences or does not. From Dylan's perspective, which is very much like that articulated by William James, one cannot choose one's destiny. Rather, one either knows that one has been transfigured or one does not, and the skepticism of those who have not experienced transfiguration, either in themselves or in others, has no bearing on the reality of the phenomenon. As it is expressed in several places in the New Testament: "He that hath ears to hear, let him hear."[716]

Thus, for Dylan, his young self, named Bobby Zimmerman, died during the mid-sixties, culminating in Dylan's motorcycle crash, which was synchronistically presaged by the death of the other Bobby Zimmerman in a motorcycle crash a few years before, regardless of whether it was 1961 or 1964. However, after the 2012 interview, *Rolling Stone* was apparently able to determine that the biker Bobby Zimmerman died "within weeks" of Robert Shelton's 1961 review of Dylan's show at Gerde's Folk City in the *New York Times*, which catapulted Dylan into the limelight, essentially marking the beginning of Dylan's public career.[717] In a roundabout way, this chronological mistake in the book from which Dylan took his information only serves to add credence to Dylan's interpretation, as naratologically speaking, the 1961 date seems even more perfectly orchestrated to confirm Dylan's conviction of his transfiguration than 1964. Indeed, the nearly five year period between September 1961 when Dylan was elevated by Shelton's review and July 1966 when he crashed his motorcycle and went into seclusion is one of the most creative, transformative half-decades that any artist has ever undergone.

Furthermore, by declaring that "it's not anything to do with the past or the future," Dylan seems to be evoking something like Bergsonian duration or Jungian synchronicity, implying that his transfiguration is partially constituted in the shift from relating to time as quantitative to understanding that moments with similar archetypal qualities resonate in a way that seems to exceed linear temporality. Although the two Bobby Zimmermans were materially unconnected, the mode of thought Dylan enacts, which appears coextensive with the generally predominant mode of thought prior to the seventeenth century, finds a more relevant connection between the young man who would become Dylan and another young man with the same name who had died years before than between Bobby Zimmerman from Hibbing and the famous singer Bob Dylan. As Dylan asserts, he can never go back to being Bobby

Zimmerman no matter how much he might want to revisit his former self, for this is apparently the price one must pay for transfiguration: it is impossible to unknow something once it has been deeply experienced. Or as Heraclitus expressed it: "You cannot step into the same river twice."

According to Dylan, this shift in perspective has been a primary factor in allowing him to do what he has done, "to crawl out from under the chaos and fly above it," as in this mode of thought, the chaotic meaninglessness of pure materialism, consisting of atoms purposelessly colliding, can be overcome by embracing a view of life as filled with cosmic significance, though hopefully tempered by intellectual rigor. As seen above, the material facts do not necessarily change in this mode of relation, though the results of approaching the world in this way "yet make all the difference" for lived experience. In his narrative of the two Bobby Zimmermans, Dylan seems to imply that something like the order of the world sacrificed another man with the same name as him to literalize the death of one of the most transformative figures in history's original identity.

This type of meaningful coincidence occurs frequently in literature and film, but our culture usually assumes that these instances are merely plot devices invented by the author rather than occurrences containing extra-textual meaning. Although there is no mode of causation that has been broadly accepted in the main streams of late modernity which could explain such a phenomenon, the ancient and well-established principles of formal and final causation offer just such an explanatory mode. From this perspective as articulated by Dylan, the literal and symbolic deaths of the two Bobby Zimmermans participate in a formal cause, the sacrificial death and rebirth of the individually embodied shamanic archetype on a mass scale apparently luring culture toward a final cause, a collective transfiguration at that moment in the mid-sixties.

EPILOGUE
"THROUGH THE MIRROR"

In being aware of the bodily experience, we must thereby be aware of aspects of the whole spatio-temporal world as mirrored within the bodily life. . . . My theory involves the entire abandonment of the notion that simple location is the primary way in which things are involved in space-time. In a certain sense, everything is everywhere at all times. For every location involves an aspect of itself in every other location. Thus every spatio-temporal standpoint mirrors the world.

Alfred North Whitehead, *Science and the Modern World*[718]

The pages above have sought to draw out particular inflections of rock and roll, and the profound historical impulse that it has carried through three primary protagonists of the genre. At this point, it seems that the most direct way to illuminate the interactions of these three rather different embodiments of rock and roll in collective discourse is to examine the qualities of encounters between Presley and the Beatles (who met only once), between the Beatles and Dylan (who became close friends, particularly Lennon and Harrison), and between Presley and Dylan (a meeting which may or may not have actually occurred, but which has apparently been alluded to in Dylan's "Went to See the Gypsy"). Ultimately, these young men all acted as mirrors for one another's transformations just as much as they mediated the collective transformation of their era.

"Long live the King!"

By the time Presley met the Beatles in 1965, the older singer appears to have long lost the initial inspiration that had impelled him essentially to create rock and roll in its primary form. It seems clear that his time in the army had forcibly knocked the rebellious fire out of Presley, reducing him from an exemplary catalyst of cultural transformation to a mere entertainer, though still an excellent and extremely popular one, as he made some great music during the sixties and seventies. However, it is also clear that Presley, as an avatar of repressed affectivity in the mid-fifties, had perhaps naively thought that he could maintain his inspired momentum within the paradigmatically hierarchical power structure of the United States Army, a notion of which he was quickly disabused.

Thus, just as he had previously been an embodiment of affect's return, in 1958 he became an embodiment of the mastering of affect by the predominant rational culture. As Lennon expressed it: "They cut off his bollocks in the army."[719]

In the years leading up to Presley's sole encounter with the Beatles in 1965, despite his public graciousness toward the younger musicians, it was apparent to Presley's crew, the "Memphis Mafia," that he was jealous of the Beatles' unprecedented success, which had suddenly eclipsed his own, definitively dethroning him from the pinnacle of cultural novelty, a deposition initiated by the army a few years before. According to Guralnick, Presley was apparently "neither interested in, nor satisfied with" the music he had been making those last few years. He was not selling as many of his new records as he had during the fifties, certainly, but perhaps even more dispiriting, he understood that his records "no longer *mattered* as they used to."

As Guralnick writes: "Presley admired the Beatles, he felt threatened by the Beatles . . . but most of all he was envious of the freedom that they evidently seemed to feel and to flaunt. He, too," Guralnick concludes, "had once enjoyed that freedom, he, too, had once been in the vanguard of the revolution, and now he was embarrassed to listen to his own music, to watch his own films."[720] Presley appears to have recognized that the "advancing" "wave-crest"[721] of novelty's ingression into culture had moved on, leaving the inventor of rock and roll behind, much like Moses who led his people to the Promised Land, but could not enter with them. As is so often the case, the figure who largely mediated the emergence of a new era of culture, who (in this case) made himself a bridge between the old rational epistemology and the emerging integrative one, remained with one foot firmly planted in the old paradigm, unable fully to leave behind the mode from which he had done so much to liberate his culture.[722]

The one time Presley and the Beatles met when they came to visit his Bel Air mansion in 1965, Presley's whole entourage was looking forward to the encounter, though the King seemed nonplussed, "sitting on the long, L-shaped white couch in the den, watching a soundless TV" when the Beatles came in. Though only thirty years old at the time of this encounter, like an aged monarch being visited by the young upstarts in the process of deposing him, Presley could not seem to muster any enthusiasm for meeting his successors. And indeed, the Beatles were "disappointed" by the meeting with their idol, Tony Barrow explaining: 'To be honest . . . I'd describe Elvis on that showing as a boring old fart—but I do know Ringo enjoyed his game of pool."[723]

As the Beatles were leaving after an evening of awkward conversation and half-hearted jamming, Lennon, who had been nervously affecting "a faux French accent," called out: "Sanks for ze music. . . . Long live the King!" After the meeting, Lennon admitted that "it was a load of rubbish," scathingly declaring: "It was like meeting Engelbert Humperdinck." As seen in numerous cases in the pages above, it is remarkable how inevitably the revolution becomes a new orthodoxy. In the context of the evolution of world views, this process required centuries before a real challenge to the hegemony of rationality could emerge, but in the case of rock and roll, the changing of the guard required less than a decade. Although Presley would go on to make excellent music, the promethean torch had been definitively, though grudgingly passed, just as Presley had seized the torch from Sinatra.[724]

However, although the new dispensation often rails against the old guard, once the new revolution has been achieved, the successful revolutionaries almost always honor their debt to the previous paradigm. Thus, when Jerry Schilling, a member of Presley's entourage, went to see the Beatles a few days after their meeting, Lennon made a point of telling Schilling "how much the evening had meant to him," asking him to tell Presley: "If it hadn't been for him I would have been nothing." According to Schilling: "I was just thrilled, of course, and I told Elvis, but he didn't say anything, he just kind of smiled. That was it." This episode continues the archetypal drama in which the son overthrows the father, but then feels a mixture of pity and reverence for his precursor and returns to pay his respects knowing that he will ultimately undergo a similar fate. Thus, while the revolution is occurring, the roles of revolutionary and reigning monarch seem starkly opposed, but once the transition is accomplished, both successive revolutionaries crowned king enter the canonical pantheon as men whose days of glory have come and gone, both left to live in the aftermath of the burdensome gift they were granted.

Subsequent to this encounter, life and music would go on for both Presley and Lennon until they both "left the building" within a few years of one another as the seventies gave way to the eighties, definitively marking the end of the classic era of rock and roll. Nevertheless, it seems to be the very revolution that overthrew Presley in the mid-sixties which impelled him to "come back" in the late sixties and seventies to make deeper, more mature, though less revolutionary music in the later years of his life. According to Guralnick, describing a conversation between Presley and producer Felton Jarvis in 1965 after Presley's meeting with the Beatles: "What Elvis wanted, he explained to Felton, was the kind of sound the Beatles and some of the other English bands were getting: it was a hotter sound; it jumped out at you, you got the sense that something was really happening. Felton eagerly nodded assent. It was a matter of feel." Having initiated the genre that took "feel" as its primary focus, Presley's interest in the further affective realms that the Beatles and their contemporaries were exploring through innovations in arrangement and recording as much as in attitude was apparently reawakened by his encounter with the younger group. And there is certainly no shame in this late rebirth of the King in partial emulation of his successors, for how many can say that they were once the bearer of a genuine cultural revolution?[725]

"Fanning the Fateful Flame"

The Beatles' discovery of *The Freewheelin' Bob Dylan* album in 1964 began an association with the American singer that would catalyze a profound transformation, not only in the group's aesthetic, but in the mode of being that they enacted. According to McCartney: "I'm sure this kind of thing found its way into our music, and into our lyrics, and influenced whom we were interested in. . . . Vocally and poetically Dylan was a huge influence." Similarly, Lennon claimed that, largely because of Dylan, "I'd started thinking about my own emotions. . . . Instead of projecting myself into a situation, I would try to express what I felt about myself." Although the Beatles were always clever lyricists, they generally paid more attention up to this point in their career to the sound of the words than to the content. By all accounts, Dylan was the largest factor in their turn away from teenage themes to more mature lyrical content.

As Lennon would later declare: "I think it was Dylan who helped me realize that . . . not by any discussion or anything, but by hearing his work." As he did for so many members of his generation, Dylan acted as a kind of spiritual mentor for Lennon, even as Lennon perhaps acted in a similar capacity for Dylan. As probably the two most revered songwriters of their time (excepting the slightly younger Bob Marley and maybe a few others), Lennon found a counterpart in Dylan of an entirely different sort than his "creative tension" with McCartney, Lennon declaring: "When I met Dylan I was quite dumbfounded." Dylan's whole demeanor, his whole aesthetic, and his approach to his music and, especially, his lyrics, proved a liberating agent for Lennon. However, perhaps the most profound effect that Dylan had on Lennon and the other Beatles was introducing them to the plant with which they would become inextricably associated.[726]

Like the Beatles, Dylan was partial to alcohol as a means of moving his center of attention from his head to his body, one friend at the University of Minnesota saying that "he used to get really fucking drunk, we all did." However, whereas the Beatles religiously used speed in their early years, particularly before their encounter with Dylan, the American singer seems to have enjoyed cannabis perhaps more than amphetamines long before he became famous. Indeed, when Dylan started hanging out with the more bohemian crowd during his year in Minneapolis, as Heylin relates: "One of the things that separated the 'new kind of people' from the 'established order' was their penchant for popping pills, smoking weed, and quaffing a carafe or two of Chateau le Plonk." And as an acquaintance that Dylan met in Madison, Wisconsin, on his rambling way from Minneapolis to New York observes, Dylan "was the first guy who had marijuana in his mitten."

Although it is not clear whether Dylan literally carried cannabis in an unfingered glove, a strikingly humorous image, this statement seems to indicate that Dylan was devoted to the plant. Certainly, this propensity for smoking cannabis explains to a large degree some of the profound differences between Dylan and the Beatles in their younger years. As Dylan describes his early use of cannabis in a 1978 interview:

> Grass was everywhere in the clubs. It was always there in the jazz clubs and in the folk-music clubs. There was just grass and it was available to musicians in those days. And in coffeehouses way back in Minneapolis. That's where I first came into contact with it, I'm sure. I forget when or where, really. . . . Being a musician means, depending on how far you go, getting to the depths of where you are at. And most any musician would try anything to get to those depths, because playing music is an immediate thing. . . . Your spirit flies when you are playing music. So, with music, you tend to look deeper and deeper inside yourself to find the music. That's why, I guess, grass was around those clubs.[727]

That Dylan was drawn to cannabis at such an early point in his career, and cultivated the mode of consciousness that smoking the plant produced, generally constellated around "depth," is indicative of the quality of his music, which was initially far more introspective, surreal, and psychologically profound than the Beatles' early mode in Hamburg and Liverpool, and through the years of Beatlemania, which demonstrated the manic intensity of speed that Dylan would come to share, but without the internal profundity and imaginative efflorescence that cannabis can induce.[728]

However, this stark difference was attenuated in a rather dramatic way soon after Dylan introduced the Beatles to what would become a kind of countercultural sacrament. At their first meeting on August 28, 1964, the Beatles took out their customary assortment of pills, offering some to Dylan. However, Dylan declined, suggesting they sample his stash of cannabis instead. After an initial moment of hesitation, the Beatles all partook and, as Harrison later remarked: "We were just legless, aching from laughter." According to Spitz: "They got right into the groove, which relaxed the recalcitrant bard, who lit joint after joint, fanning the fateful flame." And as Lennon described the situation, Dylan "kept answering our phone, saying, 'This is Beatlemania here.' . . . We were smoking dope, drinking wine and generally being rock 'n rollers, and having a laugh, you know, and surrealism. It was party time." However, although "party time" might at first sound trivial, as Spitz aptly observes, this encounter between Dylan and the Beatles was "as close to a cultural milestone as could be determined by academics . . . and nothing would ever be the same again."[729]

All cultures in all times have made alliances with certain organic substances and prohibited others. For the United States and Britain of the early sixties, the three primary drugs of choice, legally sanctioned by the powers that be, were alcohol, tobacco, and various forms of speed, sometimes in the milder form of caffeine and sometimes in more potent upper or amphetamine pill forms. Cannabis was the scientific name for a plant that had been officially named "marihuana" in 1937 by an American government seeking to link the plant with racism toward Mexicans. Although cannabis had been used for decades in American and British culture by jazz musicians, and in the fifties by beat poets and other sectors of the artistic avant garde, the Beatles' and Dylan's devotion to the plant, mutually confirmed at this "marijuana summit"[730] in 1964, did probably more than anything else to shift the broader cultural allegiance toward cannabis, or at least to make the plant nearly as acceptable as the more legislatively sanctioned psychoactive compounds.[731]

As Terence McKenna makes clear in *Food of the Gods*, the substances that a culture accepts into its diet are primary signifiers of which epistemological modes are privileged in that society. McKenna writes:

> The ways in which humans use plants, food, and drugs
> cause the values of individuals and, ultimately, whole

societies to shift. . . . Society tacitly encourages certain
behaviors that correspond to internal feelings, thereby
encouraging the use of substances that produce
acceptable behavior. . . . When thinking about drugs, we
tend to focus on episodes of intoxication, but many
drugs are normally used in subthreshold or maintenance
doses; coffee and tobacco are obvious examples in our
culture. The result of this is a kind of "ambience of
intoxication." Like fish in water, people in a culture
swim in the virtually invisible medium of culturally
sanctioned yet artificial states of mind. . . . Most of us
are unaware of the effects of plants on ourselves and our
reality, partly because we have forgotten that plants have
always mediated the human cultural relationship to the
world at large.[732]

McKenna suggests that the relationships we develop with plants largely
determine the modes through which we relate to and come to know the
world. Different plants and chemical substances seem to open up "doors
of perception" into different domains of experience: some, like caffeine,
seem to promote rationality and consensus reality,[733] and some, like
cannabis, seem to bring awareness to the constructed quality of rational
experience and to open one to intuitive modes. We often label these
latter, non-rational experiential occasions "feelings" in order to
differentiate them from thoughts though, for the predominant modern,
Western mentality, thoughts have meaningful content while feelings are
merely mute. However, the great yogis, mystics, and shamans, the many
radical empiricists of human history, have demonstrated amply that
feelings, correlated with bodily sensations, are just as complex and
interesting as rational thought, and that they can tell us just as much
about the world as intellect, though in a profoundly different domain.

As Harrison explains: "The first thing, I mean, that people who
smoked marijuana and were into music [noticed] is that somehow it
focuses your attention better on the music, and so you can hear it clearer,
or that's how it appeared to be. You can see things, or you could see
things, much different."[734] Thus, the dichotomy between caffeinated
work culture and cannabis-infused counterculture does not seem to be a
polarity of productivity and pleasure, as the predominant mentality
would have it, but between two equally valid and necessary ways of
seeing the world, one primarily oriented toward acting vigorously and
precisely within the current systems of relation, and the other on seeing
through those constructed systems to relatively unmediated experience,

allowing one to encounter the world with new eyes. Indeed, as Harrison suggests, it may be easier to hear the subtleties of music when having inhaled cannabis smoke because the plant tends to make one more aware of the silent verbal chatter that usually constitutes thought in our culture, allowing that kind of internal speech consciously to be put aside to engage directly with the music rather than having constantly to describe it and explain it to oneself in silent words.

Naming things gives those things power, grants them objective, consensus reality. The language of intellect, of science, and of rationality, circularly reinforced by the predominance of caffeine as our culture's daytime drug of choice, is highly developed and sophisticated, thus wielding enormous influence on the way our culture makes decisions. Indeed, as McKenna points out, caffeine is the only drug whose right to be used is written into every labor contract in the West as the "coffee break." Far from accidental, it is clear that caffeine is the chemical substance that perhaps most fuels the rational form of consciousness characteristic of modernity (and it did, to a great extent, in the importation of tea to Europe starting in the seventeenth century).[735]

From business to law to academia, the complex language games on which these domains run, like software in the cultural operating system, govern collective discourse, and this mode of thought is pervaded by the caffeinated ambiance just as bars, the primary place of public revelry and mate-finding for our culture, are pervaded by the ingestion of alcohol.[736] However, certain streams of thought, including those derived from thinkers like James, Jung, Bergson, and Whitehead, have been working to create a vocabulary capable of expressing the complexity of felt experience, which appears to be the domain to which cannabis can offer access, as the plant, perhaps describable as a low-grade psychedelic, seems to have the effect of dissolving cultural conditioning.

Of course, moderation is key in all things, as one can certainly go too far in the direction of affective attention just as modern Western culture has often been excessive in its attention to rationality. This imbalance, while apparently necessary for the individuation of intellect, can reach a degree where it becomes destructive, as can be seen with the environmental, social, political, and economic crises that the world is currently facing, which seem to be the product of over-rationalized ways of thinking divorced from affective domains where the innate moral sense perhaps resides. Similarly, thinking too little and feeling too much can be equally destructive as can be seen, for one rather innocuous instance, in the figure of the "stoner," the overzealous cannabis user who smokes so much so frequently that he or she has difficulty extricating himself or herself from the couch or forming a coherent sentence. By most accounts, the moderate and responsible ingestion of cannabis can emancipate one's thinking just as moderate and responsible alcohol consumption can be socially and somatically liberating. But smoking cannabis excessively can inhibit meaningful engagement with the world just as surely as excessive ingestion of whisky and beer, though there are admittedly fewer health problems associated with cannabis than with alcohol. Nevertheless, it appears that, through their devotion to cannabis, the Beatles and Dylan were half-consciously attempting to balance out the excesses of modernity and lead their culture toward a "middle way."

The cannabis-mediated encounter between Dylan and the Beatles is arguably the moment in history when some of the individuals who most embodied the trajectory of Western culture at that moment made the epochal decision to try something new, to turn in a different direction in order to counterbalance the extremes of their culture's past. The qualitatively new approach to experience that emerged out of this meeting between the Beatles and Dylan, and thus between rock and roll and cannabis, became known as the counterculture, which issued into a variety of streams after the sixties, from artistic, spiritual, and health movements to political, intellectual, and ecological ones. However, the impulse enacted in this collective movement is closely related to the work of thinkers like James, Jung, Bergson, and Whitehead, all "forerunners" who attempted to create a vocabulary as adequate to describing the internal quality of experience as a purely rationalist vocabulary is to describing quantifiable phenomena.

In their first collective encounter with cannabis, the Beatles were "aching from laughter," presumably because they were suddenly becoming aware of parts of themselves that had previously been occluded, which appears to be one of the primary phenomenological effects of the plant. As often seems to be the case with early cannabis use, it is likely that the young men suddenly became conscious of the generally unconscious tensions in their bodies because they lived in a culture that subtly and pervasively repressed such affective attention. By temporarily relocating their conscious awareness in their somatic selves rather than their minds, the Beatles' ingestion of cannabis would have opened up a new way of experiencing the culturally conditioned conceptual constructs that had been unconsciously driving and constraining them. Although they had managed to enter this mode to some extent through their use of alcohol, speed, and tobacco, the ingestion of cannabis generally seems to produce qualitatively more profound and meaning-laden effects than these other substances. And this profundity can often manifest as a heightened awareness of absurdity, for as Starr remarks: "That was the first time for me that I'd really smoked marijuana and I laughed and I laughed and I laughed. It was fabulous."[737]

Laughter would have been the Beatles' psyches' corrective response, allowing repressed content to be released and a new mode of thought based on a newly awakened awareness of affect to emerge. The Beatles were primed for this kind of experience, as they possessed an exceptionally strong collective drive toward novelty, self-transcendence, and transformation. Like the needle in the cut of a vinyl album, the covers of which would soon be customarily employed in the rolling of joints, the young men "got right into the groove," immediately realizing that the nonordinary states of consciousness they had partially learned to enter into through their excessive use of alcohol, uppers, and nicotine could be accessed more deeply and in a less destructive, more contemplative way. Thus, for a whole generation, and those following, "getting into the groove" became a multi-layered metaphor that tied rock and roll together with cannabis and the emerging counterculture in a particularly striking way.[738]

Furthermore, by answering the phone "This is Beatlemania here," Dylan was exhibiting for the Beatles the absurdity of the situation in which they found themselves. By turning them on to pot, Dylan indelibly catapulted the Beatles out of their first phase and into their second incarnation. As noted above, although "party time" may sound trivial, this phrase in fact encapsulates one inflection of the joyful experimentation and search for the overcoming of normative consciousness through which novelty is often achieved: the devotion of time and attention to enjoyment, an essential quality of human experience, not only for physical and psychological well-being, but for discovery and invention.

Thus, though it may sound slightly ridiculous in a culture that has not yet fully accepted cannabis into its legally sanctioned cornucopia (though it seems to be only a matter of months as of this writing), the Beatles smoking "grass" with Bob Dylan was one of the most significant turning points of all the moments of transformation experienced by these young men from the trajectory initiated by the Enlightenment into its dialectical complement and eventual synthesis. As Spitz notes, Lennon, in particular, "had become more and more devoted to the giddy pleasures of pot,"[739] though this "giddy" quality generally seems to apply only to early experiences with the plant. Nevertheless, in a way that was simultaneously becoming literalized by the Rastafarian religion in Jamaica, Lennon really does seem to have experienced his use of cannabis as a devotional practice through which he found a new source of inspiration.

This inspired quality is evident in what are arguably his greatest songs beginning with *Help!* and *Rubber Soul* soon after his discovery of the plant (from "Help!," "You've Got to Hide Your Love Away," "Nowhere Man," and 'Tomorrow Never Knows" to "I Am the Walrus," "Revolution," "Don't Let Me Down," and "Come Together"). Any doubts about the efficacy of cannabis as a catalyst for creativity should easily be dispelled by the extraordinary quality of the music that the Beatles produced under its influence. Of course, the exploratory impulse that the Beatles, and particularly Lennon embodied, while often gloriously creative, does not come without its shadow, as Lennon at times veered too far into pure affect to the point where he became relatively unproductive, nearly losing himself in heroin and perhaps excessive ingestion of cannabis and LSD, forcing McCartney to take the reins of the band for significant portions of their career.

Thus, the Beatles' encounter with Dylan and cannabis was not all simple, confluent liberation. This encounter also made it clear that the band's current approach to making music was inadequate to their newly expanded consciousness and their concomitantly expanded artistic ambitions. Working on their fourth album, the sardonically titled *Beatles for Sale*, had not been as easy as the previous three records as they entered what Lennon called a "lousy period" when their old, pre-cannabis and pre-Dylan mentality produced music that sounded banal and uninspired to the Beatles' newly "turned on" ears.[740] The plant-based chemical catalyst that had suddenly made the Beatles aware of vastly expanded possibilities also highlighted their previous limitations, impelling them through another difficult period of transformation in which they collectively searched for a way of being and making music that more adequately satisfied the new, apparently more profound mode of experience they had begun to explore.

Although the Beatles have generally acknowledged their debt to Dylan more effusively than Dylan has reciprocated, he was clearly influenced by them as well, declaring that "they were doing things nobody was doing. . . . Their chords were outrageous, just outrageous, and their harmonies made it all valid. . . . It seemed that a definite line was being drawn. . . . This was something that had never happened before."[741] And as Dylan describes a moment when he heard "Do You Want to Know a Secret" on the radio in the late eighties: "They were so easy to accept, so solid. . . . They offered intimacy and companionship like no other group. . . . Somehow there was nothing wussy about it."[742] Although this may seem like a bit of a backhanded compliment, one suspects that the fact that Dylan, in his memoir, is more able effusively to praise relatively minor contemporaries like Ricky Nelson or Dave Van

Ronk suggests that Dylan may have felt a bit threatened by the Beatles, was perhaps even a little jealous of them.

Similarly, in a 1971 interview, Dylan expressed his admiration for the Beatles while subtly putting them down, declaring: "Everybody else thought they were for the teenyboppers, that they were gonna pass right away. But it was obvious to me that they had staying power. I knew they were pointing the direction of where music had to go."[743] Although he was close friends with Lennon, and eventually even closer friends with Harrison, it seems likely that Dylan must have been a bit envious of the fact that the Beatles had simply sold a lot more records than he had, which is perhaps part of why he finds it difficult simply to praise them.[744]

If Dylan was the spiritual king of rock and roll, perhaps held in slightly higher regard by artists and critics than the Beatles (though it is certainly a close thing), the Beatles, along with Presley, were the worldly kings. According to various estimates, the Beatles and Presley have both sold somewhere between six-hundred million and one billion records, while Dylan has sold about seventy million, no mean feat, but not quite concomitant with the extraordinarily high regard in which Dylan is almost universally held by his peers and his critics. Thus, in an oblique way, Dylan admitting that the Beatles "offered intimacy and companionship like no other group" seems to suggest a deep and abiding, though somewhat grudging, admiration for their unparalleled ability to connect directly and profoundly with such a massive audience. Dylan seems to recognize that the Beatles are his only real competition for the top spot in the rock and roll hierarchy, though Presley will always be the one who started it all.

In an illuminating anecdote from the *No Direction Home* documentary, Allen Ginsberg describes one of the early meetings between Dylan and the Beatles:

> Dylan was down the hall with the Beatles. Then a message came that I was supposed to come in there. So I came into the room and everybody was sitting there totally stone-cold silent, frozen, paranoid. Not quite knowing my place, knowing Bob, I sat down on the side of his arm-chair. John Lennon said snidely; 'why don't you sit a little closer," and I suddenly realized they were just so naïve, they were young, so I fell over laughing onto John's lap looking up at him and asked him: "Do you ever read William Blake?" And he said: '"Never!" And his wife said: "Oh, John, stop lying." Then everybody began laughing and the ice was broken. It

struck me as funny that these guys at the summit of
power, spiritual power, musical power, world fame, '65
June, were, um, so unsure of their minds and speech.[745]

As Ginsberg's story strikingly illustrates, despite the fact that Dylan and
the Beatles were evidently at the "summit of . . . spiritual power," they
were still simply very young men, all in their mid-twenties, a time when
most people are merely trying to find their place in the world. These
youthful musicians had been given a gift that very few people are ever
given, let alone at such an early age, and it is important to remember that,
despite the profound quality of their music and their narrative, they were,
to some extent, merely young men who got extremely lucky. The
historical process required avatars of the impulse toward the
reemergence and reintegration of the repressed modes at that moment,
and these five musicians happened to be positioned perfectly to fulfill
that role.

"Went to See the Gypsy"

As with so many events in the history of rock and roll, and particularly in
the life of Bob Dylan, the question of if Dylan ever met his boyhood idol
Elvis Presley has become a subject of considerable speculation. In a 2009
interview in *Rolling Stone*, Dylan claims:

> I never met Elvis because I didn't want to meet Elvis. . .
> . I wouldn't quite say he was ridiculed, but close. You
> see, the music scene had gone past him, and nobody
> bought his records. Nobody young wanted to listen to
> him or be like him. Nobody went to see his movies, as
> far as I know. He just wasn't in anybody's mind. Two or
> three times we were up in Hollywood, and he had sent
> some of the Memphis Mafia down to where we were to
> bring us up to see Elvis. But none of us went. Because it
> seemed like a sorry thing to do. I don't know if I would
> have wanted to see Elvis like that. I wanted to see the
> powerful, mystical Elvis that had crash-landed from a
> burning star onto American soil. The Elvis that was
> bursting with life. That's the Elvis that inspired us to all
> the possibilities of life. And that Elvis had gone, had left
> the building.[746]

Unless Dylan is lying outright for reasons known only to him, it seems clear that he chose never to meet Elvis, a decision that radically differentiates Dylan from the Beatles. Indeed, this difference seems characteristic of the two artists, for while the Beatles were generally direct and honest, allowing the complex mystique of their group unity and their ironic humor to protect their enactment of transgressive modes of thought, Dylan was a man alone who found it necessary to maintain a veil of distance and obfuscation even from one of his greatest influences. It seems that whereas the Beatles wanted the real experience of meeting their hero, even if the reality failed to match their expectations, Dylan would rather maintain his image of Presley as the mythical embodiment of American liberty and vitality.[747]

While the sanctity of Presley's inspiration was invaded and mastered by the military, and the Beatles could not sustain their group mind as they grew older, married, had children, and slept with each other's wives (in the case of Harrison and Starr's wife, Maureen), Dylan is perhaps the artist who has most been able to maintain his mythical stature, even while explicitly denying that status, by constantly fostering an air of paradox. Although it is wildly inaccurate for Dylan to say that Presley "just wasn't in anybody's mind" in the sixties, as Presley remained one of the top selling artists of that decade,[748] second only to the Beatles and outselling Dylan himself, it is certainly true that Presley was no longer the leader of the counterculture as he had been for a few years in the mid-fifties. Dylan apparently knew that the form of process which he and Presley and the Beatles had created transcended all of them; he knew that the phenomenon of rock and roll was not ultimately about them, but about their image in collective consciousness, and how that image was used by the millions of fans who constantly listened to their music, talked about them, and imagined them as they went about their daily lives.

Thus, it is fitting that this narrative study should end with an analysis of Dylan's "Went to See the Gypsy"[749] from 1970's *New Morning*, a song that has long been assumed by Dylan fans to be about a meeting between the young singer and Presley, sung over a casually funky, tightly loping rhythm, but which appears to be apocryphal based on Dylan's declaration in 2009. The lyrics clearly seem to point to Presley, though if we are to believe Dylan's statement, this narrative encounter between the founding father of rock and roll and the genre's greatest prophet, between Elvis and "the Elvis of the mind,"[750] is an imaginal one, a meeting which, like formal and final causation, does not necessarily possess a direct, material reality, but a psychic, mythical, symbolic reality that has real effects on the experience of those who envision the situation, which in turn may produce material effects.

One element of the lyrics of "Went to See the Gypsy" that has apparently led to the idea that the song is about Presley is that the gypsy "can move you from the rear," a generally acknowledged property of Presley's epochally swiveling pelvis and the rhythmic physicality of his music. And the fact that the gypsy is described as having engaged in this visceral pelvic motivity in Las Vegas, a city that looms so large in Presley's later years as to be almost inseparable from the man himself, adds to the case for Presley as gypsy. Indeed, that in addition to impelling one's "rear" to "move," perhaps in dancing, that the gypsy can "drive you from your fear" and "bring you through the mirror" suggests the profound effect that Presley's music had on the generations of musicians and hipsters that followed in his wake.

That the latter phrase has been appropriated as the title of this epilogue should give some indication of its importance to the general trajectory of this study: from the initiatory query of "What's That Supposed to Mean?" to the liminal promise of "Standing in the Gateway," to the provocative dare of "You Really Don't Know Until You Step Inside," to the intrepid leap of "Through the Mirror." Clearly, passing "through the mirror" can only evoke Lewis Carroll's *Through the Looking Glass*, one of the foundational texts of the sixties counterculture, in which a proper Victorian girl enters a wild, magical, psychedelic dream world much like those evoked by Dylan and the Beatles in the mid-sixties.[751] Ultimately, it appears that this passage through the mirror constitutes a turn inward away from the narrowly rational, materialistic externality of modernity toward the internal, subjective, psychological meaningfulness of formal and final causation, though this inward turn, when followed deeply enough, seems to open out into the cosmos. Presley's embodiment of repressed affective intuition in the fifties appears to have been the precondition for the more complete reemergence of premodern modes of experience in the subsequent decades, a process still underway. Presley performed the mirror through which Dylan and his generation passed just as Dylan and the Beatles enacted the mirror through which further generations leapt.[752]

And that it is a "pretty dancing girl" who intones these qualities of the gypsy indicates that it is neither Dylan nor Presley who is the primary focus of this mode of thought, but something like the "archetypal feminine" expressive of the return of embodied, intuitive modes of engagement with experience characteristic of earlier eras.[753] In the end, the deepest significance of rock and roll does not appear to be that Presley or Lennon or Dylan were exalted geniuses demanding mass worship, though they may have been this in their best moments, but rather that their songs and their images in collective experience have provided a focus and catalyst for the return of affective bodily knowledge, of formal and final causation, and of mythic enchantment to the world. Although "the gypsy was gone," as Presley was no longer on fire with the spirit of novelty, his "door was open wide," the "gateway" which might just allow the song's narrator and his audience to cross a threshold into a radically new relational mode.

By the end of the song, even the "pretty dancing girl, she could not be found," for the gypsy figure, regardless of whether or not Dylan intended to indicate Presley, appears to be something like the Jungian *anima*, an archetypal impulse leading the historical odyssey of the West full-circle, back to the hope, wonder, and sense of possibility that appear to be symbolized for Dylan by the sun rising over "that little Minnesota town," the place of his youth where he first heard Presley's music, which itself mediated the dawn of rock and roll at Sun studio. This imaginal encounter between these men would ultimately produce some of the most profound experiences for millions upon millions of rock and roll believers around the world, the multitudes who, like me, have "watched them from the distance with the music in my ears."

NOTES

[1] Friedrich Nietzsche, *Thus Spoke Zarathustra* (Cambridge, UK: Cambridge University Press, 2006) 89.

[2] Jean Gebser, *The Ever-Present Origin* (Athens, OH: Ohio University Press, 1985) xxvii.

[3] *No Direction Home*, Dir. Martin Scorsese (Paramount Pictures, 2005).

[4] David Hajdu, *Positively 4th Street: The Lives and Times of Joan Baez, Bob Dylan, Mimi Baez Farina, and Richard Farina* (New York: North Point Press, 2001) 260.

[5] Hajdu 259-260. Several other theories have been posited to explain why the crowd was booing, including that the sound quality was poor (which does not appear to be the case based on the footage), that the set was too short (which is temporally impossible as the booing started near the beginning of the first song), and that the crowd was angry at Peter Yarrow for trying to cut Dylan's set short (again temporally impossible). Some have even claimed that there was no booing, which is simply not true (Greil Marcus, *Like a Rolling Stone: Bob Dylan at the Crossroads*, New York: PublicAffairs, 2005, 155-156).

[6] Benjamin Hedin, ed. *Studio A: The Bob Dylan Reader* (New York: Norton, 2004) 42. Hedin 42.

[7] Whereas the Newport 1965 version of "Maggie's Farm" is played in the key of D, the studio recording of the song is played in the key of G. However, this transposition would not have affected the band's ability to play the song with the same chord changes relative to the original key. On the record, the band plays an E minor transitional chord, a minor sixth for the key of G, before moving to the D, the fifth, but the minor sixth is merely a tonal shading inessential to the overall trajectory of the song, while the movement from the tonic to the dominant comprises the main action of the composition, and of the blues in general.

[8] Marcus 156.

[9] Robert Palmer, *Rock & Roll: an unruly history* (New York: Harmony Books, 1995) 105.

[10] Hajdu 260.

[11] Marcus 159.

[12] Hedin 40.

[13] Hajdu 210, 227.

[14] "The 500 Greatest Songs of All Time," *Rolling Stone* online (http://www.rollingstone.com/music/lists/the-500-greatest-songs-of-all-time-20110407).

[15] Daniel Mark Epstein, *The Ballad of Bob Dylan* (New York: Harper,

2011) 110-111.

[16] Scorsese.

[17] Daniel Mark Epstein notes that Dylan's memoir "never allows truth to get in the way of a good story, or history to interfere with the revelation of the most significant truths" (Epstein 81).

[18] Marcus 154-55.

[19] Hajdu 262-63.

[20] Scorsese

[21] Or, in the slightly more prosaic phrasing of a friend from his days in Minneapolis: "he didn't give a shit." (Heylin 46).

[22] Hajdu 276.

[23] *Chronicles* 124.

[24] Hajdu 281.

[25] Henri Bergson, *Creative Evolution* (New York: Barnes & Noble Books, 2005) 19.

[26] C.G. Jung, *Synchronicity: An Acausal Connecting Principle* (Princeton, NJ: Princeton University Press, 1973) 97.

[27] "Sam Phillips: The *Rolling Stone* Interview," *Rolling Stone* 467 (February 13, 1986) 56.

[28] This seems an opportune moment to explicate some of the theoretical and conceptual language derived from a number of theorists employed throughout the following pages:

In his *Protestant Ethic and the 'Spirit' of Capitalism*, Max Weber traces the development of the rationalized quality characteristic of Western free market capitalism, a "conceptual simplification and ordering" which he presents as having come to dominate Western societies on all levels of organization over the course of modernity, down to those societies' "fundamental attitude" of "systematic regimentation." Weber describes this ascendancy of rationalism as concomitant with the repression and othering of instinctual animality, the secular, technological, quantitative productivity that largely characterized twentieth century experience in the West effectively repressing awareness of the qualitative, intuitive physicality of "natural man" as vulgar, sinful, and even inhuman (Max Weber, *The Protestant Ethic and the 'Spirit' of Capitalism and Other Writings*, New York: Penguin Books, 2002, 26-27, 86, 104, 316-17).

If Weber's analysis reveals the ways in which predominant sectors of Western culture moved away from affective modes of experience toward rationalized "disenchantment," Sigmund Freud's "return of the repressed," which Freud saw as active in the collective domain as well as in the individual, provides an indispensable conceptual tool for understanding the titanic upheavals of the twentieth century, which occurred just as the older modes of experience seemed to be nearing complete abeyance in service to the ascendancy of the rational. Freud understood that the more fundamental domains of human affect could not be denied and ignored without profound compensatory symptoms emerging, one of which seems to have been the eruption of popular music in the twentieth century, the height of which is arguably rock and roll (Max Weber, *Max Weber's Complete Writings on Academic and Political Vocations*, Ed. John Dreijmanis, New York: Algora Publishing, 2008 and Sigmund Freud, *Moses and Monotheism*, New York: Vintage Books, 1967, 120, 130, 172).

Although Freud demonstrated the return of repressed content in culture, he focused almost exclusively on delineating the neurotic symptoms that accompany such repression. By contrast, William James, working during roughly the same period as Freud, more fully defined the intuitive epistemologies that had been repressed in their healthy, non-neurotic manifestations. James demonstrates that rational intellect is but one way of knowing the world applicable to certain domains of experience more than others, and that the materially and discursively predominant cultures in the West have systematically privileged "logical reason" over "feeling" and "intuition" for the last few centuries, particularly since the widespread acceptance in the seventeenth century of the Cartesian equation of thought with human being in general as codified in the *cogito*: "I think, therefore I am." However, while these two epistemological domains, roughly definable as rationality and affectivity, have often been constructed in modernity as fundamentally discontinuous and incommensurable, James posits that, just as they were combined in premodernity in naïve, unconscious formations, it seems that the way to attain a more complete understanding of lived experience lies in the intentional integration of these experiential domains. And this integration appears to be constituted primarily in conscious awareness of where one's attention is directed, and of which mode one emphasizes at any given moment, a synthesis that, I will contend, has been enacted to a great extent by rock and roll music (William James, *The Varieties of Religious Experience*, New York: Vintage Books, 1990, 298, 301-92, 349-50, 443-44 and William James, *Pragmatism*, Toronto: Dover, 1995, 1, 86, 94-95, 111).

Henri Bergson's work corroborates James' pragmatism, suggesting that intellect is a mode of thought that can only analyze and reduce emergent qualities to their constituent parts. As he presents it, intellect alone, with science its ultimate expression, cannot truly comprehend the emergence of anything genuinely novel without recourse to affective modes. Bergson shows that the emergence of life itself, or of human consciousness, both radically emergent properties, appear to pure intellect as merely recombinations of existing elements. In contrast, the kind of emergence that Bergson traces is qualitative, not quantitative, though qualitative shifts do often have quantitative results. Furthermore, Bergson shows that this internal quality of process has to do with the conception of time: where science generally constructs time as a linear, static, quantitative medium, Bergson demonstrates that duration, the lived experience of temporality, can also be conceived as qualitative, each moment having a quality particular to it. And this "inner movement of life" is only accessible, Bergson suggests, to intuitive forms of engaging experience. Bergson asserts that intellect and intuition are both indispensable ways of knowing the world and that, although this may seem readily apparent in practice, particularly in an early twenty-first century context when affectivity has become a primary academic concern, the academic presuppositions of the last few centuries have explicitly and in many ways rendered intuitive modes as inferior to intellect, a privileging that has been concretized in class distinctions, and even perhaps in racism as discussed elsewhere. Ultimately, Bergson sees intellect and intuition as constelling an opposition that must be reintegrated if Western culture is truly to move beyond the deepest implicit prejudices of modernity (Bergson xxii, 24-25, 37-39, 124, 135, 145, 220).

Alfred North Whitehead developed this stream of thought in what is generally referred to as his "process" philosophy, though he referred to it as a "philosophy of organism." Whatever one calls it, Whitehead's work further illuminates the domains that James and Bergson articulated as a way out of the conceptual dead-end that modernity appeared to have become by the time Whitehead began writing philosophy in the nineteen-twenties. Whitehead sees the fundamental problems articulated so profoundly by modern philosophy to be resolvable by attention to bodily experience. By leaving out this entire domain, Whitehead recognizes, rational intellect has come to focus primarily on the negative, for as he writes: "The negative judgment is the peak of mentality." Bruno Latour similarly refers to the overcoming of this exclusive modern need to denounce, unveil, unmask, negate, and critique as the realization that this mode of thought, "the critical spirit" is "one competence among others" (Bruno Latour, *We Have Never Been Modern*, Cambridge, MA: Harvard University Press, 1993, 44). As Whitehead suggests, the focus solely on intellect denies conscious access to the more fundamental kinds of meaning that rational thought can structure, analyze, and critique, but cannot engender. And Whitehead, like James and Bergson, explicitly calls for the reintegration of these two modes, going as far as to nominate this epistemological synthesis "Wisdom." While in our personal lives we may recognize the efficacy of intuitive modes, Whitehead seems to suggest that as long as these modes are "omitted" from open commerce with our explicit intellectual understanding, our culture will never attain "Wisdom" as a collectivity, but only rational knowledge, an imbalanced situation that seems to have played a large part in producing the ecological, economic, social, and political crises in which we now find ourselves. According to Whitehead, the durational domain of "instantaneous reality" between "mind" and "material" is the organismic locus of lived experience in the animal body that has been repressed by the predominant scientific mentality, but which seems to have been slowly reemerging in the twentieth century, partially through the medium of popular music, perhaps reaching a peak with rock and roll (Alfred North Whitehead, *Modes of Thought*, New York: The Free Press, 1968, 153-160; Alfred North Whitehead, *Process and Reality: Corrected Edition*, Ed. David Ray Griffin and Donald W. Sherburne, New York: The Free Press, 1985, 5; Alfred North Whitehead, *Adventures of Ideas*, New York: The Free Press, 1967, 4, 43, 47, 99, 118, 148, 159; *Science and the Modern World* vii, 2, 54, 57, 143-47, 87).

[29] Guralnick 192, 243.

[30] *New York Herald-Tribune*, August 18, 1956.

[31] Lloyd Shearer, *Parade*, July 1956.

[32] Tim Riley, *Tell Me Why: The Beatles: album by album, song by song, the sixties and after* (Cambridge, MA: Da Capo, 2002) 10.

[33] Jerry Hopkins, *Elvis* (New York: Simon and Schuster, 1971).

[34] Gerry McLafferty, *Elvis Presley in Hollywood: Celluloid Sell Out* (London: Robert Hale Ltd., 1990).

[35] Robert Palmer, *Rock & Roll: an unruly history* (New York: Harmony Books, 1995) 28.

[36] Guralnick 313.

[37] Palmer 17. The beat poets, as well as the bebop movement in jazz, have much in common with the countercultural phenomenon of rock and roll, largely defining the American "hipster" aesthetic that Presley came to exemplify. In this indirect sense, the proto-beats and bebop musicians had a profound effect on the culture that produced Presley, though the beat movement is usually marked as beginning in earnest on October 7, 1955, the occasion of Allen Ginsberg's first reading of "Howl," more than a year after the release of Presley's first single, "That's All Right."

Regardless, neither the beats nor bebop, which had begun in the forties, were on Presley's radar, so to speak. While the work of Jack Kerouac or Miles Davis allowed high cultural access to the more intuitive and somatic modes that Presley embodied, there does not seem to be a direct link between the literary movement of the beats, the intellectual aesthetic performed musically by bebop, and the music of Elvis Presley. Thus, while acknowledging that the beats and bebop enacted a similar impulse to that of rock and roll, this study is primarily concerned with the influences and cultural domains that Presley and his milieu themselves saw as their immediate precursors and contemporaries, namely, popular musicians and actors.

Certainly all of these figures—poets, actors, and different kinds of musicians—were part of a larger movement in culture away from the exclusive privileging of intellect toward intuitive and somatic modes, and these various countercultural expressions were ultimately reintegrated with intellect in complex ways. However, whereas the beats essentially enacted the trajectory toward affect from the basis of a poetic genre that implicitly privileged verbal intellect even while it pushed against it, and bebop carried jazz, which had been the previously predominant musical incarnation of the repressed epistemologies, toward intellect, Presley and his contemporaries generally embodied a more pure expression of affectivity without immediate reference to intellectual domains.

Nevertheless, there is little doubt that the original rock and rollers were ultimately reacting to this privileging, and that the further permutations of the genre, particularly those of the Beatles, Dylan, and their contemporaries, would engage with rationality much more intimately than Presley's milieu. Both the beats and bebop were explicitly in dialogue with the predominant rational mode whereas Presley and the majority of fifties rock and rollers were not in any significant way. Rather, the privileging of scientific rationality in modern discourse, exemplified in the Cartesian equation of thought with human existence in general, formed the background against which rock and roll was brought into being. Although rock and roll did implicitly gain its significance by contrast to the predominant discursive modes, the genre's relationship with the intellectually privileging main streams of culture was qualitatively different than the aesthetic modes employed by the beats and bebop.

[38] Cf. *American Cool: Constructing a Twentieth-Century Emotional Style* by Peter N. Stearns

[39] Frith writes: "The problem of populist cultural studies is less its politics than its sociology, its assumption that the 'popular' is defined by

the market. The populist position is that whatever our (class-bound) personal tastes and values may be, we have to accept that sales figures, box office returns, and record charts tell us what 'the people' want. It's only a residual academic elitism that leads us to celebrate the radical or avant-garde" (Simon Frith, *Performing Rites*, Cambridge, MA: Harvard University Press, 1996, 15).

[40] As Mark Lewisohn writes: "The entertainment business couldn't grasp that rock was the purest movement of them all because it had grown organically out of rhythm and blues, and that, at its best, it was natural and thrilling. It couldn't be deposed by artifice" (Mark Lewisohn, *Tune In: The Beatles: All These Years*, New York: Crown Archetype, 2013, 116).

[41] Anthony DeCurtis, *Rocking My Life Away* (Durham, NC: Duke University Press Books, 1999) x.

[42] Palmer 11.

[43] Guralnick 241.

[44] Glenn C. Altschuler, *All Shook Up: How Rock 'N' Roll Changed America* (New York: Oxford University Press, 2003) 8.

[45] Riley 9. Conversely, Palmer argues that, "for many of these 'first-generation rockers,' the idea of a separate category of music called rock and roll is itself inherently suspect." (7) Later, he writes: "Musically, rock and roll was not so much a departure from tradition as an evolutionary synthesis. For a hypothetical (and highly unlikely) listener well versed in the history of jazz, gospel, hillbilly, western swing, Latin music, blues, and r&b, fifties rock would have held few surprises" (141). In all fairness, Palmer does seem to draw back from this assertion in other passages, but this general attitude seems to be concomitant with the intellectual, scientific orientation described by Henri Bergson in *Creative Evolution*: "Like ordinary knowledge, in dealing with things science is concerned only with the aspect of *repetition*. Though the whole be original, science will always manage to analyze it into elements or aspects which are approximately a reproduction of the past" (24-25). Although Palmer's analysis is excellent in many ways, he tends to favor the mode which reduces novel emergent phenomena to their constituent parts rather than focusing on the synthesis that transcends the individual components.

[46] Ed. Anthony Thornton, *Uncut Legends: Elvis* (Issue no. 5, 2005) 143.

[47] Altschuler 33.

[48] Charlie Gillett, *The Sound of the City*, 25-26.

[49] Melissa Gregg and Gregory J. Seigworth, *The Affect Theory Reader*, Durham (NC: Duke University Press, 2010) 1.

[50] Cf. Lewis MacAdams, *Birth of the Cool: Beat, Bebop, and the American Avant Garde* (New York: Free Press, 2001). The quality of affective authenticity appears to bear a strong resemblance to Martin Heidegger's discussion of "Dasein" in *Being and Time*, of authentic human being in the world in contrast with rationalized, "vulgar" temporal being.

[51] Altschuler 31 and Palmer 133.

[52] Gould 17-18.

[53] *Science and the Modern World* 2.

[54] Palmer 83.

[55] Altschuler 24.

[56] Palmer 150.

[57] A number of other earlier songs have been claimed, with some justification, as the first rock and roll song, including Wynonie Harris' version of "Good Rockin' Tonight (1947), "The Fat Man" by Fats Domino (1949), and "Rocket 88" by Jackie Brenston and his Delta Cats (1951) . However, it is my contention that "That's All Right" was the song that first fully concretized the impulse toward the new genre evident in these earlier songs.

[58] *Elvis at Sun*

[59] Altschuler 26.

[60] Gould 19.

[61] As Richard Tarnas explains in *The Passion of the Western Mind*: "The spirit of nature brings forth its *own* order through the human mind when that mind is employing its full complement of faculties—intellectual, volitional, emotional, sensory, imaginative, aesthetic, epiphanic." What Tarnas nominates a "participatory epistemology" is precisely the dialectical synthesis of premodern and modern modes for which Presley was intuitively reaching, that he embodied though he did not possess the vocabulary to describe his activities as such. Even if he had possessed the inclination to master the complex philosophical or poetic discourse required to describe the deeper meaning of his musical performativity, Presley would not have had the time both to do what he was doing and to explain it to the world—that is what philosophers are for. (Richard Tarnas, *The Passion of the Western Mind: Understanding the Ideas that Have Shaped Our World View*, New York: Ballantine Books, 1991, 435)

[62] Guralnick 153, 245.

[63] The chorus from Dylan's "Like a Rolling Stone." Bob Dylan, *Highway 61 Revisited* (Columbia Records, 1965).

[64] Guralnick 335.

[65] Allen Ginsberg, *Howl and Other Poems* (San Francisco: City Lights

Publishers, 2001) 9-26.

[66] Guralnick 335-6.

[67] Guralnick 99.

[68] Altschuler 27.

[69] Guralnick 103.

[70] Altschuler 191. As Frantz Fanon writes in *The Wretched of the Earth*: "Two centuries ago, a former European colony decided to catch up with Europe. It succeeded so well that the United States of America became a monster, in which the taints, the sickness and the inhumanity of Europe have grown to appalling dimensions." Here, Fanon seems to be employing Europe as the symbolic origin of Western modernity in which slavery, segregation, racism, sexism, classism, and imperialism have formed the long shadow of the Enlightenment myth of unlimited progress and the rational "ascent of man." Indeed, as Fanon implies, this "sickness" and "inhumanity" seem to be products of the exclusive privileging of intellect divorced from affect for, as he continues: "Let us decide not to imitate Europe; let us combine our muscles and our brains in a new direction. Let us try to create the whole man, whom Europe has been incapable of bringing to triumphant birth" (Frantz Fanon, *The Wretched of the Earth*, New York: Grove Press, 2005, 236-37). Instead of continuing the primarily Western hegemony of the rational, Fanon seems to suggest that the way forward is to integrate body and mind, "muscles" and "brains," for the elicitation of novelty, which will produce the birth of "the whole man" who will maintain balance between all of the different epistemological modes necessary for healthy sustainability. These repressed modes seem to be symbolized for Fanon by what he describes as "the Third World," though this term is apparently just as applicable to marginalized groups within Europe and the United States. Fanon's project seems essentially complicit with the work of James, Jung, Bergson, and Whitehead, though in a rather different cultural domain than the ones explicated by these old, white, Eurocentric men. Indeed, Alfred North Whitehead is reported as having said: "Let Americans study Europe and see what has been done. But when it comes to creation, God bless my soul! then forget everything that has ever been done before and create!" (Lucien Price, *Dialogues of Alfred North Whitehead*, Boston: Nonpareil, 2001, 60).

Based on Fanon's work, it seems plausible that the institution of slavery and, later, of segregation, produced a situation in which African American culture was literally forced to privilege and exemplify the epistemologies that had been repressed and identified as "other" by the dominant white culture as, according to Brian Ward, whites "had long reified black culture as the perpetually fascinating but feral, alluring but alarming, sensual but sordid antithesis to the dominant white one" (Brian Ward, *Just My Soul Responding: Rhythm and Blues, Black Consciousness, and Race Relations,* Berkeley, CA: University of California Press, 1998, 39). Since most African Americans generally did not have access to literacy (with notable exceptions), and they were often forced to do physically demanding work and to live in extremely modest circumstances, whether through chattel slavery or through endemic economic and social racism, many black Americans essentially had no choice but to privilege the affective efficacy that was necessary for both physical and psychological survival under such conditions. Through the instrumentality of racial oppression, American culture seems to have literalized the larger process of the individuation of intellect by means of the repression of other epistemologies. Through an institutionalized system of cultural domination and violence, many African Americans may have been forced to privilege somatic and intuitive modes while many white Americans were coerced by somewhat more subtle cultural pressures to embody a mode that privileged science, intellect, and rationality.

However, as Amiri Baraka points out in 1963's *Blues People*, there appears already to have been a definite cultural difference before the enslavement of Africans by Europeans, which chattel slavery channeled into a hierarchical relation that had not previously existed between the two equally essential epistemological modes privileged in the two cultures. He writes:

> When black people got to this country, they were Africans, a foreign people. Their customs, attitudes, desires, were shaped to a different place, a radically different life. . . . To be brought to a country, a culture, a society, that was, and is, in terms of purely philosophical correlatives, the complete antithesis of one's own version of man's life . . . This idea seems to me one of the most important aspects of the enslavement of the African: the radically different, even opposing, *Weltanschauung's* which the colonial American and the African brought to each other. Each man, in whatever 'type' of culture he inhabits, must have a way of looking at the world—whatever that means to him—which is peculiar to his particular culture. It is extremely important to understand that these diametrically opposed

interpretations of life would be in conflict normally in the most minute human contacts. But when a man who sees the world one way becomes the slave of a man who interprets the world in an exactly opposite way, the result is, to my mind, the *worst* possible kind of slavery. . . . So-called nonliterate peoples, (called by Western man 'primitive'), whose languages, and therefore whose cultural and traditional histories, are not written, are the antithesis of Western man and his highly industrialized civilization. But the idea of the 'primordial man,' or 'undeveloped peoples,' becomes absurd if we dismiss for a change the assumption that only the ideas and attitudes which the West finds useful or analogous to concepts forwarded within its own system are of any real value or profundity (Amiri Baraka, *Blues People*, New York: Harper Perennial, 1999, 1-6).

Having acknowledged this general factor in the construction of race in America, though, it should be noted that Baraka, in his 1999 preface to *Blues People*, revised the view expressed above as an oversimplification of a more subtle process, though it would be difficult to deny that this simplified conceptual structure has not to a great extent formed the basis for discourse surrounding issues of race, culture, music, and epistemology in America. Indeed, the very mode of "conceptual simplification" is characteristic of the rationality privileged in Europe-derived cultures as opposed to the apparently more embodied modes privileged in Africa-derived cultures. As Baraka writes:

It was the contrasting aspect of the theme that first superficially captured me: That there was a body of music that came to exist from a people who were brought to this side as slaves and that throughout that music's development, it had had to survive, expand, reorganize, continue, and express itself as the fragile property of a powerless and oppressed People. . . . My deep concentration on the continuing evidence of surviving "Africanisms" and parallels between African customs and philosophies, mores, etc., and the philosophies and their Afro-American continuum were to teach myself, and whoever, that Black people did not drop out of the sky, although, "fo' sho'," they continue

> to be, despite the wildest of ironies, the most American
> of Americans. . . . For all the syncretic re-presentation
> and continuation of African mores and beliefs, even
> under the hideous wrap of chattel slavery . . . there is one
> thing that I have learned, since the original writing of
> *Blues People*, that I feel must be a critical new emphasis
> not understood completely by me in the earlier text. That
> is, that *the Africanisms are not limited to Black people,
> but indeed American culture itself, is shaped by and
> includes a great many Africanisms. So that American
> culture, in the real world, is a composite of African,
> European, and Native or Akwesasne cultures, history,
> and people* (Baraka ix-xi).

Thus, it seems that it is primarily in the collective American conception that the distinct historical bifurcation between affectively and somatically oriented African American culture and rationally and logocentrically oriented white American culture has been operative, as "American culture, in the real world," is always already a mixture and assemblage of many individuals of varying skin tones, socio-cultural milieus, attitudes, backgrounds, and beliefs. Consequently, racial bifurcation was a pervasive fiction, in which African American theorists like Fanon and Baraka also necessarily participated to some extent, which produced real effects in the American experience, a paradoxically generative and tragic narrative tension whose deconstruction was largely effected through music.

[71] Cf. Michael T. Bertrand, *Race, Rock, and Elvis* (Champaign, IL: University of Illinois Press, 2000).

[72] Guralnick 27-28.

[73] Palmer 77.

[74] *Passion* 419.

[75] Altschuler 19.

[76] Gary Kays, "Elvis Defends Low-Down Style," *Charlotte Observer*, June 27, 1956.

[77] *Tune In* 90.

[78] Altschuler 57, 63, 66.

[79] Robert Johnson, " Suddenly Singing Elvis Presley Zooms into Recording Stardom," *Memphis Press-Scimitar* (February 5, 1955).

[80] Guralnick 60, 134.

[81] Palmer 25.

[82] Palmer 21 and Altschuler 35, 48.

[83] Altschuler 51.

[84] Guralnick 135.

[85] Altschuler 30.

[86] Guralnick 195, 172.

[87] Bob Dylan, *New Morning* (Columbia Records, 1970) "Went to See the Gypsy."

[88] For one instance, fully two thirds of people watching television in America were watching Presley's appearance on *The Frank Sinatra Show* during its broadcast: "The subsequent ratings . . . representing 67.7-percent audience share." Peter Guralnick, *Careless Love: The Unmaking of Elvis Presley* (New York: Back Bay Books, 2000) 63.

[89] Cf. John Leland, *Hip: The History* (New York: Ecco, 2004).

[90] Ren Grevatt, "On the Beat," *Billboard* (September 29, 1958).

[91] Guralnick 94.

[92] *Adventures* 80.

[93] *Science and the Modern World* 1.

[94] Guralnick 94-95.

[95] Hegel 18-19.

[96] Gould 20.

[97] Guralnick 96.

[98] Trevor Cajiao interview with Scotty Moore, "We Were the Only Band Directed by an Ass," *Elvis: The Man and His Music 10* (March 1991) 19.

[99] Guralnick 96, 112.

[100] Palmer 17.

[101] Guralnick 103, 133.

[102] *Process and Reality* 25.

[103] Cf. Mihaly Csikszentmihalyi, *Flow: The Psychology of Optimal Experience* (Rider and Co, 2002) 3-4.

[104] Guralnick 133-34.

[105] Altschuler 12.

[106] Guralnick 132.

[107] "Yeh-Heh-Heh-Hes, Baby," *Time* (June 18, 1956).

[108] Guralnick 100, 102.

[109] Cajiao 19.

[110] Altschuler 5-6.

[111] *New York Times* (June 6, 1956).

[112] *New York Journal-American* (June 9, 1956).

[113] Ben Gross, *New York Daily News* (June 5, 1956).

[114] Jack O'Brian, *New York Journal-American* (November 8, 1957).

[115] Dick William, *Los Angeles Mirror-News* (November 8, 1957).

[116] Altschuler 6.

[117] John Jackson, *Big Beat Heat: Alan Freed and the Early Years of Rock & Roll* (New York: Schirmer Book, 1996) 146.

[118] Gould 75.

[119] Linda Martin and Kerry Segrave, *Anti-Rock: The Opposition to Rock 'n' Roll* (Cambridge, MA: Da Capo Press, 1993) 46-47.

[120] Palmer 144.

[121] Guralnick 286.

[122] Altschuler 46.

[123] Guralnick 384 and Altschuler 8 and Cf. Ward's *Just My Soul Responding*.

[124] Hegel 18-19.

[125] *Science and the Modern World* 47.

[126] This connection is often evoked by Bob Dylan in his consistent employment of "jester" imagery, his song "Jokerman" being the most obvious example.

[127] Palmer 147.

[128] Guralnick 79.

[129] *Tune In* 123.

[130] Altschuler 67.

[131] Guralnick 120, 171, 205, 319-320.

[132] Elvis Presley, "The Complete T.V. Guide Presents Elvis Interview," *Young Man with the Big Beat: The Complete '56 Elvis Presley Masters* (Sony Legacy, 2011).

[133] "Elvis Gives Out with Crazy Cool Interview," *Waco News-Tribune* (April 18, 1956).

[134] *Tacoma News Tribune* (September 2, 1957).

[135] Guralnick 172.

[136] *Cowboy Songs* (June 1955).

[137] Cf. Terence McKenna's *Archaic Revival* (HarperSanFrancisco, 1991).

[138] Guralnick 106, 110.

[139] I say "nearly" because there are some precursors in the reaction to Frank Sinatra or even Stravinsky's *The Rite of Spring*, accompanied at its premier by Vaslav Nijinsky's controversial choreography, though certainly not on this scale or degree of intensity.

[140] Guralnick 119.

[141] Cf. William James, *Essays in Radical Empiricism* (Mineola, NY: Dover Publications, 2003).

[142] Jerry Hopkins interview with Bob Neal

[143] Guralnick 174.

[144] *Varieties* 325.

[145] Guralnick 352-3, 151.

[146] Palmer 66.

[147] Ger Rijff, *Memphis Lonesome* (Amsterdam: Tutti Frutti Productions, 1985) 19.

[148] Guralnick 344, 110.

[149] Palmer 8.

[150] Guralnick 120, 264.

[151] *Tune In* 319.

[152] Douglas Brinkley, "Bob Dylan's America," *Rolling Stone* (May 14, 2009) 48.

[153] Robert Johnson, "Elvis Sings and Thousands Scream," *Memphis Press-Scimitar* (July 5, 1956).

[154] In his *The Making of a Counter Culture*, Theodore Roszak defines "counter culture" as "a culture so radically disaffiliated from the mainstream assumptions of our society that it scarcely looks to many as a culture at all, but it takes on the alarming appearance of a barbaric intrusion" (42). However, although this definition emphasizes the radical difference from the predominant cultural streams and the predominant culture's inevitable resistance to the counterculture, in practice, the counterculture often participates in the main streams of culture by dissenting from within the established pathways of commerce, generally seeking to transform those avenues of transmission rather than abandon them altogether. Presley, the Beatles, Dylan, and their contemporaries did not found new societies completely divorced from their cultures, but transgressed their cultures' normative assumptions enough to transform them in fundamental ways while still being able to participate in collective discourse.

It is only through this dialectical process, creating a counterculture *within* the field of the dominant discursive streams that cultures are inexorably transformed. But cultures can only transform so quickly, and those who seek to remake their culture too radically can dissolve into incoherence or lose the very things that make us human, an extreme example of which is Charles Manson and his cult, who, through tragedy, forced the sixties counterculture to complicate some of its more simplistic ideas about liberation through sex, drugs, and social organization. Ultimately, Roszak asserts, the counterculture "strikes beyond ideology to the level of consciousness, seeking to transform our deepest sense of self, the other, the environment"(49).

[155] The term "postmodern" has meant different things to different people. It was originally coined by Charles Olson, one of the Black Mountain poets, as a way of articulating the radical break from the limiting

assumptions of modernity. However, I am employing the term here in the way it has come most commonly to be used: as "an incredulity toward metanarratives," to quote Jean-Francois Lyotard.

[156] Richard Tarnas, *Cosmos and Psyche: Intimations of a New World View* (Plume, 2006) 14.

[157] Riley 20-21.

[158] As Gould sums up the impact of the phenomenon surrounding the early Beatles: "From its frenzied, inchoate beginnings in Britain and the United States, the great upsurge of adolescent fervor that the press called Beatlemania would coalesce into one of the main tributaries of a broad confluence of pop enthusiasm, student activism, and mass bohemianism that would flood the political, social, and cultural landscape of much of the industrialized world during the second half of the 1960s" (Gould 8).

[159] MacDonald 13.

[160] Ray Connelly, *Times of London*, September 6, 2008.

[161] *Tune In* 13, 133.

[162] David Sheff and G. Barry Golson, eds., *The Playboy Interviews with John Lennon and Yoko Ono* (New York: Playboy Press, 1981).

[163] *Tune In* 473.

[164] John Lennon, *The Beatles Anthology*, Dir. Geoff Wonfor and Bob Smeaton (Apple Corps, 2003).

[165] *Pragmatism* 1.

[166] MacDonald 27.

[167] Steve Turner, *The Gospel According to the Beatles* (Louisville, KY: Westminster John Knox Press, 2006) 9.

[168] Riley 12.

[169] Spitz 41.

[170] The Beatles, *The Beatles Anthology* (San Francisco: Chronicles, 2000) 11.

[171] Hunter Davies, *The Beatles* (New York: W. W. Norton & Company, 2010) 19.

[172] *Rolling Stone* (June 28, 1970).

[173] Spitz 41.

[174] Riley 13-14.

[175] However, as Palmer notes: "rock and roll genealogy . . . is never as linear and clear-cut as the beleaguered student might wish" (Palmer 72).

[176] *Tune In* 787.

[177] Spitz 49.

[178] *Tune In* 132.

[179] Spitz 38, 56, 63.

[180] Gould 62.

[181] Palmer 140.

[182] *Tune In* 167.

[183] Jann Wenner, *Lennon Remembers* (New York: Popular Library, 1971) 168.

[184] Guralnick 212.

[185] *Tune In* 8.

[186] Spitz 65.

[187] *Tune In* 99.

[188] Gould 47.

[189] Some have interpreted Lennon's willful authenticity as a kind of dilettantish pose, and not without some justification, for although Lennon would proclaim himself a "working-class hero," he was actually the most solidly middle-class member of the Beatles, McCartney declaring "John's family was rather middle-class" (*Tune In* 16). Thus, as with Bob Dylan, there was a kind of paradoxical artifice in Lennon's performance of authenticity, though, to my mind, this conceit does not detract appreciably from Lennon's art.

[190] Spitz 97.

[191] Riley 20.

[192] Spitz 98.

[193] *Beatles Anthology* (book) 12, Riley 23, and *Tune In* 11.

[194] Gould 34, Spitz 437, *Tune In* 8, and Riley 23.

[195] *Tune In* 129.

[196] Billy Shepherd, *The True Story of the Beatles* (New York: Bantam, 1964) 16.

[197] Gould 59.

[198] Spitz 110-11.

[199] MacDonald 20-21.

[200] Riley 29 and Palmer 65.

[201] Gould 68.

[202] Spitz 128.

[203] *Tune In* 108.

[204] Spitz 130-31.

[205] MacDonald 10-11 and Gould 8, 178.

[206] Riley 17.

[207] Bergson 159.

[208] *Beatles Anthology* (book) 22. As John Lennon put it: "Practically every Buddy Holly song was three chords, so why not write your own?" (*Tune In* 11).

[209] Riley 46.

[210] Spitz 132.

[211] *Tune In* 9.

[212] Gould 65-66.

[213] Spitz 133.

[214] *Process and Reality* 25, 85.

[215] Spitz 133.

[216] *Tune In* 13.

[217] *The Playboy Interviews with John Lennon and Yoko Ono* 119.

[218] MacDonald x.

[219] Riley 33.

[220] Spitz 133.

[221] *Beatles Anthology* (book) 23.

[222] *Tune In* 10.

[223] Spitz 135.

[224] Riley 8-9.

[225] Gould 42.

[226] Spitz 35-36, 142-43, 555.

[227] Riley 15.

[228] Barry Miles, *Paul McCartney: Many Years from Now* (New York: Henry Holt, 1997) 49.

[229] *Tune In* 182.

[230] John Lennon, *John Lennon/Plastic Ono Band* (Apple/EMI, 1970).

[231] Spitz 176.

[232] Riley 12.

[233] Cf. Whitehead's *The Aims of Education* for his discussion of these "stages" of "romance" and "precision."

[234] According to Lewisohn, the Beatles were "the first Liverpool rock group to go on tour" (*Tune In* 308).

[235] Spitz 190.

[236] Jody Cook and Patty Henry, *Graceland National Historic Landmark Nomination Form,* 13. (http://www.nps.gov/nhl/designations/samples/tn/Graceland.pdf, accessed 2/8/10).

[237] Spitz 190.

[238] *Tune In* 500.

[239] Gould 104.

[240] *Beatles Anthology*.

[241] Spitz 207.

[242] Artist Christian Ebert, personal communication.

[243] *Tune In* 354.

[244] Gould 78-82 and *Tune In* 366.

245 Spitz 209.

246 Gould 38.

247 MacDonald 9.

248 *Tune In* 125.

249 Spitz 209.

250 Price 59-60. Price attributes this quote to section XIII of *Science and the Modern World*, though this section does not contain such a quote, at least in the 1967 Free Press edition.

251 *Tune In* 422, 767.

252 *Beatles Anthology*

253 Spitz 210, 212.

254 According to Alain Danielou, quoted in Palmer: "A very high level of sound is useful in inducing states of trance" (Palmer 149).

255 Gould 81.

256 *Tune In* 417, 447.

257 Spitz 217 and *Tune In* 367.

258 MacDonald 9.

259 Spitz 219 and *Tune In* 445.

260 Cynthia Lennon, *A Twist of Lennon* (New York: Avon Books, 1980) 55.

261 Spitz 245.

262 McCartney describes them in the *Anthology*: "They weren't really rockers or mods like we'd seen. They were something in the middle. They called themselves "exis:" existentialists. They were art students, really." *Beatles Anthology*.

263 *Tune In* 378.

264 Riley 26.

265 Gould 87.

266 Spitz 223-24.

267 Gould 4.

268 Riley 41 and Spitz 225.

269 Spitz 234.

270 Gould 82.

271 Spitz 4-5.

272 Bergson 41.

273 Spitz 6. It should be noted that, although original rock and roll had subsided, great music was still being made in the late fifties and early sixties, particularly in the Brill Building output exemplified by Phil Spector, who strongly influenced the Beatles. However, the Beatles seem to have felt that the music of the late-fifties and early sixties lacked something of the visceral intensity and epochal novelty of mid-fifties

rock and roll. In particular, they experienced the British rock and roll scene as particularly anemic, with Cliff Richard and the Shadows its primary exemplar in that moment.

[274] *Tune In* 778.

[275] Spitz 11.

[276] *Tune In* 404.

[277] Spitz 11-12.

[278] Gould 82.

[279] Spitz 12, 202.

[280] Gould 89.

[281] Spitz 237, 300. Similarly, Gould refers to the Top Ten Club in Hamburg, where the Beatles found the peak of their early success in that city, as having been promoted "as a mecca for rock 'n' roll" (Gould 94).

[282] Riley 6.

[283] *Tune In* 695.

[284] Spitz 268.

[285] Gould 109.

[286] *Tune In* 711.

[287] Spitz 269, 274.

[288] *Tune In* 517, 839.

[289] Gould 116-117.

[290] *Tune In* 520.

[291] Spitz 279.

[292] *New York Times* (February 8, 1964) 49.

[293] Gould 129-134.

[294] Spitz 555.

[295] As Lewisohn writes: "Sometimes in life, things go right; only very rarely do that *all* go right, and so it was now—for them and for everyone and everything around them" (*Tune In* 839).

[296] *Beatles Anthology.*

[297] *Tune In* 542, 568.

[298] Spitz 279-80.

[299] *Paul McCartney* 96.

[300] *Tune In* 17.

[301] MacDonald 12-13.

[302] Spitz 280-81, 555.

[303] *Paul McCartney* 89.

[304] *Tune In* 559.

[305] *The Beatles Book Monthly* (January 1983) 7.

[306] MacDonald 34.

[307] Gould 121.

[308] Spitz 296.

[309] The story of how the Beatles came to be signed by Parlophone appears to have been rather more complex than it has usually been reported, though this complexity is not particularly relevant to the project of this book, and thus will only be alluded to here. According to Lewisohn: "Though it would remain an ingrained myth that Parlophone was the impoverished laughingstock of the record business, the perennial last pick in the playground, it had long been (and by spring 1962 clearly was) the most eclectic, diverse and fascinating record label in Britain and the world." Similarly, Kim Bennett, who worked for Sidney Colman, recalls that "the Beatles record was going to be made as a *gesture* to Sid, to give Sid Colman a sop." And according to Lewisohn, Len Wood, the managing director of EMI (Parlophone's parent company), "virtually ordered George [Martin] to record the Beatles" (*Tune In* 637, 640,). However, the statements from some of the participants seem to contradict Lewisohn's apparently authoritative judgment, so I will leave it to scholars of the Beatles' business dealings to debate these issues. Nevertheless, whether or not Martin was obliged to record the Beatles, that they won the producer to their cause in the session described below seems the most significant factor in their early recording career.

[310] George Martin, *All You Need Is Ears* (New York: St. Martin's Griffin Press, 1994) 84.

[311] Martin 122.

[312] Although the Beatles had technically already been signed by Martin to Parlophone for political reasons as discussed above, and their first meeting with him was officially a recording date, Martin "considered the session little more than a look-see, a chance to assess the group he'd signed blind" (*Tune In* 667). This session would determine how much effort and energy Martin would put into the group, and thus it really was a kind of "audition," not for a recording contract, but for Martin's enthusiastic involvement, which would prove essential to the group's success.

[313] Spitz 306, 308.

[314] Gould 112.

[315] Riley 9.

[316] *Tune In* 756. Despite the Beatles' recent immersion in the more somatic mode characteristic of both rock and roll and the Reeperbahn, the rational mode had been inculcated into them from a young age as an intrinsic part of English education. Although the Beatles' experiences in English schools had prepared them for their encounter with Abbey Road to a far greater extent than the analogy to the meeting of primitive tribe

and advanced technological civilization suggests, there does seem to have been something of this quality endemic to the situation, as apparent in descriptions of the Beatles' first encounter with Abbey Road is an evocation not only of regional prejudice, but of class distinctions between the basically working class attitude of the Beatles (belied somewhat by particularly Lennon's middle-class background) and the relatively high cultural environment of Abbey Road. The encounter between the Beatles and Abbey Road seems to have exemplified the friction, and eventual integration, of working-class and middle-class modes of relation. (*Tune In* 664, Gould 46, and MacDonald 25).

[317] The title of Ian MacDonald's book.

[318] *Beatles Anthology.*

[319] Spitz 316.

[320] Gould 121.

[321] Spitz 350.

[322] Gould 109 and Spitz 59.

[323] Turner 10,Riley 26 and Gould 14.

[324] Spitz 316, 350.

[325] Gould 122.

[326] Spitz 210.

[327] Martin 123.

[328] Gould 122-123.

[329] Martin 123.

[330] Brian Southall, *Abbey Road: The Story of the World's Most Famous Recording Studio* (Cambridge, UK: Stevens, 1982) 81.

[331] Riley 27.

[332] *Tune In* 668.

[333] Gould 123.

[334] *Tune In* 670.

[335] Spitz 318-319.

[336] William J. Dowlding, *Beatlesongs* (New York: Fireside, 1989) 35.

[337] Spitz 318-319.

[338] In Hamburg, according to Lewisohn: "The first to buy a leather jacket, George, was also the first to get the boots" (*Tune In* 395), a style which the other Beatles soon adopted.

[339] *Process and Reality* 5.

[340] *Tune In* 417-18.

[341] Gould 83, 126.

[342] Spitz 325.

[343] *Tune In* 112.

[344] Gould 309.

345 Riley 25, 44.

346 *Tune In* 719.

347 Michael Braun, *Love Me Do: The Beatles' Progress* (London: Penguin, 1964) 37.

348 *Beatles Anthology.*

349 Spitz 338-9.

350 Riley 29 and *Tune In* 71.

351 Spitz 325.

352 *Tune In* 550.

353 Riley 41-43.

354 *Tune In* 716.

355 Southall 78.

356 *Tune In* 665.

357 Spitz 352-53 and *Tune In* 648.

358 *Tune In* 672.

359 Palmer 9 and *Tune In* 582.

360 Spitz 352.

361 *Tune In* 746, 748.

362 Gould 137, 142.

363 Riley 45 and *Tune In* 731. It should be noted, however, that the Brill Building/Girl Group/Motown era in the early sixties pushed popular music, including rock and roll, toward complexity in ways that presaged "Please Please Me," though the Beatles brought the visceral intensity of early rock and roll together with the instrumental and harmonic sophistication of what Phil Spector referred to as "little symphonies for the kids" in an unprecedented manner (Palmer 37-39, *Tune In* 420).

364 *Tune In* 725.

365 Martin 130.

366 Riley 47.

367 Gould 138-141.

368 Riley 47.

369 Gould 142.

370 *Tune In* 808.

371 Spitz 363.

372 Gould 180.

373 Spitz 363.

374 Gould 92.

375 Spitz 367, 377.

376 The Clash, *London Calling* (Epic Records, 1979).

377 Spitz 371.

378 MacDonald xi-xii and *Tune In* 306, 322, 349, 661.

[379] *Tune In* 492.
[380] *Beatles Anthology.*
[381] *Beatles Book Monthly* (August 1983) 6.
[382] *Tune In* 820.
[383] Spitz 373, 375.
[384] Maureen Cleave, *Evening Standard* (February 2, 1963) 145.
[385] Gould 157.
[386] Spitz 384, 398.
[387] *Sunday Times* (November 3, 1963).
[388] David Bailey and Peter Evans, *Goodbye Baby and Amen* (New York: Coward McCann, 1969) 73.
[389] Barbara Ehrenreich, Elizabeth Hess, and Gloria Jacobs, *Re-Making Love* (Garden City, NY: Doubleday, 1986) 35.
[390] Gould 184.
[391] *Vancouver Sun* (August 24, 1964).
[392] "Beatles Bat It Out for Seattle," *Seattle Post-Intelligencer* (August 22, 1964).
[393] *Daily Mail* (October 1, 1963).
[394] Geoffrey Giuliano, *Dark Horse: The Secret Life of George Harrison* (London: Pan, 1991) 47.
[395] Jack Gould, "The Beatles and Their Audience," *New York Times* (February 10, 1964).
[396] *Washington Post* (February 10, 1964).
[397] *Newsweek* (November 18, 1963).
[398] *Herald Tribune* (February 10, 1964).
[399] *Cosmos and Psyche* xiiv.
[400] *Beatles Anthology* (book) 120.
[401] Gould 167, 233.
[402] Spitz 497.
[403] Gould 260.
[404] *Beatles Anthology.*
[405] Spitz 541-542.
[406] Wenner 106.
[407] Sheff 121.
[408] *Tune In* 4.
[409] Ray Coleman, *McCartney: Yesterday and Today* (London: Boxtree Ltd., 1998) 6.
[410] Paul Gambaccini, *Paul McCartney: In His Own Words* (London: Omnibus Press, 1993) 17-19 and Coleman 7.
[411] Spitz 62.
[412] "'HELP!' But It's Just in Fun," *NME* (July 30, 1965).

[413] Wyndam, *London Life* (December 1965).

[414] "John Lennon Slams the Critics," *NME* (August 6, 1965).

[415] *Beatles Anthology* (book) 193.

[416] "Shrieks of 55,000 Accompany Beatles," *New York Times*, August 16, 1965.

[417] Keith Badman, *The Beatles: Off the Record* (London: Omnibus Press, 2008) 169-70.

[418] "Paul McCartney as Songwriter," *Herald Tribune* (December 26, 1965) 26.

[419] "Bards of Pop," *Newsweek* (March 24, 1966) 103.

[420] *Beatles Anthology* (book) 194.

[421] Sheff, 163.

[422] *Beatles Anthology* (book) 196.

[423] Mark Lewisohn, *The Beatles: Recording Sessions* (New York: Harmony, 1988) 69.

[424] *Beatles Anthology* (book) 194.

[425] James Hillman, *Re-Visioning Psychology* (New York: HarperCollins 1975) 17.

[426] On his website in 2011, Dylan wrote: "Everybody knows by now that there's a gazillion books on me either out or coming out in the near future. So I'm encouraging anybody who's ever met me, heard me or even seen me, to get in on the action and scribble their own book. You never know, somebody might have a great book in them."[426] And in a 2012 interview for *Rolling Stone*, Dylan exhorts the interviewer: "I'm trying to explain something that can't be explained. Help me out." I believe that some "great" books have been written about Dylan, including *The Ballad of Bob Dylan: A Portrait* by Daniel Mark Epstein, David Hajdu's *Positively Fourth Street*, several books by Greil Marcus, and Dylan's own *Chronicles: Volume One*, which offers an unparalleled view into the inner workings of the man's mind. Thus, although I am not producing a whole book on Dylan, this chapter is my bid to write about him in a way in which he could recognize himself, though in doing so I will often take recourse to philosophers with whom Dylan may not be familiar (or even interested). By illuminating Dylan's artistic brilliance with the conceptual brilliance of the philosophers mentioned throughout, I hope to "help" Dylan "explain something that can't be explained" (Mikal Gilmore, "Bob Dylan Unleashed: A Wild Ride on His New LP and Striking Back at Critics," *Rolling Stone*, September 27, 2012).

In that same extraordinary 2012 interview, Dylan declares: "Everything people say about you or me, they are saying about themselves. They're telling about themselves. Ever notice that? In my case, there's a whole world of scholars, professors and Dylanologists, and everything I do affects them in some way. And, you know, in some ways, I've given them life. They'd be nowhere without me." I acknowledge that many of the things I say about Dylan in the following pages, I am also saying about myself. Certainly, one cannot write a book without revealing something of one's most fundamental preoccupations. And I humbly accept Dylan's designation as "scholar, professor, and Dylanologist," despite his seemingly derogatory intent, though I would also suggest that Dylan rather enjoys the attention, perhaps even requires it, in which case we also give him life. Writing a book about another person is like playing a cover song: the content is the subject's, but the arrangement of that content, the voice, and the interpretation are the writer's.

[427] "Bob Dylan: San Francisco Press Conference," December 1965.

[428] Bob Dylan, *Chronicles* (New York: Simon & Schuster, 2005) 45-46.

[429] Greil Marcus, *Like a Rolling Stone: Bob Dylan at the Crossroads* (New York: PublicAffairs, 2005) 18.

[430] *Rolling Stone* 2012.

[431] Kuhn writes: "almost always the men who achieve these fundamental inventions of a new paradigm have been either very young or very new to the field whose paradigm they change" (Thomas S. Kuhn, *The Structure of Scientific Revolutions*, Chicago, IL: The University of Chicago Press, 1996, 90). Furthermore, although Kuhn is explicitly referring to scientific revolutions, there is ample reason to believe that the dynamics of transformation he articulates hold true for revolutionary moments in all domains of process. As Tarnas elaborates:

> As with the evolution of scientific paradigms, so with all forms of human thought. The emergence of a new philosophical paradigm, whether that of Plato or Aquinas, Kant or Heidegger, is never simply the result of improved logical reasoning from the observed data. Rather, each philosophy, each metaphysical perspective and epistemology, reflects the emergence of a global experiential gestalt that informs that philosopher's vision, that governs his or her reasoning and observations, and that ultimately affects the entire cultural and sociological context within which the

philosopher's vision is taking form (*Passion* 439).

[432] Riley 24.

[433] *Chronicles* 240-1.

[434] *No Direction Home*, Dir. Martin Scorsese (Paramount Pictures, 2005).

[435] Epstein 49.

[436] *Chronicles* 42-43.

[437] Robert Shelton, *No Direction Home* (New York: Ballantine Books, 1987) 12.

[438] Hajdu 66.

[439] Benjamin Hedin, ed. *Studio A: The Bob Dylan Reader* (New York: Norton, 2004) 35.

[440] Hajdu 198.

[441] Hedin 24.

[442] *Playboy*, (Chicago, IL: Playboy, March 1978).

[443] Hajdu 67.

[444] *Chronicles* 95-97, 165.

[445] Hajdu 67.

[446] Shelton 32.

[447] Hajdu 11.

[448] *Chronicles* 34.

[449] Scorsese

[450] *Chronicles* 35.

[451] Gould 100. However, as Robert Palmer suggests: "Often dismissed as a dull interregnum between the original fifties rock explosion and the arrival of the 'modern pop band' in the person of the Beach Boys and the Beatles, the late fifties/early sixties was in many ways a uniquely rich time for rock and roll, and one that found the music growing in fresh and unexpected directions" (Palmer 35). Nevertheless, Dylan seems to have been significantly less interested in the sophistication and musical complexity of the Brill Building, Phil Spector, and the "girl groups" than were the Beatles.

[452] Sean Wilentz, *Bob Dylan In America* (New York: Anchor Books, 2011) 51.

[453] *Chronicles* 48.

[454] Wilentz 66.

[455] Wilentz 50.

[456] *Chronicles* 235.

[457] The other was Dylan's wife at the time, Sarah. Shelton 400.

[458] Wilentz 51.

[459] It seems to have been primarily through poststructuralism, particularly of the French variety, that the term took on its more exclusively

deconstructive tone. In particular, Olson's statement that "the job now, is to be at once archaic and culture-wise" seems to suggest the integration of premodern and modern epistemologies. (Charles Olson, *Selected Letters*, Ed. Ralph Maud, University of California, 2000, 58.)

460 *Chronicles*, 247.

461 Bob Dylan, *Highway 61 Revisited* (Columbia Records, 1965).

462 Marcus 118. Some of these other practices include meditation, yoga, the ingestion of psychoactive substances, breathwork, and various therapeutic modalities.

463 Scorsese

464 *Chronicles* 58.

465 Clinton Heylin, *Dylan: Behind the Shades Revisited* (New York: HarperCollins, 2001) 43.

466 *Passion* 434.

467 *Chronicles* 58.

468 *Chronicles* 49.

469 Anthony Scaduto, *Bob Dylan: An Intimate Biography* (New York: Grosset and Dunlap, 1971) 56.

470 "Let Us Now Praise Little Men," *Time* (May 31, 1963).

471 *Chronicles* 243-44.

472 Epstein 80 and Hedin 33.

473 Hedin 28.

474 Marcus 53.

475 Hajdu 71.

476 *Chronicles* 245.

477 Scorsese

478 *Chronicles* 248.

479 It is instructive that, in a review of *The Freewheelin' Bob Dylan*, Pankake states an unequivocal preference for Dylan's first, relatively conventional self-titled album. (Hedin 17).

480 Bergson 124.

481 *Adventures of Ideas* 159.

482 *Science and the Modern World* vii. Cf. William James, *The Will To Believe and Other Essays in Popular Philosophy, and Human Immortality*, (Digireads.com, 2010) 6.

483 *Chronicles* 250-3.

484 Wilentz 53.

485 *Chronicles* 253-4.

486 Hedin 33-34.

487 Hajdu 191.

488 Scorsese

[489] Hedin 25-26.

[490] Marcus 29.

[491] Hedin 34-35.

[492] *Chronicles* 253-4, 247.

[493] Hajdu 73.

[494] *Chronicles* 27.

[495] In his 2012 interview for *Rolling Stone*, Dylan asserts: "If you were here around that time, you would know that the early Sixties, up to maybe '64, '65, was really the Fifties, the late Fifties. They were still the Fifties, still the same culture, in America anyway. And it was still going strong but fading away. By '66, the new Sixties probably started coming in somewhere along that time and had taken over by the end of the decade. Then, by the time of Woodstock, there was no more Fifties."

[496] *Chronicles* 28, 30, 35-36. If only to bring balance to Dylan's rather negative assessment of his place of origin in the above passage, it is worthwhile to reproduce a passage from *Dialogues of Alfred North Whitehead* as reported by Lucien Price:

> "It often seems to me," Whitehead resumed, "that European man was at his best between 1400 and 1600. Since then our appreciation of beauty has become too overlaid with intellectualizing. We educated people have our aesthetic sense too highly cultivated and do not come to beauty simply enough. It is possible that the feeling for beauty is much more true and strong in unschooled people than in ourselves. The early cathedral builders—even the Norman and Romanesque—did not theorize: they *built*; and the poets went to work much more directly. We of today over-elaborate. The only place I see where another great flowering of European culture might come is in the American Middle West, where the start could be fresh and from the ground up" (Price 60).

It might be suggested that Whitehead's Midwestern "flowering of European culture," predicted in 1935, is evident in rock and roll, particularly in Dylan and Presley, as Whitehead assents to the broad definition of the Midwest suggested by Price as "between the Appalachians and the Rockies. . . . Roughly, the Mississippi Basin" (Price 68). As if designed to fulfill Whitehead's prophecy, both Memphis and Minneapolis lie along the Mississippi river, the central axis of the geographical area delineated by Whitehead and Price.

[497] As Owen Barfield explains in *Saving the Appearances: A Study in Idolatry*, the ancient Hebrews were the forerunners of modernity's crusade against a premodern world view founded primarily on formal and final causation, which Barfield terms "original participation," and which was almost completely predominant prior to the initiation of the individuation of the autonomous rational intellect by the ancient Hebrews, and subsequently by the ancient Greeks, that found its culmination in the last three centuries (Barfield 124).

[498] *Playboy* 1978.

[499] In the 1950s, there were more Jews in New York City, peaking at 2.1 million (roughly a quarter of the city's population), than any other city in the United States. Thus, it seems likely that part of the reason why Dylan was so drawn to New York is that he had grown up an outsider, part of a tiny Midwestern Jewish enclave among primarily Christians, and he was perhaps instinctively drawn to the place where he could feel the least an outsider in his own country. When he arrived in New York, it seems that he finally discovered a culture that valued his particular brand of intellectually shaded affective intensity, a quality often ascribed to Jewish people, perhaps a product of that culture's millennia-long commitment to the interpretation of language as "the people of the book." (UJA Federation of New York, *The Jewish Community Study of New York: 2011*, www.ujafedny.org, 39)

[500] *Chronicles* 37.

[501] Cf. Morris Dickstein, *Gates of Eden: American Culture in the Sixties* (Cambridge, MA: Harvard University Press, 1997).

[502] *Chronicles* 39, 99.

[503] Hedin 36.

[504] *Chronicles* 9.

[505] Scorsese

[506] *Chronicles* 55.

[507] Scorsese

[508] *Chronicles* 255, 55.

[509] Jim Slotek, "Cohen's Future is Now," *The Toronto Sun* (Nov. 19 1992) and Hedin 49.

[510] Epstein 90.

[511] *Chronicles* 9-10.

[512] *Rolling Stone* 2012.

[513] "Dylan Looks Back," *60 Minutes* (CBS News, November 13 2006).

[514] *Chronicles* 45-46, 18-19.

[515] Wilentz 2.

[516] Hajdu 71, 35.
[517] *Chronicles* 19, 20.
[518] Wilentz 9.
[519] *Chronicles* 15.
[520] Marcus 23.
[521] *Chronicles* 46.
[522] Marcus 113.
[523] Wilentz 12.
[524] Bergson 38.
[525] *Chronicles* 47, 17-18, 34-35, 56.
[526] Cf. Terence McKenna's *The Archaic Revival*.
[527] *Chronicles* 235-36, 240, 61.
[528] Hajdu 69.
[529] *Chronicles* 62, 70-72.
[530] Hedin 35.
[531] *Varieties* 325.
[532] *Chronicles* 71-73, 78.
[533] The version that Dylan may have heard, used by Scorsese in *No Direction Home*, was by Bill Monroe, though it was also covered by Hank Williams and Roy Acuff.
[534] Scorsese
[535] *Chronicles* 78-9. It is interesting to note that, as late as 1961, Dylan's name was not yet fixed for, as Robert Shelton writes of an interview with Dylan for his *New York Times* piece: "Did he want me to call him Bobby Dylan or Bob Dylan? He thought that one out, as if he were about to sign a contract. Half aloud, he repeated the two names to himself: 'Bob Dylan, Bobby Dylan, Bob Dylan, Bobby Dylan . . . Make it Bob Dylan! That's what I'm really known as,' he declared confidently" (Hedin 12).
[536] Hajdu 73-74.
[537] Hedin 48.
[538] *Eat the Document*, Dir. Bob Dylan (ABC Television, unreleased).
[539] Hajdu 281.
[540] Wilentz 13.
[541] Hedin xiv.
[542] *Chronicles* 84.
[543] *The Passion of the Western Mind* 416.
[544] *Chronicles* 89, 15, 277.
[545] Wilentz 6.
[546] *Chronicles* 253-4.
[547] Although Guthrie was certainly influential in some circles, he never achieved mainstream success in the form of a hit record.

[548] *Chronicles* 278.

[549] Heylin 74.

[550] Scorsese

[551] *Chronicles* 278-79.

[552] Epstein 99.

[553] Robert Shelton, "Bob Dylan: A Distinctive Stylist," *The New York Times*, September 29, 1961.

[554] Heylin 77.

[555] *Chronicles* 279-80, 5-8, 227.

[556] Wilentz 44.

[557] *Chronicles* 228.

[558] Heylin 47.

[559] *Chronicles* 241, 54, 229, 52, 236.

[560] Hajdu 105.

[561] Heylin 85.

[562] Scorsese

[563] Hajdu 108.

[564] Epstein 104-6.

[565] Hajdu 119 and Epstein 110.

[566] Hedin 41.

[567] Epstein 111.

[568] Hajdu 166-67. Bikel is referring specifically to an encore of "We Shall Overcome" sung by Dylan, Baez, Seeger, and others.

[569] *Rolling Stone* 2012.

[570] Epstein 113-14.

[571] Scorsese

[572] Epstein 74.

[573] Gould 207.

[574] Epstein 115-16.

[575] (http://en.wikipedia.org/wiki/Another_Side_of_Bob_Dylan)

[576] Epstein 144, 135.

[577] *Rolling Stone* 2012.

[578] Playboy, March 1978.

[579] Scorsese

[580] *Rolling Stone* 2012.

[581] Epstein 138, 145.

[582] Irwin Silber, "An Open Letter to Bob Dylan," *Sing Out!* (November, 1964).

[583] *Chronicles* 67.

[584] Scorsese

[585] Marcus 60-61.

[586] *Playboy*, March 1978.

[587] Palmer 107.

[588] Barry Miles and Pearce Marchbank, eds., *Bob Dylan: In His Own Words* (New York: Quick Fox, 1978) 46, 61, 74.

[589] *Rolling Stone* 2012.

[590] Hajdu 10 and Hedin xvi, xiii.

[591] *Chronicles* 292-3.

[592] Scorsese

[593] Epstein 163.

[594] *Don't Look Back*, Dir. D.A. Pennebaker (Docurama, 1967).

[595] *Rolling Stone* 2012.

[596] Scorsese

[597] *Varieties* 462-63.

[598] Robert N. Bellah, *Beyond Belief: Essays on Religion in a Post-Traditionalist World* (Berkley, CA: University of California Press, 1970) 21.

[599] It might also be noted that Bellah's definition of religion applies equally to reductive scientific materialism.

[600] Riley 35.

[601] Turner 10. Steve Turner explores a hypothesis in his *The Gospel According to the Beatles* closely related to that of the present chapter, though he focuses primarily on the Beatles' explicit engagement with religion, from Lennon's tenure as a choirboy to their collective adventures with meditation and Eastern thought. In contrast, this chapter focuses on the quality of language consistently used to describe the Beatles in explicitly non-religious contexts, particularly in their relation to music. Thus, while there will inevitably be some overlap in the two projects, the present chapter and Turner's book are complementary.

[602] *Rolling Stone* (June 28, 1970).

[603] *Tune In* 90.

[604] Spitz 41.

[605] *Varieties* 177.

[606] *Tune In* 9.

[607] *Beatles Anthology* (book) 22 and *Tune In* 89. For a brief moment in 1962, Lewisohn writes: "The new messiah was Luther Dixon, the producer behind the Shirelles' sound" (*Tune In* 586). It is also interesting to note that Lewisohn describes McCartney as "an adamant atheist," at least in 1962, though this atheism appears to have been primarily directed toward institutionalized religion, as many of McCartney's statements exhibit a religious quality in relation to music (*Tune In* 776).

[608] Gould 305-6.

609 *Tune In* 9.
610 Spitz 41.
611 *Tune In* 146.
612 Gould 341.
613 Riley 41, 18.
614 *Tune In* 809 and MacDonald xx.
615 Riley 33.
616 Spitz 15-16.
617 Turner 10.
618 *Tune In* 405.
619 Gould 179.
620 As Lewisohn writes: "The Beatles' return [from Hamburg] was no less explosive, locally, than the arrival of rock and roll itself in 1956. . . . Everything started to change because of them, and quickly" (*Tune In* 410).
621 *Beatles Anthology* (book) 22.
622 Spitz 34-35, 86 and Mircea Eliade, *Shamanism: Archaic Techniques of Ecstasy* (Princeton, NJ: Princeton University Press, 1964) 19.
623 Spitz 105.
624 Turner 5-6.
625 Spitz 176, 51, 92.
626 Cf. Robert N. Bellah, *Religion in Human Evolution: From the Paleolithic to the Axial Age* (Cambridge, MA: The Belknap Press of Harvard University, 2011).
627 Spitz 92.
628 *Varieties* 36.
629 Spitz 113, 210, 306.
630 Turner viii, 1.
631 *Tune In* 340, 557, 839.
632 Riley 36.
633 *Beatles Anthology* (book) 68.
634 *Pragmatism* 77-78.
635 *Will to Believe* 19.
636 *Tune In* 518.
637 Spitz 274, 284, 354.
638 *Pragmatism* 1.
639 *Science and the Modern World* 2.
640 Spitz 355.
641 Gould 79.
642 *Beatles Anthology* (book) 41.
643 The probabilistic discipline of "fuzzy logic" is an appropriate analogy

for the emerging mode of thought, and perhaps more than analogy, as instead of working solely in binary, either/or propositions, both probabilistic logic and the modes of thought articulated by James, Jung, Bergson, Whitehead, and Tarnas are concerned with partial truths like those embodied, for instance, by science and religion, and in the emergent dialectical synthesis of those truths, which appear merely incommensurable to traditional logic.

[644] Spitz 386-387, 269.

[645] Gould 4.

[646] Ellis Amburn, *Dark Star: The Roy Orbison Story* (Secaucus, NJ: Lyle Stuart Inc., 1990) 67.

[647] Spitz 300, 397. Gould similarly refers to the Top Ten Club in Hamburg, where the Beatles found the peak of their early success in that city, as having been promoted "as a mecca for rock 'n' roll" (Gould 94).

[648] Spitz 408.

[649] Gould 184, 142.

[650] Epstein 104.

[651] Spitz 422.

[652] Bergson 22.

[653] *Process and Reality* 28.

[654] *Partisan Review* (Summer 1964).

[655] Spitz 427.

[656] "The Night Carnegie Hall Went Berserk," *Melody Maker*, February 22, 1964.

[657] *New York Times*, February, 13, 1964.

[658] Spitz 553, 483, 492.

[659] J. Simpson and E. Wiener, Eds., *Oxford English Dictionary, Second Edition* (Oxford University Press, 2009).

[660] MacDonald xxii-xxiii, 20-22.

[661] Spitz 519.

[662] Nic Cohn, *Today There Are No Gentlemen* (London: Weidenfeld and Nicholson, 1971) 67.

[663] *Tune In* 740.

[664] *Passion* 429.

[665] *Science and the Modern World* 47, 143-47.

[666] Bergson 33.

[667] Edna Gundersen, "Dylan Is Positively on Top of His Game," *USA Today* (September 10, 2001).

[668] Scorsese

[669] *Chronicles* 111, 124.

[670] Epstein 34.

671 Scorsese

672 *Varieties* 36.

673 "Bob Dylan: San Francisco Press Conference," December 1965.

674 Scorsese

675 *Chronicles* 43.

676 The Rolling Stones, "You Can't Always Get What You Want," *Let It Bleed* (Decca Records, 1969).

677 Neil Hickey, *TV Guide* (September 11, 1976).

678 *Chronicles* 43-44.

679 *Will to Believe* 35, 52.

680 *Playboy*, March 1978.

681

(http://content.usatoday.com/communities/theoval/post/2010/09/obama-meets-dylan-/1#.UbIJ_iqF-_E)

682 *Chronicles* 188.

683 Marshall McLuhan, *Understanding Media: The Extensions of Man* (New York: McGraw-Hill, 1964).

684 Epstein 53.

685 *Chronicles* 245-6.

686 Rob Epstein and Jeffrey Friedman, Directors, *Howl*, 2010.

687 *Chronicles* 247-48. I would suggest that the cosmological shift toward which Dylan gestures is perhaps most directly expressed by Richard Tarnas in *Cosmos and Psyche*.

688 *Varieties* 460.

689 *Chronicles* 16.

690 "Must Be Santa," Dir. Nash Edgerton (Sony Music Entertainment, 2009).

691 Heylin 4.

692 It seems that Dylan employs "fate" and "destiny" interchangeably, though they nominate slightly different inflections of final causation: "fate" suggests lack of choice (as in "fatalism," "fatality," etc.) while "destiny" seems to imply a general trajectory that requires participation from a person with free will (as in "destination"). Dylan uses "destiny" more than "fate," which perhaps indicates an implicit recognition of this subtle difference, particularly as Dylan seems to see final causation (though he does not describe it as such) as a negotiation between teleology and conscious choice.

693 *Chronicles* 69.

694 *Science and the Modern World* 1.

695 Kuhn 5.

696 *Chronicles* 236, 51, 61-62.

[697] *"60 Minutes,"* 2004.

[698] Hedin 35.

[699] *Chronicles* 22.

[700] *Rolling Stone* 2012.

[701] *Chronicles* 71-73, 254-5.

[702] *Rolling Stone* 2012.

[703] *Chronicles* 256.

[704] Scorsese

[705] *"60 Minutes"* 2004.

[706] *Chronicles* 288.

[707] *Playboy*, March 1978.

[708] Scorsese

[709] Suze Rotolo, *A Freewheelin' Time: A Memoir of Greenwich Village in the Sixties* (New York: Broadway Books, 2008) 94.

[710] *The Evolutionary Mind* 9.

[711] My discussion of psychedelics, along with numerous other ideas expressed in these pages, has inevitably been influenced by many hours spent listening to lectures by the inimitable Terence McKenna.

[712] *Chronicles* 114-15, 186, 9.

[713] Epstein 134.

[714] *Chronicles* 79.

[715] *Rolling Stone* 2012. The book Dylan is referring to is: Sonny Barger, Keith Zimmerman, and Kent Zimmerman, *Hell's Angel: The Life and Times of Sonny Barger and the Hell's Angels Motorcycle Club* (New York: William Morrow Paperbacks, 2001).

[716] *Holy Bible: King James Version* (Nashville, TN: Holman Bible Publishers, 1979) 2 Corinthians 3:18, Matthew 11:15.

[717] "Bob Dylan: His Hells Angel Conversion," *The Guardian Music Blog* (http://www.guardian.co.uk/music/2012/sep/20/bob-dylan-hells-angel-conversion)

[718] *Science and the Modern World* 91.

[719] *Tune In* 586.

[720] *Careless Love* 207.

[721] *Varieties* 325.

[722] *Adventures of Ideas* 28.

[723] *Careless Love* 211.

[724] Spitz 582-3.

[725] *Careless Love* 212, 230.

[726] *Beatles Anthology* (book), 158.

[727] *Playboy*, March 1978.

[728] Heylin 43. Lennon and Harrison had apparently smoked cannabis

once or twice, but had not made a habit of it as Dylan had (*Tune In* 596).

[729] Spitz 536.

[730] Gould 283.

[731] Spitz 535-36.

[732] Terence McKenna, *Food of the Gods: The Search for the Original Tree of Knowledge: A Radical History of Plants, Drugs, and Human Evolution* (New York: Bantam Books, 1992) 15.

[733] I should note that, although I experimentally abstained from caffeine for a few years in my mid-twenties, this book would probably not have been possible without the heady rush of coffee, which I thoroughly enjoy.

[734] "Beatles and Drugs" (https://www.youtube.com/watch?v=91C9h_Yd_3o)

[735] *Food of the Gods* 185, 180.

[736] Terence McKenna, *Light of the Third Millennium* (Austin, TX, 1996).

[737] *Beatles Anthology* (book) 158.

[738] Gould 254.

[739] Spitz 547.

[740] *Beatles Anthology* (book) 160.

[741] Gould 251.

[742] *Chronicles* 204.

[743] Altschuler 183.

[744] (http://en.wikipedia.org/wiki/Best_selling_music_artists) As Epstein writes, in the mid-sixties, Dylan "was a niche act whose influence was out of all proportion to his popularity" (Epstein 129).

[745] Scorsese

[746] Douglas Brinkley, *Rolling Stone* (May 14, 2009) 48.

[747] That Dylan visited Woody Guthrie on his deathbed numerous times clearly demonstrates where Dylan's ultimate allegiance resided.

[748] Presley appears to have had more chart success than either Dylan or the Rolling Stones in the sixties, the Beatles being the only band to surpass him in terms of sheer numbers during that decade (http://tsort.info/music/faq_decade_artists.htm).

[749] "Went to See the Gypsy," *New Morning*

[750] Hajdu 276-277.

[751] Both Lennon and McCartney, but especially Lennon, were Lewis Carroll devotees (*Tune In* 8).

[752] *Cosmos and Psyche* 68.

[753] As Tarnas writes in *The Passion of the Western Mind*: "I believe this has all along been the underlying goal of Western intellectual and spiritual evolution. *For the deepest passion of the Western mind has been*

to reunite with the ground of its own being. The driving impulse of the West's masculine consciousness has been its dialectical quest not only to realize itself, to forge its own autonomy, but also, finally, to come to terms with the great feminine principle in life, and thus to recover its connection with the whole: to differentiate itself from but then rediscover and reunite with the feminine, with the mystery of life, of nature, of soul. And that reunion can now occur on a new and profoundly different level from that of the primordial unconscious unity, for the long evolution of human consciousness has prepared it to be capable at last of embracing its own ground and matrix freely and consciously. The *telos*, the inner direction and goal, of the Western mind has been to reconnect with the cosmos in a mature *participation mystique*, to surrender itself freely and consciously in the embrace of a larger unity that preserves human autonomy while also transcending human alienation" (*Passion* 443-4).

BIBLIOGRAPHY

"The 500 Greatest Songs of All Time." *Rolling Stone* online. April 7, 2011.

Altschuler, Glenn C. *All Shook Up: How Rock 'N' Roll Changed America*. New York: Oxford University Press, 2003.

Amburn, Ellis. *Dark Star: The Roy Orbison Story*. Secaucus, NJ: Lyle Stuart Inc., 1990.

Badman, Keith. *The Beatles: Off the Record*. London: Omnibus Press, 2008.

Bailey, David and Peter Evans. *Goodbye Baby and Amen*. New York: Coward McCann, 1969. "Bards of Pop." *Newsweek*. March 24, 1966.

Barfield, Owen. *Saving the Appearances: A Study in Idolatry*. Middletown, CT: Wesleyan, 1988. The Beatles, *Past Masters, Vol. 2*. Capitol Records, 1988.

The Beatles, *Please Please Me*. Capitol Records, 1987.

The Beatles Anthology. Dir. Geoff Wonfor and Bob Smeaton. Apple Corps, 2003.

"Beatles and Drugs," www.youtube.com.

"The Beatles and Their Audience." *New York Times*. February 10, 1964.

"Beatles Bat It Out for Seattle." *Seattle Post-Intelligencer*. August 22, 1964.

The Beatles Book Monthly. January 1983.

The Beatles Book Monthly. August 1983.

The Beatles. *The Beatles Anthology*. San Francisco: Chronicles, 2000.

Bellah, Robert N. *Beyond Belief: Essays on Religion in a Post-Traditionalist World*. Berkeley, CA: University of California Press, 1970.

Bergson, Henri. *Creative Evolution*. New York: Barnes & Noble Books, 2005.

Bertrand, Michael T. *Race, Rock, and Elvis*. Champaign, IL: University of Illinois Press, 2000.

Blake, William. "Letter to Thomas Butt." 22 November, 1802. *The Letters of William Blake*. Ed. Geoffrey Keynes. Charleston, SC: Nabu Press, 2011.

"Bob Dylan: His Hells Angel Conversion." *The Guardian Music Blog*. September 20, 2012.

"Bob Dylan: San Francisco Press Conference (Dec. 1965)" www.youtube.com.

Braun, Michael. *Love Me Do: The Beatles' Progress*. London: Penguin, 1964.

Brinkley, Douglas. "Bob Dylan's America." *Rolling Stone.* Rolling Stone, 14 May, 2009.

Cajiao, Trevor. "We Were the Only Band Directed by an Ass." *Elvis: The Man and His Music 10.* (March 1991).

Cohn, Nic. *Today There Are No Gentlemen.* London: Weidenfeld and Nicholson, 1971.

Coleman, Ray. *McCartney: Yesterday and Today.* London: Boxtree Ltd., 1998.

Cook, Jody, Patty Henry. "Graceland National Historic Landmark Nomination Form." National Park Service, National Historic Landmarks Program. February 8, 2010.

Csikszentmihalyi, Mihaly. *Flow: The Psychology of Optimal Experience.* London: Rider and Co, 2002.

The Clash. *London Calling.* Epic Records, 1979.

Daily Mail. October 1, 1963.

Davies, Hunter. *The Beatles.* New York: W. W. Norton & Company, 2010.

DeCurtis, Anthony. *Rocking My Life Away.* Durham, NC: Duke University Press Books, 1999.

Don't Look Back. Dir. D.A. Pennebaker. Docurama, 1967.

Dunbar, Dirk. "The Evolution of Rock and Roll: Its Religious and Ecological Themes." *Journal of Religion and Popular Culture.* 2 (2002): n. pag. Web. 23 April, 2012.

Dylan, Bob. *Bringing It All Back Home.* Columbia Records, 1965.

Dylan, Bob. *Chronicles.* New York: Simon & Schuster, 2005.

Dylan, Bob. *Highway 61 Revisited.* Columbia Records, 1965.

Dylan, Bob. *Infidels.* Columbia Records, 1983.

Dylan, Bob. *John Wesley Harding.* Columbia Records, 1967.

Dylan, Bob. *New Morning.* Columbia Records, 1970.

Dylan, Bob. *Slow Train Coming.* Columbia Records, 1979.

Dylan, Bob. "To my fans and followers." www.bobdylan.com. Sony Music Entertainment, 13 May 13, 2011.

"Dylan Looks Back." *60 Minutes.* CBS News, November 13 2006.

Eliade, Mircea. *Shamanism: Archaic Techniques of Ecstasy.* Princeton, NJ: Princeton University Press, 1964.

Ehrenreich, Barbara, Elizabeth Hess, and Gloria Jacobs. *Re-Making Love.* Garden City, NY: Doubleday, 1986.

Epstein, Daniel Mark. *The Ballad of Bob Dylan.* New York: Harper, 2011.

Fanon, Frantz. *The Wretched of the Earth.* New York: Grove Press, 2005.

Freud, Sigmund. *Moses and Monotheism*. New York: Vintage Books, 1967.

Frith, Simon. *Performing Rites*. Cambridge, MA: Harvard University Press, 1996.

Gambaccini, Paul. *Paul McCartney: In His Own Words*. London: Omnibus Press, 1993.

Gebser, Jean. *The Ever-Present Origin*. Athens, OH: Ohio University Press, 1985.

Ginsberg, Allen. *Howl and Other Poems*. San Francisco: City Lights Publishers, 2001.

Giuliano, Geoffrey. *Dark Horse: The Secret Life of George Harrison*. London: Pan, 1991.

Gilmore, Mikal. "Bob Dylan Unleashed: A Wild Ride on His New LP and Striking Back at Critics." *Rolling Stone*. September 27, 2012.

Gould, Jonathan. *Can't Buy Me Love: The Beatles, Britain, and America*. New York: Harmony Books, 2007.

Gregg, Melissa and Gregory J. Seigworth. *The Affect Theory Reader*. Durham, NC: Duke University Press, 2010.

Grevatt, Ren. "On the Beat." Billboard. September 29, 1958.

Gundersen, Edna. "Dylan Is Positively on Top of His Game." *USA Today*. September 10, 2001.

Guralnick, Peter. *Careless Love: The Unmaking of Elvis Presley*. New York: Back Bay Books, 2000.

Guralnick, Peter. *Last Train to Memphis: The Rise of Elvis Presley*. New York: Abacus, 2003.

Hajdu, David. *Positively 4th Street: The Lives and Times of Joan Baez, Bob Dylan, Mimi Baez Farina, and Richard Farina*. New York: North Point Press, 2001.

Hedin, Benjamin, ed. *Studio A: The Bob Dylan Reader*. New York: Norton, 2004.

Hegel, G.W.F. *Hegel's Phenomenology of Spirit*. Ed. J.N. Findlay. Oxford University Press, 1977.

Herald Tribune. February 10, 1964.

Heylin, Clinton. *Dylan: Behind the Shades Revisited*. New York: HarperCollins, 2001.

Hickey, Neil. *TV Guide*. September 11, 1976.

Hillman, James. *Re-Visioning Psychology*. New York: HarperCollins, 1975.

Holy Bible: King James Version. Nashville, TN: Holman Bible Publishers, 1979.

James, William. *Pragmatism*. Toronto: Dover, 1995.

James, William. *The Varieties of Religious Experience*. New York: Vintage Books, 1990.

James, William. *The Will To Believe and Other Essays in Popular Philosophy, and Human Immortality*. Lawrence, KS: Digireads.com, 2010.

"Jewish Cities." *The Daily Beast*. Newsweek. December 1, 2010.

"John Lennon Slams the Critics." *NME*. August 6, 1965.

Johnson, Robert. "Elvis Sings and Thousands Scream." *Memphis Press-Scimitar*. July 5, 1956.

Jung, C.G. *Synchronicity: An Acausal Connecting Principle*. Princeton, NJ: Princeton University Press, 1973.

Kuhn, Thomas S. *The Structure of Scientific Revolutions*. Chicago, IL: The University of Chicago Press, 1996.

Lennon, Cynthia. *A Twist of Lennon*. New York: Avon Books, 1980.

Leland, John. *Hip: The History*. New York: Ecco, 2004.

Lennon, John. *John Lennon/Plastic Ono Band*. Apple/EMI, 1970.

"Let Us Now Praise Little Men." *Time*. May 31, 1963.

Lewisohn, Mark. *The Beatles: Recording Sessions*. New York: Harmony, 1988.

Lewisohn, Mark. *Tune In: The Beatles: All These Years*. New York: Crown Archetype, 2013.

MacAdams, Lewis. *Birth of the Cool: Beat, Bebop, and the American Avant Garde*. New York: Free Press, 2001.

MacDonald, Ian. *Revolution in the Head*. Chicago, IL: Chicago Review Press, 2007.

Marcus, Greil. *Like a Rolling Stone: Bob Dylan at the Crossroads*. New York: PublicAffairs, 2005.

McKenna, Terence. *Food of the Gods: The Search for the Original Tree of Knowledge: A Radical History of Plants, Drugs, and Human Evolution*.

McKenna, Terence. *Light of the Third Millennium* (Austin, TX, 1996).

Martin, George. *All You Need Is Ears*. New York: St. Martin's Griffin Press, 1994.

"Must Be Santa." Dir. Nash Edgerton. Sony Music Entertainment, 2009.

Martin, Linda and Kerry Segrave. *Anti-Rock: The Opposition to Rock 'n' Roll*. Cambridge, MA: Da Capo Press, 1993.

Miles, Barry and Pearce Marchbank, eds. *Bob Dylan: In His Own Words*. New York: Quick Fox, 1978.

Miles, Barry. *Paul McCartney: Many Years from Now*. New York: Henry Holt, 1997.

Mill, John Stuart and Jeremy Bentham. *Utilitarianism and Other Essays*. New York: Penguin Books, 2004.

New York Journal-American. June 9, 1956.

The New York Times. June 6, 1956.

The New York Times. February 8, 1964.

New York Times, February, 13, 1964.

New York Times, August 16, 1965.

Nietzsche, Friedrich. *Thus Spoke Zarathustra.* Cambridge, UK: Cambridge University Press, 2006.

"The Night Carnegie Hall Went Berserk," *Melody Maker,* February 22, 1964.

No Direction Home. Dir. Martin Scorsese. Paramount Pictures, 2005.

"Obama meets Dylan: 'Gives me just a little grin, and then leaves.'" www.USAToday .com. September 29, 2010.

Olson, Charles. *Selected Letters.* Ed. Ralph Maud. University of California, 2000.

Palmer, Robert. *Rock & Roll: an unruly history.* New York: Harmony Books, 1995.

Partisan Review. Summer 1964.

"Paul McCartney as Songwriter." *Herald Tribune.* December 26, 1965.

Playboy. Chicago, IL: Playboy, March, 1978.

Presley, Elvis. *Elvis at Sun.* RCA, 2004.

Price, Lucien. *Dialogues of Alfred North Whitehead.* Boston: Nonpareil, 2001.

Riley, Tim. *Tell Me Why: The Beatles: album by album, song by song, the sixties and after.* Cambridge, MA: Da Capo, 2002.

Rolling Stone. June 28, 1970.

Rotolo, Suze. *A Freewheelin' Time: A Memoir of Greenwich Village in the Sixties.* New York: Broadway Books, 2008.

Scaduto, Anthony. *Bob Dylan: An Intimate Biography.* New York: Grosset and Dunlap, 1971.

Sheff, David and G. Barry Golson. *The Playboy Interviews with John Lennon and Yoko Ono.* New York: Playboy Press, 1981.

Shelton, Robert. *No Direction Home.* New York: Ballantine Books, 1987.

Simpson, J. and E. Wiener, Eds. *Oxford English Dictionary, Second Edition.* Oxford University Press, 2009.

Shepherd, Billy. *The True Story of the Beatles.* New York: Bantam, 1964.

Silber, Irwin. "An Open Letter to Bob Dylan." *Sing Out!* November, 1964.

Slotek, Jim. "Cohen's Future is Now." *The Toronto Sun.* 19 November 1992.

Southall, Brian. *Abbey Road: The Story of the World's Most Famous Recording Studio*. Cambridge, UK: Stevens, 1982.

Spitz, Bob. *The Beatles: The Biography*. New York: Back Bay Books, 2005.

Sunday Times. November 3, 1963.

Tarnas, Richard. *Cosmos and Psyche: Intimations of a New World View*. Plume, 2006.

Tarnas, Richard. *The Passion of the Western Mind: Understanding the Ideas that Have Shaped Our World View*. New York: Ballantine Books, 1991.

Thornton, Anthony, ed. *Uncut Legends: Elvis*. Issue no. 5, 2005.

Turner, Steve. *The Gospel According to the Beatles*. Louisville, KY: Westminster John Knox Press, 2006.

UJA Federation of New York. *The Jewish Community Study of New York: 2011*. www.ujafedny.org.

Vancouver Sun. August 24, 1964.

Ward, Brian. *Just My Soul Responding: Rhythm and Blues, Black Consciousness, and Race Relations*. Berkeley, CA: University of California Press, 1998.

Washington Post. February 10, 1964.

Washburn, Michael. *The Ego and the Dynamic Ground: A Transpersonal Theory of Human Development*. Albany, NY: State University of New York Press, 1994.

Weber, Max. *Max Weber's Complete Writings on Academic and Political Vocations*. Ed. John Dreijmanis. New York: Algora Publishing, 2008.

Weber, Max. *The Protestant Ethic and the 'Spirit' of Capitalism and Other Writings*. New York: Penguin Books, 2002.

Wenner, Jann. *Lennon Remembers*. New York: Popular Library, 1971.

Whitehead, Alfred North. *Adventures of Ideas*. New York: The Free Press, 1967.

Whitehead, Alfred North. *Modes of Thought*. New York: The Free Press, 1968.

Whitehead, Alfred North. *Process and Reality: Corrected Edition*. Ed. David Ray Griffin and Donald W. Sherburne. New York: The Free Press, 1985.

Whitehead, Alfred North. *Science and the Modern World*. New York: The Free Press, 1967.

Wilentz, Sean. *Bob Dylan In America*. New York: Anchor Books, 2011.

Wyndam, *London Life* (December 1965).

"Yeh-Heh-Heh-Hes, Baby." *Time*. June 18, 1956.

ACKNOWLEDGEMENTS

I would like to thank *The Journal of Religion and Popular Culture* for allowing me to reprint my essay, "An Extreme Sense of Destiny," in somewhat altered form, as part of the fifth chapter. I would also like to express my gratitude to Elizabeth Finkelstein for giving me permission to use her late husband Nat Finkelstein's photograph on the cover, which was taken in Andy Warhol's studio in July 1965, the same month Dylan "went electric" at the Newport Folk Festival. Thank you also to Special Rider Music for permission to reprint quotes from "Like a Rolling Stone" and "Went to See the Gypsy," to Daniel Mark Epstein for permission to reprint passages from *The Ballad of Bob Dylan*, and to Hachette Book Group for permission to reprint passages from *Last Train to Memphis*.

Thanks to all of the musicians I have played with who have taught me so much. And many thanks to friends, colleagues, and mentors (in vaguely chronological order): Sharon Boucher, Jared Rock, the late, great JR Minkel, Brandon Wiley, Rebecca Kruger, Sarah Rennick, Jessica Belasco, John Meitzen, Jeremy Liebman, Brent Pennington, Andy McCallister, Arun Nair, James Case-Leal, Stephanie Dodes and the Dodes family, Kevin Drost, Matthew Stoulil, Richard Tarnas, Jackie DiSalvo, Ammiel Alcalay, Joan Richardson, Sean Kelly, Keiron Le Grice, Gerhard Joseph, Frank Cioffi, Christian Ebert, and Marc Dolan.

And last but certainly not least, I would like to thank my family: my parents, Dan and Carol Orsborn, and my sister, Jody Orsborn, for many years of encouragement, support, and love; and my in-laws, Don and Susan Edwards (and their extended families), for treating me like their own son, for letting us live in their cabin in the woods while I wrote the bulk of this book, and for raising a beautiful, brilliant, kind, funny, chic daughter, Ginny Maxwell, the love of my life, to whom this book is dedicated.

INDEX

Abbey Road Studios, 84-88, 93, 257
Abraham, Karl, 214
Acuff, Roy, 24, 266
Alexander, Arthur, 55
Alighieri, Dante, 136
"All I Really Wanna Do," 164
Allen, Frank, 76
Allyn, David, 149
American Idol, 152
"And I Love Her," 107
Andersen, Eric, 162-63, 167, 215
Another Side of Bob Dylan, 134, 163-64
Aquinas, Saint Thomas, 217, 261
Aristarchus, 55
Aristotle, 179-80, 197
Armstrong, Louis, 24
Arnold, Jerome, 3
ayahuasca, 214

Bacchae, 192
Baez, Joan, 117, 152, 160, 165-66, 209-10, 267
"Ballad in Plain D," 164, 166
"Ballad of a Thin Man," 124, 166
"The Ballad of John and Yoko," 183
Balzac, Honoré de, 116-17, 136
Band, The (The Hawks), 3, 169-71
Bangs, Lester, 12
Baraka, Amiri, 21, 245-47
Barber, Adrian, 63, 73, 83, 91
Barger, Ralph, 217
Barnum, P.T., 104, 185
Barrow, Tony, 97-98, 102, 221
Bateson, Gregory, 22
Beach Boys, The, 111, 262
Beatles, The, 12, 16, 42, 45-118, 122, 128-30, 133, 138-40, 142-43, 155, 159, 163, 167, 172, 176-196, 202-3, 217, 220-234, 241, 250-53, 255-58, 262, 268-70, 273
Beatles for Sale, 108, 111, 114, 230
Belafonte, Harry, 160, 206-7
Bellah, Robert, 176, 268

Bennett, Kim, 256
Bennett, Tony, 152
Bergson, Henri, 38, 42, 52, 55, 72, 82, 120, 130-132, 143, 147, 191-92, 194, 198, 205, 218, 227-28, 238-40, 242, 244, 270
Berry, Chuck, 12, 24, 50, 55-56, 64-65, 118
"Besame Mucho," 80
Best, Mo, 71, 184
Best, Pete, 68, 71-72, 88, 91-93
Bikel, Theodore, 160, 267
Billboard, 103, 107
Black, Bill, 20, 29-30, 33-34
Black Mountain, 251
Black Sabbath, 69
Blake, William, 92, 231
Blonde on Blonde, 166, 198
Bloomfield, Mike, 1-3
"Blowin' in the Wind," 159-60
"Blue Moon of Kentucky," 16, 20, 31, 33
Bob Dylan, 158, 169
Boone, Pat, 123
"Boots of Spanish Leather," 163-64
Borges, Jorge Luis, 146
Bowie, David, 69
Brand, Oscar, 4
Brando, Marlon, 10, 15, 32, 136
Brenston, Jackie, 243
Brill Building, The, 255, 258, 262
Bringing It All Back Home, 1-2, 115, 134, 164, 169-70, 172, 174
Bristol, Tennessee/Virginia, 190
Brown, Alan, 86
Buddha, 184, 186, 198
Byrds, The, 111
Byrne, Johnny, 67, 73
Byron, George Gordon, 137, 143

Café Wha?, 140-41
Cage, John, 150
Cain and Abel, 171
Campbell, Joseph, 64

cannabis, 108-9, 113, 167, 224-230, 273
Canute, 44
Carroll, Lewis, 106, 234, 274
Carter, June, 168
Casbah, the, 71
Cash, Johnny, 168, 171
Castaneda, Carlos, 214
Castro, Fidel, 136
Cavern, The, 50-51, 73-75, 78, 86, 102, 105, 185, 189-90, 217
Celler, Emanuel, 35
Charles, Ray, 9, 25
Chambers Brothers, The, 1
Chess, Leonard, 24
Chess Records, 24
Chicago, Illinois, 164, 190
"Chimes of Freedom," 164
Christ, 85, 171, 183-84, 188, 217
Cinderella, 33
Civil War, The, 141, 146, 151
Clancy, Liam, 161
Clash, The, 99
Claus, Santa, 206
Cochran, Eddie, 61, 182
Cohen, David, 165, 215
Cohen, Leonard, 139
Cole, Nat King, 24
Coleridge, Samuel Taylor, 143
Colman, Sidney, 82, 256
Columbia Records, 152, 154-56, 158, 169, 172
"Come Together," 230
Como, Perry, 15
Copernicus, Nicolaus, 55, 188-89
Corso, Gregory, 123
Crickets, The, 55-56
Crosby, Bing, 15
Crudup, Arthur "Big Boy," 15, 23
Crumpacker, Chick, 9
Cuban Missile Crisis, 163
"Cumberland Gap," 126

Davis, Miles, 241
Davis, Rod, 51
Day, Doris, 15

Dean, James, 10-11, 14, 42, 124, 128, 136, 156, 160
Decca Records, 80-83, 87-89, 98, 133, 159
Descartes, Rene, 81, 188, 196, 238, 241
Devil, the, 73
Dickens, Charles, 136
DiMaggio, Joe, 136
Disney, 33
Dixon, Luther, 269
"Do You Want to Know A Secret," 230
Dominoes, the, 72
Donegan, Lonnie, 50, 56, 64
"Don't Be Cruel," 51
"Don't Let M e Down," 230
Don't Look Back, 150, 165, 169, 173
"Don't Think Twice, It's All Right," 159, 164
Doors, The, 1
Dorsey brothers, 17
"Drifting Too Far From the Shore," 148
"Drive My Car," 113-14
Duluth, Minnesota, 118
Dylan, Bob, 1-7, 12, 16-17, 27, 30, 42-43, 56-57, 75, 106, 108-9, 111, 115-174, 179, 189, 191, 197-220, 223-37

Eat the Document, 150
The Ed Sullivan Show, 26, 104, 189
Eliade, Mircea, 181, 213
Elijah, 217
Ellington, Duke, 24, 40
Elliott, "Ramblin'" Jack, 132-34, 153, 209
Elvis at Sun, 15
EMI, 82, 85, 256
Epstein, Brian, 74-83, 91, 100, 102, 185-86, 189, 202
Euripides, 192
Everly Brothers, The, 45, 96, 118

Fanon, Frantz, 21, 244, 247

Farina, Mimi Baez, 152
Farina, Richard, 4, 6, 152, 154,
Fate, Jack, 206
Feinstein, Barry, 133
Ferlinghetti, Lawrence, 123
Folklore Center, 141
Folkways Records, 152
Foreshaw, Dave, 72
Forest Hills, 6
Forster, E.M., 18
Freed, Alan, 14
The Freewheelin' Bob Dylan, 159,
    163-64, 169, 223, 263
Freud, Sigmund, 65, 237-38
"From Me to You," 111
Frost, Jack, 206
Funkadelic, 174

Galilei, Galileo, 188-89
Galveston, Texas, 142
Gaslight, The, 142-43, 155, 206
Gasoline, 122
Gentle, Johnny, 61-62
The Genuine Basement Tapes, 169
Gerde's Folk City, 218
"Gimme Some Truth," 45
Ginsberg, Allen, 18, 123-24, 204, 213,
    231-32, 240
"Girl," 113
"Girl From the North Country," 159,
    164
Glover, Tony, 168
"God," 184
Gogol, Nikolai, 136
"Good Rockin' Tonight," 16, 32, 243
Goodman, Benny, 21, 73
Goons, The, 56, 65
Gorgeous George, 201, 206-7
Griffiths, Eric, 48
Grimes, Tiny, 14-15
Grosse Freiheit, 63
Guthrie, Nora, 162
Guthrie, Woody, 126-30, 132-33, 138,
    152-53, 157-58, 160, 162, 168,
    170-71, 203-5, 267, 273

Hades, 64
Haley, Bill, 13, 26
Hamburg, Germany, 61-73, 76, 78-81,
    83, 87-88, 90, 98, 101, 107, 111,
    183, 224, 255, 257, 269-70
Hammond, John, 152-56, 158
Hanisch, Carol, 139
Hanseatic League, 62
Hanton, Colin, 57
A Hard Day's Night (album), 107
A Hard Day's Night (film), 67, 77,
    108, 110
"A Hard Day's Night," 59
Hard Rain, 150
"A Hard Rain's A-Gonna Fall," 124,
    159, 163
"Hard Travelin'," 126
Hardy, John, 142
Harris, Wynonie, 243
Harrison, George, 53, 62, 64, 69, 71,
    78, 89-91, 93, 95-96, 107-8, 111,
    113-14, 179, 193, 220, 225-27,
    231, 233, 273
Harvard University, 141
"Heartbreak Hotel," 47
Hegel, Georg Wilhelm Friedrich, 30,
    36, 129, 193
Heidegger, Martin, 243, 261
Hell's Angels, 216
Help! (album), 108-9, 113-14, 230
Help! (film), 109-10
"Help!" 114, 230
Hendrix, Jimi, 108, 150
Henry, John, 142, 144
Hentoff, Nat, 119, 134, 138, 147
Heraclitus, 55, 219
Herald, John, 141
Hercules, 64, 73
heroin, 230
Hester, Carolyn, 152-54
Hibbing, Minnesota, 117, 119, 122,
    137-38, 148, 164, 168, 201, 205,
    218, 235
Highway 61, 118
Highway 61 Revisited, 198
Hitler, Adolf, 35

Holliday, Billy, 24
Holly, Buddy, 4, 12, 50, 55-56, 59-61, 70, 121, 152, 169, 253
Homer, 206, 211
Hopkins, Lightnin', 134
"Hound Dog," 37
"How Much Is That Doggie in the Window?" 122
Howard's End, 18
Howe, Bones, 17
"Howl," 18, 122, 240
Hughes, Langston, 36
Hugo, Victor, 136
Humperdinck, Engelbert, 222
Hurricanes, The, 73

"I Ain't Got No Home," 126
"I Am the Walrus," 230
"I Lost My Little Girl," 53
"I Don't Believe You," 164
"I Don't Care If the Sun Don't Shine," 33
"I Feel Fine," 108
"I Remember You," 97
"I Saw Her Standing There," 75, 100, 104
"I Want to Hold Your Hand," 103
"If I Had a Hammer," 160
Ifield, Frank, 97
"I'm A Loser," 114
"I'm Left, You're Right, She's Gone," 16-17
"I'm So Lonesome I Could Cry," 121
Imagine, 45
"Imagine," 184
In His Own Write, 106
"In My Life," 113
Indra, the, 64
Infidels, 139, 199
"It Ain't Me Babe," 164, 166
"It Don't Mean a Thing (If It Ain't Got That Swing)," 40
"It's All Over Now, Baby Blue," 4
"I've Got a Feeling," 75

Jackass, 69

Jackson, Harry, 149
Jagger, Mick, 200
James, Billy, 155-56
James, William, 41, 43, 46, 82, 95, 145, 148, 176-77, 183, 185-87, 191, 196, 198, 202, 204-5, 218, 227-28, 238-40, 244, 244, 270
Jarvis, Felton, 222-23
Jesus, 85, 171, 183-84, 188, 217
Johnson, Lyndon B., 167
Johnson, Robert, 73, 150, 212
Johnston, Bob, 198-99
John Wesley Harding, 198
"Jokerman," 139, 249
Jolson, Al, 161
Joplin, Janis, 150
Jordan, Louis, 33
Joyce, James, 106
Juanico, June, 11, 38
"Judas!" 3, 6, 171
Jung, C.G., 198, 200, 216, 218, 227, 228, 235, 244, 270
"Just Like a Woman," 166

Kansas City, Missouri, 190
Kant, Immanuel, 261
Keisker, Marion, 31-32, 38, 43
Kennedy, John F., 104, 162-63, 167, 171
Kepler, Johannes, 188-89
Kerouac, Jack, 123, 125-26, 241
King Creole, 10
King, Jr., Martin Luther, 36
Kingston Trio, The, 160
Kinks, The, 69, 111
Kirchherr, Astrid, 70
Koerner, John, 146
Kooper, Al, 2, 6, 7
Koschmider, Bruno, 65-66, 78, 87
Kramer, Billy, 72
Kuhn, Thomas, 118, 147, 207-8, 261

Langhorne, Bruce, 169, 172, 174
Lanois, Daniel, 215
Las Vegas, Nevada, 234
Latour, Bruno, 239

Leach, Sam, 195
Lear, Edward, 106
Leave it to Beaver, 137
Led Zeppelin, 69
Lennon, Cynthia, 69
Lennon, John, 23, 30, 45-62, 65-72,
    75, 77-81, 83-85, 87, 90-94, 96-
    100, 105-6, 109-114, 118-20, 139,
    163, 176-178, 181-184, 188, 192,
    214, 220-223, 225, 229-231, 234,
    252-53, 257, 268, 273-74
Let It Be, 75
Levittown, 137
Levy, Lou, 156-57
Lewis, Jerry Lee, 26
"Like a Rolling Stone," 1, 3, 4, 6, 149,
    166, 169
Little Richard, 12, 24, 48-50, 55-56,
    61, 64, 66, 99, 118, 121, 123
Liverpool, England, 49-51, 58-59, 61,
    63-64, 67, 71-75, 78-80, 82-84, 86,
    97-98, 100-1, 107, 117-18, 140,
    179, 184, 190, 193, 224, 253
Locke, Dixie, 37
Locke, John, 135
Logic, 108
"London Calling," 99
London, England, 77, 86, 94, 97-99,
    102, 118, 170, 179-80
"The Lonesome Death of Hattie
    Carroll," 163
Longfellow, Henry Wadsworth, 137
Los Angeles, 73, 221, 232
"Lost Highway," 121
Love and Theft, 206
"Love Me Do," 95, 97, 195
Love Me Tender, 49
LSD, 108, 167, 214, 230
Luther, Martin, 135
Lynch, Kenny, 99, 101
Lyotard, Jean-Francois, 124, 251

Machiavelli, Niccolò, 136
MacLeish, Archibald, 197-98
Madison, Wisconsin, 224
Magical Mystery Tour, 70

"Maggie's Farm," 1, 134, 169, 236
Manchester Free Trade Hall, 3
Manley, Colin, 82, 99
Manson, Charles, 250
Marley, Bob, 199, 223
The Marriage of Heaven and Hell, 92
Martin, Dean, 15, 33
Martin, George, 77, 82-84, 87-91, 93-
    96, 102, 111, 114, 129, 155, 178,
    256
Masked and Anonymous, 206
"Masters of War," 159, 164
Mathis, Johnny, 152
Matthau, Walter, 10
Maupassant, Guy de, 136
"Maybelline," 12
Maymudes, Victor, 119
McCartney, Paul, 30, 37, 45-47, 51-62,
    66, 69-71, 75, 77-80, 87, 90-94, 96,
    98, 100, 104, 109-11, 113-14, 163,
    177-78, 181-84, 223, 230, 252,
    254, 269, 274
McKenna, Terence, 214, 225-27, 272
McLuhan, Marshall, 47, 203
Mecca, Saudi Arabia, 73, 190
Memphis Mafia, 221, 232
Memphis, Tennessee, 21-22, 28, 33,
    40, 44, 66, 117, 190, 265
"Michelle," 113
Midnight Special, 206
"Milkcow Blues Boogie," 15-17, 32,
    44
Milligan, Spike, 64
Minneapolis, Minnesota, 123, 125-26,
    135, 138, 149, 164, 224, 237, 265
Mississippi River, 118, 265
"Mixed-Up Confusion," 169
Monroe, Bill, 266
Monroe, Marilyn, 136, 161
Montesquieu, 135
Moondog Coronation Ball, 14-15
Moore, Scotty, 20, 28-31, 33-34, 40
Morrison, Jim, 150
Moses, 217, 221
"Motorpsycho Nightmare," 164
Motown Records, 258

"Mr. Tambourine Man," 4, 143
Muldaur, Geoff, 2
Muldaur, Maria, 6
"Must Be Santa," 206
"Mystery Train," 16

Nashville Skyline, 198
Nashville, Tennessee, 190
Nazis, the, 35, 65
Neal, Bob, 10, 41, 43, 249
Neil, Fred, 140
Nelson, Paul, 5
NEMS, 75
Neuwrith, Bobby, 168
New Morning, 198, 233
New Orleans, Louisiana, 190
New York, New York, 118, 125-26,
    136-41, 151-52, 154, 164, 170,
    190, 204, 206, 208, 213, 224, 265
New York Public Library, 151
Newport Folk Festival, 1-7, 159-61,
    166-69, 171, 236
Newton, Isaac, 188
Nijinsky, Vaslav, 249
"1913 Massacre," 158
"Norwegian Wood," 113-14
"Nowhere Man," 113-14, 230
Nuggets, 12

Obama, Barack, 3, 202
Odysseus, 64, 73, 211
Oh Mercy, 215
Oklahoma, 126, 128
Olson, Charles, 124, 251, 263
On the Road, 122-23, 125
"One Too Many Mornings," 164
"Only a Pawn in their Game," 163
Ono, Yoko, 78,
Orbison, Roy, 55, 62, 190
Ovid, 136
Owen, Alun, 107

Page, Patti, 33
Palomar Ballroom, 73
Pankake, Jon, 129-33, 152, 155, 166,
    263

Parker, Charlie, 14
Parlophone Records, 82-83, 85, 98,
    155, 185, 256
Parsons, Gram, 150
Paul Butterfield Blues Band, 1, 3
Pennebaker, D.A., 150, 164
Pericles, 136
Perkins, Carl, 55
Peter, Paul, and Mary, 1, 160
Petty, Norman, 55
Phillips, Dewey, 33-34
Phillips, Sam, 9, 20, 24-26, 28-34, 37,
    39-40, 43, 155
Picasso, Pablo, 139-40
Plastic Ono Band, 184
Plato, 31, 261
"Please Please Me," 95-97, 113, 258
Poe, Edgar Allen, 137
"Positively Fourth Street," 166
Preludin, 69
Presley, Elvis, 9-45, 47-56, 58-59, 61-
    66, 68, 70, 72, 75, 77-78, 88, 92,
    97-99, 104, 106, 108, 117-23, 126-
    28, 130, 138-39, 150, 154-55, 167,
    169, 176-79, 183-84, 189-90, 214-
    15, 220-23, 231-35, 240-41, 243,
    248, 250, 265, 273
Preston, Billy, 48
Pretty Polly, 144
Pro Tools, 108
Punk'd, 69
Pythagoreans, 55

Quarry Men, The, 50, 56, 59

Radio Luxembourg, 181
"Ramblin' Man," 121
Ray, 9
Ray, Robert, 127
RCA, 9
Rebel Without a Cause, 124
Reeperbahn, the, 63-64, 66, 71, 73, 76,
    184, 257
Remo Four, the, 72, 82, 99
Renaldo and Clara, 212
Republic, 31

"Revolution," 230
Richard, Cliff, 55-56, 66, 77, 93, 255
Richards, Ron, 88, 90, 93-95
Rickenbacker, 107
Rimbaud, Arthur, 147, 212
The Rite of Spring, 249
Robinson, Jackie, 21
Robinson, Smokey, 55
"Rock Around the Clock," 13
"Rocket 88," 243
Rolling Stones, The, 69, 72, 111, 180, 191, 273
Roszak, Theodore, 250
Rothchild, Paul, 1
Rotolo, Suze, 153, 161, 164, 213
Rousseau, Jean-Jacques, 135
Royal Albert Hall, 102, 170
Rubber Soul, 75, 107, 111, 113-15, 172, 230

San Francisco, California, 63, 200
Sartre, Jean-Paul, 125
Savio, Mario, 123
Scorsese, Martin, 4, 6, 122, 124, 128, 134, 148, 153, 159, 165, 168, 197-98, 200, 211, 266
Schilling, Jerry, 222
Seattle, Washington, 190
Second World War, 63, 119, 135, 197
Seeger, Mike, 146-47, 151, 208
Seeger, Pete, 6, 119, 153, 160, 168, 267
Self Portrait, 198
Sgt. Pepper's Lonely Hearts Club Band, 70
Shadows, The, 55, 74, 93, 255
Shakespeare, William, 206
"She Loves You," 111
Shea Stadium, 67, 112
"The Sheik of Araby," 80
Sheldrake, Rupert, 214
Shelley, Percy Bysshe, 137
Shelton, Robert, 119, 153-54, 218, 266
Sheridan, Tony, 68, 76
Shirelles, The, 269
Shotton, Pete, 47-49, 51, 53, 181

Silber, Irwin, 167-68
Sinatra, Frank, 15, 35-36, 104, 222, 248-49
Sing Out!, 167
Small Faces, The, 77
Smith, Norman, 88-89
Smith, Mike, 80
Snow, Jimmie Rodgers, 38-39
"Song to Woody," 157-58
A Spaniard in the Works, 110
Spector, Phil, 255, 258, 262
Stage Show 17
Stagger Lee, 144
Star-Club, 83, 183
Starkey, Maureen, 233
Starr, Ringo, 67, 77, 91-93, 95-96, 113-15, 181, 228, 233
Statue of Liberty, 43
Stone, Sly, 174
Storm, Rory, 73
Stravinsky, Igor, 249
"Subterranean Homesick Blues," 169, 173
Sun Studio, 15-16, 20, 25, 27-28, 33-34, 56, 235
Sutcliffe, Stuart, 68, 70, 83, 114
Svedberg, Andrea, 161-62

Tacitus, 136
Talmud, The, 183
Tarnas, Richard, 22, 82, 105, 125, 195, 243, 261, 27-71, 274
Taylor, Alistair, 74-76
Taylor, Cecil, 150
"Thank You Girl," 111
"That'll Be the Day," 12, 59, 178
"That's All Right," 12-13, 15-17, 28, 31-34, 40, 43, 65, 97, 108, 169, 241, 243
"Think for Yourself," 113
"This Land is Your Land," 204
Thomas, Dylan, 149
Thornton, Big Mama, 15
"Three Cool Cats," 80
Through the Looking Glass, 234
Thucydides, 136

Thurber, James, 106
"Ticket To Ride," 109
The Times They Are A-Changin', 163-64
"The Times They Are A-Changin'," 163, 173
Tin Pan Alley, 54
Titanic, 142
"Tomorrow Never Knows," 59, 230
Top Ten Club, The, 255, 270
Traum, Happy, 140
Tupelo, Mississippi, 24, 190
"Turn, Turn, Turn," 160
"Tutti Frutti," 12
"Twist and Shout," 102

Valentino, Rudolph, 103
Van Ronk, Dave, 161, 230
Vienna, Austria, 190
Vietnam War, 163, 171
Vincent, Gene, 61, 70, 182
"Visions of Johanna," 166
Voltaire, 135

Wally, Nigel, 182
Warren, Earl, 136
WDIA, 23
Weber, Max, 13, 47, 79, 137, 144, 195, 237-38
Welch, Bruce, 110
"Went to See the Gypsy," 220, 233-34
"Where Have All the Flowers Gone?" 160
The White Album, 110

Whitehead, Alfred North, 14, 28, 32, 37, 56, 65, 82, 90, 109, 131-32, 145, 186, 191-92, 196, 198, 205, 207, 227-28, 239-40, 244, 264-65, 270
Who, The, 69, 72, 77, 111, 180
Williams, Alan, 64-66
Williams, Big Joe, 134
Williams, Hank, 120-21, 126, 150, 266
Williams, Larry, 55
Williams, Paul "Huckleback," 14-15
Wilson, Tom, 127
"With God on Our Side," 163-64
With the Beatles, 106
Woodstock, Festival, 264
Woodstock, New York, 169
Wooler, Bob, 76, 92, 99, 180, 185-86
"The Word," 75, 113
World War II, 63, 119, 135, 197

Yale University, 141, 155
Yardbirds, The, 111, 180
Yarrow, Peter, 1, 236
"Yesterday," 110, 114
"You Can't Always Get What You Want," 200
"Your Hit Parade," 15
"Your Cheatin' Heart," 121
"You've got to hide your love away," 230

Zimmerman, Keith and Kent, 217
Zimmerman, Robert, 121, 148-49, 161, 184, 216-19

Made in United States
North Haven, CT
19 October 2022

25652511R00163